INDEX TO BRITISH
LITERARY BIBLIOGRAPHY

II

SHAKESPEARIAN BIBLIOGRAPHY AND TEXTUAL CRITICISM

A BIBLIOGRAPHY

T. H. HOWARD-HILL

OXFORD
AT THE CLARENDON PRESS
1971

Oxford University Press, Ely House, London W. 1

GLASGOW NEW YORK TORONTO MELBOURNE WELLINGTON
CAPE TOWN SALISBURY IBADAN NAIROBI DAR ES SALAAM LUSAKA ADDIS ABABA
BOMBAY CALCUTTA MADRAS KARACHI LAHORE DACCA
KUALA LUMPUR SINGAPORE HONG KONG TOKYO

PRINTED IN GREAT BRITAIN

PREFACE

G. R. PROUDFOOT of King's College, London, gave me invaluable advice when I was preparing the manuscript, and John Simmons, Fellow of All Souls, gave further help and also read revises. They have saved me from many errors and I am most grateful for their friendly counsel. Any errors which remain are my own. If readers would send me, care of the publishers, notes of any omissions and errors they may discover, I would be happy to acknowledge their assistance in a revised edition, should one be called for.

The Bibliography is as complete to the end of 1969 as it could be made. I am especially grateful to the Delegates of the Oxford University Press for accepting this second volume for publication, and to the Printer for enabling the manuscript to be published so quickly after completion.

T. H. H.

Trevenny, Noke, Oxford
December 1969

CONTENTS

8   CONTENTS

BIBLIOGRAPHY OF BRITISH LITERARY BIBLIOGRAPHIES:

INTRODUCTION

THE first volume of the *Index to British Literary Bibliography* listed checklists and bibliographies on subjects likely to be of interest to students of English literature and printing and publishing. The third volume, which will be complete to the end of 1969, will record books and articles on subjects relating to the history of British printing and publishing and the bibliographical and textual study of English literature. This second volume —*Shakespearian Bibliography and Textual Criticism*—covers the Shakespeare bibliographies and checklists which were excluded from the first volume and adds a chronicle of the bibliographical and textual investigation of his works. The history of Shakespeare's text after 1890 is so closely connected with that of bibliographical discussion of his works that they can scarcely be distinguished, and the literature is so extensive that there is some advantage in combining bibliographies and analytical studies in a single volume.

SHAKESPEARIAN BIBLIOGRAPHY
AND TEXTUAL CRITICISM

I. SCOPE. The general considerations which have governed the selection of items have been set out fully in the introduction to the earlier volume (*Bibliography of British Literary Bibliographies*. Oxford, Clarendon pr., 1969, p.xi–xiii). If the principles on which the present volume has been arranged do not appear clearly here, the reader should find that the more extensive general introduction in the first volume will assist him in his inquiry.

The kinds of publication which were excluded by rule from the present volume (unless there were particular reasons why an item should be listed) are similar, namely, '(a) catalogues of manuscripts, and of (b) letters . . . (d) library accessions lists, (e) theses, (f) exhibition catalogues less than 10p. in extent . . . (h) booksellers' catalogues, and (i) auction and sale catalogues . . .'. When auction or sale catalogues are exceptionally interesting or extensive, or have a certain standing in the literature, they have been included despite the general rule. I cannot guarantee, however, that even this limited coverage is complete. Further, I have taken no account of notes on the text prefixed to individual editions of Shakespeare's works.

Much important textual criticism and for many plays the sole modern evaluations of the text are to be found in the introductions to such comprehensive editions as the New Arden edition. It is consistent with my practice in the other volumes not to take account of such material. I expect that readers need no further warning that they would be unwise to neglect the textual introductions to the New Cambridge and Arden editions, and editions of single plays, such as Pollard's *Richard II* and Greg's *Merry Wives of Windsor*.

In addition, there are some special subjects which I have not attempted to cover in the present volume. Some may find a place in the last volume whereas others, such as iconography, of which the bibliographical interest is slight and tangential, will not be covered at all. Save for one or two general contributions, works which discuss Shakespeare's printers and publishers have been reserved to the third volume, but sections of books on individual printers and publishers which treat of the printing and publication of particular Shakespearian works have been included. The literature of Shakespearian forgeries, to which such writers as Law, Stamp, Race, and Tannenbaum have contributed conspicuously, has also been reserved to the next volume where it will form part of the larger survey of which it is an indistinguishable fragment. Only the hard-core apocrypha (*STM*, *TNK*, and *Ed3*, to use the abbreviations sanctioned recently) have been mentioned here; such plays as *Arden of Feversham* and *Cardenio* will be included in the next volume.

Other notes which bear on scope should be consulted under the third section of this introduction. The principle of excluding books and articles in foreign languages, already eroded in the first volume, is here further relaxed to allow inclusion of some material written in European languages.

II. STYLE OF ENTRY. There is little alteration to the style of entry as described on p.xiii–xvi of the preceding volume. However, the reader's attention is drawn to the style of the annotation.

The most important innovation in the present volume is the provision of notes describing the contents of the articles listed. These brief notes, largely abstracted from the articles themselves, are therefore often in the language of the author, and do not purport to be critical: I have been content in most cases to note simply what the author set out to do, or what conclusions he has come to. Under some subject headings the reader will thus find a conspectus of bibliographical or textual examination of a problem as it has developed over the years. Regrettably, such summary annotation does little justice to an author who has had no unusual conclusions to present but who has drawn upon important new evidence in support of an old view or has presented novel arguments in favour of an old conclusion. Also, many articles are listed here of which the point is uncertain, or which do not readily lend themselves to either summary or abstract; however, readers should not assume that an item without annotation is of such a kind, for when the substantial content of an article has been conveyed by its title, I have not added to the entry.

Many bibliographical arguments are so detailed that an expository kind of annotation could not avoid, within the small space which could be allowed, doing injustice to the author's exposition. I have therefore limited the annotation to descriptive notes, and because similar considerations apply to monographs, I have usually eschewed annotation in favour of supplying a summary of the contents of the book, drawn from its contents page. Usually, this is sufficient to enable the reader to assess the scope, nature, and conclusions of the author's book, and to decide whether it is relevant to his inquiry. Where a list of contents is enigmatic, or lacking, a short description of the author's intentions has been supplied.

When an article has distinctive and informative subheadings in the text, I have listed them beneath the main entry. They will often reveal the steps of the author's exposition and show how the item is relevant to the reader's inquiry in much the same way as the table of contents in a monograph.

III. ARRANGEMENT OF ENTRIES. The main division of the bibliography between 'Works' and 'Textual studies' attempts to distinguish between the works of Shakespeare as physical objects which can be collected, counted, and described, and the texts as products of processes of transmission, which attract a different kind of study. The reader will see at once that only studies which relate to the physical features of the manuscript and printed sources of the text and its transmission from the author to the reader have been listed here. Consequently, this bibliography records only a small portion of the literature on which a scholar must call when dealing with the text of any one of Shakespeare's works. Nowhere does the central theme of this bibliography appear more clearly than in the selection of entries representing the textual or bibliographical study of the famous cruxes. The reader, and especially the unpractised student, must be reminded continually that besides bibliographical considerations the editor and student of the text will need to draw upon a far wider range of linguistic and literary material than is listed here when he attempts to elucidate a crux. For example, in dealing with such widely disputed cruxes as Mistress Quickly's 'babled' in *H5* or Hamlet's 'dram of eale', I have listed here only such papers as draw on physical or 'bibliographical' evidence in their attempts to determine the correct reading.

It has seemed preferable to arrange the entries under broad and comprehensive headings rather than to attempt more detailed classifications. The existing Shakespeare bibliographies offer no good guide to the proper arrangement of these materials. Detailed classification may afford some *post hoc* intellectual satisfaction, but is likely more often than not to frustrate the search of the reader who may not have as precise an idea of the content of the item he requires, and of the subheadings under which it should properly have been listed, as the compiler had when working with the book or article before him. Even a comprehensive table of contents will not greatly aid a reader if he must refer to the bibliography under a number of different subheadings before coming upon the entry which satisfies his inquiry. Of course, every reader should start his search with the Index, but many readers prefer to open a book in the general vicinity of the item they seek and read up to it. Serendipity brings compensations.

One disadvantage of a general arrangement under broader headings is that sometimes it is not easy to see how an entry is related to others on the more particular subject. Experiments with more detailed arrangements have led me to accept this disadvantage which the Index, one hopes, will help to overcome.

The arrangement, then, consists of a few main categories together with some particular headings, most of which are the titles of Shakespeare's works. As a rule, the entries are arranged in chronological order, with the bibliographies relating to the subject heading being listed directly after it. Because the subject arrangement is simple and the number of headings is small, it is not expected that the reader will have much difficulty in using the bibliography; nevertheless, the following notes should help to make the classification clearer.

The first section, *General bibliographies and guides*, records some basic items which will lead to the broader pastures of Shakespeare studies should the reader find that his needs cannot be met entirely by the items in this list itself. Checklists and catalogues of Shakespeariana (that is, lists of works about or relating to Shakespeare, rather than of his plays and poems in their several editions) are also listed in this section, where, for convenience, I have included lists of Shakespearian literature and translations published abroad. The reader should not expect to find an exhaustive list of bibliographies of translations, for translations do not come within the general scope of the *Index*. However, the main items are listed and the inquirer with more specialist needs will be greatly aided by the *Shakespeare Quarterly* annual bibliography.

General surveys of aspects of Shakespeare studies, or appraisals of Shakespearian scholarship over periods of years, have not been listed unless the subject of the survey was substantially bibliographical or textual.

The section on *Works* lists writings on the early printings and principal collected editions of Shakespeare's works, and the collections and libraries in which they might be found and studied. This section is headed by a list of bibliographies, checklists, and catalogues which enumerate Shakespeare's works in general with varying amounts of bibliographical description. For bibliographies of particular works (or subjects) the reader should consult the appropriate heading. Checklists and exhibition catalogues issued by libraries have been included in this section when they mention a fair number of early editions; otherwise they have been listed in the preceding section.

Under 'Collections' are items which describe the main libraries for the study of Shakespeare, together with some general items dealing with private collections, or exhibitions of the works, which cannot properly be listed under more detailed headings. Under the heading 'Quartos' are the bibliographies of the first printings of Shakespeare's works, and articles which deal with the quartos (including the nature of the 'bad' quartos) in general. I could also have put under this heading the items relating to the individual quartos published before 1623 (such as *LLL* and *Ado*), but it seems best for the reader to refer to a single heading for discussions of quarto and folio texts of these plays. Therefore they have been listed together in the last section.

Textual studies, the last section, under which studies of the separate works have been listed, records the literature of the textual and bibliographical examination of all Shakespeare's canonical works. I have not attempted to distinguish between 'textual' and 'bibliographical' articles, since it is likely that readers will be interested to learn of all the papers on a text and will prefer to find them under a single heading.

The limitations of the annotation to which I referred earlier are nowhere more evident than when it is applied to papers on a single textual point, under the heading of the particular work. For such papers, I have merely indicated as concisely as possible what reading the author has chosen to adopt. The act, scene, and line references in the titles of the articles are those of the original paper, but I have supplied the Globe reference where necessary for consistency of reference. The Index gives the Globe act and scene reference, and the Folio through-line-number for the entries which discuss textual points.

IV. INDEX. Apart from the innovation mentioned above, the Index maintains the conventions of the previous volume. The subheading 'Text' under the titles of Shakespeare's works introduces index references to the discussions of textual points; these are arranged in text order.

TABLE OF ABBREVIATIONS

Abstrs	Abstracts
Acad	Academia; Academy, etc.
Ado	*Much ado about nothing*
Ag	August
Am	America/n
Angl	Anglia; Anglaises
Ann	Annual/s
anr.	another
Ant.	*Antony and Cleopatra*
Antiqu	Antiquarian
Ap	April
Assn	Association/s
attrib.	attributed
Auc	Auction
AUMLA	Australasian universities' language and literature association journal
Austral	Australasian
AWW	*All's well that ends well*
AYL	*As you like it*
BBC	British broadcasting corporation
Beibl	Beiblatt
Bib	Bibliographical
bibliogr.	bibliography; bibliographical
Bk/s	Book/s
Bkmn	Bookman
Bksllr	Bookseller
BM	British museum
Bod	Bodleian
Brit	British
Bull	Bulletin/s
c.	*circa*
CBEL	*Cambridge bibliography of English literature*
Cent	Century
Chron	Chronicle
cm.	centimetre/s
co.	company
Coll	College; Collection
Coloph	Colophon
comp.	compiled; compiler/s
Comp	Comparée
Conn.	Connecticut
Connois	Connoisseur
Contemp	Contemporary
Cor.	*Coriolanus*
Crit	Criticism
C.U.P.	Cambridge university press

Cym.	*Cymbeline*
D	December
Dept.	Department
descr/s.	description/s
diagr/s.	diagram/s
ed.	edited; editon/s; editor/s
Educ	Education/al
Ed3	*Edward 3*
Eng	English
enl.	enlarged
Err.	*Comedy of errors*
F	February; Folio/s
facsim/s.	facsimile/s
f./ff.	following
Fortn	Fortnightly
Gen	General
Germ	German/ic
Graph	Graphic
Ham.	*Hamlet*
hft	Heft
Hist	Historical; History
H.M.S.O.	His/Her majesty's stationery office
Hndbk	Handbook
H5	*Henry 5*
H6	*Henry 6*
H8	*Henry 8*
ib.	*ibidem*
illus.	illustrated; illustrations
Illus	Illustrated
It.	Italian
J	Journal
Ja	January
Jahrb	Jahrbuch
JC	*Julius Caesar*
Je	June
Jl	July
Jn.	*King John*
l.	leaf/leaves
Lang	Language/s; Langues
LC	*Lover's complaint*
ld.	lord
Lib	Library/ies
Lit	Literature; Literary
Litt	Littérature
LLL	*Love's labour's lost*
Lond	London
Lr.	*King Lear*
ltd.	limited
Luc.	*Lucrece*
Mac.	*Macbeth*
Mag	Magazine
Mass.	Massachusetts
Merc	Mercury

Mich.	Michigan
MM	*Measure for measure*
MND	*Midsummer night's dream*
Mnth	Month
Mod	Modern; Modernes
Mr	March
ms/s.	manuscript/s
Mthly	Monthly
Mus	Museum
MV	*Merchant of Venice*
My	May
N	Note/s; News; November
n.d.	no date
Newsl	Newsletter
News-sh	News-sheet
Ninet	Nineteenth
N.J.	New Jersey
no/s.	number/s; numero/s, etc.
Notebk	Notebook
Nth	North
N.Y.	New York
N&Q	Notes and queries
Oc	October
O.E.D.	Oxford English dictionary
Opp	Opportunities
Oth.	*Othello*
O.U.P.	Oxford university press
p.	page/s
Pa	Papers
Per.	*Pericles*
Philol	Philological
Philos	Philosophical
port/s.	portrait/s
PP	*Passionate pilgrim*
pr.	press
Proc	Proceedings
pt	part/s
ptd.	printed
ptg.	printing
Ptg.	Printing
ptr.	printer/s
pub.	published
Pub	Public; Publication/s
Q	Quarterly; quarto/s
R	Review/s; Revue
Rec	Record/s
Renaiss	Renaissance
repr.	reprint/ed
Res	Research
rev.	revised
Rev:	Review/s
rf.	refer

R.I.	Rhode Island
Rom.	*Romeo and Juliet*
R2	*Richard 2*
R3	*Richard 3*
S	September
Sat	Saturday
Sci	Science/s
SD	stage-direction/s
ser	series
Sevent	Seventeenth
Sh	Shakespeare/'s
Shr.	*Taming of the shrew*
sig/s.	signature/s
Soc	Society/ies
Son.	*Sonnets*
SP	speech prefix/es
St.	Saint
Statesm	Statesman
Sth	South
Sthly	Southerly
STM	*Sir Thomas More*
Stud	Studies
Supp	Supplement
Surv	Survey
TGV	*Two gentlemen of Verona*
Theat	Theatre/er
Tim.	*Timon of Athens*
Tit.	*Titus Andronicus*
TLS	*Times literary supplement*
Tmp.	*Tempest*
TN	*Twelfth night*
TNK	*Two noble kinsmen*
TP	title-page
trans.	translated; translation/s
Trans	Transactions
transcr/s.	transcription/s
Tro.	*Troilus and Cressida*
Twent	Twentieth
Univ	University
U.P.	University press
v.	volume/s
Ven.	*Venus and Adonis*
Wisc.	Wisconsin
Wiv.	*Merry wives of Windsor*
WT	*Winter's tale*
1H4	*Henry 4, part 1*
1H6	*Henry 6, part 1*
2d	second
2H4	*Henry 4, part 2*
2H6	*Henry 6, part 2*
3d	third
3H6	*Henry 6, part 3*
8°	octavo

INDEX TO BRITISH
LITERARY BIBLIOGRAPHY

II

*Shakespearian bibliography
and textual criticism*

GENERAL BIBLIOGRAPHIES OF
AND GUIDES TO
SHAKESPEARIAN LITERATURE

PRINCIPAL PERIODICALS

1 **New Shakespeareana,** a critical, contemporary, and current review of Shakespearean & Elizabethan studies. 1no1–1no4. S–D. New York, Shakespeare society, 1901–11.

2 **Shakespeare Association Bulletin.** 1–24. Je–Oc. New York, 1924–49. (Continued as Shakespeare Quarterly)

3 **Shakespeare Jahrbuch.** Deutsche Shakespeare-Gesellschaft, Jahrbuch. 1–60. Weimar, 1865–1924; 61–99. Leipzig, 1925–63; 100/1– . Weimar, 1964/5– .

4 **Shakespeare Newsletter.** 1– . New York, 1951– .

5 **Shakespeare Quarterly.** 1– . Bethlehem, Pa., Shakespeare association of America, 1950– .

6 **Shakespeare Research Opportunities;** report of the Modern language association conference. 1– . Riverside, Calif., Dept. of English, University of California, 1965– .

7 **Shakespeare Studies (Tokyo).** 1– . Tokyo, Shakespeare society of Japan, 1962– .

8 **Shakespeare Studies,** an annual gathering of research, criticism, and reviews. 1– . Cincinnati, 1965–8; Dubuque, Iowa, W. C. Brown, 1969– .

9 **Shakespeare Survey,** an annual survey of Shakespearian study and production. 1– . Cambridge, C.U.P., 1948– .

PRINCIPAL CUMULATED INDEXES

15 **Shakespeare** survey. General index to volumes 1–10. Sh Surv 11:171–223 '58.

16 —— Index to volumes 11–20. *ib.* 21:171–219 '68.

17 **Deutsche Shakespeare-Gesellschaft.** Gesamtverzeichnis für die Bände 1–99 des Shakespeare-Jahrbuchs . . . bearbeitet von Marianne Rohde. Heidelberg, Quelle & Meyer, 1964. 158p. 23cm.

18 **Smith, Martin Seymour-.** Cumulative index to the Shakespeare quarterly, volumes 1–15, 1950–1964. New York, Ams pr. [1969] 276p. 25cm.

SERIAL BIBLIOGRAPHIES

20 'Shakespeare and his contemporaries in the literature of 1934[-48], a classified bibliography' *in* **Shakespeare Association Bulletin.** 1–24. New York, Shakespeare association of America, 1924–49.

Comp. by Samuel A. and Dorothy Tannenbaum, 1935–49; various issues; continued in Shakespeare Quarterly.

21 'Shakespeare, an annotated bibliography for 1949[–]' *in* **Shakespeare Quarterly.** 1– . Bethlehem, Pa., Shakespeare association of America, 1950– .

22 **McManaway, James Gilmer.** Textual studies. (The year's contributions to Shakespearian study.) Sh Surv 1:127–31 '48; 2:145–53 '49; 3:143–52 '50; 4:153–63 '51; 5:144–52 '52; 6:163–72 '53; 7:147–53 '54; 8:153–9 '55; 9:148–56 '56; 10:151–8 '57; 11:149–55 '58; 12:146–52 '59; 13:162–9 '60; 14:157–66 '61; 15:175–82 '62; 16:172–81 '63; 18:186–92 '65; James Kirkwood Walton 19:154–63 '66; 20:170–9 '67; 21:157–63 '68; G. Richard Proudfoot 22:176–83 '69.

23 'Shakespearean work in progress' *in* **Shakespeare Research Opportunities.** 1– . Riverside, Calif., 1965– .

24 **Barroll, J. Leeds.** 'Significant articles, monographs, and reviews' *in* **Shakespeare Studies.** 1– . Dubuque, Iowa, 1965– .

GENERAL BIBLIOGRAPHIES AND GUIDES

30 **Wyman, W. H.** Bibliography of the Bacon–Shakespeare controversy, with notes and extracts. Cincinnati, P. G. Thomson, 1884. 124p. 23cm.

31 **Shakespeare memorial library**, STRATFORD-UPON-AVON. Interesting & important donation from the Indian government. [Stratford-upon-Avon, 1890] 1 l. 31cm.
List of translations into the languages of India.

32 **Harris, Edward B.** Mr. Sidney Lee's Life of Shakespeare. N&Q ser9 3:42–3 Ja '99.
Notes on points of bibliogr. interest.

33 **Deutsche Shakespeare-Gesellschaft. Bibliothek.** Katalog der Bibliothek der Deutschen Shakespeare-Gesellschaft. Weimar, R. Wagner, 1900. 56p. 23cm.
Earlier catalogues were issued in 1865, 1876, 1899; see no.81.

34 **Jaggard, William,** comp. 'Folklore, superstition and witchcraft in Shakespeare, a bibliography' in Lucy, Margaret. Shakespeare and the supernatural. Liverpool, 1906. p.34–8.

35 **Deutsche Shakespeare-Gesellschaft. Bibliothek.** Katalog. . . . Weimar, R. Wagner, 1909. vi,88p. 24cm.

36 **Lee, sir Sidney.** A Shakespeare reference library. [London] 1910. 12p. 25cm. Covertitle. (English association. Leaflet no.15)
See no.60.

37 **'Shakespeare'** in Ward, sir Adolphus W. and A. R. Waller, ed. The Cambridge history of English literature. Cambridge, 1910. V.5, p.426–72.
Superseded by the bibliogr. in CBEL: see no.75a.

38 **Wigan. Public library.** William Shakespeare, a list of books and papers relating to Shakespeare preserved in the reference department . . . by Henry Tennyson Folkard. Wigan, J. Starr, 1910. 37p. 25cm.

39 **Marks, Percy J.** Australasian Shakespeareana, a bibliography of books, pamphlets, magazine articles, &c. that have been printed in Australia and New Zealand dealing with Shakespeare and his works. Sydney, Tyrell's, 1915. 34p. 26cm.

40 **Meyer, H. H. B.** A brief guide to the literature of Shakespeare. Chicago, American library association publishing board, 1915. 61p. 17cm.

41 **Wheatley, Henry Benjamin.** Shakespeare as a man of letters. Bib Soc Trans 14pt1:109–32 '15/16.
'Technique' (p.111–24): discussion of Shakespeare's use of book terms, and understanding of books and printing.

42 **Baroda. Central library.** Shakespeare tercentenary, 1616–1916. . . . Books in stock. [Baroda, 1916] 13p. 18cm.

43 **Bolton. Public libraries.** Shakespeare tercentenary, 1616–1916; hand-list of books in the central reference and lending libraries on Shakespeare and his works. [Bolton, Glensdale, ptr., 1916] 20p. facsim. 19cm.

44 **Chicago. Public library.** William Shakespeare, 1616–1916; selected list of books. . . . [Chicago, 1916] 32p. 15cm.
Rev. from Chicago Pub Lib Bk Bull 5n08:137–8, 151–4 Oc '15.

45 **Jersey City, N.J. Public library.** William Shakespeare, 1616–1916; list of books in the Free public library of Jersey City. Jersey City, N.J., 1916. 30p. 16cm. Covertitle.

46 **Lynn, Mass. Public library.** Special list: William Shakespeare Mar. 1, 1916. [Lynn, 1916] 10p. 26cm. Headtitle.

47 **New York. Public library.** The Shakespearian festival. New York, 1916. 22p. 15cm.
Chronol. checklist of ana comp. by Jacqueline M. Overton.

48 **Northup, Clark Sutherland.** Shakespeare bibliographies and reference lists. Pa Bib Soc Am 10n02:92–100 Ap '16.
Specimen of his Register of bibliographies, 1925.

49 **Rochdale. Public libraries, art gallery and museum.** Catalogue: Shakespeare tercentenary exhibition, April 14–May 28, 1916. [Rochdale, 1916] 36p. illus., facsim. 22cm.

50 **Southwark. Public libraries and museums.** 'Catalogue of exhibits' *in* A paper on Shakespeare and Southwark by Robt. W. Bowers . . . together with a catalogue of the exhibition . . . in the Reference department of the Central library. [London, 1916] p.27–33.

51 **Stephen, George Arthur.** William Shakespeare, an annotated catalogue of the works of William Shakespeare and the books relating to him in the Norwich public library. Norwich Pub Lib Readers' Guide 5n02:32–53 Mr '16.

52 **Watkins, Marie O.** Guide to the literature of Shakespeare in the library. St. Louis Pub Lib Mthly Bull new ser 14n03:79–135 Mr '16.

53 **West Ham. Public libraries.** Shakespeare tercentenary, 1916. Aids to the study of Shakespeare in the Central library, Stratford. West Ham, 1916. 8p. illus. 15cm. Covertitle.

54 **Brooke, Charles Frederick Tucker.** The Shakespeare tercentenary. Pa Bib Soc Am 11n03/4:123–35 Jl/Oc '17.
Survey of publications associated with tercentenary celebrations.

55 **Sparke, Archibald.** New Shakspere society's publications. N&Q ser12 4:77 Mr '18; W. A. B. Coolidge; St. Swithin *ib.* 4:143 My '18; A. Sparke; R. A. Shrimpton 4:170 Je '18; W. Jaggard 4:338 D '18; A. Sparke 5:162 Je '19.

56 **Czeke, Marianne.** Shakespeare-Könyvtár. Budapest, M. Kir. Tudománye-gyetemi Nyomda, 1920. 208p. 23cm. (A Budapesti Királyi Magyar Tudo-mányegyetemi könyvtár címjegyzékének mellékletei, II)

56a **Price, Lawrence Marsden.** 'Shakespeare in Germany' *in* English German literary influences: bibliography and survey. Berkeley, Calif., 1920. p.51–81.
See also no.87a.

57 **Ruppert y Ujaravi, Ricardo.** 'Índice cronológico de las traducciones e imitaciones' *in* Shakespeare en España; traducciones, imitaciones e influencia de las obras de Shakespeare en la literatura española. Madrid, 1920. p.[103]–6.

58 **Ward, Annette P.** Abbey's illustrations of Shakespeare's comedies. Bull Bib 11:141–2 My/Ag '22.

   Checklist of Edwin A. Abbey's illus. to essays by Andrew Lang in Harper's Magazine, D 1889–Ag '95.

59 **Sellers, Harry.** A working Shakespeare bibliography. Lib Assn Rec new ser 1n02:106–13 Je '23; 1n03:157–64 S '23.

60 **Lee, sir Sidney** and **sir E. K. Chambers.** A Shakespeare library. 2d ed. [London] 1925. (First pub. 1910) 18p. 25cm. (English association. Pamphlet no.61)

61 **Boas, Frederick Samuel.** Shakespeare societies, past and present. Sh R 1n05: 315–21 S '28.

62 **Dubeux, Albert.** 'Liste chronologique des traductions et adaptations françaises de Shakespeare' *in* Les traductions françaises de Shakespeare. Paris, 1928. p.[49]–81.

63 **Popović, Vladeta.** 'Bibliography. I. Translations of Shakespeare into Serbian.—II. Serbian essays, etc. on Shakespeare . . .' *in* Shakespeare in Serbia. London, 1928. p.[125]–8.

64 **Par, Alfonso.** Contribución a la bibliografía española de Shakespeare; catálogo bibliográfico de la colección del autor. Barcelona, 1930. 136p. 17cm. (Instituto del teatro nacional. Publicaciones, no.7)

65 **Ebisch, Walther** and **L. L. Schücking.** A Shakespeare bibliography. Oxford, Clarendon pr., 1931. xviii,294p. 25cm.

   Classified list of Shakespeariana with some critical notes. For the Supplement, *see* no.70.
   Rev: N&Q 160:468 Je '31; H. S[ellers] Mod Lang N 47:486 '32.

66 **Shakespeare association of Japan.** Catalogue of the exhibition of Shakesperiana . . . held at Maruzen co. ltd., Tokyo, from 20th to 29th May, 1933. [Tokyo, 1933] 82p. 22cm.

67 **Jaggard, William.** Shakespeare once a printer and bookman; lecture one of the twelfth series of printing trade lectures at Stationers' Hall, London. Stratford-upon-Avon, Shakespeare pr. [1934] 34p. facsims. 26cm.

   Mainly a glossary of printing and bookish terms in Shakespeare's works.

68 **Rānjī G. Shāhānī.** 'Essai bibliographique' *in* Shakespeare vu par les Orientaux. Paris [1934?] p.124–55.

   List of Hindi translations.

69 **Paul, Henry Neill** and **G. E. Dawson.** Shakespeare bibliography. TLS 28 F '35:124.

   Announcement of bibliogr. of 'literary editions (i.e. those intended primarily for readers) between 1709 and 1865, and of stage versions, . . . between 1660 and 1865'.

70 **Ebisch, Walther** and **L. L. Schücking.** Supplement for the years 1930–1935 to
A Shakespeare bibliography. Oxford, Clarendon pr., 1937. (Repr. New York,
B. Blom [1964]) 104p. 25cm.

See also no.65, 110.

Rev: N&Q 172:288 '37; S. C. Chew N.Y. Herald Tribune Bk R 4 Ap '37:37; H. S[ellers]
Library ser2 18:119 '37; I. A. Williams Lond Merc 35:506 '37; W. Keller Sh Jahrb 73:171
'37; P. Alexander Mod Lang R 33:581–2 '38; H. S[ellers] Mod Lang N 53:77 '38.

71 **H., O. N.** Shakespeare in Greek and Latin. N&Q 175:350 N '38; D. Cacla-
manos; C. Kessary; W. Jaggard ib. 175:389–90 N '38; P. Morgan; O. F.
Babler 175:409 D '38; L. G. H. Horton-Smith 175:464 D '38.

72 **Clendening, Logan.** A bibliographic account of the Bacon–Shakespeare controversy. Coloph new graphic ser 1no3:25–32 S '39. facsims.

Rev: TLS 6 Ja '40:12.

73 **Minoru, Toyada.** Shakespeare in Japan, an historical survey. Japan Soc
London Trans 36:77–175 '39.

'A Japanese Shakespeare bibliography' (p.163–75). Earlier compilations by Ichikawa Sanki
and Yamaguchi Takemi (1931–3), and Yamaguchi Takemi (1933), noted in this item have
not been located.

74 **Einarsson, Stefán.** Shakespeare in Iceland, an historical study. Eng Lit Hist
7no4:272–85 D '40.

75 **Minoru, Toyada.** 'A Japanese Shakespeare bibliography' in Shakespeare in
Japan, an historical survey. Tokyo; Southern Pasadena, 1940. p.121–39.
(Not seen)

75a '**Shakespeare**' in The Cambridge bibliography of English literature. Cambridge, 1940–57. V.1, p.539–608, by Frederick W. Bateson; v.5 (Supplement,
ed. G. G. Watson, 1957), p.257–93, by James C. Maxwell, J. M. Nosworthy
and D. M. Malone.

76 **Fucilla, Joseph Guerin.** Shakespeare in Italian criticism; a supplement to the
bibliographies compiled by Ebisch and Schücking. Philol Q 20no4:559–72
Oc '41.

77 **Guttman, Selma.** The foreign sources of Shakespeare's works, an annotated
bibliography of the commentary on this subject between 1904 and 1940,
together with lists of certain translations available to Shakespeare. New
York, King's crown pr., 1947. (Repr. New York, Octagon books, 1968)
xxi,168p. 24cm.

Rev: TLS 27 Mr '48:182; H. W. Herrington Symposium 2:300–2 '49; F. Baldensperger R
Litt Comp 22:589–91 '49; E. E. Willoughby Sh Assn Bull 23:204–5 '49; P. Reyher Lang
Mod 42:296 '49; R. T. H. Bks Abroad 23:79 '49; A. M. C. Latham R Eng Stud new ser
1:91 '50.

78 **Downs, Brian W.** Anglo-Danish literary relations, 1867–1900. Mod Lang R
43no2:145–74 Ap '48.

'Shakespeare and other British dramatists' (p.154–7)

78a [**Bibliography** of German editions of Shakespeare since 1945] in Mitteilungen
der Deutschen Shakespeare-Gesellschaft 1 Ag '49. 12p. (Not seen: after
Sh Q)

79 **Galland, Joseph Stanislaus.** Digesta anti-Shakespeareana. Ann Arbor, University microfilms, 1949. iii,1663 l. ([University microfilms, Ann Arbor, Mich.] Publication no.1175) Microfilm copy of typewritten manuscript.

'A descriptive bibliography of books and articles on the various controversies. . . . The 4509 items are listed alphabetically by authors' (Microfilm Abstrs 9no2:199 '49). Originally doctoral dissertation, University of Wisconsin, 1914.

80 **Cordasco, Francesco G. M. and K. W. Scott.** A brief Shakespeare bibliography for the use of students. New Orleans, Phoenix pr., 1950. iii,26p. 23cm.

81 **Deutsche Shakespeare-Gesellschaft. Bibliothek.** Katalog . . . nach dem Stand vom 31. März, 1951. [Weimar, 1951] 357p. 19cm.

82 —— Nachtrag, 1950–1960. Weimar, 1960. 116p. 19cm.

83 **Lüdeke, H.** Shakespeare-Bibliographie für die Kriegsjahre 1939–1946, England und Amerika. Archiv 187:25–36 '50; 188:8–40 '51.

84 **Downs, Brian W.** Anglo-Norwegian literary relations, 1867–1900. Mod Lang R 47no4:449–94 Oc '52.

'Shakespeare' (p.455–7)

85 **Fermor, Una Ellis-.** English and American Shakespeare studies, 1937–1952. Angl 71hft1:1–49 '52.

'I. Textual and bibliographical studies' (p.5–22)

86 **Halliday, Frank Ernest.** A Shakespeare companion, 1550–1950. London, G. Duckworth [1952] xiv,742p.+16 l. of plates. illus., diagrs., ports., facsims. 20cm.

See no.127.

87 **Newcastle-upon-Tyne. Public libraries.** William Shakespeare: select catalogue of books. [Newcastle, 1952] 35p. 20cm.

87a **Price, Lawrence Marsden.** 'Shakespeare in Germany' *in* English literature in Germany. Berkeley, Calif., 1953. p.444–81.

Expansion of no.56a.

88 **Mez, John Richard.** Edward de Vere, or Shakespeare, a bibliography. [Ruvigliana, Suisse, 1954] 3 l. 28cm. Headtitle. (Duplicated typescript)

89 **Brown, John Russell.** 'A select Shakespeare bibliography' *in* Sisson, Charles J. Shakespeare. London [1955] p.33–50.

90 **Chambers, sir Edmund Kerchever.** 'General classified bibliography' *in* Encyclopædia Britannica. Chicago [n.d., 1955?] V.20, p.453.

No item later than 1927.

91 **Heun, Hans Georg.** Probleme der Shakespeare-Übersetzungen. Sh Jahrb 92:450–63 '56.

92 **Eckhoff, Lorentz.** Shakespeare in Norwegian translations. Sh Jahrb 92:244–54 '56.

93 **Molin, Nils.** Shakespeare translated into Swedish. Sh Jahrb 92:232–43 '56.
'List of translations' (p.239–43)

94 **Bloch, Joshua.** Shakespeare in Hebrew garb. Jewish Bk Ann 14:23–31 '56/7.
'Hebrew versions of Shakespearean writings' (p.27–31)

95 **Fogel, Adah Boraisha-.** Shakespeare translations in Yiddish. Jewish Bk Ann 14:32–7 '56/7.
'Bibliography' (p.37)

96 **Smith, Gordon Ross.** Shakespeare bibliography. Sh Newsl 7no5:36 N '57.
Note on his Classified Shakespeare bibliography: no.110.

97 **Hahn, Wiktor.** Shakespeare w Polsce: bibliografia. Wrocław, Zakład Narodowy im. Ossolińskich, 1958. xix,386p. 25cm.
Rev: W. Weintraub Sh Q 11:217–19 '60.

98 **Deutsche Shakespeare-Gesellschaft. Bibliothek.** Bibliothek der Deutschen Shakespeare-Gesellschaft bei der Stadtbücherei Bochum; ein Verzeichnis. Bearbeitet von Gertrud König. [Bochum, 1959] 53p. 14×21cm.

99 **Hares, R. R.** Shakespeare glossaries and concordances: bibliography. London, University of London School of librarianship and archives, 1960.

100 **Steensma, Robert C.** Shakespeare and the army, a bibliography. Sh Newsl 10no3:28 My '60.

101 —— Shakespeare and medicine, a bibliography. Sh Newsl 10no4/5:36–7 S/N '60.

102 —— Shakespeare and religion, a bibliography. Sh Newsl 10no6:46 D '60.

103 **Marder, Louis.** Shakespearean biography, a bibliography. Sh Newsl 11no3:20–1 My '61.

104 **Moreira Gomes, Celuta** and **Thereza da Silva Aguiar.** William Shakespeare no Brasil: bibliografia. Rio de Janeiro, Biblioteca nacional, 1961. 352p. 26cm. Covertitle. (Brasil. Ministério da Educação e cultura. Biblioteca nacional. Anais, v.79 (1959))

105 **Marder, Louis.** A bibliography of Shakespearean bibliographies. Sh Newsl 12no3:24–5 My '62.

106 **Steensma, Robert C.** Shakespeare and the supernatural, a bibliography. Sh Newsl 12no4:32 S '62.

107 **Riffe, Nancy Lee.** Shakespeare's stage, a bibliography. Sh Newsl 12no5:40 N '62.

108 **Steensma, Robert C.** Shakespeare and women, a bibliography. Sh Newsl 12no2:12 Ap '62.

109 **Monval, Madeleine Horn-.** Les traductions françaises de Shakespeare, à l'occasion du quatrième centenaire de sa naissance, 1564–1964. Paris, Centre national de la recherche scientifique, 1963. 104p. illus. 26cm.

110 **Smith, Gordon Ross.** A classified Shakespeare bibliography, 1936–1958. University Park, Pennsylvania State U.P., 1963. lviii,784p. 28cm.

Unindexed continuation of Ebisch and Schücking, nos.65, 70.

Rev: G. B. Evans J Eng Germ Philol 63:165–6 '64; S. Barnet Coll Eng F '64:392; S. F. Johnson Renaiss N 17:4–8 '64; C. Leech Univ Toronto Q 33:315–16 '64; J. W. Velz Eng Stud 45:189–91 '64; H. Howarth J Gen Educ 16:72–4 '64; H. Heuer Sh Jahrb 100:311–13 '64; R. Berman Kenyon R 26:564 '64; R. C. Bald Mod Philol 62:68–9 '64; C. C. Mish Sevent Cent N 22:50 '64; R. W. Dent Sh Q 16:247–55 '65; N. J. Szenczi Sh Stud 2:366–9 '66.

111 **Steensma, Robert C.** and **L. Marder.** Shakespeare's fools, a bibliography. Sh Newsl 13no1:6 F '63.

112 **Steensma, Robert C.** Shakespeare and history, a bibliography. Sh Newsl 13no2:14 Ap '63.

113 —— Shakespeare on the eighteenth-century stage, a bibliography. Sh Newsl 13no4:29 S '63.

114 —— Shakespearean criticism in eighteenth-century England, a bibliography of modern studies. Sh Newsl 13no5:39 N '63.

115 —— Shakespeare and law, a bibliography. Sh Newsl 13no6:48 D '63.

116 **Adout, Jacques.** Shakespeare en Suisse romande. Schweizer Theat Jahrb 30:153–6 '64.

117 **Albert, Gábor.** Selected bibliography of Shakespeare's works published in Hungarian. New Hungarian Q 5no13:112–18 '64.

118 **Alexander, Peter,** *ed.* Studies in Shakespeare; British academy lectures by H. S. Bennett [and others] London, O.U.P., 1964. 246p. 19cm.

Includes 'The treatment of Shakespeare's text by his earlier editors, 1709–1768', by Ronald B. McKerrow. (p.103–31)—'Edward Capell and his edition of Shakespeare', by Alice Walker. (p.132–48)

119 **And, Metin.** Shakespeare in Turkey. Theat Res 6no2:75–84 '64. illus.

'Table of Shakespeare productions and translations in Turkey' (p.79–84)

120 **Boustead, Alan.** Music to Shakespeare, a practical catalogue of current incidental music, song settings and other related music. [London] O.U.P., distributor [1964] v,40p. 25cm.

121 **British book centre,** NEW YORK. Shakespeare, 1564–1964; reference list. New York [1964] [12]p. 21cm. Covertitle.

122 **Brown, John Russell.** 'A select Shakespeare bibliography' *in* Shakespeare, the writer and his work. [London, 1964] p.416–91.

123 **Dean, Winton, Dorothy Moore**, and **Phyllis M. Hartnoll,** *comp.* 'Catalogue
of musical works based on the plays and poetry of Shakespeare' *in* Hartnoll,
Phyllis M., *ed.* Shakespeare in music; essays by John Stevens [and others]
London, Macmillan, 1964. (Repr. London; New York, 1967) p.243–321.
'Check-list of composers' (p.291–321)

124 **Duţu, Alexandru.** Shakespeare in Rumania, a bibliographical essay. Bucha-
rest, Meridiane, 1964. 239p. illus., facsims. 16cm.
'Index of translations and adaptations' (p.221–39)

125 **Filipović, Rudolf.** Shakespeare in Croatia, an annotated bibliography.
Studia Romanica et Anglica Zagrabiensia 17/18:73–101 Jl/D '64.

126 **Great Britain. Public record office.** Shakespeare in the public records.
London, H.M.S.O. [1964] 40p. facsims. 24cm. (Public record office hand-
books, no.5)
Checklist of documents with extensive notes by N. E. Evans.

127 **Halliday, Frank Ernest.** A Shakespeare companion, 1564–1964. [Rev. ed.]
[Harmondsworth, Middlesex] Penguin books [1964] (First ed. [1952])
565[1]p. diagrs. 19cm. (Penguin reference books R27)
'Bibliography' (p.545–[66]). Useful for quick access to basic bibliogr. information.

128 **Hastings. Public library.** A Shakespeare booklist, published in commemoration of the quatercentenary of the birth of William Shakespeare. [Hastings,
1964] [12]p. 18cm.

128a **India. National library,** CALCUTTA. Shakespeare in India, an exhibition of
books and illustrations to celebrate the fourth birth centenary of William
Shakespeare. Calcutta, 1964. vi,45p. (Not seen)
Includes list of trans. into Indian languages.

129 **Instituto Britânico em Portugal,** LISBON. Shakespeariana Portuguesa: ex-
posição, abril–maio 1964. [Lisbon? 1964] iii,37p. 19cm. (Duplicated typescript)

130 **Leamington. Public library.** Shakespeare, a catalogue. [Leamington, 1964]
13p. 25cm. Covertitle. (Duplicated typescript)

131 **[Levidova, Inna Mikhailovna]** *ed.* Shekspir; bibliografiya russkikh perevodov
i kriticheskoi literatury na russkom yazyke, 1748–1962. [Shakespeare, a
bibliography of Russian translations and literature on Shakespeare in
Russian, 1748–1962] Moscow, Kniga, 1964. 708p. 21cm.
Chronol. classified checklist, in Russian. The 'bibliographic appendices' include 'Payne
Collier and Russian translators of Shakespeare', by V. P. Komarova; 'The reactions of
British scholars to the edition of Complete Shakespeare . . . of S. A. Vengerov, 1902–
1904', by Yu. D. Levin.
Rev: V. Baskakov Russkaya literatura 1:216–20 '65; N. Nikiforovskaya Sovetskaya
bibliografiya 4:78–83 '65; P. Zaborov Izvestiya Akad nauk SSSR (Lit & Lang ser) 24:262–4
'65; G. Gibian Sh Q 17:94–6 '66.

131a —— 'Shekspir na russkom yazyke (bibliografiya perevodov i kriticheskikh
rabot)' *in* Vil'yam Shekspir: k chetyrekhsotletiyu so dnya rozhdeniya,
1564–1964: issledovaniya i materialy. Moskva, 1964. p.403–76.
Checklist of trans. and critical works in Russian to 1963; *see also* no.156a.

132 **McManaway, James Gilmer.** Shakespeare in the United States. Pub Mod Lang Assn 79no5:513–18 D '64.
General survey of American Shakespeareana, mainly bibliogr.

133 **Mangini, Nicola and G. Biadene,** *comp.* [Catalogue of editions exhibited] *in* Mostra bibliografica Shakespeariana, Venezia. Venezia, 1964. p.13–40. (Not seen)

134 **Marder, Louis.** American & German doctoral dissertations. Sh Newsl 14no2/3:51–5 Ap/My '64.
Checklist of c.550 items, 1867–1963.

135 **Moreira Gomes, Celuta.** 'Shakespeare em traduções brasileiras: bibliografia' *in* Melo, Barbara and O. Monat, *ed.* William Shakespeare. Rio de Janeiro, 1964. (Not seen)

135a **Neumann, Walter.** Shakespeare; Werke u. Sekundärliteratur aus d. Beständen d. Stadtbücherei in Bielefeld. Bielefeld, 1964. 55p. (Not seen)

136 **St. Pancras. Public libraries.** William Shakespeare, a book list . . . new compiled and imprinted . . . to mark the 400th anniversary of his birth in 1564. [London] 1964. 11p. 23cm.
Comp. by Martin Underwood.

137 **Scunthorpe. Public libraries.** Shakespeare quatercentenary, 1564–1964: Shakespeare, a catalogue of books about the man, his times and his works. [Scunthorpe, 1964] 20p. 18cm. Covertitle.

138 **Shakespeare** in France. Yale French Stud 33:127–30 '64.

139 **Sideris, Joannis.** Shakespeare in Greece. Theat Res 6no2:85–99 '64.

140 **Warsaw. Uniwersytet. Biblioteka.** Szekspir w literaturze i plastyke polskiej. . . . Katalog wystawy opracował S. Helsztyński z udziałem Jana Dąbrowskiego. Warszawa, 1964. 34p. 19cm. (Duplicated typescript)

141 **Helsztyński, Stanisław.** Polish translations of Shakespeare in the past and today. Sh Jahrb 100/1:274–93 '64/5.
'Polish translations of Shakespeare' (p.289–93)

142 **Berman, Ronald.** A reader's guide to Shakespeare's plays, a discursive bibliography. Chicago, Scott, Foreman [1965] 151p. 22cm.

143 **Levidova, Inna Mikhailovna** Shekspir na russkom yazyke v sovetskikh izdaniyakh k 400-letiyu so dnya rozhdeniya V. Shekspira. [Shakespeare in Russian in Soviet editions; on the occasion of the quatercentenary of Shakespeare's birth] Kniga (Moscow) 10:253–71 '65.

144 **Moreira Gomes, Celuta and Thereza da Silva Aguiar.** William Shakespeare no Brasil; bibliografia das commemorações do 4° centenário 1964. Rio de Janeiro, Divisão de publicações e divulgação, Biblioteca nacional, 1965. 251p. illus. 27cm.

145 **Páříková, M.** and **J. Kuncová,** *ed.* William Shakespeare 1564–1616; Shakespearovo dílo a literatura ve fondech Mlk. Praha, 1965. 2v. (Duplicated typescript) (Not seen)

'Mimeographed bibl. of the Prague Municipal Library's holdings in *Shak.* editions and books . . . and periodical articles and essays.' (Sh Q)

146 **Barcia, Pedro Luis,** *comp.* 'Bibliografía Shakespeariana; publicaciones hechas en la Argentina' *in* La Plata. Universidad nacional. Facultad de humanidades y ciencias de la educación. Departamento de letras. Instituto de literaturas extranjeras. Shakespeare en la Argentina. La Plata [1966] p.[99]–115.

146a **Campbell, Oscar James,** *ed.* The reader's encyclopedia of Shakespeare. New York, Crowell [1966] xv,1014p. illus., facsims., tables, ports. 26cm.

147 **Greg, sir Walter Wilson.** Collected papers, edited by J. C. Maxwell. Oxford, Clarendon pr., 1966. xii,449p. facsims. 21cm.

Includes sometimes revised reprs. of '13. Shakespeare's hand once more.—14. A question of plus or minus.—18. The function of bibliography in literary criticism illustrated in a study of the text of King Lear.—26. The printing of Shakespeare's Troilus and Cressida in the First folio.' These papers are listed herein under the date of first publication.

Rev: TLS 28 S '67:924; *rf*. J. C. Maxwell *ib*. 5 Oc '67:938.

148 **Shakespeare** in Israel: a bibliography for the years ca.1950–1965. Sh Q 17n03:291–306 '66.

149 **Sotonová, Vlastamila** and **L. Venyš,** *comp.* 'A bibliography of Czech writings and lectures on Shakespeare by members of the teaching staff of Charles university from 1882–1964' *in* Stříbrný, Zdeněk, *ed.* Charles university on Shakespeare; essays. Prague, 1966. p.159–70.

150 **Bate, John.** How to find out about Shakespeare. Oxford, Pergamon pr. [1968] xv,161p. facsims. 17cm.

1. Shakespeare's England.—2. The life of Shakespeare.—3. Shakespeare's theatre and productions.—4. The text of Shakespeare's works.—5. Shakespeare's sources.—6. Literary criticism.—7. Special themes and subjects.—8. The sonnets and poems.—9. Commentaries on individual plays.—10. The bibliographical apparatus.

151 **McNamee, Lawrence F.** 'William Shakespeare' *in* Dissertations in English and American literature: theses accepted by American, British and German universities, 1865–1964. New York, 1968. p.216–55.

'Bibliographies of Shakespeare' (p.218–19); 'The text of Shakespeare' (p.232–3)

152 **Marder, Louis.** Shakespeare glossaries, 1710–1948. Sh Newsl 18n03:22–3 My '68.

153 **Shakespeare-Literatur** in Bochum. Aus den Beständen des englischen Seminars des Germanistischen Instituts und der Universitätsbibliothek der Ruhr-Universität Bochum, der Deutschen Shakespeare-Gesellschaft West und der Stadtbücherei Bochum. [Bochum] Stadtbücherei Bochum, 1968. 236p. 18cm. (Not seen)

154 **Velz, John W.** Shakespeare and the classical tradition, a critical guide to commentary, 1660–1960. Minneapolis, University of Minnesota pr.; London, O.U.P., 1968. xvii,459p. 28cm.

Rev: TLS 15 My '69:532; J. C. Maxwell N&Q 214:148–50 '69.

155 **Elton, William R.** Shakespeare and renaissance intellectual contexts: a selective annotated list, 1967–1968. Sh Res Opp 4:122–202 '68/9.

156 **Stensgaard, Richard.** Shakespeare, Paracelsus, and the plague of 1603: an annotated list. Sh Res Opp 4:73–7 '68/9.

156a **Levidova, Inna Mikhailovna.** 'Bibliografiya perevodov i kriticheskoi literatury o Shekspire na russkom yazyke, 1963–1964' *in* Shekspirovskiy sbornik 1967. Moskva [1969] p.356–68.
Continuation of no.131a.

157 **Payne, Waveney R. N.** A Shakespeare bibliography. London, Library association, 1969. 93p. 22cm.

158 **Wells, Stanley.** Shakespeare, a reading guide. London, English association, 1969. 44p. 25cm. (2d issue, with addenda, 1970.)

WORKS

BIBLIOGRAPHIES

170 **Shakespeare memorial library,** STRATFORD-UPON-AVON. A list of the editions of Shakespeare's works published in America. Printed for the Council of the Shakespeare memorial association. Stratford-on-Avon, J. Morgan, ptr. [1890] 6p. 21cm. Covertitle.

171 **[Phillipps, James Orchard Halliwell-.]** A calendar of the Shakespearean rarities, drawings & engravings, formerly preserved at Hollingbury Copse. . . . 2d ed. enl. Ed. by Ernest E. Baker. London, Longmans, Green, 1891. (First pub. 1887) xviii,170p. 23cm.

172 **The critical** editions. Shakespeariana 10no1:59–61 Ja '93.
Checklist of 55 items.

173 **British museum. Dept. of printed books.** Catalogue of printed books. Shakespeare, William. London, Ptd. by W. Clowes, 1897. 232 col. 35cm.

174 **[Brassington, William Salt]** Hand-list of collective editions of Shakespeare's works published before the year 1800. Stratford-upon-Avon, J. Morgan, 1898. [5]p. 25cm. Covertitle.

175 **Jonas, Maurice.** Early Shakspearian books. N&Q ser9 1:225 Mr '98.
Checklist of Q and ana in his collection.

176 **[Wheeler, F. A.]** *comp.* A catalogue of Shakespeareana with a prefatory essay by Sidney Lee. London, Ptd. for presentation only, at the Chiswick pr., 1899. 2v.(xlviii,504p.) 30cm.
Unindexed, extensively annotated short-title catalogue of 922 entries, largely purchased by M. J. Perry.

177 **Birmingham. Public libraries. Shakespeare memorial library.** An index to the Shakespeare memorial library, by A. Capel Shaw. Birmingham, P. Jones, 1900–3. viii,265p. 25cm.
Rev: H. G. Fiedler Angl Beibl 15:123–6 '04.

178 **Cambridge. University. Trinity college. Library.** Catalogue of the books presented to the library of Trinity college in Cambridge, compiled by W. W. Greg. Cambridge, Ptd. for Trinity college at University pr., 1903. viii,172p. 23cm.
Rev: A. Brandl Sh Jahrb 41:223–4 '05.

179 **Sotheby, Wilkinson and Hodge, ltd.,** LONDON. Catalogue of a very valuable and important collection of Shakespeareana which will be sold by auction . . . the 7th day of December, 1903. . . . London, Dryden pr., J. Davy [1903] 11p.+12 plates. illus., facsims.(part.fold.) 23cm.

180 **Lambert, D. H.** Cartae Shakespeareanae; Shakespeare documents, a chronological catalogue of extant evidence relating to the life and works of William
Shakespeare, collated and chronologically arranged. London, G. Bell, 1904.
xxi,107p. illus., facsims. 17cm.

181 **Irving, sir John Henry Brodribb-.** Catalogue of the valuable library of sir
Henry Irving and a collection of old play-bills . . . sold by auction. Rev. ed.
[London, Christie, Manson & Woods, 1905] 69p. 23cm.
'Shakespeare and Shakespeareana' (p.46–59)

182 **Sotheby, Wilkinson and Hodge, ltd.,** LONDON. Catalogue of a valuable
collection of books by or relating to Shakespeare, his works, times, and
influence on subsequent writers, including early editions of his plays . . .
which will be sold by auction . . . Thursday, the 25th of May, 1905, and two
following days. . . . London, J. Davy, Dryden pr. [1905] 132p. 25cm.
761 items.

183 **Newcastle-upon-Tyne. Public libraries.** . . . William Shakespeare: handlist
of editions, commentaries, etc. Newcastle upon Tyne, Easey & Best, ptr.,
1906. 11p. 25cm. (Not seen)

183a **Eton college. Library.** A descriptive catalogue of the early editions of the
works of Shakespeare preserved in the library of Eton college. London, Ptd.
for the college, 1909. (Anr. issue: London, H. Frowde, O.U.P. [1909])
viii,27p. 25cm.
Comp. by sir Walter W. Greg.
Rev: M. Förster Sh Jahrb 46:306 '10.

184 **Pollard, Alfred William.** Shakespeare folios and quartos, a study in the
bibliography of Shakespeare's plays, 1594–1685. London, Methuen, 1909.
vii,175p. facsims. 37cm.
1. The conditions of publishing in Shakespeare's day.—2. A bibliography of the quarto
editions of Shakespeare's plays published previously to 1623, with the entries relating to
them in the register of the Stationers' company, and notes, 1594–1622.—3. The good and
the bad quartos.—4. The quartos of 1619.—5. The Folio of 1623: I. Bibliographical
description. II. The collection of the copy. III. The editing. IV. The printing.—9. Bibliography, 1624–1685.—10. The later folios and quartos.—Additional appendix. . . . Mr.
G. W. Cole's census of the quartos of 1619.
Rev: Nation 90:9–10 '10; TLS 21 Ap '10:137–8; N&Q ser11 1:338–9 '10; A. Brandl Sh
Jahrb 46:269–71 '10.

185 **Shakespeare's birthplace,** STRATFORD-UPON-AVON. Catalogue of the books,
manuscripts . . . at present exhibited in Shakespeare's birthplace. Stratford-
upon-Avon, Ptd. for the trustees, 1910. xv,134p. illus., ports., facsims.
17cm.
Comp. by Richard Savage; *see* no.212.

186 **Sutton, Albert.** Shakespeare and the drama; a catalogue of Shakespearian
and dramatic literature on sale. . . . Manchester [n.d., c.1910] 60p. facsims.
21cm. Covertitle. (His [Catalogue] no.167)

187 **Jaggard, William.** Shakespeare bibliography; a dictionary of every known
issue of the writings of our national poet and of recorded opinion thereon

in the English language. Stratford-on-Avon, Shakespeare pr., 1911. (Repr. New York, Ungar, 1959) xxi,729p. illus., ports., facsims. 23cm.

'. . . something more than a bibliography; in fact, an encyclopædia of Shakespearean information and stage history . . .'; in dictionary form. 'Addenda and corrigenda'. (p.702–29)

Rev: A. W. P[ollard] Library ser3 2:331–5 '11; Athenæum 27 My '11:610–11; Nation 93:9–10 '11; N&Q ser11 4:59 '11; N.Y. Times Bk R 16:351 '11; D. Figgis Bkmn 40:254–5 '11; TLS 4 My '11:176; A. G. Newcomer Dial 51:192–4 '11; C. S. Northup J Eng Germ Philol 11:218–30 '12.

188 **Northup, Clark Sutherland.** On the bibliography of Shakespeare. J Eng Germ Philol 11no2:218–30 Ap '12.

Largely rev. of Jaggard's Bibliography, with substantial corrigenda.

189 **Dobell, Bertram, ltd.,** LONDON. Shakespearian catalogue, a collection of various editions of the works of Shakespeare, books illustrative of his life and times, textual and other criticism . . . offered for sale. . . . [London, R. Stockwell, ptr.] 1914. 35p. 20cm. Covertitle. (His [Catalogue] no.229)

848 items.

190 **Boston. Public library.** Shakespeare tercentenary, 1616–1916; an exhibition, free lectures, selected list of working editions and works relating to Shakespeare, offered by the public library of the city of Boston. Boston, 1915. 44p. 15cm.

191 **Cardiff. Public libraries.** Catalogue of the Shakespeare tercentenary exhibition held in the Reference library, 1916. Cardiff, Ptd. by the Western mail for the Libraries committee, 1916. 32p. 20cm.

Rev: TLS 11 My '16:223.

192 **Grolier club,** NEW YORK. Catalogue of an exhibition illustrative of the text of Shakespeare's plays as published in edited editions; together with a large collection of engraved portraits of the poet. New York, 1916. xiv,115p. ports. 24cm.

193 **John Rylands library,** MANCHESTER. Catalogue of an exhibition of the works of Shakespeare, his sources and the writings of his principal contemporaries. . . . Tercentenary of the death of Shakespeare, 1616, April 23, 1916. Manchester, Manchester U.P.; London, Longmans, Green, 1916. xvi,169p. facsims. 23cm.

Rev: TLS 11 My '16:223.

194 **New York. Public library.** Exhibition of Shakespeariana, April 2–May 31, 1916. New York, 1916. 22p. 15cm.

Comp. by Henrietta C. Bartlett.

195 **Oxford. University. Bodleian library.** A catalogue of the Shakespeare exhibition held in the Bodleian library to commemorate the death of Shakespeare, April 23, 1616. Oxford, Ptd. for the Bodleian library by F. Hall, 1916. xv,99p. illus., facsims. 27cm.

Rev: A. W. P[ollard] Library ser3 7:176 '16.

196 **Princeton university. Library.** Special exhibits in the Princeton university library, 1. Shakespeare tercentenary: exhibit relating to the life of

Shakespeare, important early editions of his works, original illustrations by Cruikshank, contemporary editions of Shakespeare's sources, 1916. Princeton, N.J., 1916. 7p. 24cm. Covertitle.

197 **Redwood library and athenæum,** NEWPORT, R.I. The Redwood library guide to an appreciation of Wm. Shakespeare, his works and fame; being a few explanatory notes on an exhibition of books and manuscripts selected from the collection of mr. Marsden J. Perry. Providence, Ptd. at the sign of the standard, 1916. 37p. 23cm.

198 **Victoria and Albert museum,** SOUTH KENSINGTON, LONDON. Shakespeare exhibition, 1916. [London, 1916] ii,20p. illus. 15cm.

199 —— [Same]: [2d ed., rev.] July 1916.
Preface by Cecil Smith.

200 **Wales. National library,** ABERYSTWYTH. Shakespeare tercentenary, 1916: annotated catalogue of books, etc. exhibited at the University college of Wales, Aberystwyth, May, 1916. Aberystwyth, 1916. 19p. 18cm.

201 **The Shakespeare** tercentenary catalogues. TLS 5 Oc '16:476; 7 D '16:588.
1. Great Britain.—2. The United States.
Comprehensive review article with interesting notes on copies of early ed.

202 **New York. Public library.** Catalogue of the exhibition of Shakespeareana held at the New York public library . . . in commemoration of the tercentenary of Shakespeare's death. Comp. and arranged by Henrietta C. Bartlett. New York, 1917. 161p. 25cm.
Rev: A. W. Pollard Library ser3 8:183-6 '17.

203 **[Hazlitt, William Carew]** Catalogue of the Shakespeare library formed by an English collector. To be sold. . . . New York, Anderson galleries [1918] 215p. illus. 24cm. (Not seen)
969 entries, mainly before 1700.

204 **Dix, Ernest Reginald McClintock.** Earliest printing of Shakespeare's plays in Ireland. Bib Soc Ireland Pub 2no1:18-20 '21.
'List of Shakespeare's plays printed in Ireland before 1801' (p.19-20)

205 **Bartlett, Henrietta Collins.** Mr. William Shakespeare: original and early editions of his quartos and folios, his source books and those containing contemporary notices. New Haven, Yale U.P.; London, H. Milford, O.U.P., 1922. xxviii,217p. 24cm.
Introduction.—The key to owners.—Shakespeare's works.—Spurious plays assigned to Shakespeare and adaptations of his works.—Source books.—Contemporary notices.
Rev: New Statesm 15 Jl '22:422; Sat R 134:178-9 '22; I. A. Williams Lond Merc 6:524 '22; TLS 15 Je '22:389; B. da C. Greene Lit R 16 S '22:30; A. M. Thorndike N.Y. Times Bk R 9 Jl '22:2; C. F. T. Brooke Yale R new ser 12:634-5 '23; T. S. Graves Stud Philol 20:257-8 '23.

206 **Nicoll, John Ramsay Allardyce.** 'A brief bibliography of Shakespeare adaptations, 1660-1700' *in* Dryden as an adapter of Shakespeare. London, 1922. p.[26]-34.

207 **British museum.** British museum Shakespeare exhibition, 1923. Guide to the mss. & printed books exhibited in celebration of the tercentenary of the First folio Shakespeare. [London] Ptd. by order of the trustees, 1923. 77p. facsims.(1 fold.) 21cm.

Introduction by A. W. Pollard.

208 **Cardiff. Public libraries.** Catalogue of the exhibition of Shakespeariana . . . in commemoration of the First folio centenary, 1623–1923. Cardiff, Ptd. for the Libraries committee by the Educational publishing co., 1923. 52p. 22cm.

209 **Durham. University. Armstrong college,** NEWCASTLE-UPON-TYNE. Catalogue of an exhibition of the early editions of the works of Shakespeare held in commemoration of the tercentenary of the First folio 1623. With a preface by Gordon Craig. [Newcastle upon Tyne] 1923. 19p. 23cm.

210 **Maggs bros.,** LONDON. Shakespeare and Shakespeareana, a catalogue issued in commemoration of the tercentenary of the First folio Shakespeare, A.D. 1623–1923. London, 1923. 339p. illus., facsims. 21cm. (Catalogue 434)

See no.215.

211 **Shakespeare association,** LONDON. In commemoration of the First folio centenary, a resetting of the preliminary matter of the First folio, with a catalogue of Shakespeariana exhibited in the hall of the Worshipful company of stationers, illustrative facsimiles, and introduction by sir Israel Gollancz. London, Published for the Shakespeare association by H. Milford, O.U.P., 1923. (Anr. issue: Published for the Worshipful company of stationers, 1923) 54p. illus., facsims. 26cm.

'Exhibits' (p.47–54)

212 **Shakespeare's birthplace,** STRATFORD-UPON-AVON. Catalogue of the books, manuscripts . . . exhibited in Shakespeare's birthplace, compiled by Frederick C. Wellstood. Stratford-upon-Avon, 1925. 176p. illus., facsims. 19cm.

See no.223.

213 **Spencer, Hazelton.** Improving Shakespeare; some bibliographical notes on the restoration adaptations. Pub Mod Lang Assn 41no3:727–46 S '26.

Classified checklists of 'A. Bibliographies of the restoration alterations.—B. First editions of altered stage versions of Shakespeare's plays, 1660–1710.—C. Plays sometimes mistaken for altered versions of Shakespeare', with bibliogr. notes and discussion. See no.217.

214 **Madan, Falconer,** *ed.* A catalogue of Shakespeareana, with some notes and a preface. . . . London, Ptd. for presentation only, 1927. (Anr. issue: London, G. Michelmore [1927]) vii,209p. 26cm.

215 **Maggs bros.,** LONDON. Shakespeare and Shakespeareana. [London, Ptd. by the Courier pr., 1927] 519[21]p. illus., facsims. 25cm. (Catalogue 493)

Indexed catalogue of 1,383 items.

216 **Oxford. University. Bodleian library.** Specimens of Shakespeariana in the Bodleian library at Oxford. [Oxford] Ptd. by J. Johnson, ptr. to the University, 1927. 68p. port., facsims. 23cm.

217 **Spencer, Hazelton.** 'Bibliography' *in* Shakespeare improved, the restoration versions in quarto and on the stage. Cambridge [Mass.] 1927. p.[381]–90.

Checklists of 'A. First editions of the altered versions.—B. Bibliographies and general works on the altered versions.—C. Works on adaptations of single plays.—D. Select bibliography of works on the restoration theatre'.

218 **Stockwell, La Tourette.** Shakespeare and the Dublin pirates. Dublin Mag new ser 4no3:21–45 Jl/S '29.

'A handlist of the editions of Shakespeare printed in Ireland during the 18th century' (p.33–45): title checklist with TP transcrs. and locations of copies.

219 **Babcock, Robert Witbeck.** A preliminary bibliography of eighteenth-century criticism of Shakespeare. Stud Philol extra ser 1:58–98 My '29.

Primary texts of Shakespeare criticism in the eighteenth century.—The restoration.—The early nineteenth century.—Collections of eighteenth-century critical texts.—A secondary bibliography of Shakespeare criticism in the eighteenth century.

220 —— 'Primary texts of Shakespeare criticism in the eighteenth century' *in* The genesis of Shakespeare idolatry, 1766–1799. . . . Chapel Hill, 1931. (Repr. New York, Russell & Russell, 1964) p.[244]–67.

Rev. from no.219. 'A secondary bibliography of Shakespeare criticism in the eighteenth century' (p.[268]–95). *See also* no.230.

221 **Ford, Herbert Lewis.** Shakespeare 1700–1740; a collation of the editions and separate plays, with some account of T. Johnson and R. Walker. Oxford, O.U.P., 1935. (Repr. New York, B. Blom [1968]) [6]145p. ports., facsims. 23cm.

Full discursive descrs., from Rowe's first to Theobald's second ed.

Rev: R. B. McK[errow] Library ser4 17:117–21 '36; TLS 1 F '36:100.

222 **Westfall, Alfred Van Rensselaer.** 'Chronological list of American editions of Shakespeare, 1787–1865' *in* American Shakespearean criticism, 1607–1865. New York, 1939. (Repr. New York, B. Blom, 1968) p.[168]–84.

64 items.

223 **Shakespeare's birthplace,** STRATFORD-UPON-AVON. Catalogue of the books, manuscripts . . . exhibited in Shakespeare's birthplace, compiled by the late Frederick C. Wellstood. New ed., with a supplementary list of recent additions. Stratford-upon-Avon, 1944. 180p. illus., facsims. 18cm.

224 **Sprague, Arthur Colby.** 'Bibliographical notes [on eighteenth and nine-teenth century prompt-books]' *in* Shakespeare and the actors. Cambridge, Mass., 1944. p.[335]–50.

225 **Austria. Nationalbibliothek,** VIENNA. Katalog der Shakespeare-Ausstellung. Wien, H. Bauer [1947] 93p.+facsims. 16cm.

226 **Dawson, Giles Edwin.** Three Shakespeare piracies in the eighteenth century. Stud Bib 1:49–58 '48. facsims.

TP transcrs. and facsims. of 3 ed. and their pirated versions; *Ham.*, 1723; *Oth.*, 1724; and *Mac.*, 1729, ptd. 1729–31.

227 **France. Bibliothèque nationale,** PARIS. **Dépt. des imprimés.** Catalogue des ouvrages de William Shakespeare conservés au Département des imprimés,

et dans les bibliothèques de l'Arsenal, Mazarine, Sainte-Geneviève, de l'Institut, et de l'Université de Paris. Paris, Imprimerie nationale, 1948. 423p. 26cm.

2,077 items.

228 **Illinois. University. Library.** Shakespeare at Illinois; notes on an exhibition of the Ernest Ingold folios and other Shakspereana in the University of Illinois library. Prepared by Thomas W. Baldwin and Isabelle Grant. Urbana, University of Illinois pr., 1951. 22p. facsim. 21cm.

229 **Rosenbach company,** PHILADELPHIA. William Shakespeare, a collection of first and early editions of his works, 1594 to 1700. Philadelphia, 1951. v,22p. illus., facsims. 26cm.

230 **Wiley, Margaret Lee.** A supplement to the bibliography of Shakespeare idolatry. Stud Bib 4:164–6 '51/2.

Babcock addenda: see no.220.

231 **O'Hegarty, Patrick Sarsfield.** Some Irish eighteenth-century editions of Shakespeare not recorded by Jaggard, Stockwell or Ford. Irish Bk Lover 32no1:4–7 Je '52.

232 **Stone, M. W.** Shakespeare and the juvenile drama. Theat Notebk 8:65–6 Ap/Je '54.

List of juvenile drama adapted from Sh., with a note of publishers.

233 **Fisher, Sidney T.** An exhibition of Shakespeare books, from the collection of mr. Sidney Fisher of Montreal, exhibited at the Stratford Shakespearean festival, 1956, Stratford, Ontario. Montreal, Halcyon pr., 1956. 38p. facsims. 16cm.

Rev: F. R. Goff Sh Q 8:125–6 '57.

234 **Royal Shakespeare theatre,** STRATFORD-UPON-AVON. **Library.** Shakespeare memorial library. Items of interest to theatre research workers. [Stratford-upon-Avon, 1957] 4 l. 33cm. Headtitle. (Duplicated typescript)

235 **Parker, R. B.** 'Old books and Elizabethan printing' *in* Jackson, B. A. W., *ed.* Stratford papers on Shakespeare. Toronto [1962] p.[30]–104. facsims.

An introduction to the Fisher collection, with a general account of Elizabethan printing practices and techniques of bibliographical study. 'An exhibit of Shakespeare books from Sidney Fisher's collection.' (p.97–104)

236 **Hastings, William T.** The richest Shakespeare collection. Bks at Brown 19:113–42 My '63.

Purchase of Thomas Rodd's collection in 1845 for the library of Brown university.

237 **Birmingham. Public libraries.** Eighteenth century attitudes to Shakespeare; the catalogue of an exhibition of books in the Birmingham library to celebrate the 400th anniversary of the birth of William Shakespeare. [Birmingham] 1964. 16p. 19cm.

Comp. by Charles Parish.

238 **Birmingham. Public libraries. Shakespeare memorial library.** Shakespeare exhibition to celebrate the four hundredth anniversary of his birth and the centenary of the library. Birmingham, 1964. 59p. illus., facsims. 19cm.

239 **British museum. Dept. of printed books.** Shakespeare, an excerpt from the General catalogue of printed books. London, Trustees of the British museum, 1964. 517 col. 34cm.

240 **Farmer, Geoffrey A. J.** A checklist of the collected editions of the works of William Shakespeare held in the major Australian libraries. Adelaide, Libraries board of South Australia, 1964. [iii]25[5]p. 24cm. (Duplicated typescript)
   Rev: S. Musgrove Austral Univ Mod Lang Assn 22:301–3 '64; G. A. Wilkes Sthly 3:213–15 '64; J. P. Whyte Southern R 1:95 '65.

241 **Fisher, Sidney T.** An exhibit of Shakespeare books, a loan exhibition from the collection of mr. Sidney Fisher of Montreal, exhibited at the Stratford Shakespearean festival, Stratford, Ontario. Montreal, 1964. 26p. facsims. 17cm.

242 **Gordan, John Dozier.** The bard and the book; editions of Shakespeare in the seventeenth century, an exhibition. New York, New York public library, 1964. 23p. 26cm.
   Repr. from N.Y. Pub Lib Bull 68n07:462–76 S '64.
   Shakespeare the poet.—Shakespeare the dramatist.—The Pavier quartos.—The First folio.—Quartos between 1623 and 1632.—The second folio.—Quartos between 1632 and 1663.—The third folio.—Attributions.—Adaptations.—The fourth folio.

243 **Henry E. Huntington library and art gallery, SAN MARINO, CALIF.** William Shakespeare, 1564–1616, an exhibition commemorating the four hundredth anniversary of Shakespeare's birth, April 23 1564. San Marino, Calif., 1964. [6]24[2]p. illus., facsims. 18cm.
   Comp. by William A. Parish and Dorothy Bowen.

244 **Lehigh university, BETHLEHEM, PA. Library.** A guide to an exhibition of rare books relating to Shakespeare on the occasion of the quadricentennial of his birth. Bethlehem, Pa., 1964. 48p. 23cm.
   Comp. by Frank S. Hook.

245 **Milwaukee. Public library.** William Shakespeare, his editors and editions; a commentary on the major editions of Shakespeare's works. [Milwaukee] 1964. 68p. illus. (Not seen)
   Comp. by Orval Liljequist and L. Sherill.

246 **Oxford. University. Bodleian library.** William Shakespeare, 1564–1964: a catalogue of the quatercentenary exhibition in the Divinity school, Oxford. Oxford, 1964. iv,83p. 19cm.
   Rev: TLS 24 S '64:885; J. G. McManaway Sh Q 17:439–40 '66.

247 **Scotland. National library, EDINBURGH and Edinburgh. University. Library.** Shakespeare, an exhibition of printed books to mark the quater-centenary of his birth, drawn from the resources of the National library of Scotland and of the library of the University of Edinburgh. Edinburgh, 1964. 40p. 24cm. (Scotland. National library. Catalogue, no.3)

248 **South Australia. Libraries board.** [Four hundred years of Shakespeare, 1564–1964] An exhibition of the main editions of William Shakespeare arranged by the Libraries board of South Australia for the third Adelaide festival of arts. [Adelaide, 1964] 32p. facsim. 24cm.

Comp. by Colin J. Horne.

249 **Kendall, Lyle H.** 'Shakespeare collections, quartos, source and allusion books in the W. L. Lewis collection' *in* Corder, Jim W., *ed.* Shakespeare 1964. Fort Worth [1965] p.113–77.

Quasifacsim. TP transcrs., collations, bibliogr. notes and refs. for 100 items, including a bound set of Pavier Q; 'Index of provenance' (p.176–7)

250 **Shattuck, Charles Harlen.** The Shakespeare promptbooks, a descriptive catalogue. Urbana, Illinois U.P., 1965. vii,553p. 25cm.

Chronol. checklist by title of 'marked copies of Shakespeare used in English language, professional theatre productions from the 1620's to 1961', with descr. notes.

Rev: A. Gerstner-Hirzel Erasmus 18:94–5 '66; R.-M. Moudouès R d'Hist Théât 18:244–5 '66; H. Heuer Sh Jahrb 102:265–6 '66; P. M. Hartnoll N&Q 211:313–14 '66; W. A. Bacon Lib Q 36:258 '66; Choice 3:412 '66; Antiqu Bkmn 37:526; A. Nicholson Bks Today 30 Ja '66:11; A. E. Kalson Mod Lang R 62:511–12 '67.

251 **Waseda university,** TOKYO. **Tsubouchi memorial theatre museum.** Catalogue of books in the Shakespeare collection of the Theatre museum, Waseda university. [Tokyo] 1966. iv,146p. 26cm.

COLLECTIONS AND LIBRARIES

270 **Timmins, Samuel.** What the rarities are. Shakespeariana 7no1:34–7 Ja '90.

Appraisal of the Halliwell–Phillipps collection.

271 **The Shakspeare** exhibition in the British museum. Athenæum 3992:562 Ap '04.

272 **Ballinger, John.** Shakespeare and the municipal libraries. Library ser2 7no26:181–91 Ap '06.

General account of some major public library Sh. collections, with a classified checklist of recommended books.

273 **Francis, John Collins.** Earl Howe's Shakespeare quartos and folios. N&Q ser10 9:4–5 Ja '08.

274 **The Britwell** Shakespeares. (Notes on sales) TLS 25 D '19:784.

275 **Shakespeariana** in New York. (Notes on sales) TLS 3 Ap '19:188.

Account of Herschel V. Jones sale, with many early Q.

276 **Burton, Richard Francis.** Description of an extraordinary volume of Shakespeareana, the property of Richard Francis Burton of Longner Hall, near Shrewsbury . . . sold by auction by messrs. Sotheby, Wilkinson & Hodge . . . 23rd of March, 1920. . . . London, J. Davy, Dryden pr. [1920] 7p. facsims. 25cm.

Included *PP* 1599, *Luc.* 1600, Middleton's Ghost of Lucrece 1600, *Ven.* 1599, and one other.

277 **Continental** editions of Shakespeare. (Notes on sales) TLS 13 D '23:884.

Listed in G. Michelmore's catalogue Two hundred . . . books, 1923.

278 **The Warwick** Castle Shakespeares. (Notes on sales) TLS 25 Oc '23:712.

Probable that the whole of the extensive Warwick collection went to Folger.

279 **From** Folger to the nation. Sh Assn Bull 3no1:23–4 Ap '28.

Note on the presentation of the Folger collection.

280 **Smith, Robert Metcalf.** The formation of Shakespeare libraries in America. Sh Assn Bull 4no3:65–74 Jl '29.

Informal account of principal American collectors of Sh.

281 **Shakespeare** prices. (Notes on sales) TLS 27 N '30:1020.

Survey of prices fetched in recent sales for early F and Q.

282 **Whicher, George Frisbie.** Henry Clay Folger [and the Shakespeare library Amherst Graduates Q 20:4–16 '30.

283 **Henry C.** Folger, 18 June 1857, 11 June 1930. New Haven, Privately ptd., 1931. 114p. port. 26cm.

Includes Biographical sketch, by George E. Dimock.—The significance of the Folger Shakespeare memorial, an essay toward an interpretation, by William Adams Slade.— Henry C. Folger as a collector, by A. S. W. Rosenbach.

284 **Slade, William Adams.** The Folger Shakespeare library. Lib J 57no13:601–7 Jl '32. illus.

285 **Whicher, George Frisbie.** The Folger Shakespeare library. Theat Arts Mthly 16no2:108–16 F '32.

286 **Folger Shakespeare library,** WASHINGTON, D.C. The Folger Shakespeare library, Washington. [Amherst, Mass.] Published for the trustees of Amherst college, 1933. 36p.+36 plates. 27cm.

The library, by Joseph Quincy Adams.—The building, by Paul Philippe Cret.

Rev: TLS 8 Mr '34:163.

287 **Schelling, Felix Emmanuel.** The Horace Howard Furness memorial. Univ Pennsylvania Lib Chron 1no1:6–7 Mr '33.

288 —— Shakespeare books in the library of the Furness memorial. Univ Pennsylvania Lib Chron 3no3:33–41 Oc '35.

289 **Smith, Robert Metcalf.** The Willis Vickery sale. Sh Assn Bull 8no2:89–91 Ap '33.

Auction sale of Shakespeariana by American art association, Mr '33.

290 **Willoughby, Edwin Eliott.** Cataloguing the early printed English books of Folger Shakespeare library. Lib J 62no8:330–1 Ap '37.

291 —— The classification of the Folger Shakespeare library. Lib Q 7no3:395–400 Jl '37. table.

292 **Bartlett, Henrietta Collins.** Shakespeare census. TLS 4 Je '38:386.
On her forthcoming bibliogr.: *see* no.385.

293 **Willoughby, Edwin Eliott.** Cataloging and classifying the Folger Shakespeare library. Wilson Bull 13no6:378–82,387 F '39. illus.

294 **Folger Shakespeare library,** WASHINGTON, D.C. The Folger Shakespeare memorial library administered by the trustees of Amherst college; a report on progress, 1931–1941 by Joseph Quincy Adams. [Amherst, Mass.] Trustees of Amherst college, 1942. 61p. illus. 23cm.
Rev: TLS 1 Ag '42:384; sir F. C. Francis Library ser4 23:148–50 '43; H. B. Charlton John Rylands Lib Bull 27:70–3 '43.

295 **A Shakespeare** collection. (Sales and bibliography) TLS 3 Ja '42:12.
Nine folios, including Lee's no.XCVI, and many Q, from the Darwin P. Kingsley collection.

296 **Scouten, Arthur H.** [Two recent exhibitions] II. Shakespeare. Lib Chron Univ Texas 1no3:12–13 '45.

297 **McManaway, James Gilmer.** The Folger Shakespeare library. Sh Surv 1:57–78 '48; *rf.* S.Y.E. N&Q 193:388 S '48. illus.
Extensive detailed account of the Library's holdings and activities.

298 **Dawson, Giles Edwin.** The resources and policies of the Folger Shakespeare library. Lib Q 19no3:178–85 Jl '49.

299 **Folger Shakespeare library,** WASHINGTON, D.C. The Folger Shakespeare library . . . [a brief description] [Amherst, Mass.] Published for the trustees of Amherst college, 1949. 13p. illus. 20cm.
Also issued in 1951, 1959.

300 **Francis, sir Frank Chalton.** The Shakespeare collection in the British museum. Sh Surv 3:43–57 '50. facsim.
The Garrick library.—Royal and other collections.—The museum's holdings of quartos and folios.—Later editions.—Elizabethan and Jacobean manuscripts.—Source and allusion books.—Background literature.—Early music.

301 **Birmingham. Public libraries. Shakespeare memorial library.** The Shakespeare memorial library, a brief description. [Birmingham, 1951] 6p. facsim. 21cm.
Also issued in 1964.

302 **Foster, Joseph T.** Folger; biggest little library in the world. Nat Geog Mag 100no3:411–24 S '51. illus.

303 **Hanson, Laurence William.** The Shakespeare collection in the Bodleian library, Oxford. Sh Surv 4:78–96 '51. facsims.

Detailed analysis of Bodleian holdings, with notes on material in college libraries.

304 **Adams, Herbert Mayow.** The Shakespeare collection in the library of Trinity college, Cambridge. Sh Surv 5:50–4 '52.

305 **Fleming, John F.** The Rosenbach–Bodmer Shakespeare folios and quartos. Sh Q 3no3:257–9 Jl '52.

Account of sale of A. S. W. Rosenbach collection to Martin Bodmer, Geneva.

306 **Folger** library loan exhibit of folios and quartos. Sh Q 3no2:142 Ap '52.

307 —— [Same]: *ib.* 4no2:210–11 Ap '53.

List of exhibiting institutions.

308 **Hayward, John Davy.** The Rosenbach–Bodmer Shakespeare collection. Bk Coll 1no2:112–16 '52.

309 **$1,000,000** Shakespeare collection sold to Swiss collector. Sh Newsl 2no3/4:9 Mr/Ap '52.

310 **Wright, Louis Booker.** The Folger library as a research institution. Coll Res Lib 13no1:14–17 Ja '52.

311 **Davies, Godfrey.** The Huntington library. Sh Surv 6:53–63 '53.

312 **Payne, Waveney R. N.** The Shakespeare memorial library, Birmingham. Sh Newsl 3no1:5 F '53.

313 **Patrick, F. J.** The Birmingham Shakespeare memorial library. Sh Surv 7:90–4 '54.

314 **Shakespeare** collection to Texas Christian university. Sh Q 5no1:101 Ja '54.

Gift to Burnett library of early ptd. texts, including Pavier Q, formerly owned by William M. Lewis.

315 **Rare** Shakespeare editions at Texas Christian university. Sh Q 6no4:477–8 '56.

A fuller account than that preceding.

316 **Savage, Henry L.** The Shakespearean library of Henry N. Paul, '84. Lib Chron Univ Princeton 17no1:49–50 '55.

317 **Bonnard, Georges Alfred.** Shakespeare in the Bibliotheca Bodmeriana. Sh Surv 9:81–5 '56. facsim.

Account of Martin Bodmer's library at Geneva.

318 **Wells, Henry W.** New Shakespeare collection at Columbia. Sh Newsl 7no4:27 S '57.

319 **Wright, Louis Booker.** The Harmsworth collection and the Folger library. Bk Coll 6no2:123–8 '57.

Account of acquisitions from Harmsworth library and their relation to the existing collections.

320 **Payne, Waveney R. N.** The Shakespeare memorial library, Birmingham. Lib Assn Rec 6ono4:120–2 Ap '58. illus.

321 **Shakespeare** in the Sutro library. Sh Q 9no2:214 '58.
Report of F, early Q and J. O. Halliwell-Phillipps's Shakespeare–Stratford mss. collection.

322 **Fox, Levi.** The Shakespeare memorial library, Stratford-upon-Avon. Ohio State Univ Theat Coll Bull 6:5–7 '59.

323 **Folger Shakespeare library,** WASHINGTON, D.C. The Folger library, a decade of growth, 1950–1960. Washington, 1960. 49p. illus. 23cm.
By Louis B. Wright.
Rev: J. G[erritsen] Eng Stud 41:198–9 '60.

324 **Wright, Louis Booker.** A working library of sixteenth- and seventeenth-century history [the Folger Shakespeare library]. Libri 10no3:169–91 '60.

325 —— Huntington and Folger, book collectors with a purpose. Atlantic Mthly 209no4:70–4 Ap '62.

326 **Shakespeare** in the library, a symposium. Open Access 10no2:1–11 Ja '62.
1. The Shakespeare collections of Shakespeare's birthplace and the Royal Shakespeare theatre, Stratford-upon-Avon, by Levi Fox.—2. The Birmingham university Shakespeare institute library, Stratford upon Avon, by Maria Dubno.—3. The Shakespeare memorial library, Birmingham public libraries, by Waveney R. N. Payne.

327 **Folger** traveling exhibits of Shakespeariana. Sh Q 14no2:190 '63.

328 **Les collections** shakespeariennes dans le monde. Theat Res 5no3:169–75 '63.
Preliminary tabulation of libraries with substantial Sh. collections.

329 **Alden, John Eliot.** America's first Shakespeare collection. Pa Bib Soc Am 58:169–73 '64.
On the collection and activities of Thomas Pennant Barton whose collection is now in the Boston public library.

330 **Birmingham. Public libraries. Shakespeare memorial library.** Shakespeare memorial library, a brief description. [Birmingham] 1964. (First issued 1951) 8p. illus., facsims. 21cm. Covertitle.

331 **Fleming, John F.** 'A book from Shakespeare's library discovered by William van Lennep' *in* McManaway, James G., *ed.* Shakespeare 400; essays by American scholars. . . . New York, 1964. p.25–7. facsim.

332 —— [Same]: Sh Q 15no1:25–7 '64.
Copy of Surrey's Songes and sonnettes, 1557, presented by Sh. to a contemporary; now in collection of Arthur Houghton.

333 **Hewlett, Horace W.** The Folger Shakespeare library. Wilson Lib Bull : 630–5 Ap '64. (Not seen)

334 **McManaway, James Gilmer.** The Folger Shakespeare library. Univ Pennsylvania Lib Chron 30no2:72–6 '64.

335 **Rachow, Louis A.** The Walter Hampden memorial library. Wilson Lib Bull :656–9 Ap '64. (Not seen)

'History and *Shak*. holdings of this library at The Players, New York City.' (Sh Q)

336 **Schmidt, Werner.** Centre of Shakespeare research. GDR R 3:25 '64. illus. (Not seen)

'Information about the Weimar *Shak*. Library.' (Sh Q)

337 **Schmidt, Werner.** Die Bibliothek der Deutschen Shakespeare-Gesellschaft. Marginalien 16:15–26 '64. (Not seen)

338 **Shakespeare**-documents. Theat Res 6no1:50–8 '64.

Includes The Shakespeare collection in the British museum, by sir Frank C. Francis, extracted from no.300.

339 **Shakespeare** exhibition. John Rylands Lib Bull 47no1:3–6 S '64.

340 **Willard, Helen D.** Shakespeare in the Harvard theatre collection. Theat Res 6no3:168–72 '64.

341 **Woods, V. H.** The Birmingham Shakespeare memorial library. Central Lit Mag 39no7:13–17 Ap '64.

Repr. in Restor & 18th Cent Theat Res 3no2:49–55 '65.

342 **Wright, Louis Booker.** The Folger Shakespeare library, repository of Tudor and Stuart history. Connois 155no626:231–7 Ap '64.

343 **Ingram, William.** The Furness library. Sh Newsl 15no3:20 My '65.

344 **The Shakespeare** library of Yerevan. Sh Newsl 16no5/6:46 N/D '66.

345 **Wright, Louis Booker.** The Folger library; two decades of growth, an informal account. Charlottesville, Published for the Folger Shakespeare library by the University pr. of Virginia; London, O.U.P., 1968. xi,300p. 24cm.

Reprs. of occasional newsletters describing Library acquisitions and activities.

GENERAL

360 **Krebs, H.** Date of Shakespeare concordance. N&Q ser8 11:188 Mr '97; R. M. Spence; E. H. Marshall; J. Radcliffe *ib*. 11:313 Ap '97.

361 **Plomer, Henry Robert.** The printers of Shakespeare's plays and poems. Library ser2 7no26:149–66 Ap '06.

General survey.

362 **Woollen, Henry.** An early Shakesperian concordance. TLS 8 Je '16:273; F. Blackburn *ib.* 5 Je '16:285; T. R. Smith 6 Jl '16:321; L. G. R.; W. Powell 13 Jl '16:334.

Ayscough's Index in his 3v. 1791 ed. of the Works, and 8° in 1790.

363 **Spencer, Hazelton** [and] **J. R. A. Nicoll.** The restoration playlists. R Eng Stud 1n04:443–6 Oc '25.

Discussion of Allardyce Nicoll's suggestion that lost prompt-books or corrected quartos, the sources of restoration versions of Sh. plays, might be discovered.

364 **A Shakespeare** centenary. (Notes on sales) TLS 15 S '27:628.

Account of John Wilson's Catalogue of all the books . . . relating to Shakespeare, 1827, the first Sh. bibliogr.

365 **Sáinz de Robles, F. C.** Los manuscritos de versiones de Shakespeare en la Biblioteca municipal de Madrid. Revista de la Biblioteca Archivo y Museo [del ayuntamiento de Madrid] 8:420–32 '31. (Not seen)

366 **Bald, Robert Cecil.** Shakespeare on the stage in restoration Dublin. Pub Mod Lang Assn 56n02:369–78 Je '41.

Descr. of collection of F3 texts used as prompt-books, formerly owned by J. O. Halliwell-Phillipps and now in Folger Sh. library.

367 **Parker, W. M.** Shakespeare concordances. TLS 12 My '45:228.

General survey of principal lists.

368 **McManaway, James Gilmer.** Additional prompt-books of Shakespeare from the Smock Alley theatre. Mod Lang R 45n01:64–5 Ja '50.

369 **Dain, Neville E.** Notes on the editing and collecting of Shakespeareana. Librarian S '56:149–53. (Not seen)

370 **Race, Sydney.** [Shakespearian discovery] N&Q 202:457–8 Oc '57.

Was account in N&Q 1860 of discovery of Sh. mss. a hoax?

371 **Evans, Gwynne Blakemore.** The Douai manuscript; six Shakespearean transcripts, 1694–95. Philol Q 42n01:158–72 Ja '62.

Descr. of ms. in Douai public library containing transcrs. of *TN, AYL, Err., Rom., JC,* and *Mac.,* made from an annotated F2.

372 —— New evidence on the provenance of the Padua prompt-books of Shakespeare's Macbeth, Measure for measure, and Winter's tale. Stud Bib 20:239–42 '67.

New evidence suggests that the association of these prompt-books with sir Edward Dering's group is 'questionable, though still not impossible'. (p.239)

373 **Dent, Robert W.** 'Reflections of a Shakespeare bibliographer' *in* McNeir, Waldo F. and Thelma N. Greenfield, *ed.* Pacific Coast studies in Shakespeare. 1967. p.303–15. (Not seen)

374 **Hill, Trevor Howard Howard-.** The Oxford old-spelling Shakespeare concordances. Stud Bib 22:143–64 '69.

380 **Wagner, Albrecht.** Eine Sammlung von Shakespeare-Quartos in Deutschland. Angl 25:518–32 N '02.

Discursive account, with quasifacsim. TP transcrs. of 9 items.

381 **Lee, sir Sidney.** Four quarto editions of plays by Shakespeare, the property of the trustees and guardians of Shakespeare's birthplace. Stratford-upon-Avon, Trustees and guardians of Shakespeare's birthplace, 1908. 63p. facsims. 20cm. Covertitle.

Discursive descrs. of *MV* 1600, *MND* 1600, *Lr.* 1608, and *Wiv.* 1619.
Rev: Athenæum 4208:761 '08.

382 **Wheatley, Henry Benjamin.** Post-restoration quartos of Shakespeare's plays. Library ser3 4no15:237–69 Jl '13.

Discursive bibliogr. notes on later Q, in title order.

383 **Bartlett, Henrietta Collins** and **A. W. Pollard.** A census of Shakespeare's plays in quarto, 1594–1709. New Haven, Yale U.P.; London, H. Milford, O.U.P., 1916. xli,153p. tables. 31cm.

See no.385.

384 **Bartlett, Henrietta Collins.** First editions of Shakespeare's quartos. Library. ser4 16no2:166–72 S '35. table.

Supplements the Census. 'Present location of the first separate editions' (p.169–71); 'List of owners'. (p. 171–2)

385 —— and **A. W. Pollard.** A census of Shakespeare's plays in quarto, 1594–1709. Rev. and extended by Henrietta C. Bartlett. New Haven, Yale U.P.; London, H. Milford, O.U.P., 1939. v,165p. tables. 26cm.

Descrs. of 'every known copy of each edition and issue' of the Q ptd. before 1623 (except *Per.*, First part of the Contention, and The true tragedy), and *JC*, *Mac.*, and *Shr.*, with its 'history from publication until January 1939'; with a list of unidentified copies, and detailed index. 1222 copies with descrs. and notes, and notes of provenance.

Rev: G. E. Dawson Mod Lang N 55:226–7 '40; H. Sellers Library ser4 20:432–3 '40; TLS 2 Mr '40:115; J. Q. Adams J Eng Germ Philol 39:405–7 '40; sir W. W. Greg R Eng Stud 16:208–11 '40; B. M. Philol Q 19:413–14 '40; N&Q 178:161–2 '40; A. E[sdaile] Lib Assn Rec 42:132 '40; E. M. Albright Mod Philol 39:101–2 '41.

390 **The Shakspere** quarto facsimile series. Acad 39:466–7 My '91; F. J. Furnivall *ib*. 39:491 My '91.

On the Griggs–Praetorius facsimiles.

391 **Dewischeit, Curt.** Shakespeare und die Stenographie. Sh Jahrb 34:170–220 '98.

392 **Jonas, Maurice.** Shakspearian quartos. N&Q ser9 2:506 D '98.
On the number of existing copies of the various Q.

393 **Quarto** publishers. Shakespeariana 9no1:124–5 Ap '92.
Table repr. from the introduction to the Bankside Shakespeare, v.14.

394 **Spence, R. M.** A Shakespearian desideratum. N&Q ser8 9:268 Ap '96; W. A. Henderson; W. F. Prideaux *ib.* ser8 9:476–7 Je '96; R. M. Spence; A. H. 10:32 Jl '96; A. G. C. 10:105 Ag '96.
Discussion of the available Q facsims.

395 **Five** Shakspere quartos. Athenæum 4056:113 Jl '05.
Sale from library of George Carrington, Great Missenden.

396 **Two** Shakspere quartos. Athenæum 4052:796 Je '05.
Sale of *Leir* and *R3* 1605 at Sotheby's.

397 **Pollard, Alfred William.** Shakespeare in the remainder market. Acad 1778: 528–9 Je '06.
Account of discovery of the Gwynn set of Pavier Q.

398 **Axon, William Edward Armytage.** Shakespeariana at Douai. N&Q ser10 7:421 My '07; E. S. Dodgson; H. W. D. *ib.* 7:516–17 Je '07.
Collection of dramatic texts assigned to 18th century, from the collection of the English Benedictines; *see* no.371.

399 **Are** the dates on certain of the Shakespeare quartos spurious? New Shakespeareana 7no3:69–74 Jl '08.
Largely drawn from Greg's Library articles.

400 **Furnivall, Frederick James.** Pope's Shakespeare quarto. N&Q ser10 10:107 Ag '08.
Seeks Q claimed to have been seen by Pope, in which 'the parts [were] divided into lines and the actors' names in the margin'.

401 **Greg, sir Walter Wilson.** On certain false dates in Shakespearian quartos. Library ser2 9no34:113–31 Ap '08; 9no36:381–409 Oc '08. facsims., tables.
'Designs used in Shakespeare watermarks' (facing p.380)
Numerals, devices and the common paper stock show that the Pavier Q were falsely dated. The second part replies to critics, and discusses the possibilities of false imprints in other works.

402 **Huth, Alfred Henry.** Shakespeare's quartos. Acad 74:864–5 Je '08; sir W. W. Greg *ib.* 74:889–90 Je '08.
On the watermarks of the Pavier Q.

403 **Phin, John.** The Shakespeare quartos. Nation 86no2240:510 Je '08.
On the devices in the Pavier Q.

404 **The Shakspeare** quartos. Athenæum 4201:544 My '08; sir S. Lee *ib.* 4202:574 My '08; sir W. W. Greg 4205:669–70 My '08; sir S. Lee 4236:14 Ja '09; A. W. Pollard 4237:43–4 Ja '09; sir S. Lee 4238:73 Ja '09; sir W. W. Greg; A. H. Huth 4239:100–1 Ja '09; sir W. W. Greg 4240:132 Ja '09.
More on the Pavier Q.

405 **Baker, George P.** [and] **G. W. Cole.** Some bibliographical puzzles in Elizabethan quartos. Pa Bib Soc Am 4:9–23 '09.
Cole's comments on Baker's paper list Pavier Q in Britain and U.S.A.; the uniformity of the numbers of surviving copies, and of their measurements, disposes of Pollard's 'remainder' theory.

406 **Jaggard, William.** False dates in Shakespearian quartos. Library ser2 10no38:201–7 Ap '09.
Lists 27 books, mostly ptd. by Jaggard, with watermarks similar to those noted by Greg in the Pavier Q, together with note of other occurrences of ornaments, and notes on recent sales of these Q.

407 **Huth, Alfred Henry** [and] **A. W. Pollard.** On the supposed false dates in certain Shakespeare quartos. Library ser3 1no1:36–53 Ja '10.
Argues against the Greg and Pollard exposure of the Pavier Q, with rejoinder.

408 **Neidig, William J.** False dates on Shakspere quartos: a new proof applied to a controversy of scholars. Century Mag 80no6:912–19 Oc '10. illus., facsims.
The first presentation of his demonstration that the separately dated TP of the Pavier Q used the same settings of type.

409 **Neidig, William J.** The Shakespeare quartos of 1619. Mod Philol 8no2:145–63 Oc '10. facsims.
Conclusive photographic evidence from similarities of TP type disposition that Q dated 1600 and 1608 were 'printed within a few days of the quartos bearing the date 1619'.

410 **Pollard, Alfred William.** False dates in Shakespeare's quartos. Library ser3 2no5:101–7 Ja '11.
Review article on Neidig's 1910 articles.

411 **Fitzgerald, James D.** Three pirated plays of Shakespeare. Roy Philos Soc Glasgow Proc 47:138–73 '15/16. table.
Q1 of *H5*, *Wiv.*, and *Ham.* attributed to the one dishonest actor-reporter.

412 **Shakespeare** quartos. (Notes on sales) TLS 16 My '18:236; *rf.* 20 Je '18:292.
F1 not recorded by Lee, and 1619 Q, from ld. Vernon's library, Sudbury Hall.

413 **The Marsden** J. Perry library. (Notes on sales) TLS 20 N '19:680.
Descr. of important Sh. ed., including Gwynn set of Pavier Q.

414 **Pollard, Alfred William** and **J. D. Wilson.** The stolne and surreptitious Shakespearian texts. TLS 9 Ja '19:18; 16 Ja '19:30; Charlotte C. Stopes *ib.* 23 Ja '19:56; A. W. Pollard 30 Ja '19:56; D. Salmon 6 F '19:69–70; J. D. Fitzgerald 20 F '19:98.
1. Why some of Shakespeare's plays were pirated.—2. How some of Shakespeare's plays were pirated. *See also* nos.1311, 1565 and 1708.

415 **Pollard, Alfred William** and **J. D. Wilson.** What follows if some of the good quarto editions of Shakespeare's plays were printed from his autograph manuscripts. Bib Soc Trans 15pt2: 136–9 '19.

Summary of paper read 16 D '18; *see also* Report. Bib Soc News-sh 2–4 Ja '19.

416 **Bartlett, Henrietta Collins.** Undescribed Shakespeare quartos. TLS 17 Je '20:384.

Descrs. of 16 early Q in Holford collection at Dorchester House.

417 **Fitzgerald, James D.** Transcription in the pirated plays of Shakespeare. TLS 13 My '20:303; sir W. W. Greg *ib.* 20 My '20:320; J. D. Fitzgerald 3 Je '20:352.

418 **The Shakespearian** find. (Notes on sales) TLS 26 F '20:144.

Account of discovery at Longner Hall of volume containing *Ven., Luc., PP*, etc.: *see also* no.276.

419 **Unrecorded** editions of Shakespeare. (Notes on sales) TLS 30 N '22:788; F. E. Bastian *ib.* 7 D '22:823; F. D. M. 14 D '22:842; Notes on sales 28 D '22:876.

Common Tonson reprs. of 1734–5 in bookseller's catalogue.

420 **Matthews, William.** Shorthand and the bad Shakespeare quartos. Mod Lang R 27no3:243–62 Jl '32. tables.

'. . . Bright's Characterie . . . was an impracticable system in which to report plays.' (p.262)

421 —— [Same]: A postscript. Mod Lang R 28no1:81–3 Ja '33.

Brief account of the unsuitability of Peter Bales's Brachygraphy for reporting plays.

422 **Willoughby, Edwin Eliott.** 'XII. The falsely dated Shakespeare quartos of 1619' *in* A printer of Shakespeare, the books and times of William Jaggard. London, 1934. p.125–39.

423 **Hutcherson, Dudley.** The forged quartos. TLS 3 Ja '35:9.

The University of Virginia set of Pavier Q, destroyed by fire, had been in iv. in the original binding.

424 **Lawrence, William John.** 'The secret of the bad quartos' *in* Those nut-cracking Elizabethans; studies of the early theatre and drama. London, 1935. p.153–74. facsims.

They were illicitly prepared texts, abbreviated for touring country companies.

425 **Matthews, William.** Shakespeare and the reporters. Library ser4 15no4: 481–98 Mr '35.

Bright's Charactery was an imperfect system liable to produce many mistakes in transcription; the errors in Q cannot be attributed to the use of Charactery.

426 **Price, Hereward Thimbleby** [and] **W. Matthews.** Shakespeare and the reporters. Library ser4 17no2:225–30 S '36.

Argument over the use of Bright's system for the production of reported texts.

427 **Förster, Max.** Shakespeare and shorthand. Philol Q 16no1:1–29 Ja '37. table.

Supports the theory of stenographic reporting of plays.

428 **Hart, Alfred.** Stolne and surreptitious copies, a comparative study of Shakespeare's bad quartos. [Melbourne] Melbourne U.P., 1942. xi,478p. tables. 21cm.

1. Bibliography of the parallel texts.—2. Length.—3. Vocabularies of the bad quartos.—4. The rarer words of Shakespeare's plays.—5. Compounds.—6. Vocabulary and the theory of double revision.—7. State of the quarto texts.—8. The plots of the bad quartos.—9. Style of the bad quartos.—10. Non-Shakespearean verse.—11. Abridgment, official and unofficial.—12. The first sketch theory.—13. Blunders that bear witness.—14. Verse structure of the bad quartos.—15. Rhymed lines.—16. Composite lines.—17. Emendations of Shakespeare's text from the bad quartos.—18. Repetition of lines, etc.—19. Play-reporting and reporters.—20. Inter-play borrowings—The Pembroke group of plays.—21. Inter-play borrowings of the later bad quartos.—22. Stage directions.—23. Summary.—Appendix. Did Marlowe write the plays on Henry VI.

Rev: TLS 1 My '43:216; G. I. Duthie R Eng Stud 19:416–18 '43; E. T. Clark Sh Fellowship Q 5:6–8 '44; L. Kirschbaum Mod Lang N 59:196–8 '44; M. Doran Mod Lang R 39:190–3 '44.

429 **Sisson, Charles Jasper.** Shakespeare quartos as prompt-copies; with some account of Cholmeley's players and a new Shakespeare allusion. R Eng Stud 18no70:129–43 Ap '42.

Support for Pollard's theory that Q were used as prompt-books following delivery of the ms. copy to the printer, although 'there is no certain instance of such a usage by any company of its own plays in quarto form, or in the last decade of the sixteenth century'. (p.143)

430 **Danks, Kenneth B.** [The good and bad quartos] Eng 6no33:154 '46.

The 'diuerse . . . stolne copies' were the 1619 Pavier Q.

431 **Hodgson and co., ltd.,** LONDON. The remarkable story of the Shakespearian quartos of 1619, being a brief record of the unravelling of a puzzle in Shakespearian bibliography and an account of the unlooked-for discovery of a set of the quartos of 1619. London, 1946. 12p. illus., facsims. 25cm. Covertitle.

Account by J. E. H[odgson] of the Girsby Manor Pavier Q now at Texas Christian university, Fort Worth: *see* no.249.

432 **A treasure** restored. TLS 18 My '46:235.

The Girsby Manor Pavier Q.

433 **Stevenson, Allan H.** Shakespearian dated watermarks. Stud Bib 4:159–64 '51/2.

The Pavier Q Sir John Oldcastle '1600' and *H5* '1608' show watermarks dated 1608 and 1617 or 1619 respectively.

434 **Kirschbaum, Leo.** Shakespeare and the stationers. Columbus, Ohio state U.P., 1955. x,421p. 23cm. ([Graduate school monographs. Contributions in languages and literature, no.15])

The problem of the stolen Shakespeare quartos.—The Stationers' company in operation.—Surreptitious publication in Shakespeare's day.—A conjectural history of the relations between Shakespeare's fellows and the stationers, 1594–1623.—Appendix A: copyright and publication history of the bad quartos.—Appendix B: trade biographies of the publishers of the bad quartos.—Corrections and additional notes.

Rev.: H. E. Rollins J Eng Germ Philol 55:147–9 '56; A. Brown Sh Q 7:426–9 '56; K. Brunner Sh Jahrb 92:427–31 '56; C. Blagden Library ser5 11:54–6 '56; R. E. Hill Mod Lang R 51:97–8 '56; G. E. Dawson Mod Philol 54:58–61 '56; S. F. Johnson Renaiss N 10:43–4 '57.

435 **Danks, Kenneth B.** What Heminges and Condell really meant. N&Q 200: 16–19 Ja '55; 201:11–13 Ja '56.

'Stolne and surreptitious copies' refers to the Pavier Q only.

436 **Martin, Burns.** Shakespeare quartos. TLS 21 S '56:553; sir W. W. Greg *ib.* 28 S '56:569.

On the Shakespeare association's Q facsimiles.

437 **Stevenson, Allan H.** Thomas Thomas makes a dictionary. Library ser5 13no4:234–46 D '58. illus., facsims.

Huntington library copy of STC 24531 contains an annotated ptd. sheet of copy for the first ed. of Thomas's Dictionarium, 1587, with printing-house markings. Stevenson discusses the implications of this for the study of Sh. texts set up from rev. Q copy.

438 **Craig, Hardin.** 'Revised Elizabethan quartos, an attempt to form a class' *in* Bennett, Josephine W., O. Cargill and V. Hall, *ed.* Studies in the English renaissance drama in memory of Karl Julius Holzknecht. New York, 1959. p.43–57.

439 **Danks, Kenneth B.** The bibliographical and psychological fallacies in Pollard's second proposition. N&Q 204:439–40 D '59.

Argues against Pollard's proposition 'that the entry of a drama in S.R. to one person and its assignment to another person on the day or date argued improper trade conduct'. (p.439)

440 —— Decem rationes, a Shakespearean monograph. London, Winterson, 1959. 44p. 18cm.

Identifies the Pavier Q as the 'stolne and surreptitious copies'.

Rev: TLS 19 F '60:110; C. Hoy Sh Q 11:377–8 '60; R. A. Foakes Eng 13:22–3 '60.

441 **Cairncross, Andrew S.** Pembroke's men and some Shakespearian piracies. Sh Q 11no3:335–49 '60.

Suggests Q *2H6* (Contention), Q *3H6* (True tragedy), Q *R3* and Q *Rom.* 'now generally recognised as memorial versions of the corresponding Shakespearian plays, were made by the same group of actor-reporters, on the same occasion' (p. 335), i.e. 'in the summer of 1593'.

442 **Craig, Hardin.** A new look at Shakespeare's quartos. Stanford, Calif., Stanford U.P.; London, O.U.P., 1961. vi,134p. 22cm. (Stanford Stud Lang Lit XXII)

1. Classification and misclassification.—2. Some effects of erroneous or imperfect theories.—3. Inadequate methodology in textual criticism.

Rev: R. E. Knoll Coll Eng 23:163 '61; K. Muir Stud Eng Lit 2:254 '62; W. C. McAvoy Manuscripta 6:115–16 '62; F. D. Hoeniger Queen's Q 68:697 '62; J. K. Walton Mod Lang R 57:247 '62; D. E. Jones Drama Surv 2:226–7 '62; R. K. Turner Sth Atlantic Bull Mr '62:14–15; A. Brown Renaiss N 15:337–8 '62; G. W. Williams Sth Atlantic Q 61:118 '62; P. A. Jorgensen Personalist 43:124 '62; C. P. Lyons Pa Bib Soc Am 56:125–6 '62; A. B. Weiner Q J Speech 48:211 '62.

443 **Bentley, Gerald Eades.** Eleven Shakespeare quartos. Princeton Univ Lib
Q 30n02:69–76 '69. facsims.
Presented by Daniel Maggin.

FOLIOS

460 **Smith, Robert Metcalf** and **H. S. Leach.** The Shakespeare folios and the
forgeries of Shakespeare's handwriting in the Lucy Packer Linderman
memorial library of Lehigh university; with a list of original folios in American libraries. Bethlehem, Pa., 1927. 47p. facsims. 23cm. (Lehigh university.
Publications 1n02 Mr '27. Institute of research. Circular no.7. Studies in
humanities, 1)

1. The Lehigh university Shakespeare folios.—2. Preceding owners of the Lehigh folios.—
3. First folios in America.—4. Shakespeare folios in American libraries.—5. The condition of First folios.—6. The increasing value of Shakespeare folios.—7. Bibliographical
description of the Lehigh folios.—8. The Shakespeare signature and notes forged by
William Henry Ireland.

Rev: G. Binz Angl Beibl 38:319–21 '27.

461 **Bald, Robert Cecil.** The Shakespeare folios. Bk Hndbk 1n02:100–5 '47.
facsims.
Introductory essay to the next item.

462 **Horrox, Reginald.** Tables for the identification and collation of the Shakespeare folios. Bk Hndbk 1n02,4,8/9:105–12,113–26,129–76 '47–50. facsims.

463 **[Livingston, Luther Samuel]** The four folios of Shakespeare's plays; an
account of the four collected editions. Together with a census of known
perfect copies of the First folio. A description of an exceptionally desirable
set now offered for sale by Dodd, Mead and co. [New York, 1907] 32p.
24cm. (Not seen)

464 **Thornton, Richard H.** Shakespeariana, the three folios. N&Q ser13 1:249
S '23.
Notes that irregularities of spacing in F1 are followed by F2, 3.

465 **Shakespearian** literature. (Notes on sales) TLS 28 Jl '27:524.
Sale of ld. Leigh's set of folios, including Lee LXXXII, and other works.

466 **Kelmscott,** Shakespeare and Kipling. (Notes on sales) TLS 29 N '28:944.
Two sets of folios, including the Hacket copy (Lee CXXXI) and another incomplete,
unrecorded F from Toft Hall, Knutsford.

467 **Shakespeare** folios. (Notes on sales) TLS 2 Ag '28:572.
Sale of Ingleby (Lee CX) F, and Halsey copy of F2.

468 **Smith, Robert Metcalf.** Notes on Shakespeariana. Sh Assn Bull 4n04:121–5
Oc '29.

469 —— [Same]: *ib.* 5n03:140–1 Jl '30.

470 —— [Same]: *ib.* 6n04:178–80 Oc '31.
Account of recent migration of folios.

471 **Shakespeare** folios from America. (Notes on sales) TLS 21 F '35:112;
7 Mr 35:148.
Sale of four F from Massachusetts General hospital, including Lee XXXI.

472 **Müllertz, Mogens.** De fire Shakespeare Folioer. Bogvennen ny række 4:9–59
'49. illus., facsims.
Ben Jonson giver ideen.—The company of stationers.—Første folio's besværlige og
langsomme forberedelse.—Den første folio.—Den anden folio.—Den tredie folio.—Den
fjerde folio.—De senere folioer.—Epilog.—Summary (in English)
'Johnson's folio, being the first collected edition of plays in England, is the occasion for
and the prototype of the edition of the collected works of Shakespeare.' (p.41)

473 **Gift** of Shakespeare folios. Sh Q 3n04:392–3 Oc '52.
Bequest of four F to State teachers' college, West Chester, Pennsylvania, by William Pyle
Philips; with a note of other educational institutions possessing sets of the folios.

474 **Dawson, Giles Edwin.** Shakespeare folios at Cornell. Sh Q 4n04:487 Oc '53.
Report of donation by William G. Mennen to Cornell university library: *see* no.476.

475 **Shakespeare** folios at Haverford college. Sh Q 4n01:107–8 Ja '53.
Bequest of set of F by William Pyle Philips.

476 **Cornell university. Library.** The Shakespeare folios in the Cornell university
library given by William G. Mennen, '08. Ithaca, N.Y., Published under the
auspices of the Cornell library associates, 1954. 16p. 23cm.
Comp. by William R. Keast.

477 **Folger** library makes permanent loan of four folios. Sh Newsl 10n04/5:32
S/N '60.
To libraries of St. Andrews and British Columbia universities.

478 **Falconer, A. F.** The Shakespeare folios. Spectrum 1n04:40–1 Mr '61.
Permanent loan of Folger nos.9, 31, 14, and 11 to St. Andrews university.

490 **Lee, sir Sidney,** *ed.* Shakespeare's comedies, histories & tragedies: a supplement to the reproduction in facsimile of the First folio edition ... containing a census of extant copies with some account of their history and condition. Oxford, Clarendon pr., 1902. 45[1]p. 38cm.

Introduction.—The census: Class I. Perfect copies.—Class II. Imperfect copies.—Class III. Defective copies.—Class IV. Copies otherwise unclassed owing to lack of full description.—Index.

491 —— Notes & additions to the Census ... Rev. to 24th May, 1906. London, H. Frowde, 1906. 30p. 24cm.

Repr. from Library ser2 7no26:113–39 Ap '06.

492 **Marder, Louis.** First folio reproductions past & present: a brief bibliography. Sh Newsl 18no4/5:33–4 S/N '68.

---

500 **A collation** of the First folio. Shakespeariana 10no1:30–3 Ja '93.

501 **Fleming, William H.** American spelling. Shakespeariana 10no1:41–4 Ja '93; *rf.* T. R. Lounsbury *ib.* 10no2:115–16 Ap '93.

On spelling and compositors in F1.

502 **Thornton, Richard H.** Shakespeare, the 1623 Folio. N&Q ser8 8:306 Oc '95; H. P. Stokes; H. Ingleby *ib.* 8:353 N '95; J. Malone 8:429–30 N '95.

On the mispagination associated with the late insertion of *Tro.*

503 **Jonas, Maurice.** Shakespeare's First folio. N&Q ser8 10:23 Jl '96; R. R[oberts?] *ib.* 10:71 S '96.

Discussion of variants amongst copies, with reference to *Oth.* proofsheet.

504 **St. Swithin.** S. I. N&Q ser8 11:383 My '97; R. R[oberts?] *ib.* 12:31–2 Jl '97.

On Johnson–Theobald–Irving copy of F, with inscription attributed to Samuel Ireland, and subsequent discussion of other inscribed copies.

505 **Ingleby, Holcombe.** The First folio of Shakespeare. N&Q ser8 12:63,222 Jl,S '97; R. R[oberts?] *ib.* 12:281–2 Oc '97; H. Ingleby; W. J. Jaggard; J. Murray; A. J. Rudolph 12:413 N '97; R. R[oberts?]; E. A. Petherick; ld. Aldenham ser9 1:449–50 Je '98; R. R[oberts?] 2:211 S '98.

Owners and locations of copies.

506 **Lee, sir Sidney.** Some bibliographical problems connected with the Elizabethan drama. Bib Soc Trans 4pt2:149–50 '98.

Principally concerned with characteristics of Sheldon and Daniel copies of F1.

507 **Kok, Abraham Seyne.** Shakespeare's First folio. Nederlandsche Spectator 25:200–2 Juni '99.

508 **Lee, sir Sidney.** Shakespeare's First folio, some notes and a discovery. Cornhill Mag new ser 6no34:449–58 Ap '99. facsim.

Account of the Vincent–Sibthorp copy now in the Folger Shakespeare library.

509 **Lee, sir Sidney.** An undescribed copy of the Shakspeare First folio. Athenæum 3747:266–8 Ag '99.

Discussion of seventeenth-century ms. emendations in newly found copy.

510 **Ward, C. S.** Shakespeare: the First folio. N&Q ser9 4:496 D '99.

Quotes Quaritch's Catalogue no.194 on prices of F.

511 **Lee, sir Sidney.** Some undescribed copies of the First folio Shakespeare. Bib Soc Trans 5pt2:166–74 '99/00.

Summary of paper read 18 D '99; also in Bib Soc News-sh 2–3 Ja '00.

Notes on copies owned by William Phelps, Dursley, Glos.; Coningsby Sibthorp, Sudbrooke Holme, Lincs.; and an annotated copy purchased by 'a Glasgow collector' at Christie's sale, Jl '98.

512 **Highest** price ever paid for a First folio. New Shakespeareana 1no1:27–8 S '01.

MacGeorge copy, with survey of earlier prices.

513 **Lee, sir Sidney.** The Shakspeare First folio. Athenæum 3829:347 Mr '01.

Solicits information for his Census, no.490.

514 **Morgan, Appleton [and] sir S. Lee.** The cataloguing of First folios from an American point of view. New Shakespeareana 1no1:18–22 S '01; *rf. ib.* 2no1:32–3 Ja/Mr '03.

515 **Lee, sir Sidney.** Extant copies of the Shakspeare First folio. Athenæum 3893:722 Je '02.

A final appeal for details of copies.

516 **The Shakespeare** First folio. TLS 26 D '02:386–7; W. Day *ib.* 2 Ja '03:5; H. Hart 9 Ja '03:11; sir H. T. Wood 16 Ja '03:17; H. Hart 23 Ja '03:25.

General essay on the occasion of the publication of the Lee facsimile, with discussion of facsimile processes.

517 **The First** folio of Shakspeare: facsimile. Athenæum 3923:19 Ja '03.

Review article on the Lee facsimile.

518 **Greg, sir Walter Wilson.** The bibliographical history of the First folio. Library ser2 4no15:258–85 Jl '03.

Corrections to and observations on Lee's introduction to the Folio facsimile.

519 **Leeper, Alexander.** The reduced facsimile of the First folio Shakespeare. N&Q ser9 11:429 My '03.

The Chatto and Windus facsim. of 1876 was made from Lee's no.LXXXVI, later sold to Robert Roberts, Boston, Lincs.

520 **Two** hundred and eighty years' appreciation in prices of the First folio. New Shakespeareana 2no1:26–8 Ja/Mr '03.

Table of prices and estimate of cost of production.

521 **Jaggard, William.** Shakspeare First folio facsimile. Athenæum 4017:559–60 Oc '04.

Notes ornament mentioned by Lee is also found in Wilson's Christian dictionary.

522 **[Madan, Falconer]** The original Bodleian copy of the First folio of Shakspeare. Athenæum 4035:241–2 F '05. diagr.

Description of the volume.—Condition and binding.

523 —— [Same]: Repr. with illus. *in* Bk Auc Rec 2pt2:1–3 '05. illus., diagr.

Collation and descr. of the original Stationers' company deposit copy, known as the Turbutt copy.

524 **[Oxford. University. Bodleian library]** The original Bodleian copy of the First folio of Shakpeare: the Turbutt Shakespeare. Oxford, Clarendon pr., 1905. 13p.+6 plates. illus., facsims., tables. 39cm.

1. General account, by F. Madan.—2. History of the volume in the 18th and 19th centuries.—3. Technical description of the volume.—4. The portrait and verses, by G. M. R. Turbutt.—5. The preliminary leaves, by F. Madan and G. M. R. Turbutt.—6. The binding of the Turbutt Shakespeare, by S. Gibson.

525 **Roberts, William.** Shakspeariana. Athenæum 4038:347–8 Mr '05.

Review of items of Sh. interest in current booksellers' catalogues.

526 **Lee, sir Sidney.** Mr. Lee's Census of Shakspeare First folios. Athenæum 4081:52 Ja '06.

On an error in the record of preliminary leaves of the Leiter copy.

527 **Cole, George Watson.** The First folio of Shakespeare; a further word regarding the correct arrangement of its preliminary leaves. Pa Bib Soc Am 3:65–83 '08. diagrs., tables.

Discussion of four forms of arrangement, with solution based largely on evidence of watermarks. 'Literature of the subject' (p.83)

Rev: Library ser3 1:211–17 '10.

528 **Harris, Edward B.** The First folio Shakespeare: earliest reference to and pictorial representation of. N&Q ser11 7:8–9 Ja '13; W. Jaggard *ib.* 7:56 Ja 13; E. B. Harris 7:94–5 F '13; M. H. Spielmann 7:137 F '13; W. Jaggard 7:217 Mr '13.

529 **Shakespeariana.** Bod Q Rec 1no1:24–5 Ap '14.

Bodleian spellings of Sh. name when entering F in 1623; worn pages as indication of reading habits, 1623–42.

530 **Spielmann, Marion Harry.** The Bodleian (Malone) First folio. TLS 4 My '16:213; *rf.* The book of homage *ib.* 25 My '16:249.

Bodley's copy contains a proof state of the Droeshout engraving later than the Halliwell-Phillipps (Folger) proof. *See* no.569.

531 **Carter, Pierson Cathrick.** Heminges and Condell. TLS 11 Oc '17:492.

Reassertion of their predominant share in editing F1.

532 **Guthkelch, Adolph Charles Louis.** Two notes on the First folio of Shakespeare. Mod Lang R 12no1:78–81 Ja '17.

Tro. was re-located in the histories section of F1 to achieve a balanced distribution of pages amongst the three divisions.—In *Ham.* and *Lr.*, the only F texts substantially shorter than Q, F 'omissions' occur mainly in the latter half of each play, another attempt to equalize the sections.

533 **Baugh, Albert Croll.** A note on the Shakespeare First folio. Mod Lang N 33no8:505 D '18.
Corrects Lee's Census, no.XX, the Sheldon copy.

534 **Greenwood, sir Granville George.** Heminge and Condell and mr. Dugdale Sykes. TLS 29 Ja '20:68–9.
On the interpretation of the Preface, written by Jonson and merely signed by Heminge and Condell.

535 **Satchell, Thomas.** The spelling of the First folio. TLS 3 Je '20:352.
Distribution of spellings in *Mac.* suggests either that ms. copy was the work of two scribes, or that the text was set up by two compositors, A and B.

536 **Abrahams, Aleck.** George Daniel's First folio Shakespeare. N&Q ser12 9:308 Oc '21.
Notes on the sale and provenance of the Daniel–Burdett Coutts copy.

537 **The library's** First folio Shakespeares. N.Y. Pub Lib Bull 25no12:799–801 D '21. facsims.
Cursory account of N.Y. Public library's four copies, mainly drawn from Lee's Census.

538 **Notes** on sales. [Sale of Longe copy, with the cancelled page of *Rom.*] TLS 4 Ag '21:504.

539 **Rhodes, Raymond Crompton.** The arrangement of the First folio. TLS 29 D '21:875.
'... the plays were made up in the playhouse in batches for the printer, and ... each batch consisted of homogeneous texts.'

540 **The Burdett** Coutts library. (Notes on sales) TLS 30 Mr '22:216; 25 My '22:348.
Includes account of the Daniel–Burdett Coutts F1, and other ana.

541 **Brooke, Charles Frederick Tucker.** The Folio of 1623. Yale R new ser 13no1:130–43 Oc '23.
Repr. in his Essays on Shakespeare and other Elizabethans. New Haven; London, 1948. p.[78]–92.

541a **Brunelli, B.** L'in-folio Shakespeariano della Bibliotheca universitaria di Padova. Marzocco 28no20 '23. (Not seen)

542 **The First** folio. TLS 19 Ap '23:253.
Centenary article.

543 **Guppy, Henry.** A brief summary of the history of the First-folio edition of Shakespeare's dramas, 1623–1923, in commemoration of the tercentenary of the publication of the First-folio, 1623–1923. Manchester, Manchester U.P.; London, Longmans, Green, 1923. 31p. facsims. 26cm.
Repr. from John Rylands Lib Bull 7no3:457–79 Ag '23.

544 **Kempling, William Bailey.** The tercentenary of the First folio. Fortn R 119:584–8 Ap '23.

545 **Porter, Charlotte.** The First folio. Lit R 6 Oc '23:109; *rf.* T. M. Parrott *ib.* 22 D '23:398. (Not seen)

546 **Rhodes, Raymond Crompton.** Shakespeare's First folio. Oxford, B. Blackwell; New York, D. Appleton, 1923. 147p. 23cm.

1. The pious fellows of Shakespeare.—2. The Company of stationers & printers.—3. The Pavier Shakespeare.—4. The unblotted papers.—5. Divers stolne & surreptitious copies. —6. Shakespeare's first company.—7. The catalogue of plays.—8. The editorial policy.

Rev: C. F. T. Brooke Lit R 1:308 '23; Contemp R 123:799–801 '23; E. Shanks Lond Merc 8:322 '23; TLS 21 Je '23: 421; sir E. K. Chambers Mod Lang R 18:485–6 '23; G. Sampson Bkmn 64:150–1 '23; New Statesm 21:212 '23; Sat R 135:740 '23; T. S. Graves Stud Philol 21:437–8 '24.

547 —— William Jaggard and the First folio. TLS 22 Mr '23:198; W. B. Kempling *ib.* 5 Ap '23:233; sir W. W. Greg 12 Ap '23:247; R. C. Rhodes; W. B. Kempling 19 Ap '23:270; sir W. W. Greg; W. B. Kempling 26 Ap '23:288; W. B. Kempling 17 My '23:340.

On rights in the copy for F1 and the circumstances of Jaggard's association with its publication.

548 **Stoll, Elmer Edgar.** On the anniversary of the Folio. Nth Am R 218no816: 646–59 N '23.

549 **[Veale, C. J.]** A First folio in India. (Notes on sales) TLS 5 Jl '23:460.

Copy of letter repr. in Pioneer Mail (Allahabad), 8 Je '23, describing F1 in library of Thomason engineering college, Roorkee, not described by Lee.

550 **Shakespeare association,** LONDON. 1623–1923: studies in the First folio written for the Shakespeare association in celebration of the First folio tercentenary . . . by M. H. Spielmann, J. Dover Wilson, sir Sidney Lee, R. Crompton Rhodes, W. W. Greg, Allardyce Nicoll, with an introduction by sir Israel Gollancz. London, H. Milford, O.U.P., 1924. xxxvi,182p. illus., facsims. 25cm.

General introduction, by sir Israel Gollancz.—Shakespeare's portraiture, by M. H. Spielmann.—The task of Heminge and Condell, by J. Dover Wilson.—A survey of First folios, by sir Sidney Lee.—The First folio and the Elizabethan stage, by R. Crompton Rhodes.—The First folio and its publishers, by W. W. Greg.—The editors of Shakespeare from First folio to Malone, by Allardyce Nicoll.

Rev: TLS 23 Ap '25:280; Oxford Mag 43:446–9 '25; F. S. Boas Mod Lang R 20:470–3 '25; New Statesm 24:750 '25; R. B. McKerrow R Eng Stud 1:492–4 '25; N&Q 148:287–8 '25; Library ser4 6:182–5 '25; S. C. Chew Nation 121:193–4 '25; E. Deckner Angl Beibl 37:103–15 '26.

551 **Wilson, Frank Percy.** The Jaggards and the First folio of Shakespeare. TLS 5 N '25:737; 12 N '25:756.

F1 advertised in Frankfurt book fair catalogue.

552 **Morgan, Appleton.** Shakespeare's First folio. N&Q 150:435–6 Je '26.

Suggests that copy for F1 was obtained surreptitiously by Richard James, second husband of Shakespeare's widow.

553 **Detmold, C. Charles.** Publication of First folio. N&Q 153:478 D '27; G. A. Taylor *ib.* 154:124 F '28.

Discussion of the sources of copy for F1.

554 **E., R.** The Bodleian First folio. N&Q 153:100 Ag '27; Foras *ib.* 156:121,446 F,Je '29.

555 **Shakespeare** and Garrick. (Notes on sales) TLS 28 Je '28:492.
Wynne FI sold for £8,500.

556 **The Wantage-Crawford** First folio. (Notes on sales) TLS 2 F '28:84.
Sold to unnamed American collector.

557 **Willoughby, Edwin Eliott.** The heading Actus primus, Scæna prima in the First folio. R Eng Stud 4no15:323–6 Jl '28. table.
Analysis of the distribution of forms of this heading reveals that Jaggard's compositors used the same setting of type on many occasions.

558 —— An interruption in the printing of the First folio. Library ser4 9no3: 262–6 D '28.
Bibliogr. evidence, mainly from ornaments, shows that Jaggard's printing of Favyn's Theatre of honour and FI was suspended at the 'end of quire b, the second page of Richard II' to speed the publication of Vincent's Discovery of errors.

559 **Noble, Richmond.** The facsimile Folio texts. TLS 8 Ag '29:624.
Plea for use of facsimile texts by producers and actors as corrective for 'corruptions, introduced into the text by editors'.

560 **Willoughby, Edwin Eliott.** A note on the typography of the running titles of the First folio. Library ser4 9no4:385–7 Mr '29.
Reoccurrence of damaged letters shows that FI compositors used the same settings of type to print the headtitles of successive plays.

561 —— The typography of the act-headings of the First folio. R Eng Stud 5no18:198–200 Ap '29.
Jaggard's compositors left space for the headings which were inserted from standing type before printing.

562 —— A note on the pagination of the First folio. Mod Lang N 44no6:373–4 Je '29.
The division of FI into three separately paged sections was 'a convenience to the printer'

563 —— Phrases marking the terminations of acts in the First folio. Mod Lang N 45no7:463–4 N '30.
'Finis Actus Primus' and the like in F *TGV, LLL,* and *TN.*

564 **White, Frederick C.** A First folio of Shakespeare burnt as rubbish. N&Q 159:458 D '30.
Report of destruction of count Gondomar's copy.

565 **Willoughby, Edwin Eliott.** The printing of the First folio of Shakespeare. [Oxford] Ptd. at the O.U.P. for the Bibliographical society, 1932. xiii,70p. facsims., tables. 21cm. (Bib Soc Trans Supplement, no.8)
Introduction.—Some typographical practices.—The history of the printing of the First folio.—The composition and proof-reading.
Rev: TLS 13 Jl '33:476; H. S[ellers] Mod Lang N 50:139 '35.

566 **A First** folio. (Notes on sales) TLS 16 N '33:800.
Lee XCI.

567 **Leslie, sir Shane.** The Folger folios. TLS 20 S '34:636.
Some notes on the copies; *see also* no.570.

568 **Willoughby, Edwin Eliott.** 'XIV. The printing of the First folio of Shakespeare' *in* A printer of Shakespeare, the books and times of William Jaggard. London, 1934. p.157–74.

569 **Smith, Robert Metcalf.** Fly specks and folios. Coloph new ser 1no1:25–32 Jl '35. facsims.
On the apparent colon after 'Copies' in the Halliwell-Phillipps proof of the Droueshout engraving. *See* no.530.

570 —— The Folger folios. TLS 7 Mr '35:143.
Corrections to Leslie (no.567) gathered during preparation of a new census of copies.

571 —— An interesting First folio. Sh Assn Bull 10no1:58–9 Ja '35.
Table of ms. readings in unnamed copy discovered Ag '34.

572 **Tannenbaum, Samuel Aaron.** An immortal fly-speck. Sh Assn Bull 10no4: 247–8 Oc '35.
See no.569.

573 **Casson, Leslie F.** Notes on a Shakespearean First folio in Padua. Mod Lang N 51no7:417–23 N '36.
Descr. and discussion of revision and cutting of *MM*, *WT*, and *Mac*. for acting, c.1680–94.

574 **Jackson, Wilfrid S.** A cheap Folio. TLS 26 S '36:768.
Plea for a cheap repr. of F1.

575 **A Shakespeare** discovery. (News and notes) TLS 30 Jl '38:501.
Imperfect copy found in Devon.

576 **Smith, Robert Metcalf.** The pursuit of the First folio. Coloph new ser 3no1:41–53 '38.
Detailed account of Folger's purchase of the Vincent–Sibthorp copy.

577 —— Why a First folio Shakespeare remained in England. R Eng Stud 15no59:257–64 Jl '39.
Account of Folger's efforts to acquire the Turbutt copy now in the Bodleian.

578 **Hastings, William T.** Shakespeare Ireland's First folio. Coloph new graphic ser 1no4:75–86 Ja '40. illus., facsims.

579 —— [Same]: Repr. in Bks at Brown 2no3:1–12 F '40.
The make-up of the Folio.—The manuscript notes.

580 **Dawson, Giles Edwin.** A bibliographical problem in the First folio of Shakespeare. Library ser4 22no1:25–33 Je '41. diagr.
Development of Adams's account of the irregularity in sig. gg and the ptg. of *Tro*.

581 **Hinman, Charlton J. K.** A proof-sheet in the First folio of Shakespeare. Library ser4 23no2/3:101–7 S/D '42. facsims., tables, diagr.
Discussion of proof-sheet in Jonas copy (Folger 47) of *Oth*. vv4^v:3, p.336:333.

582 **Philbrick, Norman.** Act and scene division in the first edition of Shakespeare. Theat Ann 1944:36–46 '45. (Not seen)

583 **Hinman, Charlton J. K.** Why 79 First folios? A paper read before the Bibliographical society of the University of Virginia, June, 1947. [Charlottesville, Va., 1947] 12p. 28cm. Headtitle. (Duplicated typescript)

584 **Robinson, A. M. Lewin.** The Grey copy of the Shakespeare First folio. Q Bull Sth African Lib 5no1:11–16 S '50.

'The Shakespeare First folio: detailed collation' (p.14–16): Lee CXLIX.

585 **Hinman, Charlton J. K.** Mark III: new light on the proof-reading for the First folio of Shakespeare. Stud Bib 2:143–53 '51. facsims.

Discusses proof-sheet of qq6ᵛ, *Lr.*, p.292, and its conjugate forme-page, *Ham.*, p.281.

586 **Saga** of the stolen Folio. Sh Newsl 1no3:10 My '51.

Theft and restoration of copy in the Chapin library.

587 **Muir, Kenneth.** Split lines in the First folio. N&Q 197:271–2 Je '52.

Lines split for typographical convenience by F compositors should be restored to full length.

588 **Walker, Alice.** Textual problems of the First folio: Richard III, King Lear, Troilus & Cressida, 2 Henry IV, Hamlet, Othello. Cambridge, C.U.P., 1953. viii,170p. tables. 17cm. (Shakespeare problems, VII)

Examination of 'what lay between Shakespeare's manuscript and the Folio texts of these six plays and what the editorial implications are of the use of corrected quartos as Folio copy' (p.12). Much F corruption must be attributed to compositor B, setting from corrected Q copy.

Rev: TLS 24 Jl '53: 482; N&Q 198:454–5 '53; P. Williams Sh Q 4:481–4 '53; R. A. Foakes Eng 9:220–1 '53; P. Edwards Mod Lang R 49:365–7 '54; M. A. Shaaber Mod Lang N 69: 436–8 '54; G. B. Evans J Eng Germ Philol 53:127–30 '54; J. G. McManaway Pa Bib Soc Am 48:105–7 '54; P. Williams Sth Atlantic Q 53:272 '54; J. M. Nosworthy Library ser5 9:63–5 '54; G. B. Harrison Dublin R 118:226–8 '54; H. Heuer Sh Jahrb 90:324–6 '54; A. Koszul Études Angl 7:321–2 '54; J. W. Beach J Eng Germ Philol 53:127–30 '54; J. G. McManaway Sh Surv 7:152–3 '54; H. T. Price Sh Q 5:112 '54; P. Alexander R Eng Stud new ser 9:188–93 '58; J. Gerritsen Eng Stud 41:269–70 '60.

589 **Flatter, Richard.** Der Setzer der ersten Shakespeare-Folio. Das Antiquariat 9no1/2:5–6 Ja '53; 11no23/4:275–6 D '55.

590 **Hinman, Charlton J. K.** Variant readings in the First folio of Shakespeare. Sh Q 4no3:279–88 Jl '53.

Progress report on collation of F, noting that 'the press-corrections in the First Folio ordinarily do not show reference to copy'. (p.286)

591 **Editing** the First folio. Sh Newsl 4no5:41 N '51.

592 **Hinman, Charlton J. K.** The Halliwell-Phillipps facsimile of the First folio of Shakespeare. Sh Q 5no4:395–401 '54.

The facsimile, published in 1876, derives from the Roberts copy (Lee LXXXVI, Folger 33) throughout the comedies through part of *1H4*, thereafter from the Staunton facsim. of 1866 which was based on copies in BM and Bridgewater House (ld. Ellesmere).

593 —— Variant readings in First folios. Sh Newsl 4no5:41 N '54.

594 **Kökeritz, Helge,** *ed.* Mr. William Shakespeares comedies, histories, & tragedies, a facsimile edition. . . . New Haven, Yale U.P.; London, G. Cumberlege, O.U.P. [1954] xxix[20]889p. facsims., diagrs. 28cm.

The reviews contain interesting observations on facsimiles and facsimile reproduction in general.

Rev: Sh Newsl 4:40 '54; T. E. Cooney Sat R 18 D '54:12; K. J. Holzknecht Pa Bib Soc Am 49:190–1 '55; F. T. Bowers Mod Philol 53:50–7 '55; L. Marder Am Schol 24:241–2 '55; E. D. O'Brien Illus Lond N 23 Jl '55:164; H. B. Charlton Manchester Guardian Wkly 14 Jl '55:10; J. I. M. Stewart New Statesm 30 Ap '55:622; D. F. Foxon Bk Coll 3: 261–2 '55; TLS 14 Oc '55:612; sir W. W. Greg, R. C. Bald *ib.* 28 Oc. '55:629; G. Freedley Lib J 80:83 '55; A. Brown Library ser5 11:57–9 '56; H. Heuer Sh Jahrb 92:393–4 '56; F. R. Johnson Sh Q 7:114–15 '56; Dublin Mag 31:32–4 '56; J. G. McManaway Mod Lang R 51:588–90 '56.

595 **Bowers, Fredson Thayer.** The Yale facsimile and scholarship. Mod Philol 53n01:50–7 Ag '55.

Detailed, unfavourable examination of the Kökeritz–Prouty facsimile, with a note of errors in *Jn.*

596 **Eisenman, Alvin.** The Yale facsimile edition of the Shakespeare First folio. Ptg & Graph Arts 3n01:15–21 F '55.

Account of the ptg. of the Yale facsim., with survey of earlier facsim. ed.

597 **Greg, sir Walter Wilson.** The Shakespeare First folio, its bibliographical and textual history. Oxford, Clarendon pr., 1955. xvi,496p. 22cm.

1. Planning the collection.—2. Questions of copyright.—3–5. Editorial problems.— 6. The printing.—Postscript.

Rev: J. Wain Spectator 15 Jl '55:101; H. B. Charlton Manchester Guardian Wkly 14 Jl '55:10; R. A. Foakes Eng 10:227–8 '55; D. Daiches Twent Cent 158:180–3 '55; N&Q 200:412–13 '55; TLS 14 Oc '55:612; A. Brown Listener 53:1037–8 '55; Times Wkly R 16 Je '55:12; K. J. Holzknecht Pa Bib Soc Am 50:88–95 '56; W. R. LeFanu Bk Coll 4:332–4 '56; C. J. K. Hinman Sh Q 7:97–101 '56; H. Heuer Sh Jahrb 92:385–90 '56; A. Walker Library ser5 11:56–7 '56; K. Muir Mod Lang R 51:97 '56; J. G. McManaway Sh Surv 9:148–9 '56; Dublin Mag 31:32–4 '56; B. Martin Dalhousie R 36:289–91 '56; H. S. Wilson Univ Toronto Q 26:271–2 '57; P. Alexander R Eng Stud new ser 9:69–70 '58.

598 —— The Shakespeare First folio. TLS 21 Oc '55:621; R. C. Marsh; C. L. Quinton *ib.* 21 Oc '55:621; sir W. W. Greg; R. C. Bald 28 Oc '55:639.

Incidental comment on Greg's book.

599 **Hinman, Charlton J. K.** Cast-off copy for the First folio of Shakespeare. Sh Q 6n03:259–74 '55. facsims.

Because F was set by formes, copy required to be cast off; this entailed a degree of precision which affected the setting into type.

600 **Mackenzie, Barbara.** Shakespeare's First folio. Q Bull Sth African Lib 10:57–60 '55/6.

601 **Akrigg, G. P. V.** The arrangement of the tragedies in the First folio. Sh Q 7n04:443–5 '56.

'The tragedies were arranged according to what Condell and Heminge took to be the order of their composition.' (p.443)

602 **First** folio in Siberia. Sh Q 7n04:460 '56.

Copy found in Tomsk; present location unknown.

603 **Flatter, Richard.** Some instances of line-division in the First folio. Sh Jahrb 92:184–96 '56.

Distinction between short lines in copy and lines divided by F compositors because they were too long for the measure.

604 **Hart, James D.** 'On the First folio' *in* California. University. University at Berkeley. Library. Two million: several addresses given. . . . Berkeley, 1956. p.4–9.

Some references to the Library's Crocker copy.

605 **Shroeder, John W.** The great Folio of 1623: Shakespeare's plays in the printing house. [Hamden, Conn.] Shoe string pr., 1956. xi,125p. facsims., diagrs. 25cm.

1. Publication and printing.—2. The Folio irregularities.—3. . . . addenda.—4. Copyright, copy, and cancels.—5. Conclusion.

Rev: R. A. Foakes Eng Stud 39:261–3 '57; sir W. W. Greg Library ser5 12:130–3 '57; C. J. K. Hinman Sh Q 8:219–22 '57; sir W. W. G[reg] Bk Coll 6:95 '57; I. B. Cauthen J Eng Germ Philol 56:631–3 '57; G. W. Williams Renaiss N 11:33–5 '57.

606 **Hinman, Charlton J. K.** The prentice hand in the tragedies of the Shakespeare First folio: compositor E. Stud Bib 9:3–20 '57. tables.

Discussion of work of apprentice compositor in *Tit., Rom., Tro., Ham., Lr.,* and *Oth.*

607 **Nathan, Norman.** Compositor haste in the First folio. Sh Q 8no1:134–5 '57.

The author's experience as a time-and-motion study engineer suggests it to be unlikely the 'haste of the compositor' will be 'demonstrable from a consideration solely of the textual characteristics'. (p.135)

608 **Barton, Thomas Pennant.** The library's First folio of Shakespeare. Boston Pub Lib Q 10no2:63–77 Ap '58. facsim.

Repr. of Description of a copy, 1860.

609 **Hook, Frank S.** The manuscript alterations in the Honeyman First folio. Pa Bib Soc Am 53:334–8 '59.

Tabulation and comparison with modern readings of 106 contemporary ms. alterations.

610 **Hinman, Charlton J. K.** Six variant readings in the First folio of Shakespeare. Lawrence, University of Kansas libraries, 1961. 17p. 22cm. ([University of Kansas publications. Library series, 13])

'. . . there are two corrections in the Folio that must have been made by reference to copy; and there are some five or six others that may have been.' (p.17)

Rev: TLS 4 Ag '61:488; A. Walker Library ser5 17:180–1 '62.

611 —— The printing and proof-reading of the First folio of Shakespeare. Oxford, Clarendon pr., 1963. 2v. facsims., tables. 26cm.

Part I: Introductory considerations: needs, tools, methods. 1. Introduction: old problems and new needs.—2. The First folio: preliminary data. A. Jaggard books of 1621–3. B. Copyrights in the plays. C. The First folio as published. D. Edition size and speed of production. E. Standard printing-house procedures; the forme.—3. The kinds of evidence and their uses. A. Types. B. Other kinds of evidence useful in determining order. C. Spellings, cases, and compositors. D. Press variants: the proof-reading. E. The chronology of the printing.—Appendixes. A. Spellings. B. Types. C. Centre rules.—Part II: The printing, a detailed analysis. Introduction.—1. The histories.—2. The tragedies.—3. The comedies.—4. The printing of the First folio in review. A. On questions of order. B. On compositor study. C. How the work progressed: a tabular synopsis. D. The printing, a general summary.

Rev: F. Kermode New Statesm 65:944 '63; TLS 12 Jl '63:516; R. A. Foakes Eng 14:239 '63; J. Crow Bk Coll 12:376,379 '63; G. B. Evans Eng Lang N 1:140–4 '63; J. C. Maxwell R Eng Stud new ser 15:79–81 '64; D. F. M[cKenzie] Cambridge R 8 F '64:255; A. Arnold Personalist 45:276–7 '64; P. Edwards N&Q 209:152–3 '64; C. Leech Univ Toronto Q 33: 316–17 '64; G. R. Smith Sevent Cent N 22:10 '64; R. Hosley Arizona Q 20:78–81 '64; J. Gerritsen Eng Stud 45:184–7 '64; H. Heuer Sh Jahrb 100:313–15 '64; J. Robertson Oxford Mag 13 F '64:197; G. W. Williams J Eng Germ Philol 63:778–80 '64; J. H. P. Pafford Mod Lang R 59:628–30 '64; S. F. Johnson Renaiss N 17:224–30 '64; A. Yamada Sh N 3:11–12; W. C. McAvoy Manuscripta 8:146–8 '64; H. E. Hulme Essays Crit 15:220–3 '65; J. B. Fort Études Angl 18:74–5 '65; C. Hoy Pa Bib Soc Am 59:445–9 '65; G. Lambrechts Bull Faculté Lettres Strasbourg 43:1061–3 '65.

612 **Doyle, Anthony Ian H.** The Cosin First folio. Durham Univ J 56n02:85 Mr '64.

613 **Kunze, Horst.** Die Shakespeare First folio von 1623 in der Deutschen Staatsbibliothek. Marginalien 16:27–8 '64. (Not seen)

614 **Baldwin, Thomas Whitfield.** On act and scene division in the Shakspere First folio. Carbondale, Southern Illinois U.P., 1965. xi,179p. 21cm.

The marking of acts and scenes in printed Latin drama.—The marking of acts and scenes in English manuscripts of Shakspere's time.—Comedies with acts and scenes marked in the First folio.—Theories of assembled texts.—Comedies with acts only in the First folio.—Irregular speech headings.—Histories and tragedies in the First folio.—The heart of the matter.—Literary genetics of the phrase 'maimed and deformed'.—Shakspere's autograph.—Appendix: Rights in Shakspere's plays.

Rev: W. M. Jones Coll Eng 27:339–40 '65; TLS 29 Jl '65:654; M. Crane J Eng Germ Philol 65:182–3 '66; J. A. Barish Stud Eng Lit 6:361–2 '66; T. H. Howard-Hill R Eng Stud new ser 17:310–12 '66.

615 **Craven, Alan E.** Justification of prose and Jaggard compositor B. Eng Lang N 3n01:15–17 S '65.

Compositor B 'habitually used long and short forms' of he, she, be, etc.

616 **Hill, Trevor Howard Howard-.** Ralph Crane's parentheses. N&Q 210:334–40 S '65. tables.

Includes discussion of frequency of parentheses in some F texts, and compositorial practices.

617 **King, T. J.** The 1623 reprint of Thomas of Reading, a computer analysis. Sh Newsl 15n06:54 D '65.

Analysis of compositorial changes in Jaggard's reprint, with application to F1.

618 **Why** is the famous ornament of the dogs and archers famous? Bks & Lib Univ Kansas 3n01:5 Mr '66. illus.

619 —— More on dogs and archers. *ib.* 3n02:3 Ap '66.

Migrations of ornament in F between 1583 and 1677.

620 **Pafford, J. H. P.** The Methuen facsimile, 1910, of the First folio, 1623. N&Q 211:126–7 Ap '66.

The facsimile was made from a copy (Lee II) in the Guildhall library, London.

621 **Kable, William S.** The influence of justification on spelling in Jaggard's compositor B. Stud Bib 20:235–9 '67.

Some notes on B's spellings in the Pavier Q, and their application to the study of F1.

622 **Kable, William S.** Compositor B, the Pavier quartos, and copy spellings. Stud Bib 21:131–61 '68. tables.

623 **Marder, Louis.** The new Norton–Hinman standard folio: its aim, background, and predecessors. Sh Newsl 18no4/5:31–3 S/N '68.

Plea for through line numbers (TLN).—Sidney Lee, 1902.—The Hinman–Norton–Folger Folio.—Different Folio states.—Original random proofreading.—The Folio errors.—Previous composite folios.—Through line numbers.—19th century TLN.—19th century TLN plea.—Complications of the new system.—Digression on act & scene abolition.

FOLIOS—SECOND

640 **Smith, Robert Metcalf.** The variant issues of Shakespeare's second folio and Milton's first published poem, a bibliographical problem. [Bethlehem, Pa., Lehigh university, 1928] 62p. facsims. 23cm. (Lehigh university publications, 2no3 Mr '28. Institute of research. Circular no.14. Studies in the humanities, 4)

1. The bibliographical status of the second folio.—2. The title pages of the second folio.—3. Milton's epitaph on Shakespeare.—4. The paper and water-marks of the title pages and effigies leaves.—5. A list of second folios.—6. The value of second folios and notable copies.

Rev: G. Binz Angl Beibl 39:339–40 '28.

645 **Jones, A. B. Bence-.** The second folio Shakspeare. Athenæum 3847:104 Jl '01; E. Hartley *ib*. 3849:168 Ag '01; P. A. Daniel 3850:200 Ag '01; E. Hartley 3852:264 Ag '01.

Variations in pagination and TP.

646 **Smith, C. Alphonso.** The chief difference between the First and second folios of Shakespeare. Eng Studien 30no1:1–20 N '01.

F2 represents a new ed., rather than a repr. of F1, designed to 'make the language conform to the needs of written style rather than to the demands of oral delivery'. (p.4)

647 **Herpich, Charles A.** The second folio Shakespeare. N&Q ser9 10:181–3 S '02; H. C. L. Morris *ib*. ser9 10:371 N '02.

Discursive collation, with distinction of 6 TP variants, from copies in N.Y. Public library.

648 **Clarke, Cecil.** Shakespeare second folio in Switzerland. N&Q ser10 11:366 My '09.

Report of copy now in Basle Public library.

649 **Shakespeare,** the second folio. Athenæum 4275:393-4 Oc '09.
Observations on the text.

650 **McElwaine, P. A.** Star-ypointing: Milton's epitaph on Shakespeare. N&Q
ser11 7:227 Mr '13; E. Durning-Lawrence *ib.* 7:456 Je '13; W. Jaggard
8:11-12 Jl '13; E. Durning-Lawrence 8:141-2 Ag '13; J. R. Magrath;
W. F. Prideaux 8:196 S '13; E. Durning-Lawrence 8:232-2 S '13; C. A.
Herpich; J. T. Curry 8:294-5 Oc '13; W. E. Baxter 8:317 Oc '13; E. Durn-
ing-Lawrence 9:11-12 Ja '14; J. D. Parsons; T. Bayne; C. C. B.; E. Bensly;
E. Durning-Lawrence 9:73-4 Ja '14; H. M. Smith 9:114 F '14; E. Durning-
Lawrence; E. Bensly; W. H. Pinchbeck 9:172-3 F '14; D. L. Galbreath;
J. D. Parsons 9:217 Mr '14; T. Bayne 9:237-8 Mr '14; W. B. S. 9:257 Mr
'14; E. Durning-Lawrence 9:294-5 Ap '14; J. D. Parsons 9:353 My '14.
The discussion is mostly concerned with the nature of F2.

651 **Spielmann, Marion Harry.** The Royal society's Shakespeare second folio.
TLS 23 Ap '25:284; F. S. Ferguson *ib.* 30 Ap '25:300; M. H. Spielmann 7
My '25:316.
Peculiarities of the text and portrait on TP suggest it to be a trial proof.

652 **Lee, sir Sidney.** 'Shakespeare and the inquisition, a Spanish second folio'
in Elizabethan and other essays. Selected and edited by Frederick S. Boas.
Oxford, 1929. p.[184]–95. facsim.
Descr. of Inquisitor's censoring of passages in F2 in library of English college at Valla-
dolid. Rev. from The Times 10,11 Ap '22.

653 **O'Hegarty, Patrick Sarsfield.** Shakespeare, 1632. Dublin Mag new ser
14:70 Ja/Mr '39.
Descr. of copy formerly owned by rev. Thomas Butler, d.1793.

654 **Including** Blake water-colours: illustrations from the British museum's
newly-acquired second folio. Illus Lond N 225:1163 D '54. facsims.

655 **Dawson, Giles Edwin.** Second folio variants. TLS 1 F '47:65.
Two TP variants amongst Folger copies additional to those recorded by Smith, no.640.

656 **Robinson, A. M. Lewin.** The Grey copy of the Shakespeare second folio.
Q Bull Sth African Lib 6no4:120-5 Je '52.
'The Shakespeare second folio, 1632: detailed collation.' (p.121-5)

657 **Todd, William Burton.** The issues and states of the second folio and Milton's
epitaph on Shakespeare. Stud Bib 5:81-107 '52/3. facsims., tables.
The order of issues.—The order of variants in the first issue.—The size and distribution
of issues.—The effigies leaf.—Historical associations: the Charles I copy.—Tabulation of
variants.—Register of copies.
Rev: P. Edwards Sh Q 4:185-6 '53; H. T. Price *ib.* 5:120 '54.

658 **McManaway, James Gilmer.** The colophon of the second folio of Shakespeare. Library ser5 9no3:199-200 S '54.
Folger 34 lacks the colophon, Folger 35 has two, showing that the colophon was added
to sheets first ptd. without it.

659 **Boase, T. S. R.** An extra-illustrated second folio of Shakespeare. Brit Mus Q 20no1:4–8 Mr '55.

BM copy with water-colour or pencil extra-illustrations by early 19th-century artists, including Blake.

FOLIOS—THIRD

670 **J., D.** Shakespeare: a remarkable folio. N&Q ser10 5:427 Je '06.

Copy of F3 in Victoria and Albert museum, with autographs of Leigh Hunt, Words-worth, Browning, and Dickens.

671 **Harris, Edward B.** The third folio Shakespeare. N&Q ser10 9:241–2 Mr '08; A. Abrahams *ib.* 9:314–15 Ap '08.

Maintains that there was only one issue of F3.

672 —— Shakespeare third folio: the Jones copy. N&Q ser11 1:244 Mr '10.

The copy referred to in no.670 has facsim. TP.

673 **The third** folio Shakespeare. (Notes on sales) TLS 27 Ja '21:64.

General account, with a table of the 1663 F which 'have come into the London salerooms during the last 242 years'.

674 **The third** folio Shakespeare. (Notes on sale) TLS 4 Ap '29:279.

Copy from ld. Malmesbury's library.

675 **Danks, Kenneth B.** Chetwind's folios. TLS 17 Jl '48:401.

Query concerning the reason for Chetwind's second issue.

676 **McManaway, James Gilmer.** A miscalculation in the printing of the third folio. Library ser5 9no2:129–33 Je '54.

Two unique extra leaves bound between 2F5 and 2F6 in J. F. Neylan copy show aborted setting from Q 1639.

677 **McGinn, Donald J.** The third folio. Rutgers Univ Lib J 27no2:60–2 Je '64.

FOLIOS—FOURTH

680 **Reynolds, Theodore.** Fourth folio Shakespeare. N&Q ser8 12:69 Jl '97.

Inquiry about ptg. of p.123–4 (*LLL*) in smaller type.

681 **Bowers, Fredson Thayer.** Robert Roberts, a printer of Shakespeare's Fourth folio. Sh Q 2no3:241–6 Jl '51.

Finds 'two-section simultaneous printing' and identifies Roberts as the ptr. of the first text section. 'A note on the device in the Fourth folio.' (p.245–6)

682 **Dawson, Giles Edwin.** Some bibliographical irregularities in the Shakespeare fourth folio. Stud Bib 4:93–103 '51/2. table.

Collation and pagination.—Reprinted sheets.—Sig. Ll, pp.123–4, section 1: bibliographical analysis.

OTHER EDITIONS

690 **Shakespeare's** American editors. VI. Henry Norman Hudson. Shakespeariana 7no4:248–50 Oc '90. port.

691 **Fleming, William H.** The editors of Shakespeare. XIX. William Harness. Shakespeariana 8no2:116–18 Ap '91.

692 —— The editors of Shakespeare. XX. Alexander Dyce. Shakespeariana 8no3:169–74 Jl '91.

693 [Note on the publication of the 1891 edition of Aldis Wright's Cambridge Shakespeare] Acad 39:112 Ja '91.

694 **Hudson, William Henry.** Early mutilators of Shakespeare. Poet-Lore 4no6/7:360 '92.

695 **Adee, Alvey A.** The Bankside reference canon of the Shakespeare plays, a plea for its adoption for all the plays. Shakespeariana 10no3:152–76 Jl '93.

696 **Bennet, Norman.** Warburton's Shakespear. N&Q ser8 3:141–2 F '93; 3:2–3 Mr '93; 3:262–3 Ap '93.

Table of Warburton's ms. readings from a copy of his ed.

697 **Scammon, F. J.** The completion of the Bankside Shakespeare. Shakespeariana 10no1:21–7 Ja '93.

698 **Spingarn, J. E.** Singer's plagiarism. N&Q ser8 4:5 Jl '93.

Thirteen 'canons of criticism' in S. W. Singer's Text of Shakespeare vindicated, 1854, are 'taken nearly literally' from Thomas Edwards' Canons of criticism, being a supplement to mr. Warburton's edition of Shakespear.

699 **Collins, John Churton.** 'The Porson of Shakespearian criticism' in Essays and studies. London, 1895. p.[263]–315.

Rehabilitation of the editorial activities of Lewis Theobald.

700 **F., F. J.** Who murdered Shakespeare again, about 1730? N&Q ser8 7:9 Ja '95; W. A. Henderson *ib.* 7:95 F '95.

Reference to Royal remarks, c.1730, taken as referring to Tate but more likely Pope's ed

701 **Henderson, W. A.** The worst edition of Shakespeare. N&Q ser8 7:9 Ja '95.

That ed. by Francis Gentleman.

702 **Jonas, Maurice.** An error in the Vale press Shakespeare. N&Q ser9 6:104 Ag '00.

'He dies' for 'He faints' in *Oth.*, 2.3.

703 **Butler, James D.** The Temple Shakespeare. N&Q ser9 11:407 My '03; C. C. B. *ib.* 12:13 Jl '03.

Based on the text of the Globe ed.

704 **Dix, Ernest Reginald McClintock.** The earliest Dublin edition of Shakspeare's plays. Athenæum 3928:117 F '03.

Ham., *Oth.*, and *JC* ptd. by Grierson in 1721.

705 **Lounsbury, Thomas R.** The first editors of Shakespeare (Pope and Theobald); the story of the first Shakespearian controversy and of the earliest attempt at establishing a critical text of Shakespeare. London, D. Nutt, 1906. xxii,579p. 22cm.

Also published New York, Scribner's, 1906, with title: The text of Shakespeare, its history from the publication of the quartos and folios down to and including the publication of the editions of Pope and Theobald.

1. The dramatic situation in Shakespeare's time.—2. Attitude towards plays of the playwrights.—3. Differences of the early texts.—4. The earliest editions of Shakespeare.—5. Pope's edition of Shakespeare.—6. Pope's treatment of the text.—7. The early career of Theobald.—8. Theobald's dramatic ventures.—9. Shakespeare restored.—10. Theobald's attitude towards Pope.—11. Pope's preliminary attack.—12. The original Dunciad.—13. The Dunciad of 1729.—14. Errors about the Dunciad.—15. Shakespeare controversy of 1728.—16. Arrangements for Theobald's edition.—17. Warburton's attack on Pope.—18. The allies of Pope.—19. The Grub-street journal.—20. The attack on verbal criticism.—21. Theobald's edition and its reception.—22. The spread of Pope's influence.—23. Difficulties in Pope's way.—24. Defects of Theobald's edition.—25. Theobald's later reputation.

Rev: A. R. Waller Mod Lang R 2:265 '06; Nation 83:416–17 '06; Sh Jahrb 43:26–7 '07. W. Dibelius Dial 42:39–41 '07.

706 **Jaggard, William.** Shakespeare edited by Scott. N&Q ser10 7:428 Je '07.

Inquiry after third v. of abortive Scott ed.

707 **Sherzer, Jane.** American editions of Shakespeare, 1753–1866. Pub Mod Lang Assn 22no4:633–96 '07.

Chronol. account of ed., with some bibliogr. and textual notes.

Rev: C. S. Northup J Eng Germ Philol 17:314–15 '18.

708 **V., Q.** Rowe's Shakespeare. N&Q ser10 7:69 Ja '07; S. Butterworth; W. Jaggard *ib.* 7:117–18 F '07.

Query and discussion about the number of plates.

709 **Wheatley, Henry Benjamin.** Johnson's edition of Shakspeare. Athenæum 4272:298 S '09.

Documents relating to financial arrangements between Tonson and Johnson.

710 **Abrahams, Aleck.** Shakespeare illustrators. N&Q ser11 1:327 Ap '10; W. Scott *ib.* 1:414 My '10; J. F. Palmer 1:474 Je '10.

Inquiry and discussion concerning predecessors of Thurston as illustrators of complete ed.

711 **B., W. C.** Shakespeare: chronological edition. N&Q ser11 2:348 Oc '10; T. Jones; W. Scott *ib.* 2:431 N '10.

Discussion concerning ed. in which plays are arranged in order of composition, e.g. Furnivall's Leopold, 1877, and the Royal Shakespeare, 1880–4, editions.

712 **Furness, Horace Howard.** Shakespearian editors, past and present. Lib J 35no3:112–13 Mr '10.

713 **Adee, Alvey A.** The Bankside reference canon of the Shakespeare plays, a plea for its adoption for all editions. New Shakespeareana 10no3:69–93 Ag/Oc '11.

714 **Connell, George.** Shakespeare: Tallis & co.'s edition. N&Q ser11 3:367 My '11.

715 **Brooks, Charles Stephen.** 'The worst edition of Shakespeare' *in* Journeys to Bagdad. New Haven, Conn., 1915. p.23–42.

Repr. from Yale R new ser 4no2:368–77 Ja '15. Literary essay on Bell's 1774 ed.

716 **Spielmann, Marion Harry.** Robert Inglis's edition of Shakespeare. N&Q ser11 11:188 Mr '15.

Seeks identity of artist and engraver of plates.

717 **Aitken, George Atherton.** Shakespeare's first editor. TLS 11 My '16:225.

Extracts from sale catalogue of Rowe's library.

718 **Burd, Henry Alfred.** 'Joseph Ritson and some eighteenth-century editors of Shakespeare' *in* Wisconsin. University. Dept. of English. Shakespeare studies. Madison [Wisc.] 1916. p.253–75.

719 **Steeves, Harrison Ross.** 'American editions of Shakespeare' *in* Matthews, Brander, and A. H. Thorndike, *ed.* Shaksperian studies by members of the Department of English and comparative literature in Columbia university. New York, 1916. (Repr. New York, Russell & Russell, 1962) p.[345]–68.

720 **Wheatley, Henry Benjamin.** Shakespeare's editors, 1623 to the twentieth century. Bib Soc Trans 14pt2:145–73 '16/17.

Summary report in Bib Soc News-sh 1–4 N '16.

721 **Jones, Richard Foster.** Lewis Theobald, his contribution to English scholarship with some unpublished letters. New York, Columbia U.P., 1919. xi,363p. 20cm. (Columbia university. Studies in English & comparative literature)

Includes 2. The rage for emending.—3. Shakespeare restored.—5. The edition of Shakespeare.—7. The progress of the method.

722 **Woodbridge, Homer E.** The Yale Shakespeare. J Eng Germ Philol 19no3: 426–30 Je '20.

General survey of some v. of this ed.

723 **Boas, Frederick Samuel.** 'Three hundred years of Shakespeare at Oxford and Cambridge' *in* Shakespeare & the universities and other studies in Elizabethan drama. Oxford, 1923. p.42–83.

Includes accounts of Sh. editors and scholars, and other bibliographica.

724 **Owen, Daniel E.** 'Dr. Furness's method in editing the New variorum' *in* Schelling anniversary papers by his former students. New York, 1923. p.227–32.

725 **Nicoll, John Ramsay Allardyce.** 'The editors of Shakespeare from First folio to Malone' *in* Shakespeare association, London. 1623–1923: Studies in the First folio. London, 1924. p.157–78.

726 **Mertz, Wendel.** Die Shakespeare-Ausgabe von Theobald, 1733. Gießener Beiträge zur Erforschung der Sprache und Kultur Englands und Nordamerikas 2n02:193–248 '25.

727 **Cuming, A.** A copy of Shakespeare's works which formerly belonged to dr. Johnson. R Eng Stud 3n010:208–12 Ap '27.

Copy of Pope's 1747 ed. now at University college, Aberystwyth, with Johnson's notes.

728 **Smith, David Nichol.** Shakespeare in the eighteenth century. Oxford, Clarendon pr., 1928. 91p. 17cm.

Three lectures, the second of which deals with the treatment of Sh. text by the eighteenth-century ed. (p.29–60)

729 **Boswell** and Shakespeare problems. (Notes on sales) TLS 16 My '29:408.

Notes bibliogr. variants in a copy of Rowe's 1709 ed.

730 **Jackson, Alfred.** Rowe's edition of Shakespeare. Library ser4 10n04:455–73 Mr '30. illus.

General account of 1709 and 1714 ed., with TP transcrs., and lists of illustrations.

731 **Tannenbaum, Samuel Aaron.** Textual errors in the Furness variorum. Mod Lang N 45n08:510–14 D '30.

Tables of errors.

732 **Wilson, John Dover.** Thirteen volumes of Shakespeare: a retrospect. Mod Lang R 25n04:397–414 Oc '30.

Classification and selection of texts: definition of copy.—Act and scene division.—Punctuation and stage-directions.—Spellings, misprints, and emendation.—Notes and glossary.

733 **Boyce, Benjamin.** Alderman Boys, illustrator of Shakespeare. N&Q 160:172 Mr '31; E. E. Newton *ib.* 160:210–11 Mr '31.

Account of Boydell's illustrated ed., 1802– .

734 **Wagenknecht, Edward.** The first editor of Shakespeare. Coloph 8:[12]p. '31. illus., facsims.

General account of Rowe's 1709 ed.

735 **McKerrow, Ronald Brunlees.** The treatment of Shakespeare's text by his earlier editors, 1709–1768. Proc Brit Acad 19:89–122 '33. (Annual Shakespeare lecture) Also issued separately.

The early folios, Rowe, Pope, Theobald, Johnson, and Capell. Repr. in no.118.

Rev: Library ser4 14:360–2 '33; H. S[ellers] Mod Lang R 29:369 '34; G. W. Fischer Angl Beibl 45:116–17 '34; A. E. DuBois Sewanee R 42:240–4 '34.

736 —— Rowe's Shakespeare, 1709. (Bibliographical notes) TLS 8 Mr '34:168.

Distinction and discussion of repr. ed. of 1709.

737 **Madan, Falconer.** The first Oxford Shakespeare. Bod Q Rec 7no83:474 '34.

Hanmer's ed., 1744.

738 **Paul, Henry Neill.** Johnson's Shakespeare, 1765. Univ Pennsylvania Lib Chron 2no1:1–3 Mr '34.

Distinction of two 1765 ed.

739 **Campbell, Olwen W.** and **Stella C. Campbell.** Wanted, a pocket Shakespeare. TLS 20 Je '35:399; M. R. Ridley; W. Jaggard *ib.* 27 Je '35:416; P. Alexander; O. W. and S. C. Campbell 4 Jl '35:432; M. R. Ridley 18 Jl '35:464; P. Alexander 1 Ag '35:489.

Discussion of and note of misprints in New Temple ed.

740 **Cook, Davidson.** A fictitious Shakespeare editor. TLS 23 N '35:776.

Account of ed. issued by Charles Daly, nominally ed. by 'A. C. Cunningham'.

741 —— An unchronicled Shakespeare edition. TLS 2 N '35:697.

Popular dramatic works issued by Vernor, Hood & Sharpe, 1800, in 6v.

742 **Crosse, Gordon.** Charles Jennens as editor of Shakespeare. Library ser4 16no2:236–40 S '35.

743 **Dawson, Giles Edwin.** The Arlaud-Duchange portrait of Shakespeare. Library ser4 16:290–4 D '35. facsims.

Examination of the portrait in Rowe's 1709 and Theobald's 1733 ed. *See also* no.748.

744 **Senex.** Faking. N&Q 168:466 Je '35.

Discussion of 'improved' copies of early Sh. ed.

745 **Shaaber, Matthias A.** The Furness variorum of Shakespeare. Am Philos Soc Proc 75:281–5 '35.

General survey of its history.

746 **Paul, Henry Neill.** Billy Jones' Shakespeare. (Notes and queries) Coloph new ser 1no3:461–2 '36.

Rare 1826 ed.

747 **Beaujon, Paul,** *pseud.* Some recent editions of Shakespeare's works. Signat 7:17–32 N '37. facsims.

Typographical appreciation of modern ed.

748 **Dawson, Giles Edwin.** A note on the Arlaud-Duchange portrait of Shakespeare. Library ser4 18no3:342–4 D '37.

Further bibliogr. discussion: *see* no.743.

749 **Willoughby, Edwin Eliott.** The reading of Shakespeare in colonial America. Pa Bib Soc Am 31pt1:45–56 '37.
Survey of ed. available to colonists, and their use.

750 **Bakeless, John Edwin.** The most famous edition of Shakespeare, the Furness variorum. Commonweal 28:637–8 '38. (Not seen)

751 **Hazen, Allen Tracy.** Johnson's Shakespeare, a study in cancellation. (Antiquarian notes) TLS 24 D '38:820.
Cancels designed to soften Johnson's comments on some Warburtonian conjectures.

752 **Summers, Alphonse Montague Joseph-Mary Augustus.** The first illustrated Shakespeare. Connois 102no448:305–9 D '38. facsims.
Rowe's ed.

753 **Cancels** in Johnson's Shakespeare. Bod Lib Rec 1no3:42–3 F '39.
Acquisition of copy containing cancellanda.

754 **Limited editions club,** NEW YORK. Shakespeare, a review and a preview. . . . New York, 1939. 25[44]p. illus. (part col.) 30cm.
Part I. Review: 1. What we know about Shakespeare, by J. W. Mackail.—2. What has been said of Shakespeare, by John Milton and others.—3. Landmarks in the publishing of Shakespeare, by Mark G. Holstein.—Part II. Preview: 4. A note upon a new Shakespeare, by George Macy.—5. The text of the new Shakespeare, by Herbert Farjeon.—6. The format of the new Shakespeare, by Bruce Rogers.—7. Pages and pictures from the new Shakespeare.
Followed by: Some notes upon a project for an illustrated Shakespeare; a note upon the format, by mr. Bruce Rogers; a note upon the text, by mr. Herbert Farjeon; a note upon the project, by mr. George Macy.

755 **Thompson, Lawrance.** The Boydell Shakspeare, an English monument to graphic arts. Princeton Univ Lib Chron 1no2:17–24 F '40. facsim.

756 **Wilcox, John.** McKerrow's New Shakspere text. Sh Assn Bull 15no1:59–60 Ja '40.
General note.

757 **Schmitz, R. Morrell.** Scottish Shakspere. Sh Assn Bull 16no4:229–36 Oc '41.
Discussion of ed. by Hugh Blair, 1753–95.

758 **Spencer, Hazelton.** Shakespearean cuts in restoration Dublin. Pub Mod Lang Assn 57no2:575–6 Je '42.

759 **Suling, Karl-Heinz.** Die Shakespeareausgabe Nicholas Rowes, 1709. Würzburg-Aumühle, K. Triltsch [1942] 111p. 23cm.
Einleitung: Die Shakespearetexte des 17. Jahrhunderts.—Hauptteil: Rowes Shakespeareausgabe. 1. Die verschiedenen Texte. — 2. Die einleitenden Prosakapitel. — 3. Die vierte Folio als Grundlage de Roweschen Ausgabe. — 4. Die Abweichungen Rowes von der vierten Folio. — 5. Zusammenfaßung.

760 **Sutherland, James Runcieman.** The dull duty of an editor. R Eng Stud 21no83:202–15 Jl '45.
On the conflicting ed. attitudes of Pope and Theobald.

761 **A gift** from the Delegates of the Press. Bod Lib Rec 2no24:127–8 Jl '46.

F2 with ms. collations of F1 and F3 by Thomas Hawkins, the overseer of the ptg. of Hanmer's Sh., 2d ed., 1771.

762 **Byrne, Muriel St. Clare.** Bell's Shakespeare. TLS 31 Ja '48:65.

Discussion of ed. issued in parts, 1773–6.

763 **Eastman, Arthur M.** Johnson's Shakespearean labors in 1765. Mod Lang N 63no8:512–15 D '48.

764 **Dawson, Giles Edwin.** Warburton, Hanmer, and the 1745 edition of Shakespeare. Stud Bib 2:35–48 '49.

Unassigned emendations in Hanmer's 1744 ed., which the 1745 ed. substantially reprints, are there attrib. to Warburton, by himself.

765 **Evans, Gwynne Blakemore.** The text of Johnson's Shakespeare, 1765. Philol Q 28no3:425–8 Jl '49.

Theobald's 1757 issue, not just a repr. as was previously thought, was used as copy for *1H6* in Johnson's ed., and possibly for twenty-five other plays.

766 **Eastman, Arthur M.** Johnson's Shakespeare and the laity, a textual study. Pub Mod Lang Assn 65no4:1112–21 D '50.

On the general characteristics of the text.

767 —— The texts from which Johnson printed his Shakespeare. J Eng Germ Philol 49no2:182–91 Ap '50. tables.

Distribution of Johnson's use of Theobald's 1757 and Warburton's 1747 ed. by play.

768 **Horne, Colin J.** Malone and Steevens. N&Q 195:56 F '50.

Steevens on the lack of profit from his ed.

769 **Sherbo, Arthur.** Dr. Johnson on Macbeth: 1745 and 1765. R Eng Stud new ser 2no5:40–7 Ja '51.

Discussion of the differences between Johnson's notes in his Miscellaneous observations on the tragedy of Macbeth, 1745, and in his 1765 ed.

770 **Sampson, Anthony.** The printing of Shakespeare's plays. Signat new ser 15:40–54 '52. facsims.

Observations on the typography of the main ed. since F.

771 **Sherbo, Arthur.** The proof-sheets of dr. Johnson's Preface to Shakespeare. John Rylands Lib Bull 35no1:206–10 S '52. table.

Sigs. A and a only, about half the Preface.

772 —— Warburton and the 1745 Shakespeare. J Eng Germ Philol 51no1:71–82 Ja '52.

'. . . a comparison of Warburton's early notes and emendations on Shakespeare with the attributions of those same notes and emendations in the 1745 edition; second, an examination of all the attributions in one play of those same notes and emendations for each of the six volumes of the 1745 edition; and third, an investigation of accusations brought against Warburton in a contemporary pamphlet for stealing . . . from the 1745 edition.' (p.71)

773 **Monoghan, T. J.** Johnson's additions to his Shakespeare for the edition of 1773. R Eng Stud new ser 4no15:234–48 Jl '53.
'List of Johnson's additions.' (p.247–8)
Rev: A. Sherbo Philol Q 33:283–4 '54.

774 **Nowottny, Winifred M. T.** 'Editors, editions and critics' *in* Sisson, Charles J., *ed.* William Shakespeare, the complete works. London; New York [1954] p.xxv–xxxiii.

775 **Sherbo, Arthur.** Dr. Johnson's Dictionary and Warburton's Shakespeare. Philol Q 33no1:94–6 Ja '54.
Copy of Warburton's 1747 ed. marked up for the Dictionary.

776 **Sisson, Charles Jasper.** A new edition of Shakespeare is always a major venture. Bksllr 2518:1016–18 Mr '54. illus., facsims.
The design for the new edition.—The text for the edition.

777 **Willoughby, Edwin Eliott.** A deadly edition of Shakespeare. Sh Q 5no4: 351–7 '54. facsims.
Biography, and general account of William Dodd's unpublished ed., now in Folger Shakespeare library.

778 **Rare** edition of Shakespeare to University of Texas. Sh Q 6no2:198 '55.
J. O. Halliwell-Phillipps 16v. ed., 1853–65, extra-illustrated by Abraham Coles.

779 **Supplements** to the New variorum Shakespeare. Sh Q 6no3:247 '55.
Announcement.

780 **Mr.** Anonymous. Editing Shakespeare. TLS 8 Je '56:345.
On Sisson's ed.

781 **Sherbo, Arthur.** Samuel Johnson, editor of Shakespeare. . . . Urbana, University of Illinois pr., 1956. xii,182p. tables. 26cm. (Illinois studies in language and literature, v.42)
Genesis and progress.—The Dictionary and Johnson's reading.—Johnson's indebtedness to others.—The preface.—The notes.—General observations.—Later editions.—Appendixes: Johnson's reading; Johnson's borrowings; The preface; Critical terminology; Numerical analysis of the notes of the 1765 edition; Revisions in later editions; Selected notes.
Rev: A. M. Eastman Sh Q 8:548–9 '57; *rf.* A. Sherbo *ib.* 9:433 '58; M. R. Ridley R Eng Stud new ser 9:91–3 '58; W. K. Wimsatt Mod Lang N 73:214–17 '58; N&Q 202:88–9 '58.

782 **Weitenkampf, Frank.** American illustrators of Shakespeare. N.Y. Pub Lib Bull 60no2:70–2 F '56. illus.

783 **Eastman, Arthur M.** In defense of dr. Johnson. Sh Q 8no4:493–500 '57.
Defends Johnson from Sherbo's charge of plagiarism.

784 **Hoeniger, F. David.** Dowden marginalia on Shakespeare. Sh Q 8no1:129–32 '57.
Edward Dowden's textual notes in incomplete Arden ed., now in Folger Shakespeare library.

785 **Rosenberg, Marvin.** Reputation, oft lost without deserving. . . . Sh Q 9n04: 499–506 '58.
General essay on the editorial procedures of Thomas Bowdler and James Plumptre.

786 **Sherbo, Arthur.** Sanguine expectations: dr. Johnson's Shakespeare. Sh Q 9n03:426–8 '58.
Johnson's pre-1745 work on Sh., with a list of 19 early notes in the 1765 ed.

787 **Yonge, Stanley.** Two Thomas Bowdlers, editors of Shakespeare. N&Q 203:383–4 S '58.

788 **Dawson, Giles Edwin.** 'Robert Walker's editions of Shakespeare' *in* Bennett, Josephine W., O. Cargill and V. Hall, *ed.* Studies in the English renaissance drama in memory of Karl Julius Holzknecht. New York, 1959. p.58–81.

789 **Avon** swans among the Penguins. TLS 8 Ap '60:227; R. Fisher *ib.* 6 My '60:289.
Survey of contemporary paperback ed.

790 **Scholes, Robert E.** Dr. Johnson and the bibliographical criticism of Shakespeare. Sh Q 11n02:163–71 '60.
Johnson anticipated the direction of modern textual and bibliogr. scholarship.

791 **Sen, Sailendra Kumar.** Capell and Malone, and modern critical bibliography. Calcutta, K. L. Mukhopadhyay, 1960; London, Probsthain, 1961. 52p. 22cm.
Appendix: A. Capell, from the introduction to his edition of Shakespeare, 1768.—B. Malone, from the preface to his edition of Shakespeare, 1790.—C. Capell, from the preface to Prolusions, 1760.—D. Tyrwhitt, from his appendix to his preface to the edition of The Canterbury tales, 1775–1778. (p.36–52)
Rev: J. George N&Q 206:399 '61; A. Walker Library ser5 16:310–11; TLS 3 Mr '61:144; D. E. Karr Sh Q 13:582–3 '62.

792 **Walker, Alice.** Edward Capell and his edition of Shakespeare. Proc Brit Acad 46:131–45 '60. (Annual Shakespeare lecture) Also issued separately.
Study of the life, and contribution to biblio-textual criticism, of the originator of scientific criticism of the text. Repr. in no.118.

793 **Wolf, Edwin.** A signed American binding on the first American edition of Shakespeare. Sh Q 12n02:152–4 '61. facsim.
Binding by John Lightbody of Bioren and Madan ed. of 1795–6, now at Philadelphia Library co.

794 **Barnet, Sylvan.** Editions of Shakespeare, a right copious industry. Coll Eng 22n06:434–41 Mr '61.
Text.—Apparatus.—1. Complete works in a single volume.—2. 1–23 plays per volume.—3. Collections of a few works.
Assessment of modern editions.

795 **Eddy, Donald D.** Samuel Johnson's editions of Shakespeare, 1765. Pa Bib Soc Am 56:428–44 '62. diagr., tables.
Discussion and distinction of three 1765 ed.

796 **Gilbert, Vedder M.** Thomas Edwards and the bad edition of Shakespeare. Union Coll Symposium 25–7 '64. (Not seen)
'On the Edwards–Warburton controversy over the latter's revision of Pope's *Shak.*' (Sh Q)

797 **Hillier, Richard L.** The bard in paper. Lib J 89no2:193–8 Ja '64.
Classified checklist of ed. and criticism available in paperback editions.

798 **Muir, Kenneth.** Editions of Shakespeare. R Eng Lit 5no4:59–62 Oc '64.

799 **Sale, Roger.** The Shakespearean market place; modern texts for modern readers. Antioch R 24no1:124–35 '64.

800 **Wilson, John Dover.** How I took to editing Shakespeare. TLS 23 Ap '64:323.
Reminiscences of setting out on the New Cambridge ed.

801 **Brown, Arthur.** The great variety of readers. Sh Surv 18:11–21 '65.
Survey of popular ed.

802 **Rao, Balakrishna.** Scott's proposed edition of Shakespeare. Indian J Eng Stud 6:117–19 '65.
Discussion of Scott's aborted ed., c.1822–7.

803 **Ribner, Irving.** On re-editing Kittredge's Shakespeare. Sh Newsl 15no5:47 N '65.

804 **Marder, Louis.** Systematizing Shakespeare studies and editing the Variorum Shakespeare. Sh Newsl 16no1:1–3 F '66.

805 **Perrin, Noel.** The real Bowdler. N&Q 211:141–2 Ap '66.
The Family Shakespeare begun by miss Henrietta Maria Bowdler and continued by Thomas Bowdler.

806 **Wilson, John Dover.** The Cambridge New Shakespeare. TLS 9 Je '66:515.

807 **Gomme, A. H.** Shakespeare for the sixties. TLS 6 Jl '67:599; J. C. Maxwell; C. Clark *ib.* 13 Jl '67:619; A. H. Gomme 20 Jl '67:639; J. C. Maxwell 3 Ag '67:707; G. B. Harrison 17 Ag '67:743; J. C. Maxwell 31 Ag '67:781.
On the textual value of the Penguin ed.

808 **Clark, Charles.** Shakespeare plain. TLS 13 Je '68:628.
On the new Penguin Shakespeare.

809 **Kalson, Albert E.** Eighteenth-century editions of Colley Cibber's Richard III. Restor & 18th Cent Theat Res 7no1:7–17 My '68.
Quasifacism. TP transcrs. and some bibliogr. notes.

810 **Dobrée, Bonamy.** 'How to edit Shakespeare' *in* Jefferson, D. W., *ed.* The morality of art; essays presented to G. Wilson Knight. . . . London [1969] p.33–40.
On 18th-century editors and editing.

TEXTUAL STUDIES

830 **Walder, Ernest.** Shakespearean criticism, textual and literary, from Dryden to the end of the eighteenth century. Bradford, T. Brear, 1895. 135p. 19cm. (Not seen)

831 **Skeat, Walter William.** Motto for a corrector of the text of Shakespeare. N&Q ser8 12:305 Oc '97.

> 'But ill for him who, bettering not with time,
> Corrupts the strength of heaven-descended Will,
> And ever weaker grows thro' acted crime,
> Recurring and suggesting still!'   Tennyson, Will.

832 **Van Dam, Bastiaan Adriaan P.** and **C. Stoffel.** 'Criticism of the text of Shakespeare' *in* William Shakespeare, prosody and text; an essay in criticism being an introduction to a better editing and a more adequate appreciation of the works of the Elizabethan poets. Leyden; London [1900] p.269–432.

> 13. Causes of mistakes in the text.—14. First group of the old Shakespeare-texts [*Ven., Luc., Son., LC, Per., Tmp., TGV, MM, Err., AYL, AWW, TN, WT, Jn., 1H6, H8, Cor., Tim., JC, Mac., Ant., Cym.*].—15. Second group of the old Shakespeare-texts [*R2, 2H4, R3, Tro., Tim., Lr., Oth.*].—16. Third group of the old Shakespeare-texts: high value of the surreptitious quartos [*H5, 2H6, 3H6, Rom., LLL, Ham.*].

833 **Collins, John Churton.** 'The text and prosody of Shakespeare' *in* Studies in Shakespeare. Westminster, 1904. p.297–331.

Review article on Van Dam.

834 **Proelss, Robert.** Von den ältesten Drucken der Dramen Shakespeares und dem Einflusse, den die damaligen London-Theater und ihre Einrichtungen auf diese Dramen ausgeübt haben. Leipzig, F. A. Berger, 1905. 141p. 20cm.

835 **Walder, Ernest.** 'The text of Shakespeare' *in* Ward, sir Adolphus W. and A. R. Waller, *ed.* The Cambridge history of English literature. Cambridge, 1910. V.5, p.[259]–82.

'Appendix. Genealogy of the text of Richard III.' (p. [281]–2)

836 —— [Same]: [Cheap ed.] Cambridge, 1932. V.5, p.[259]–82.

837 **Pollard, Alfred William.** The manuscripts of Shakespeare's plays. Library ser3 7no27:198–226 Jl '16.

> '. . . it is bibliographically probable that some of the First Quarto Editions of Shakespeare's plays were printed from the author's own autograph manuscript, which had previously been used as a prompt-copy; that the actors replaced their manuscript prompt-copy by a copy of the printed quarto, which in its turn received additional stage-directions and also readings representing some of the variants which were adopted by individual actors: that in 1622 a copy of the last Quarto on the market was sent to the playhouse to be roughly collated with the printed prompt-copy; and that the copy so corrected was the source of the Folio text of a normal play originally printed in a duly registered Quarto.' (p.226)

838 **Pollard, Alfred William.** The improvers of Shakespeare. Library ser3 7no28:265–90 Oc '16.

Examination of work of later editors in light of three 'deductions of some importance' arising from his previous paper; namely, 'the readings of any edition of a play . . . subsequent to the first duly registered Quarto cannot have any shred of authority'; 'the first authorized edition of any play is likely to be nearer than any other to what the editor wrote'; 'the First folio must be regarded as an *edited* text'.

839 —— Shakespeare's fight with the pirates and the problems of the transmission of his text. London, A. Moring, 1917. vii,115p. 26cm.

Repr. of the Library papers (nos.837–8); *see also* no.844.

Rev: TLS 30 Ag '17:414.

840 S. The text of Shakespeare's plays. TLS 6 S '17:429; J. D. Fitzgerald *ib.* 6 S '17:429; A. W. Pollard; The reviewer; S. 13 S '17:441; S.; H. J. Massingham 20 S '17:453; The reviewer; A. W. Pollard 27 S '17:465; S.; J. D. Fitzgerald 4 Oc '17:477; The reviewer 11 Oc '17:491–2.

Arguments about Pollard's Shakespeare's fight.

841 **Bayfield, M. A.** Shakespeare's versification and the early texts. TLS 23 My '18:242; 6 Je '18:265; 13 Je '18:277; P. Simpson *ib.* 27 Je '18:301; J. D. Wilson 4 Jl '18:313; G. O'Neill 11 Jl '18:325; M. A. Bayfield 1 Ag '18:361–2; P. Simpson 5 S '18:417; M. A. Bayfield 26 S '18:455–6.

On the application of scansion to the detection of textual error and anomaly.

842 —— Abbreviations in Shakespeare's prose. TLS 20 Je '18:291.

Certain common elisions and abbreviations have been introduced into the text by 'the actors and copyists, and the reviser or revisers of the Folio'.

843 **Greg, sir Walter Wilson.** The Hamlet texts and recent work in Shakespearian bibliography. Mod Lang R 14no4:380–5 Oc '19.

844 **Pollard, Alfred William.** Shakespeare's fight with the pirates and the problems of the transmission of his text. 2d ed., rev. with introduction. Cambridge, C.U.P., 1920. (Repr. 1937) xxviii,110p. 17cm. (Shakespeare problems [1])

Introduction.—The regulation of the book trade in the sixteenth century.—Authors, players and pirates in Shakespeare's day.—The manuscripts of Shakespeare's plays.— The improvers of Shakespeare.

Rev: TLS 2 S '20:563; *rf.* S. *ib.* 16 S '20:600; C. R. Baskervill Mod Philol 18:511 '21; W. Keller Sh Jahrb 59/60:187–92 '24; H. T. Price Angl Beibl 35:113–15 '24; P. Aronstein Eng Studien 59:440–4 '25.

845 **Gray, Henry David.** Shakespeare's punctuation. TLS 14 Jl '21:452.

846 **Greenwood, sir Granville George.** Shakespeare's fight with the pirates. New World 4no22:297–304 Mr '21.

Review article on Pollard.

847 **Poel, William.** Shakespeare's prompt copies; a plea for the early texts. TLS 3 F '21:75–6.

Plea for the association of actors in the establishment of the new text (the New Cambridge ed.) on the basis of Pollard's conclusions.

848 **Pollard, Alfred William.** Shakespeare, a standard text. TLS 10 F '21:91; R. Noble *ib.* 10 F '21:91–2; H. Granville-Barker; P. Simpson 17 F '21:107;

W. Poel 24 F '21:127; P. Simpson 3 Mr '21:144; G. B. Shaw 17 Mr '21:178;
A. W. Pollard 24 Mr '21:196; G. B. Shaw 31 Mr '21:211; A. W. Pollard;
M. Montgomery; J. D. Wilson; G. F. Abbott 7 Ap '21:228; G. B. Shaw;
W. Poel 14 Ap '21:244; A. W. Pollard; J. D. Wilson 21 Ap '21:259.

Elaboration of and discussion of Poel's suggestion.

849 **Rhodes, Raymond Crompton.** Shakespeare's prompt-books. TLS 21 Jl '21:
467; 28 Jl '21:282; W. Poel *ib.* 4 Ag '21:500; R. C. Rhodes 11 Ag '21:516;
W. Poel 18 Ag '21:532; R. C. Rhodes 1 S '21:564; W. Poel 8 S '21:580.

1. Stage-directions.—2. The curtains.
Classification of texts according to the evidence of their association with the theatre.

850 **Lawrence, William John.** Assembled texts. TLS 12 Ja '22:28.

851 **Poel, William.** A one volume Shakespeare. TLS 31 Ag '22:557; W. Jaggard
ib. 7 S '22:569.

Advocates a new one-volume ed.

852 —— Shakespeare, a standard text. TLS 26 Ja '22:60.

Notice of a meeting to be held to consider a memorandum on the editing of Sh.; the
memorandum is printed.

853 **Rhodes, Raymond Crompton.** 'The assembled texts' *in* The stagery of Shakespeare. Birmingham, 1922. p.[59]–67.

TGV, Wiv., MM, WT, and *Jn.* 'which have no stage-directions, or very few . . . cannot
therefore have been set up by the printer from the prompt-book'.

854 **Simpson, Percy.** The bibliographical study of Shakespeare. Oxford Bib Soc
Proc 1pt1:19–53 '22/3. facsims.

'Bibliographical list.' (p.[50]–3)

855 **Herford, Charles Harold.** '2. The publication of Shakespeare's works: the
stage and the press' *in* A sketch of recent Shakesperean investigation, 1893–
1923. London [1923] p.8–25.

856 **Lawrence, William John.** The theory of assembled texts. TLS 11 Ja '23:28.

There is no basis for the theory of assembling from parts and plots. Shakespeare's plays
were not kept continuously in repertory; revision meant revisal so plots and parts were
not kept.

857 **Pollard, Alfred William.** . . . The foundations of Shakespeare's text. London, Published for the British academy by H. Milford, O.U.P. [1923] 18p.
24cm. (Annual Shakespeare lecture)

At head of title: The British academy. Tercentenary of the First folio.
Repr. from Proc Brit Acad 10:379–94 '21/3. *See also* no.874.
Rev: Sir E. K. Chambers Mod Lang R 18:484–5 '23; T. S. Graves Stud Philol 21:435
'24; F. Liebermann Archiv 149:113–14 '25.

858 **Chambers, sir Edmund Kerchever.** The disintegration of Shakespeare.
London, Published for the British academy by H. Milford, O.U.P. [1924]
22p. 24cm. (Annual Shakespeare lecture)

Repr. from Proc Brit Acad 11:89–108 '24/5; repr. in Aspects of Shakespeare, being
British academy lectures. . . . Oxford, 1933. p.[23]–48; and in his Shakespearian gleanings.
[Oxford] 1944. p.1–21.

General analysis of disintegrationalist claims, with attention to revision, metrical tests, evidence from vocabulary and style, and notice of the bibliogr. arguments of Pollard and Dover Wilson.

Rev: N&Q 147:237 '24; TLS 11 S '24; A. E. Morgan Mod Lang R 21:86–9 '26.

859 **Gaw, Allison.** Actors' names in basic Shakespearean texts, with special reference to Romeo and Juliet and Much ado. Pub Mod Lang Assn 40no03:530–50 S '25.

Rather than being additions by the prompt-book keeper, these are mainly authorial in origin.

860 **Kellner, Leon.** Restoring Shakespeare, a critical analysis of the misreadings in Shakespeare's works. Leipzig, Tauchnitz; London, G. Allen & Unwin, 1925. xvi,216p. facsims. 24cm.

1. Introductory.—2. The Elizabethan handwriting.—3. Individual letters misread.—4. Abbreviation as a source of mistakes.—5. Wrong division.—6. Endings confused.—7. Pronouns confused.—8. Prefixes confused.—9. Transposition.—10. Substitution.—11. Double writing (dittography).—12. Single writing (haplography).—13. Contrasting words substituted.—14. Deliberate alterations.—15. Multiplicity of forms as a source of mistakes.—16. Intrusions into the text.

Rev: Sir W. W. Greg R Eng Stud 1:463–78 '25; TLS 23 Jl '25:493; Lond Merc 13:215–16 '25; B. A. P. Van Dam Eng Stud 7:150–4 '25; J. W. Draper J Eng Germ Philol 25:578–85 '26; E. Ekwall Moderna Språk 20:244–6 '26; S. C. Chew Nation 121:436–8 '26; E. Ekwall Angl Beibl 37:166–72 '26; M. J. Wolff Eng Studien 60:342–4 '26; K. Brunner Archiv 151:116–18 '26.

861 **Van Dam, Bastiaan Adriaan P.** Textual criticism of Shakespeare's plays. Eng Stud 7no04:95–115 Ag '25.

862 **Hunter, sir Mark.** Act- and scene-division in the plays of Shakespeare. R Eng Stud 2no07:295–310 Jl '26.

As 'all regular plays . . . were normally constructed with a five-act plan', the F by introducing divisions was restoring omissions in Q.

863 **Chambers, sir Edmund Kerchever.** The unrest in Shakespearean studies. Ninet Cent 101no600:255–66 F '27.

Repr. in his Shakespearian gleanings. [Oxford] 1944. p.22–34.

864 **Wilson, John Dover.** Act- and scene-divisions in the plays of Shakespeare, a rejoinder to sir Mark Hunter. R Eng Stud 3no12:385–97 Oc '27.

Hunter's view is consistent with his own, and his treatment of scene-division in the New Cambridge ed.; act divisions derive from change in practice in the early 17th century, and the translation of Shakespeare's company to Blackfriars.

865 **Greg, sir Walter Wilson.** Act-divisions in Shakespeare. R Eng Stud 4no14:152–8 Ap '28. table.

Analysis of all extant plays, 1591–1610, shows that 'of plays acted by men's companies in the public theatres, the undivided texts are four times as numerous as the divided'. (p.157)

866 —— Principles of emendation in Shakespeare. Proc Brit Acad 14:147–216 '28. (Annual Shakespeare lecture) Also separately published.

See no.872. Assigns the plays to textual groups according to their textual history, and considers limitations on the freedom to emend, and editorial practice.

Rev: TLS 4 Oc '28:705; Life & Letters 1:526–7 '28; N&Q 155:378 '28; W. Keller Sh Jahrb 65:192 '29.

867 **Chambers, sir Edmund Kerchever.** William Shakespeare, a study of facts and problems. Oxford, Clarendon pr., 1930. 2v. illus., facsims., tables. 22cm.

Includes 4. The book of the play.—5. The quartos and the First folio.—6. Plays in printing-house.—9. Plays of the First folio.—V.2: F. Shakespearean fabrications.—G. Table of quartos.

868 **Adams, Joseph Quincy.** Elizabethan playhouse manuscripts and their significance for the text of Shakespeare. Johns Hopkins Alumni Mag 21:21–52 '32. (Not seen)

869 **Alexander, Peter.** Shakespeare's punctuation. TLS 17 Mr '32:195.

Differences between the punctuation of Q and F texts, and between the poems and *STM* 'indicate that Shakespeare's pointing varies in fullness with the occasion'.

870 **Orsini, G. N. Giordano.** Nuovi orientamenti della filologia shakespeariana. Civiltà Moderna 4n04/6:503–46 D '32.

General survey of modern Sh. textual history. 'Appendice: Le cancellature dell'in-folio di Padova.' (p.[544]-6)

871 **Price, Hereward Thimbleby.** 'On some peculiarities in Shakespearean texts' *in* Michigan. University. Dept. of English. Essays and studies in English and comparative literature. Ann Arbor, 1932. p.75–9.

Comments on the corrupting effects of performances on the text.

872 **Greg, sir Walter Wilson.** 'Principles of emendation in Shakespeare' *in* Aspects of Shakespeare, being British academy lectures. . . . Oxford, 1933. p.[128]–201.

'Postscript: June, 1932' (p.154). Repr. from no.866. Repr. in Bradby, Anne B., *ed.* Shakespeare criticism, 1919–35. London [1936] p.78–108.

873 **Pollard, Alfred William.** The bibliographical approach to Shakespeare; notes on new contributions. Library ser4 14n03:348–52 D '33.

874 —— 'The foundations of Shakespeare's text' *in* Aspects of Shakespeare, being British academy lectures. . . . Oxford, 1933. p.[1]–22.

'Postscript, 1932' (p.21-2). Repr. from no.857.

875 —— 'Shakespeare's text' *in* Barker, Harley Granville- and G. B. Harrison, *ed.* A companion to Shakespeare. Cambridge, 1934. (Repr. 1946; Garden City, N.Y., Anchor books, 1960) p.[263]–86. facsims.

876 **Thorndike, Ashley H.** Parentheses in Shakespeare. Sh Assn Bull 9n01:31–7 Ja '34. table.

Attributes copy for seven plays in which parentheses are most frequent (in order, *2H4, WT, Wiv., Cym., Oth., TGV,* and *H8*) to transcribers, and depreciates the influence of author or compositor in these texts.

877 **Lewis, Clive Staples.** The genuine text. TLS 2 My '35:288; F. W. Bateson *ib.* 9 My '35:301; J. D. Wilson 16 My '35:313; C. S. Lewis; W. J. Lawrence 23 My '32:331; J. D. Wilson; M. R. Ridley 30 My '35:348; sir W. W. Greg; W. J. Lawrence 6 Je '35:364; J. D. Wilson 13 Je '35:380.

'We must either reject the conception of a Shakespeare who "thought in terms of the stage" and replace it with that of a literary author to whom performance was as accidental as to Milton or Tennyson: or we must define the "genuine text" to be "the whole performance in so far as Shakespeare did not explicitly disclaim it". If we do the first, then the manuscript is the genuine text: if we do the second, we must cease to talk of theatrical "contamination": we must start with the assumption that the prompt-book is genuine, and the *onus* will lie on anyone who says that it is corrupt.' (p.288)

878 **McKerrow, Ronald Brunlees.** A suggestion regarding Shakespeare's manuscripts. R Eng Stud 11n044:459–65 Oc '35.

Plays in which speech prefixes do not vary from form to form were ptd. from some sort of fair copy, perhaps scribal, whereas plays in which speech prefixes are irregular were ptd. from the author's original ms.

879 **Black, Matthew W.** Shakespeare's seventeenth century editors. Am Philos Soc Proc 76n05:707–17 '36.

'Analysis of the textual difference between the successive folios . . . reveals a consistent and successful effort to improve the text, on the part of editors employed by the printing houses.'

880 —— and **M. A. Shaaber.** Shakespeare's seventeenth-century editors, 1632–1685. New York, Modern language association of America; London, O.U.P., 1937. xii,420p. tables. 24cm.

1. Introduction.—2. Editorial changes in the second, third, and fourth folios.—Changes in the second folio, 1632: Changes adopted by many or all modern editors; Changes which restore the reading of an earlier text; Superseded changes; Intelligible changes not adopted by most modern editors; Mistaken and arbitrary changes.—Changes in the third folio, 1664. . . .—Changes in the fourth folio, 1685. . . . Appendix: Cotgrave and Poole as editors of Shakespeare.

Rev: K. Wittig Angl Beibl 49:150–4 '38; H. Spencer Mod Lang N 53:450–3 '38; R. M. Smith J Eng Germ Philol 37:305–7 '38; Sh Assn Bull 13:62 '38; F. E. Budd Mod Lang R 33:460 '38; W. Keller Sh Jahrb 74:186–7 '38; G. Connes Études Angl 3:42 '39; W. Clemen Eng Studien 73:395–6 '39; D. F. Sat R Lit 14 Ja '39:19,22; J. Bennett Mod Lang R 34:636–7 '39.

881 **Hastings, William T.** To the next editor of Shakspere: notes for his prospectus. Coloph new ser 2n04:487–503 '37.

General essay on the arrangement and treatment of the text for an ed. of Sh.

882 **Mavrogordato, John.** Shakespeare, a suggestion. TLS 10 Ap '37:275; R. W. Chapman *ib.* 17 Ap '37:292; A. J. Hawkes 24 Ap '37:308.

Plea for one-volume Sh. in the old spelling.

883 **Shakespeare** scholars at work: an age of discovery and advance. TLS 1 My '37:334–5.

The life.—Shakespeare's theatre.—The text and canon.—Criticism.

884 **Harrison, George Bagshawe.** 'Editing Shakespeare' *in* Introducing Shakespeare. Harmondsworth, Middlesex, 1939. (Repr. 1941, 1948, 1957) p.154–81.

See no.959.

885 **McKerrow, Ronald Brunlees.** Prolegomena for the Oxford Shakespeare, a study in editorial method. Oxford, Clarendon pr., 1939. (Repr. 1969) xiv,110[3]p. 23cm.

The plan of this edition.—1. The basis of a reprint.—2. The degree of exactitude to be aimed at in reproducing the copy-text.—3. The recording of the readings of other editions than the copy-text.—Appendix A: Minor typographical abnormalities. . . .—Appendix B. The descent of editions. . . .—Two specimen pages from the Oxford Shakespeare.

Rev: TLS 27 My '39:315; R. W. Zandvoort Eng Stud 21:169–71 '39; F. P. Wilson Library ser4 20:234–9 '39; W. Keller Sh Jahrb 75:145–6 '39; G. Connes Études Angl 3:377 '39; J. B. Leishman R Eng Stud 16:92–5 '40; P. Alexander Mod Lang R 35:386–7 '40; H. E. Rollins Mod Lang N 55:150–1 '40; J. Wilcox Sh Assn Bull 15:59–60 '40; W. Kalthoff Angl Beibl 51:76–8 '40; M. Priess Eng Studien 85:236–41 '42.

885a **Tannenbaum, Samuel Aaron.** The mystery of the Shakspere manuscripts. Sh Assn Bull 14no3:190–1 Jl '39.

Report of broadcast lecture on the reasons why Sh. mss. have not survived.

886 **Crundell, H. W.** Actors' parts and Elizabethan play-texts. N&Q 180:350–1 My '41.

Notes references by Pope and Colman to the theory of assembled texts.

887 **Greg, sir Walter Wilson.** McKerrow's Prolegomena reconsidered. R Eng Stud 17no17:139–49 Ap '41.

888 **Doran, Madeleine.** An evaluation of evidence in Shakespearian textual criticism. Eng Inst Ann 1941:95–114 '42.

889 **Greg, sir Walter Wilson.** The editorial problem in Shakespeare, a survey of the foundations of the text. The Clark lectures, Trinity college, Cambridge, Lent term, 1939. Oxford, Clarendon pr., 1942. lv,210p. table. 21cm.

Second ed. 1951: *see* no.903.

Prolegomena; on editing Shakespeare.—1. Introduction: the Folio and the quartos, good and bad.—2. Theatrical manuscripts.—3. The bad quartos.—4. Two doubtful quartos.— 5. The good quartos.—6. The First folio.—Appendix of stage directions.—Addenda.— Summary.—Table.

Rev: P. Mueschke N.Y. Times Bk R 1 Ag '43:22; J. Berryman Nation 157:218–19 '43; G. I. Duthie Mod Lang R 38:255–7 '43; P. Maas R Eng Stud 19:410–13 '43; 20:73–7 '43; TLS 1 My '43:216; N&Q 184:29–30 '43; M. A. Shaaber Mod Lang N 59:139–41 '43; T. James Life & Letters 36:72 '43.

890 —— The editorial problem in Shakespeare. R Eng Stud 20no78:159–60 Ap '44.

On observations on the theory of copy-text in P. Maas's review.

891 **Alexander, Peter.** Shakespeare's punctuation. Proc Brit Acad 31:61–84 '45. (Annual Shakespeare lecture) Also issued separately.

Account of editors' attitudes to the punctuation of the early texts, and examination of the treatment of the punctuation in light of modern textual theory.

Rev: J. D. Wilson R Eng Stud 23:70–8 '47; *rf.* P. Alexander *ib*. 23:263–6 '47.

892 **Wilson, Frank Percy.** 'Shakespeare and the new bibliography' *in* [Francis, sir Frank C.] *ed.* The Bibliographical society, 1892–1942: studies in retrospect. London, 1945. p.76–135.

See also nos.898, 965.

1. The beginnings to 1909.—2. The publication of plays.—3. The printing of plays.— 4. Dramatic manuscripts.—5. The copy for the quartos and the Folio.—6. Principles of textual criticism.

893 **Dawson, Giles Edwin.** 'The copyright of Shakespeare's dramatic works' *in* Prouty, Charles T., *ed.* Studies in honor of A. H. R. Fairchild. Columbia [Miss.] 1946. p.9–35.

Account of the transmission of the copyright to 1774.

894 **Flatter, Richard.** Modern stage-directions in Shakspere. Sh Assn Bull
21n03:116–23 Jl '46.

Adverse comment on expansion and invention of new SD's in the New Cambridge ed.

895 **Kirschbaum, Leo.** Shakespeare's hypothetical marginal additions. Mod
Lang N 61n01:44–9 Ja '46.

'The use of irregularly lined verse in a quarto as evidence that the copy for the quarto was
Shakespeare's own papers does not seem to me admissible.' (p.48)

896 **Wilson, John Dover.** New ideas and discoveries about Shakespeare. Virginia Q R 23n04:537–42 '47.

897 **Brooke, Charles Frederick Tucker.** 'Shakespeare and the *textus receptus*' *in*
Essays on Shakespeare and other Elizabethans. New Haven; London, 1948.
p.[103]–7.

Repr. from Henry IV, part I (Yale Shakespeare, 1947)

898 **Parrott, Thomas Marc.** Shakespeare and the new bibliography. Library
ser5 3n01:63–5 Je '48.

Comments on F. P. Wilson's no.892.

899 **Shaaber, Matthias A.** Problems in the editing of Shakespeare: text. Eng
Inst Essays 1947:97–116 '48.

900 **Wilson, John Dover.** Shakespeare and his world; the text of the plays.
Listener 42:262–4 Ag '49. facsims.

901 **McManaway, James Gilmer.** Where are Shakespeare's manuscripts? New
Coloph 2pt8:357–69 F '50.

'. . . through the year 1700 not one dramatic manuscript of any authorship that went to
a print shop has survived.' (p. 367); Sh. had no rights in his mss. and they were not his to
dispose of.

902 **Bowers, Fredson Thayer.** The revolution in Shakespeare criticism. Chicago
Alumni Mag 11–14 N '51. (Not seen)

903 **Greg, sir Walter Wilson.** The editorial problem in Shakespeare . . . 2d ed.
Oxford, Clarendon pr., 1951. a–i,lv,210p. table. 21cm.

First pub. 1942; *see* no.889. 'Preface to the second edition.' (p.[a]–g)

904 —— [Same]: 3d ed. Oxford, Clarendon pr., 1954. a–i,lv,210p. table. 21cm.

Substantially same as the 2d ed.

Rev: TLS 27 Ap '51:262; C. J. Sisson Mod Lang R 47:100–1 '52; J. C. Maxwell R Eng
Stud new ser 3:200 '52; A. Koszul Études Angl 7:322 '54; TLS 4 Mr '55:139; H. Heuer
Sh Jahrb 92:385 '56.

905 **Alexander, Peter.** Restoring Shakespeare, the modern editor's task. Sh
Surv 5:1–9 '52.

Repr. in Ridler, Anne B. (B.), *ed.* Shakespeare criticism, 1935–60. London, 1963. p.117–31.
Largely a simple discussion of some familiar cruxes.

906 **Bonnard, Georges Alfred.** Suggestions towards an edition of Shakespeare
for French, German and other continental readers. Sh Surv 5:10–15 '52.

907 **Flatter, Richard.** The true originall copies of Shakespeare's plays; outline of a new conception. Leeds Philos Soc Proc 7:31–42 Jl '52.

908 **Bowers, Fredson Thayer.** 'A definitive test of Shakespeare: problems and methods' *in* Matthews, Arthur D. and C. M. Emery, *ed.* Studies in Shakespeare. Coral Gables, Fla., 1953. p.11–29.

909 **Feuillerat, Albert G.** The composition of Shakespeare's plays: authorship, chronology. New Haven, Yale U.P.; London, G. Cumberlege, O.U.P., 1953. viii,340p. tables. 24cm.

Introduction.—1. 2 and 3 Henry VI.—2. Titus Andronicus.—3. Richard II.—4. Richard III.—5. Romeo and Juliet.—A retrospect.

Suggests that these plays are Shakespeare's reworking of earlier material, and that Ralph Crane was the editor of F.

Rev: H. Smith Yale R 43:121–5 '53; G. B. Harrison Sat R 10 Oc '53:20; F. T. Bowers Mod Philol 51:132–3 '53; TLS 5 Mr '54:154; P. Williams Sth Atlantic Q 53:270–2 '54; A. Koszul Études Angl 7:213–19 '54; K. Muir R Eng Stud new ser 5:411–13 '54; M. A. Shaaber Mod Lang N 69:427–30 '54; J. Swart Neophilol 38:221–4 '54; P. Alexander Sh Q 5:70–7 '54; G. E. Bentley Mod Lang R 49:496 '54; H. Heuer Sh Jahrb 90:326–8 '54; Virginia Q R 30:17–18 '54; J. Vallette Langues Modernes 49:90–1 '55; W. Clemen Archiv 191:88–9 '55; R. A. Law Texas Stud Eng 34:43–7 '55; L. L. Schücking Angl 73:527–32 '56.

910 **Walker, Alice.** Textual problems of the First folio. Cambridge, 1953. *See* no.588.

911 **Bowers, Fredson Thayer.** Shakespeare's text and the bibliographical method. Stud Bib 6:71–91 '54.

'. . . as scholars we have been most delinquent in failing to utilize the bibliographical method to its fullest extent and in preferring the easier delights of armchair critical speculation to the rigors of first ascertaining the fullest body of facts by bibliographical investigation.' (p.91)

912 **Nowottny, Winifred M. T.** 'The canon and the text' *in* Sisson, Charles J., *ed.* William Shakespeare, the complete works. London; New York [1954] p.xviii–xxiv.

913 **Wilson, John Dover.** The new way with Shakespeare's texts: an introduction for lay readers. I. The foundations. Sh Surv 7:48–56 '54.

An occasionally autobiographical account of modern bibliogr. history. *See also* nos.928, 930, and 1733.

914 —— 'On editing Shakespeare, with special reference to the problems of Richard III' *in* Garrett, John W. P., *ed.* Talking of Shakespeare. London [1954] p.231–57.

General account of editorial problems and procedures with a survey of the text, leading towards a consideration of *R3* in light of A. Walker's Textual problems.

915 **Bowers, Fredson Thayer.** McKerrow's editorial principles for Shakespeare reconsidered. Sh Q 6no3:309–24 S '55.

916 —— On editing Shakespeare and the Elizabethan dramatists. [Philadelphia] Published for the Philip H. and A. S. W. Rosenbach foundation by the University of Pennsylvania library, 1955. 131p. 21cm.

1. The texts and their manuscripts.—2. The function of textual criticism and biblio graphy.—3. The method for a critical edition.

See also no.956.

Rev: Virginia Q R 31:104 '55; H. W. Winger Lib Q 26:141 '56; C. J. Sisson Mod Lang R 51:242–4 '56; J. G. McManaway Sh Surv 9:149–50 '56; TLS 28 D '56:788; H. Davis Mod Lang N 71:521–3 '56; sir W. W. Greg Sh Q 7:101–4 '56; J. C. Maxwell R Eng Stud new ser 8:293–8 '57; R. Stokes J Eng Germ Philol 56:142–4 '57; L. L. Schücking Angl 76:312–13 '58.

917 **Simpson, Percy.** 'Textual criticism' *in* Encyclopædia Britannica. . . . Chicago [n.d., 1955?] V.20, p.447.

Concise survey, referring to literature not later than 1927, under Shakespeare entry.

918 **Walker, Alice.** Compositor determination and other problems in Shakespearean texts. Stud Bib 7:3–15 '55.

Demonstrates 'the need for as broadly based an analysis of compositor's spellings as possible' (p.13) with references to texts ptd. by Jaggard, Roberts and Danter; stresses the importance of printing-house spelling for an old-spelling ed., and discusses the need for compositor determination 'as one means of assessing the number and kind of substantive errors a compositor may have made'. (p.13)

919 **Bolton, Joseph S. G.** Worn pages in Shakespeare's manuscripts. Sh Q 7no2:177–82 '56.

F *Ham.*, *Oth.*, *Lr.*, *Tro.*, *R3* and *2H4* restore Q passages in 'irregular pairs separated by some forty or fifty lines'. Lists 'all the examples I can find of omitted lines, half lines, and longer passages that, coming at forty- or fifty-line intervals, might conceivably have been written back to back on single leaves of paper'. (p.178): *see* his p.181–2.

920 **Brown, Arthur.** Editorial problems in Shakespeare: semi-popular editions. Stud Bib 8:15–26 '56.

920a **Ōtsuka, Takanobu.** On the text of Shakespeare; special lecture at the English literary society. Shikoku, Kochi Joshi Daigu, 1956. (Not seen)

'Process of deciding authentic text by comparative study of *Shak.*'s signature and early editions.' (Sh Q)

921 **Williams, Philip.** New approaches to textual problems in Shakespeare. Stud Bib 8:3–14 '56.

Discussion of the application of compositor, mainly spelling, analysis to the study of the text.

922 **Danks, Kenneth B.** Are there any memorially reconstructed texts in the Shakespeare First folio. N&Q 202:143–4 Ap '57.

The characteristic features of memorially reconstructed texts do not imply illicit origin; they also appear in F texts.

923 **Walker, Alice.** Principles of annotation: some suggestions for editors of Shakespeare. Stud Bib 9:95–105 '57.

Suggests more selective annotation from material in O.E.D., with illustrative examples from *Ant*.

924 **Wilson, John Dover.** The new way with Shakespeare's texts: an introduction for lay readers. III. In sight of Shakespeare's manuscripts. Sh Surv 9:69–80 '56.

Analysis of the *STM* fragment and its influence on textual scholarship.

925 **Willoughby, Edwin Eliott.** 'Bibliography and the transmission of the text' *in* The uses of bibliography to the students of literature and history. Hamden, Conn., 1957. p.81–100.

926 **Craig, Hardin.** 'Criticism of Elizabethan dramatic texts' *in* Allen, Don C., *ed.* Studies in honor of T. W. Baldwin. Urbana, 1958. p.3–8.

927 **Hulme, Hilda E.** Shakespeare's text; some notes on linguistic procedure and its relevance to textual criticism. Eng Stud 39no2:49–56 Ap '58.

928 **Wilson, John Dover.** The new way with Shakespeare's texts: an introduction for lay readers. IV. Towards the high road. Sh Surv 11:78–88 '58.
Survey of developing understanding of foul papers, prompt-books, the ptd. texts, and their interrelationships.

929 **Bowers, Fredson Thayer.** 'The new textual criticism of Shakespeare' *in* Textual & literary criticism. Cambridge, 1959. (Repr. 1966) p.66–116.

930 **Wilson, John Dover.** The new way with Shakespeare's texts, an introduction for lay readers. Sh Newsl 9no3:21 My '59.
Abstracted by George W. Williams.

931 **Brown, Arthur.** The rationale of old-spelling editions of the plays of Shakespeare and his contemporaries: a rejoinder. Stud Bib 13:69–76 '60.
Denies that photographic facsim. ed. will serve purposes J. R. Brown claimed, and supports position of critical old-spelling ed.

932 **Brown, John Russell.** The rationale of old-spelling editions of the plays of Shakespeare and his contemporaries. Stud Bib 13:49–67 '60.
Discusses facsim. reprints, old-spelling critical ed., and the photographic and the modernized ed., and the uses to which each might be put. Concludes that photographs and fully responsible modernized critical texts best fit modern requirements.

933 **Ellis, Bradbury Pearce.** The true original copies. Tulane Drama R 5no1: 113–16 S '60.
F1 does not represent '*the* authentic version of the plays, but *one complete* version'.

934 **Wilson, John Dover.** 'The texts' *in* Gittings, Robert W. V., *ed.* The living Shakespeare. London, 1960. p.39–43.
Based on BBC broadcast talk.

935 **Bateson, Frederick Wilse.** Modern bibliography and the literary artifact. Eng Stud Today 2:67–77 '61.
Discursive appraisal of the use of bibliogr. techniques in literary criticism, with some references to 'sallied/sullied/solid'.

936 **Dawson, Giles Edwin.** What happened to Shakespeare's manuscripts. Texas Q 4no3:169–79 '61.

937 **Bateson, Frederick Wilse.** Shakespeare's laundry bills; the rationale of external evidence. Sh Jahrb 98:51–63 '62.
The application of relevant fact and relevant opinion are distinct stages in a single process: theory of editing illustrated by cruxes, including *H5* 'a babbled'.

938 **Bowers, Fredson Thayer.** What Shakespeare wrote. Sh Jahrb 98:24–50 '62.
Repr. in no.956.

939 **Partridge, Astley Cooper.** New light on the descent of Shakespeare's texts. Eng Stud Africa 6no2:186–90 S '63.
Review article on H. Craig's A new look at Shakespeare's quartos, no.442.

940 **Dawson, Giles Edwin.** Four centuries of Shakespeare publication. Lawrence, University of Kansas libraries, 1964. 24p. 23cm. (University of Kansas publications. Library ser 22)
Rev: A. Edinborough Sh Q 16:360–1 '65.

941 **Hill, Trevor Howard Howard-.** Computer analysis of Shakespearean texts. Sh Newsl 14n06:79 D '64.

942 **Muir, Kenneth.** 'Shakespeare: texts and criticism' in Spencer, Terence J. B., ed. Shakespeare, a celebration, 1564–1964. [Harmondsworth, Middlesex, 1964] p.54–66. facsims.

943 **Partridge, Astley Cooper.** Orthography in Shakespeare and Elizabethan drama, a study of colloquial contractions, elision, prosody and punctuation. London, E. Arnold [1964] viii,200p. tables. 20cm.
1. The meaning of orthography and its use in Shakespearian textual criticism.—2. The rise of clipped forms in speech in the fifteenth and sixteenth centuries; their importation into printed drama. . . .—3. Henry Porter and The two angry women of Abington.—4. Classification of contraction types and summary of conclusions.—5. The contractions and other characteristics of a manuscript play of the fifteen-nineties, John a Kent.—6. The manuscript play Thomas of Woodstock.—7. The manuscript play Sir Thomas More: list of contractions in dramatic use by 1600.—8. Shakespeare's apparent orthography in Venus and Adonis, and some early quartos.—9. Shakespeare's versification and the editing of the First folio.—10. Italian prosodists and types of dramatic elision in the English drama of the sixteenth and seventeenth centuries.—11. Syllabic variation in the quarto and folio texts of Shakespeare; its effect upon prosody in Hamlet and Troilus and Cressida.—12. Readings in plays of more than one authority for an original-spelling edition of Shakespeare: Othello. Compositor analysis.—13. Editorial revision and corruption of Shakespeare's First folio texts: Coriolanus and Antony and Cleopatra.—14. Dramatic punctuation in Elizabethan drama.—15. The punctuation of Shakespeare and Ben Jonson.—16. Henry VIII: linguistic criteria for the two styles apparent in the play.—Appendices: Chronology of Shakespeare's plays and poems. Substantive texts of the Shakespeare canon, in probable order of composition. Classification of First folio texts according to the probable nature of copy procured by Heminge and Condell. The hands in Sir Thomas More. The orthographical characteristics of Ralph Crane. New light on seventeenth-century pronunciation. Shakespeare and The two noble kinsmen. The historical development of punctuation marks.
Rev: TLS 11 Je '64:512; R. A. Foakes Eng 14:112 '64; C. Spencer Coll Eng 26:416–17 '65; C. A. Gibson AUMLA 23:131–4 '65; C. Hoy Sh Stud 1:334–5 '65; T. H. Howard-Hill R Eng Stud new ser 16:195–6 '65 ; J. B. Gabel J Eng Germ Philol 64:725–7 '65; V. T. Personalist 46:556–7 '65; J. B. Fort Études Angl 19:180–2 '66; M. A. Shaaber Sh Q 17:87 '66.

944 **Turner, Robert Kean.** Shakespearean scholarship and analytical bibliography. Sh Newsl 14n02/3:37 Ap/My '64.
Revolutionary changes in attitudes.—Relationship of early editions.—Evaluation of the printing process.—Hinman's study of the First folio.

945 —— Analytical bibliography and Shakespeare's text. Mod Philol 62n01: 51–8 Ag '64.
Review article on Hinman's Printing and proof-reading, no.611, with general comments on recent work.

946 **Walker, Alice.** The shifting text. TLS 23 Ap '64:355.
General survey of the treatment of textual matters from the earliest editors.

947 **Wilson, John Dover.** Shakespeare 1964: a scholar at work. Viewpoint 1:17–19 '64. (Not seen)

948 **Hill, Trevor Howard Howard-**. 'Shakespeare, Crane and the computer' *in* 1965 International conference on computational linguistics. Proceedings. New York, 1965. 11p. (Duplicated typescript)

949 **Hinman, Charlton J. K.** Shakespeare's text, then, now and tomorrow. Sh Surv 18:23–33 '65.

General assessment of bibliogr. scholarship; discussion of accuracy with which various compositors reproduced their copy; the textual implications of setting by formes, and report on Q thus set: *Tit.* 1594, *R3* 1597, *1H4*, *MND*, and *R2* 1597.

Summary report *in* International Shakespeare conference, Stratford-upon-Avon, 11th. Report. [Stratford-upon-Avon, 1965] p.16–17.

950 **Honigmann, Ernst Anselm Joachim.** Shakespeare's quatercentenary. Forum for Mod Lang Stud 1no4:358–75 Oc '65.

'III. Shakespeare's text.' (p.372–5)

951 —— The stability of Shakespeare's text. London, E. Arnold [1965] xi,212p. facsims. 21cm.

1. The new bibliography and the stability of Shakespeare's text.—2. The transmission of dramatic manuscripts. (Note A: foul papers. Note B: intermediate fair copies.)—3. The unblotted papers. (Note A: Blount, Jonson, Digges and Mabbe.)—4. Shakespeare's instability, some examples. (Note A: dramatis personæ lists and Othello.)—5. Other authors and their instability.—6. Troilus and Cressida. (Note A: Troilus and Cressida: quarto omissions and additions.)—7. Othello. (Note A: the Othello quarto: compositors and copyists.)—8. King Lear.—9. Some other Shakespearian texts.—10. Shakespeare's alternative numbers.—11. Order of writing.—12. Editorial policy. The new corrective editing. The eclectic text. The optimism of the new bibliography.—Appendices: A. The dramatist's rights in his play. B. George Wilkins and Pericles. C. The captives, foul papers or copy?

Rev: A. C. Partridge Eng Stud Africa 9:98–9 '66; J. B. Fort Études Angl 9:79–81 '66; C. A. Pennel Coll Eng 27:577–8 '66; J. A. Barish Stud Eng Lit 6:367–70 '66; L. A. Beaurline Renaiss N 19:262–5 '66; T. H. Howard-Hill R Eng Stud new ser 17:310–12 '66; A. T. Tsai Educ Theat J 18:291–4 '66; K. Chujo Sh Stud (Tokyo) 4:89–92 '66; R. W. Van Fossen Sh Q 18:85–6 '67.

952 **Muthuswami, B.** 'Shakespeare's text' *in* Andhra university. Shakespeare quatercentenary celebrations souvenir. Waltair, 1965. p.15–30. (Not seen)

'Review of attempts of scholars to establish the "text" of *Shak.*'s plays.' (Sh Q)

953 **Nosworthy, James M.** Shakespeare's occasional plays, their origin and transmission. London, E. Arnold; New York, Barnes and Noble [1965] 238p. 21cm.

1. Macbeth: date, scope and integrity.—2. . . . the scope and nature of augmentation.—3. . . . prompt-book and Folio copy.—4. Troilus and Cressida: the multiplicity of problems.—5. . . . Quarto and Folio.—6. . . . the Shakespearian versions.—7. The Merry wives of Windsor: traditions and problems.—8. . . . Shakespeare and Porter.—9. . . . Shakespeare's revising hand.—10. Hamlet: the general textual problems.—11. . . . the occasion and the Folio text.—12. . . . the Globe version and the first quarto.—Conclusion.—Appendix 1: Alternative endings.—Appendix 2: The songs in The witch and Ralph Crane.

Rev: J. B. Fort Études Angl 19:288–90 '66; TLS 10 Mr '66:202; R. A. Foakes Eng 16:64–5 '66; Choice 3:310 '66.

954 **Palmer, Arnold.** Monumental mistakes. TLS 23 S '65:832; A. J. Sambrook *ib.* 4 N '65:988.

On the text of the inscription on the Sh. monument in Westminster abbey.

956 **Bowers, Fredson Thayer.** On editing Shakespeare. Charlottesville, Virginia U.P. [1966] ix,210p. 21cm.

The texts and their manuscripts.—The function of textual criticism and bibliography.—The method for a critical edition.—What Shakespeare wrote.—Today's Shakespeare texts, and tomorrow's.

Repr. of the 1954 Rosenbach lectures (no.916) with the addition of nos.938 and 957.

Rev: E. A. J. Honigmann Library ser5 23:264-5 '68; T. H. Howard-Hill Sh Stud 4:380-3 '68.

957 **Bowers, Fredson Thayer.** Today's Shakespeare texts, and tomorrow's. Stud
; Bib 19:39-65 '66.

958 **Byrne, Muriel St. Clare.** Prompt book's progress. Theat Notebk 21no1: 7-12 '66.

On the value of prompt-book study for the establishment of the text and determination of acting and production history.

959 **Harrison, George Bagshawe.** 'Editing Shakespeare' *in* Introducing Shakespeare. 3d ed., rev. and expanded. [Harmondsworth, Middlesex, 1966] p.[193]-219.

First pub. 1939 (no.884); rev. ed. 1954, and various reprs.

960 **Hill, Trevor Howard Howard-.** Computer analysis of Shakespearean texts, II. Sh Newsl 16no1:7 F '66.

961 **Honigmann, Ernst Anselm Joachim.** On the indifferent and one-way variants in Shakespeare. Library ser5 22no3:189-204 S '67.

Orthographical variants between Q/F *R3*, *Oth.*, and *Lr.* mainly, largely stem from copyists and tend to rehabilitate Q.

962 **Waller, Frederick O.** 'The use of linguistic criteria in determining the copy and dates for Shakespeare's plays' *in* McNeir, Waldo F. and Thelma N. Greenfield, *ed.* Pacific Coast studies in Shakespeare. 1967. p.1-19. (Not seen)

963 '**Textual** criticism' *in* Encyclopædia Britannica. Chicago [1968] V.20, p.333-5.
1. Texts.—2. The language of Shakespeare's time.—3. Shakespeare and his printers.

964 **Wilson, John Dover.** 'How I came to edit Shakespeare' *in* Milestones on the Dover road. London [1969] p.153-87.

965 **Wilson, Frank Percy.** Shakespeare and the new bibliography. Rev. and ed. by Helen Gardner. Oxford, Clarendon pr., 1970. xi, 136p. 20cm.

See no.892.

HANDWRITING AND PALÆOGRAPHY

1000 **Furnivall, Frederick James.** On Shakspere's signatures. J Soc Archivists 1:1-3 Je '95.

1001 **Lee, sir Sidney.** Shakespeare's handwriting; facsimiles of the five authentic autograph signatures of the poet extracted from Sidney Lee's Life of William Shakespeare. London, Smith, Elder, 1899. 11p. facsims. 18cm. Covertitle.

Rev: N&Q ser9 3:299 '99.

1002 **Yeatman, John Pym.** Is William Shakspere's will holographic . . . and photographs of the poet's will. [2d ed.] Darley Dale, 1901. 72,8p. fold. facsims. 24cm. Covertitle.

The 2d is apparently the only ed.

1003 **Haines, C. Reginald.** Shakespeare autograph. N&Q ser10 2:107 Ag '04; W. Jaggard ib. 2:248 S '04; Lucy T. Smith 2:332 Oc '04.

On three signatures in a black-letter prayerbook, 1596.

1004 **Frost, Edwin Collins.** Autographs of Shakespeare in the United States. New Shakespeareana 4n02:49–62 Ap '05. facsims.(part fold.)

1. The autograph in the Boston public library.—2. The Marsden J. Perry autographs.—3. The Gunther autograph.

1005 **R., L. M.** Shakespeare's Bible. N&Q ser11 2:365 N '10; T. Jones; W. Jaggard ib. 2:430–1 N '10.

Discussion of copy of 1580 Bible, L. Thomson's trans., in the Shakespeare memorial exhibition, Whitechapel art gallery, and other bibles assigned to Shakespeare's library.

1006 **Wallace, Charles William.** Shakespeare's signature. Nation 90n02333: 259–61 Mr '10.

1007 **J., D.** Shakespeare's signatures. N&Q ser11 5:490 Je '12; W. S. Brassington ib. 6:72–3 Jl '12; E. D. Lawrence 6:153–4 Ag '12; W. B. 6:255 S '12; E. D. Lawrence 6:338 Oc '12; T. Bayne; A. R. Bayley 6:437 N '12.

Discussion of Durning Lawrence's assertion of the signatures' falsity.

1008 **Thompson, sir Edward Maunde.** 'Handwriting' in Shakespeare's England, an account of the life & manners of his age. Oxford, 1916. V.1, p.[284]–310. facsims.

General account of sixteenth-century handwriting, with 'An analysis of Shakespeare's autograph signatures' (p.299–309)

Rev: TLS 17 Ag '16:391.

1009 —— Shakespeare's handwriting, a study. Oxford, Clarendon pr., 1916. xii,63p. facsims. 23cm.

Includes facsims. and transcript of Hand D's portion of the STM ms.

Rev: N&Q ser12 3:18–19 '17; TLS 1 Mr '17:100; J. A. Herbert Library ser3 8:97–100 '17; A. Schröer Sh Jahrb 55:183–4 '19; B. Fehr Angl Beibl 35:97–102 '24.

1010 **Greenwood, sir Granville George.** Sir E. Maunde Thompson on Shakespeare's handwriting. TLS 8 Mr '17:117.

1011 **Madan, Falconer.** Shakespeariana. Bod Q Rec 2n013:25–7 Ap '17.

1. The fourth folio [copy presented by Louis Duveen].—2. Editors' spelling of their author's name.—3. Comparative popularity of certain plays [evidence from copy of F2]. —4. A Shakespeare signature (?) [in the Aldine Ovid, 1502: arguments for its authenticity]

1012 **Thompson, sir Edward Maunde.** Two pretended autographs of Shakespeare. Library ser3 8no31:193–217 Jl '17. facsims.
Negative assessment of the validity of signatures in Florio's Montaigne, and Ovid's Metamorphoses, with facsims. of authentic signatures.

1013 **Madan, Falconer.** Two lost causes and what may be said of them. Library ser3 9no34:89–105 Ap '18.
'B. A supposed Shakespeare autograph' (p.97–105): analysis of the Ovid's Metamorphoses signature and inscription in light of Maunde Thompson's findings; concludes that the question of authenticity is not finally settled.

1014 **Haines, C. Reginald.** Shakespeare signatures. N&Q ser12 5:207 Ag '19.
Signatures in his so-called prayerbook.

1015 **Thompson, sir Edward Maunde.** Shakespeare's handwriting. TLS 12 Je '19: 325; Charlotte C. Stopes *ib.* 19 Je '19:337.

1016 **Haines, C. Reginald.** A lost autograph of Shakespeare. TLS 14 Oc '20:668; W. Jaggard; C. R. Haines *ib.* 21 Oc '20:684.
Inquiry after *another* Sh. signature in a copy of Montaigne from Parham House, Sussex.

1017 **Stevenson, W. H.** Shakespeare's schoolmaster and handwriting. TLS 8 Ja '20:21.
Rebuts Lee's suggestion that Shakespeare's preference for the secretary hand 'testified to his provincial education'.

1018 **Michelmore, G.** A book annotated by Shakespeare (?) TLS 10 Ag '22:521.
Notes in a copy of Golding's trans. of Caesar, 1565, formerly in library of Richard Farmer.

1019 **Chambers, Raymond Wilson.** The spurred A. TLS 27 Ag '25:557; sir E. M. Thompson *ib.* 17 S '25:600; S. A. Tannenbaum 24 S '25:619; 22 Oc '25:698; sir G. G. Greenwood 12 N '25:756.
Its occurrence in a Chapman signature denied by Thompson.

1020 **Greenwood, sir Granville George.** The Shakespeare signatures. TLS 15 Ja '25:40; J. A. Fort; H. D. Simpson *ib.* 22 Ja '25:56; sir G. G. Greenwood 29 Ja '25:71.
On the order of signing the pages of the will.

1021 —— Shakespeare's handwriting and the Northumberland manuscript; the latest Shakespeare mare's nest. London, Watts, 1925. 31p. 18cm.
Reply to Thompson, no.1023.

1022 **Tannenbaum, Samuel Aaron.** Reclaiming one of Shakspere's signatures. Stud Philol 22no3:392–411 Jl '25. facsims.
The signature in Florio's trans. of Montaigne is 'unquestionably genuine'.

1023 **Thompson, William.** Shakespeare's handwriting. Q R 244no484:209–26 Ap '25. facsims.
Perceives Shakespeare's hand in the Northumberland ms. *See also* no.1021.

1024 **Tannenbaum, Samuel Aaron.** A new study of Shakspere's will. Stud Philol 23n02:117–41 Ap '26; *rf.* sir G. G. Greenwood *ib.* 23n04:473–6 Oc '26.

1025 —— [Same]: Reprinted from Studies in Philology, volume 23; augmented with three pages of notes and additions. Baltimore, 1926. 117–41[3]p. 23cm.

1026 **Greg, sir Walter Wilson.** Shakespeare's hand once more. TLS 24 N '27:871; 1 D '27:908; S. A. Tannenbaum *ib.* 12 Ja '28:28.

Review of Tannenbaum's Problems in Shakspere's penmanship, and The booke of Sir Thomas Moore, in which Greg traverses and amends Maunde Thompson's case for the identification of Shakespeare's hand. Repr. in no.147.

1027 **Tannenbaum, Samuel Aaron.** Problems in Shakspere's penmanship, including a study of the poet's will. New York, Century co. for the Modern language association of America; London, H. Milford, O.U.P., 1927. xvi,241p. illus., facsims. 22cm.

1. Introduction.—2. The deposition signature.—3. The warranty signature.—4. The mortgage deed signature.—5. Shakspere's will.—6. The signature on page 1 of the will.—7. . . . on page 2 of the will.—8. . . . on page 3 of the will.—9. The signature in Montaigne's Essays.—10. Folios 8 and 9 of the Booke of Sir Thomas Moore.—Appendix A: transcript of the will.—Appendix B: transcripts of facsimile reproductions in the text.

Rev: Nation 125:318 '27; sir W. W. Greg TLS 24 N '27:871; 1 D '27:908; C. J. Sisson Mod Lang R 23:231–4 '28; C. F. T. Brooke Yale R 17:406–10 '28.

1028 **Manwaring, G. E.** A missing autograph of Shakespeare. TLS 3 Oc '29:766; C. R. Haines *ib.* 10 Oc '29:794; S. A. Tannenbaum 14 N '29:926; C. R. Haines 21 N '29:978; W. T. Smedley 12 D '29:1058.

On a signature reported in Stephens's A world of wonders, 1607.

1029 **Rendall, Gerald H.** Shakespeare's handwriting and orthography. TLS 25 S '30:757–8.

'. . . the autograph text of the Sonnets, in almost every particular of script and spelling, confirmed to the pattern of Edward de Vere.' (p.758)

1030 **Tannenbaum, Samuel Aaron.** Two new Shakspere autographs (?) Sh Assn Bull 7n03:113 Jl '32. facsims.

Notes, with facsims. (p.102), on signatures in 1579 Plutarch's Lives, and Jewitt scrap, now in Folger Shakespeare library.

1031 **Carter, G. E. L.** A Shakespeare holograph. Lib Assn Rec 38n08:424–6 Ag '36. facsim.

Claims bookseller's warranty by William Aspley in Florio's World of words, 1598, is in Shakespeare's hand.

1032 **Tannenbaum, Samuel Aaron.** New Shakspere signatures. Sh Assn Bull 13n01:63–4 Ja '38.

Signature 'discovered somewhere by a friend of . . . B. Roland Lewis' denounced as 'in all probability either a forgery, a hoax, or an innocent imitation'.

1033 **Marks, Seymour.** Signatures of Shakespeare. TLS 10 Je '39:341.

> Advertised in 1866 as 'written under the imprint at the end of a Black Letter Tome, Pageant of Popes'.

1034 **Ewen, Cecil Henry L'Estrange.** What Shakespere signatures reveal; a chapter from an unpublished book. Paignton, 1940. 6p. facsims. 18cm. Covertitle.

> *Rev*: TLS 25 Ja '40:47.

1035 **Stalker, Archibald.** Is Shakespeare's will a forgery? Q R 274no544:248–62 Ap '40.

> Shakespeare's will forged by its discoverer, Joseph Greene.

1036 **Tannenbaum, Samuel Aaron.** Shakspere's will. Sh Assn Bull 15no2:126–7 Ap '40. facsim.

> A facsimile copy.

1037 **Tannenbaum, Samuel Aaron.** Self-deception, hoax or fraud? Sh Assn Bull 16no4:254–5 Oc '41.

> Marginal annotations in a copy of Holinshed's Chronicle bear 'not the slightest resemblance . . . to the . . . signatures'.

1038 **Adams, Joseph Quincy.** A new signature of Shakespeare? John Rylands Lib Bull 27no2:256–9 Je '43.

> Signature in Folger library copy of Lambarde's Archaionomia.

1039 **Dawson, Giles Edwin.** Authenticity and attribution of written matter. Eng Inst Ann 1942:77–100 '43. facsims.

> Includes discussion of the signature in Lambarde's Archaionomia, and facsims. of the authentic signatures.

1040 **Ewen, Cecil Henry L'Estrange.** A new Shakespere signature. N&Q 185:196 S '43; sir A. Heal; R. L. Eagle; W. Jaggard *ib.* 185:263–4 Oc '43.

> That in Lambarde's Archaionomia.

1041 **One** of Shakespeare's books? TLS 1 My '43:216.

> Lambarde's Archaionomia.

1042 **Shakespeare** in Washington. Theat Arts Mthly 27no4:248–51 Ap '43.

> Account of the discovery of the signature in Lambarde's Archaionomia.

1043 **A., H.** Shakespeare's will. N&Q 188:127 Mr '45; W. Jaggard *ib.* 188:174 Ap '45.

1044 **Caldiero, Frank.** Shakespeare's signature in Lambarde's APXAIONOMIA. N&Q 188:162–3 Ap '45.

> Cites Malone's statements on the usual spelling of Shakespeare's name in support of the signature's authenticity.

1045 **Ashe, Geoffrey.** Shakespeare's first manuscript? The Month new ser 6no4: 236–40 Oc '51. facsim.

> Ms. verse c.1584 in letter addressed to Walsingham, attrib. to Sh.

1046 **Price, Hereward Thimbleby.** Shakespeare's classical scholarship. R Eng Stud new ser 9no33:54–5 F '58.

Shakespeare's signature in Lambarde's Archaionomia shows that he owned at least one book.

COLLECTED EMENDATIONS

1060 **[Orson, S. W.]** Shakespeare emendations. [London, 1891] 6 l. 18 cm. Headtitle. (Duplicated typescript)

1061 **Dey, Edward Merton.** Department of textual criticism. New Shakespeareana 2no2/3:145–52 Ap/Jl '03; 3no1:19–29 Ja '04; 3no2:64–70 Ap '04; 3no3:98–102 Jl '04; 3no4:134–9 Oc '04; 4no2:63–9 Ap '05; 4no3:103–6 Jl '05; 4no4:121–6 Oc '05; 5no1:17–20 Ja '06; 5no2:55–8 Ap '06; 5no3:87–92 Jl '06; 5no4:135–8 Oc '06; 6no1:18–20 Ja '07; 6no2/3:69–71 Ap/Jl '07; 6no4:123–6 Oc '07; 7no3:75–7 Jl '08; 7no4:111–14 Oc '08.

Emendations by various hands, but mainly by Dey.

1062 **Stewart, Charles D.** Some textual difficulties in Shakespeare. New Haven, Yale U.P.; London, H. Milford, O.U.P., 1914. ix,251p. 19cm.

Rev: Yale R new ser 4:851–7 '15; G. C. M. Smith Mod Lang R 10:98–100 '16.

1063 **Donovan, Thomas.** The true text of Shakespeare and of his fellow playwrights. London, Macmillan, 1923. 31p. 21cm.

Rev: TLS 13 S '23:600.

1064 **Cuningham, Henry.** Textual notes on Shakespeare. N&Q 151:273–5 Oc '26; 152:43–5,184–5,256–7,292–4 Ja–Ap '27; F. H. Underwood *ib.* 152:104 F '27.

1065 **Tannenbaum, Samuel Aaron.** Some emendations of Shakspere's text. Sh Assn Bull 6no3:105–10 Jl '31. illus.

1066 —— 'Some emendations of Shakspere's text' *in* Shaksperian scraps and other Elizabethan fragments. New York, 1933. p.87–117. illus.

'. . . the more important of the emendations . . . which I have published from time to time in various periodicals.'

1067 **Koszul, A.** Some notes on Shakespeare's text. Eng Stud 31no6:215–17 D '50; J. C. Maxwell *ib.* 32no1:30 F '51.

Emendations suggested for *Err.* 3.1.65; *1H6* 1.5.29, and *AWW* 2.1.110.

1068 **Parsons, Howard.** Shakespeare emendations. N&Q 196:27–9 Ja '51.

1069 **Parsons, Howard.** Emendations to three of Shakespeare's plays: The merry wives of Windsor; Love's labour's lost; Comedy of errors. London, Ettrick pr., 1953. 18p. 22cm.

1070 —— Shakespearian emendations and discoveries. [London] Ettrick pr., 1953. 136p. 16cm.

As you like it.—A midsummer night's dream.—Hamlet.—The tempest.—Romeo and Juliet.—Macbeth.—Othello.—The identity of I. M.—Shakespeare and the scholars.—The history of the First folio. . . .

Largely repr. from N&Q.

Rev: N&Q 199:275–6 '54; E. G. Salter Contemp R 186:126 '54; New Statesm 29 My '54:710; C. E. Raven *ib.* 5 Je '54:733; I. B. Cauthen Sh Q 5:423–4 '54; TLS 29 Ja '54:78; H. Heuer Sh Jahrb 91:345–7 '55.

1071 **Sisson, Charles Jasper.** New readings in Shakespeare. Cambridge, C.U.P., 1956. (Repr. 1961; anr. issue: London, Dawsons, 1961) 2v. facsims. 17cm. (Shakespeare problems, VIII)

1. Introduction; the comedies; the poems.—2. The histories; the tragedies.

'This book is an attempt to survey the principal proposals made during the lifetime of its readers for the restoration of the true text of Shakespeare. It includes an explanation and defence of the readings put forward in my own recent edition.'

Rev: Q R 294:271–2 '56; A. A. Stephenson Month new ser 15:294–300 '56; Dublin Mag new ser 31:34–6 '56; N&Q 201:272 '56; H. Peschmann Eng 11:69 '56; A. C. Sprague Theat Notebk 11:31–2 '56; F. S. Boas Contemp R 190:58 '56; Listener 55:521,523 '56; J. G. McManaway Sh Surv 10:153 '57; L. L. Schücking Angl 74:371–3 '57; A. Harbage Mod Lang N 72:53–5 '57; H. T. Price Mod Philol 55:53–5 '57; A. Walker R Eng Stud new ser 8:298–301 '57; A. Brown Library ser5 12:60–2 '57; G. E. Dawson Mod Lang R 52:97–100 '57; M. A. Shaaber Sh Q 8:104–7 '57; J. A. Bryant Sewanee R 65:152–60 '57; F. T. Bowers Mod Lang Q 18:156–7 '57; H. Heuer Sh Jahrb 94:284 '58.

1072 **Lambrechts, Guy.** Proposed new readings in Shakespeare: the comedies. Bull de la Faculté des Lettres de Strasbourg 43no8:945–58 Mai/Juin '65.

INDIVIDUAL TEXTS—ALL'S WELL THAT ENDS WELL

1080 **Newcomer, Alphonso Gerald.** A Shakespeare crux. Mod Philol 11no1: 141–4 Jl '13.

Reads 'ropes' for 'rope's' at 4.2.38.

1081 **Cuningham, Henry.** All's well that ends well. IV.2,38—III.2,111. TLS 21 N '29:978.

For 'make rope's in such a scarre' suggests 'may broke's in such a cause', and reads 'still creeping' for 'still-peering' at 3.2.113.

1082 **Hastings, William T.** Notes on All's well that ends well. Sh Assn Bull 10no4:232–44 Oc '35.

1083 **Brooke, Charles Frederick Tucker.** Men may grope's in such a scarre.
Mod Lang N 58no6:426–8 Je '43.

1084 **Tannenbaum, Samuel Aaron.** Removing a scar from All's well, IV.ii.38–39.
Sh Assn Bull 18no3:133–6 Jl '43.
Reads 'sturre' for 'scarre', with an extensive list of earlier conjectures.

1085 **Jones, Harold Whitmore.** All's well, IV.ii.38 again. Mod Lang R 55no2:
241–2 Ap '60.
Reads 'men may compass 's in such a snare'.

INDIVIDUAL TEXTS—ANTONY AND CLEOPATRA

1090 **Sanderson, Thomas James Cobden-.** Anthony and Cleopatra. TLS 16 My
'12:206; 23 My '12:218.
Suggests transposing SP at 1.1.58–9.

1091 —— Note on a passage in Anthony & Cleopatra. Sh Jahrb 49:146–7 '13.
The compositor has transposed SP at 1.2.65–6.

1092 **Sampson, John.** An arme-gaunt steede. TLS 29 Ap '20:272.
Reads 'armigerent' at 1.5.48.

1093 **Bronson, Bertrand Harris.** Arme-gaunt. TLS 8 Oc '38:644; D. E. Yates *ib.*
22 Oc '38:678.
Reads 'wing-borne' at 1.5.48.

1094 **Maxwell, James C.** Shakespeare's manuscript of Antony and Cleopatra.
N&Q 196:337 Ag '51.
Comment on the spelling of Ventigius, and on 3.10.28–9.

1095 **Galloway, David.** I am dying, Egypt, dying: Folio repetitions and the
editors. N&Q 203:330–5 Ag '58.
Since the case for corruption in 4.15 'rests not on bibliographical evidence or critical
acumen but on two "repetitions" ' (p. 334) there is no need to depart from the F readings.

1096 **Thomas, Mary Olive.** The repetitions in Antony's death scene. Sh Q
9no2:153–7 '58.
Suggests repetitions reveal later interpolations rather than (after Dover Wilson) incorrect cuts in 4.15.

1097 **Muir, Kenneth.** Anthony and Cleopatra, III.xiii.73–8. N&Q 206:142 Ap '61.
Reads 'Till' for 'Tell him' at 3.13.75.

INDIVIDUAL TEXTS—AS YOU LIKE IT

1103 **Knowles, Richard.** Rough notes on editions collated for As you like it. Sh Res Opp 4:66–72 '68/9.
Comments on ed. seen for New variorum ed.

1105 **Grierson, sir Herbert John Clifford.** A note on the text of As you like it, II,i,5. Mod Lang R 9no3:370–2 Jl '14.

1106 **Tannenbaum, Samuel Aaron.** An emendation of As you like it, II.vii,73. Mod Lang N 44no7:428–30 N '29.
Reads 'necesserie' for 'wearie verie'.

1107 **Fellowes, Edmund H.** It was a lover. TLS 5 Ja '33:9; R. Noble *ib.* 12 Ja '33:24; F. C. Lathrop 2 F '33:76.
Discussion and comparison of the text of the song in Thomas Morley's setting with the F text. *See also* no.1109.

1108 **Newdigate, Bernard Henry.** A line in As you like it. TLS 7 N '42:550.
Reads 'waues' for 'meanes' at 2.7.73.

1109 **Fellowes, Edmund H.** It was a lover and his lass; some fresh points of criticism. Mod Lang R 41no2:202–6 Ap '46.
On the relation of the texts in Thomas Morley's First book of airs, 1600, and F, with some reference to the ms. in the National library of Scotland, Edinburgh.

1110 **Seng, Peter J.** The forester's song in As you like it. Sh Q 10no2:246–9 '59.
'... the rest shall beare this burthen' at 4.2.13 is 'an interjected line of dialogue.' (p.248)

INDIVIDUAL TEXTS—CORIOLANUS

1120 **Cuningham, Henry.** Coriolanus. TLS 17 Ag '22:533.
Reads 'being tender wounds, do craue' for 'being gentle wounded' at 4.1.8.

1121 **Rhodes, Raymond Crompton.** A reading of Coriolanus. TLS 31 Ag '22:557.
At 4.1.42, 'followes' should be deleted; it is a misplaced SD.

1122 **Cowling, George Herbert.** A Coriolanus crux. TLS 22 Ja '25:56; H. C. Lawrence *ib.* 19 F '25:120.
For 'appear'd' reads 'appeer'd' meaning 'confirmed', at 4.3.9.

1123 **King, A. H.** Notes on Coriolanus. Eng Stud 19no1:13–20 F '37; 20no1: 18–25 F '38.

1124 **F1** Coriolanus fragment found in 17th century binding. Sh Newsl 16no2:11 Ap '66.
Parts of sig. bb1 and bb6 in Hakewill's An apology, 1627, at the Kansas State university library.

INDIVIDUAL TEXTS—CYMBELINE

1130 **Tannenbaum, Samuel Aaron.** The Jay of Italy. Sh Assn Bull 12no3:193–4 Jl '37.
A5 3.4.52, reads, 'Whose maker' for 'Whose mother'.

1131 **Collins, Rowland L.** The simplest emendation of Cymbeline III.iv.132–5. Sh Q 15no4:448–9 '64.
Reads 'harsh noble,' for 'harsh, noble,' at 3.4.135.

INDIVIDUAL TEXTS—HAMLET

1140 **Raven, Anton Adolph.** A Hamlet bibliography and reference guide, 1877–1935. Chicago, Ill., University of Chicago pr.; Cambridge, C.U.P. [1936] (Repr. New York, Russell and Russell, 1966) xvi,292p. 23cm.
Rev: TLS 26 D '36:1070; J. S. Wilson Virginia Q R 12:636–40 '36; Lib Q 6:448–9 '36; W. Keller Sh Jahrb 72:148 '36; B. M. Philol Q 16:89–90 '37; F. Delattre R Belge de

philol et d'histoire 16:987–8 '37; H. Spencer Mod Lang N 52:437–42 '37; L. L. Schücking R Eng Stud 13:484–5 '37; W. Fischer Angl Beibl 48:105–7 '37; R. M. Smith Sh
Assn Bull 12:35–40 '37; E. Welsford Mod Lang R 33:122 '38.

1145 **Reynolds, W.** Still another reading of the dram of eale. Shakespeareana
8no2:108–9 Ap '91.
Reads 'over doubt' for 'of a doubt' at 1.4.38.

1146 **Jonas, Maurice.** Hamlet, 1603. N&Q ser8 11:46 Ja '97.
Notes copy in Warwick castle collection.

1147 **Redway, G. W.** Curious feature in Macready's copy of Hamlet. N&Q ser9
4:209 S '99.
'Murder' written eight times at 1.5 in a copy in the Dyce and Forster collection.

1148 **Poel, William.** The first quarto Hamlet. Athenæum 3776:316 Mr '00.
Account of textual revision for performance from Q1.

1149 **Westenholz, F. P. von.** Die Hamlet-quartos. Eng Studien 34no3:337–50
D '04.

1150 **Furnivall, Frederick James.** Hamlet, I.iv.36: dram of eale. N&Q ser10
4:285 Oc '05; sir M. Hunter *ib.* 5:264–5 Ap '06.
Hunter doubts Furnivall's view that 'eale' and 'deale' were true variants of 'evil' and
'devil', and suggests that they were misprints.

1151 **Miller, Aura.** The sixth quarto of Hamlet in a new light. Mod Philol
4no3:501–5 Ja '07. table.
Collation derived from Cambridge ed. (1892) shows Q6 incorporated variants from the
folios.

1152 —— The sources of the text of Hamlet in the editions of Rowe, Pope, and
Theobald. Mod Lang N 22no6:163–8 Je '07. tables.
Rowe ptd. from F4, Pope from Rowe's 2d ed., and Theobald from Pope's 2d ed.; tables
of readings.

1153 **Allen, Edward A.** The First folio of Shakespeare and the New English
dictionary. Mod Lang N 24no2:38–43 F '09.
Discussion of errors in *Ham.*

1154 **Fitzgerald, James D.** The first quarto of Hamlet, a literary fraud. Roy
Philos Soc Glasgow Proc 41:181–218 '10.
Q1 is a 'fraudulent' copy, memorially reconstructed.

1155 **Greg, sir Walter Wilson.** The Hamlet quartos, 1603, 1604. Mod Lang R
5no2:196–7 Ap '10.
Q1 *Wiv.* at sig. F2, l. 1188 contains a line from *Ham.*, 5.1.312.

1156 **Gray, Henry David.** The first quarto of Hamlet. Mod Lang R 10no2:171–80
Ap '15.
'. . . the pirated quarto was based upon a very corrupt version of the acted play supplied
to the publisher by the player who acted the part of Marcellus.' (p.174)

1157 **Van Dam, Bastiaan Adriaan P.** 'Are there interpolations in the text of Hamlet?' *in* Gollancz, sir Israel, *ed.* A book of homage to Shakespeare. [Oxford, 1916] p.473–80.
Actors' material and additions from prompt-book.

1158 **Gollancz, sir Israel.** Hatching the cock's-egg of Polonius. TLS 28 N '18: 583; P. Simpson; D. W. Thompson; M. A. Bayfield; W. D. Sargeaunt; J. Rose *ib.* 5 D '18:599–600; J. D. Wilson 2 Ja '19:10; A. D. Wilde 9 Ja '19:21.
Offers 'coragio' in place of Dover Wilson's 'cockney' for Q2 'courage' at 1.3.65.

1159 **Hubbard, Frank G.** The Marcellus theory of the first quarto of Hamlet. Mod Lang N 33no1:73–9 Ja '18.
Examination of Gray's suggestion; *see* no.1156.

1160 **Wilson, John Dover.** The copy for Hamlet, 1603. Library ser3 9no35:153–85 Jl '18.
1. The composite nature of the copy.—2. The Voltemar copy.—3. Tertium quid.
Parts of Q1 derive directly from Shakespeare's ms., parts were pirated by an actor, but the nature of Q1 suggests 'some intermediate text which will link the early Hamlet with its posthumous apparition in 1603' (p.185). *See* no.1162.

1161 —— The copy for Hamlet, 1603 and The Hamlet transcript, 1593. London, A. Moring, De la More pr., 1918. 64p. 25cm.
Repr. of Library papers; *see* nos.1160, 1162.
Rev: TLS 10 Jl '19:374.

1162 —— The Hamlet transcript, 1593. Library ser3 9no36:217–47 Oc '18.
1. Shortening.—2. Pirate and stage-adaptor.—3. Prose printed as blank-verse lengths.—4. Date and company.
Further examination of the intermediate ms. posited in his previous paper. '. . . our intermediary was a shortened copy of Shakespeare's partially revised manuscript made for a touring company' (p.218) about 1591–2. *See* no.1160.

1163 —— Hamlet's solid flesh. TLS 16 My '18:233; C. L. D. *ib.* 23 My '18:245; W. D. Sargeaunt; W. E. Wilson 18 Jl '18:337–8; J. D. Wilson 25 Jl '18:349; W. D. Sargeaunt 5 S '18:417–18.
'Sallied', despite the frequency of its occurrence in Sh., is a misreading of 'sullied', the correct reading at 1.2.129.

1164 **Fitzgerald, James D.** The first quarto of Hamlet. TLS 7 Ag '19:425.
Shakespeare's true text is contained in the words shared, in proper order, by both Q.

1165 **Sargeaunt, W. D.** The Hamlet quartos. TLS 13 F '19:83; sir G. G. Greenwood *ib.* 20 F '19:98; W. D. Sargeaunt 27 F '19:113; sir G. G. Greenwood 6 Mr '19:126; W. D. Sargeaunt 3 Ap '19:184; sir G. G. Greenwood 10 Ap '19:201.

1166 **Wilson, John Dover.** Dramatic and bibliographical problems in Hamlet. Mod Lang R 15no2:163–6 Ap '20.
Reference to bibliogr. aspects of *Ham.*, and to Greg's survey, no.843.

1167 **Cuningham, Henry.** Some passages in Hamlet. TLS 29 Je '22:428; 6 Jl '22: 444; R. Noble *ib.* 13 Jl '22:460; H. Cuningham; J. S. H. 3 Ag '22:508; sir W. W. Greg 17 Ag '22:533; H. Cuningham 12 Oc '22:648.

1168 **Greg, sir Walter Wilson.** Textual criticism in Hamlet. TLS 26 Oc '22:687; H. Cuningham *ib.* 2 N '22:707.

Condemnation of Cuningham's methods of textual criticism.

1169 **Poel, William.** The first quarto Hamlet, an Elizabethan actor's emendations. N&Q ser12 11:301–3 Oc '22.

'Q1. is a cut-down and rearranged text, adapted from the playhouse copy which appeared in print, twenty years later, in the first folio.' (p.301)

1170 **De Groot, Hendrik.** The first quarto of Hamlet. TLS 8 Mr '23:160.

Textual indications of faulty revision in the Corambis–Montano scene.

1171 —— Hamlet, its textual history. Amsterdam, Swets & Zeitlinger, 1923. 143p. 25cm.

1. The Ur-Hamlet.—2. The relation between the second quarto, 1604, and the First folio, 1623.—3. The relation between the quarto of 1603 (Q1) and that of 1604 (Q2).—4. Is there any direct connection between Q1 and F1?—5. The piracy.—Conclusion.
Rev: B. Fehr Angl Beibl 35:141–5 '24; A. W. Pollard Eng Stud 6:38–9 '24; B. A. P. Van Dam Museum 31:301–5 '24; sir W. W. Greg Mod Lang R 19:228–30 '24; T. S. Graves Stud Philol 21:427 '24;

1172 —— New Shakespeare criticism. Neophilol 8:284–95 Jl '23.

Largely an examination of Dover Wilson's no.1161.

1173 **Haworth, Peter.** Hamlet's dram of eale. TLS 5 Ap '23:232; N. W. Hill; L. Kellner *ib.* 3 My '23:304; P. Haworth 14 Je '23:404.

1174 **Hubbard, Frank G.** The readings of the first quarto of Hamlet. Pub Mod Lang Assn 38no4:792–822 D '23. tables.

Variations among the three texts, Q1, Q2, F1.—Readings from the first quarto in editions before 1825.—Readings from the first quarto in editions later than 1825.—Other readings and emendations [from Q1] whose adoption is proposed.

1175 **Spencer, Hazelton.** Hamlet under the restoration. Pub Mod Lang Assn 38no4:770–91 D '23.

1. The source.—2. The state of the text.—3. Authorship.
Analysis of D'Avenant's 1676 Q, altered from Q6 (1637)

1176 **Wilson, John Dover.** Spellings and misprints in the second quarto of Hamlet. Essays & Stud 10:36–60 '23.

Classification of misreadings and spellings, and consequential emendations.

1177 **Van Dam, Bastiaan Adriaan P.** The text of Shakespeare's Hamlet. London, J. Lane, Bodley head, 1924. 380p. 27cm.

1. The QS, the stolne and surreptitious quarto printed in 1603.—2. The interpolations in the Q and in the F.—3. The formal and verbal variations between the Q, the F, and the original text.—4. The omissions in the Q, and in the F.—5. What is the Q and what is the F?—6. Prosody.—7. The relation between rhyme, blank verse, broken verse and prose.—8. Shakespeare's Hamlet.—9. Other plays studied in the light of knowledge obtained.
Rev: TLS 25 S '24:592; *rf.* B. A. P. Van Dam *ib.* 9 Oc. '24:631; A. W. Pollard Eng Stud 6:221–5 '24; *rf.* B. A. P. Van Dam *ib.* 7:21–3 '25; E. Shanks Lond Merc 10:59,545–6 '24; sir W. W. Greg Mod Lang R 20:83–8 '25; H. Craig Philol Q 4:187–8 '25; K. Malone J Eng Germ Philol 25:142–3 '26; H. T. Price Museum 33:151–2 '26; E. Deckner Angl Beibl 37:360–72 '26.

1178 **Cuningham, Henry.** Textual notes on some passages in Hamlet. N&Q
151:75–6, 93–4, 147–9, 176–7, 248 Jl–Oc '26; F. H. Underwood *ib.* 151:138
Ag '26; J. A. Knowles 151:193–4 '26.

1179 **Underwood, F. H.** Hamlet, an amendment. N&Q 150:422 Je '26; C. F.
Hardy *ib.* 151:66–7 Jl '26; F. H. Underwood 153:102–3 Ag '27.
Reads 'oile' for 'eale' at 1.4.36, with references to *STM*.

1180 **Gray, Henry David.** Thomas Kyd and the first quarto of Hamlet. Pub Mod
Lang Assn 42no3:721–35 S '27.
'. . . throughout the play X [the editor of Q1] made a presentable text by putting into
shape those parts of M's [Marcellus, the actor-reporter] manuscript which could not
serve for an acting version.' (p.735)

1181 **Lawrence, William John.** 'The mystery of the Hamlet first quarto' *in*
Shakespeare's workshop. Oxford, 1928. (Repr. New York, Haskell house,
1966) p.110–23.
Rev. from Criterion 5no2:191–201 My '27.
Q1 represents an ur-Hamlet with Sh. embellishments introduced by a pirate for a pro-
vincial company in 1601.

1182 **Manning, H. C.** A famous Shakespearean riddle; essay. [Dorchester, F. G.
Longman, Friary pr., 1927] [9]p. illus. 22cm.
Reads 'The barme of ale / Doth all the noble substance of a dough / To his owne scandle.'
at 1.4.36–8.

1183 **Mackail, J. W.** The text of Hamlet, I.ii.129. TLS 4 Oc '28:710; J. D. Wilson *ib.* 18 Oc '28:759; L. J. Potts 25 Oc '28:783; J. D. Wilson 1 N '28:806;
sir M. Hunter 15 N '28:859; W. Marschall 22 N '28:910; M. Montgomery
29 N '28:938.
Reads 'solid'; 'sallied' is a rendering of It. 'saldo'.

1184 **Schaubert, Else von.** He's fat and scant of breath. Angl 52:93–6 Mr '28.

1185 **Willoughby, Edwin Eliott.** A note on the relationship of the first and second
quartos of Hamlet. Angl 52:288 S '28.
The spelling 'pre thee' at 1.2.177 shows that some passages of Q2 were set up from Q1.

1186 **Wilson, John Dover** [and] **H. D. Gray.** Hamlet Q1 and mr. Henry David
Gray. Pub Mod Lang Assn 43no2:575–82 Je '28.
Controversy on the 'reporter' theory, and priority.

1187 **Bone, Gavin.** The clue of pronounciation. TLS 21 Mr '29:241; W. S.
Weeks *ib.* 4 Ap '29:276.
'F "solid" for Q "sallied" . . . is likely to be a printer's instinctive normalization of what
(rightly or wrongly) he took to be a phonetic spelling' at 1.2.129.

1188 **Tannenbaum, Samuel Aaron.** Five notes on Hamlet. Angl 52:373–81 Ja '29.

1189 **Ramello, Giovanni.** The tragicall historie of Hamlet prince of Denmarke,
1603; con un'appendice sul testo anonimo Der bestrafte Brudermord. . . .
Turin, Bocca, 1930. 292p. tables. 23cm. (Studi sugli apocrifi Shake-
speariani)
Forme e problemi del testo. — Le anomalie del Q1 studiate nella loro genesi. — Origine

unitaria degli elementi spuri. — Come nacque il Q1. — La posizione del testo-base del Q1 di fronte al Q2 e al F. — La fortuna critica del Q1. — Appendice.

'. . . when W. Roberts entered *Hamlet* on the Stationers' Register in July, 1602, he already had in his possession the manuscript, probably in Shakespeare's autograph, which he printed towards the close of 1604. This manuscript was thus removed from all influence of the theatre, while the copy, ultimately used for the text of 1623, took its place and became familiar to the actor who, later in 1602 or in 1603, compiled the text published in the latter year of the Quarto.' (from TLS)

Rev: TLS 12 Je '30:492; P. Alexander Mod Lang R 26:199–200 '31; H. D. Gray Mod Lang N 46:410–12 '31.

1190 **Greg, sir Walter Wilson.** A question of plus or minus. R Eng Stud 6no23: 300–4 Jl '30.

Discussion of repeated lines bracketing either insertions or deletions in Q1, and elsewhere. Repr. in no.147.

1191 **Tannenbaum, Samuel Aaron.** Hamlet's pajock reconsidered. Sh Assn Bull 7no3:127–30 Jl '32.

Reads 'puttock' at 3.2.295.

1192 **Parrott, Thomas Marc.** Errors and omissions in the Griggs facsimile of the second quarto of Hamlet. Mod Lang N 49no6:376–9 Je '34.

Comparison of facsims. of 3 extant copies with the Griggs facsimile.

1193 **Paul, Henry Neill.** Players' quartos and duodecimos of Hamlet. Mod Lang N 49no6:369–75 Je '34. table.

Theobald's stage edition of 1743.—The Bettertonian text of 1683.

1194 —— Mr. Hughs' edition of Hamlet. Mod Lang N 49no7:438–43 N '34.

History of 12° ed. pub. in 1718, with list of later printings (p.442)

1195 **Stone, George Winchester.** Garrick's long lost alteration of Hamlet. Pub Mod Lang Assn 49no3:890–921 S '34.

'A comparison of cuts in acting copies of Hamlet' (p.903); 'Record of performances of Garrick's alteration of Hamlet' (p.904–5)

1196 **Tannenbaum, Samuel Aaron.** [Hamlet's too too solid flesh] Sh Assn Bull 9no4:217–18 Oc '34.

Sh. 'wrote "saltie"; the scribe read "sallid"; the compositor set it up as "sallied"; the Folio editor bungled it into "solid"'. (p.218)

1197 **Wilson, John Dover.** The manuscript of Shakespeare's Hamlet and the problems of its transmission, an essay in critical bibliography. Cambridge, C.U.P.; New York, Macmillan, 1934. (Repr. 1963) 2v.(xviii,435p.) tables. 17cm. (Shakespeare problems [IV])

Volume I: The texts of 1605 and 1623.—1. Introduction.—2. The character of the Folio Hamlet.—3. The character of the second quarto text.—4. Shakespeare and the Globe.— Volume II: Editorial problems and solutions.—1. Introduction.—2. The framework of the text.—3. The choice of variants.—4. Emendation.—Appendices: A. The textual evidence of Q1. B. Readings in F1 claimed by dr. Greg as deliberate alterations or corrections in the prompt-book. C. A classified list of the F1 readings departed from in the Cambridge Shakespeare text of Hamlet in 1866. D. A comparative table of stage-directions and speech-headings in Q2, F1 and Q1, together with parallels from the Globe Shakespeare. E. A table of variants in the dialogue of Hamlet, Q2 and F1.

Rev: TLS 16 Ag '34:563; *rf*. W. E. Whiting *ib*. 20 S '34:636; W. J. Lawrence Spect 153:198 '34; N&Q 167:161–2 '34; Nation 139:516 '34; I. Brown Observer 26 Ag '34; sir W. W. Greg Mod Lang R 30:80–6 '35; L. C. Knights New Criterion 14:506–11 '35;

L. L. Schücking Angl Beibl 46:97–104,129–37 '35; C. F. T. Brooke Yale R 24:618–22 '35; Commonweal 21:382 '35; P. M. Jack N.Y. Times Bk R 2 F '36:2,24; T. M. Parrott Mod Lang N 52:382–6 '37; M. Deutschbein Sh Jahrb 73:172–5 '37; N. B. Allen Sh Assn Bull 16:154–65 '41.

1198 **Alexander, Peter.** The text of Hamlet. R Eng Stud 12n048:385–400 Oc '36.

Substantially an examination of the system of punctuation in the New Cambridge ed. of *Ham.*

1199 **Allen, Percy.** Stage or study? TLS 11 Ap '36:316; sir W. W. Greg *ib.* 2 My '36:379; P. Allen 9 My '36:400; L. L. Schücking 16 My '36:420.

Discussion, centring on *Ham.*, on the question of whether Shakespeare wrote plays only for the stage, with no thought for a reading public.

1200 **Cairncross, Andrew S.** The problem of Hamlet, a solution. London, Macmillan, 1936. xix,205p. 17cm.

1. The problem.—2. The second quarto.—3. The First folio.—4. The first quarto.— 5. The ur-Hamlet.—6. The date of Hamlet.—7. The piracy: Shakespeare's first company. —8. The topical references.—9. The German Hamlet.—10. Further conclusions.—11. Lear and Leir.—12. A note on Macbeth.—13. Shakespearian chronology.—Appendix: Parallels between the first quarto of Hamlet and The contention and The true tragedy.

Ham., represented by Q2, was written for the Queen's men late 1588 or early 1589; this version was shortened for the stage, to form the F text; Q1 is a memorial piracy of the 'cut' version, made about Ag–S, 1593. The following plays, from which the pirate included echoes in Q1, were therefore written and acted before August 1593: *Jn., TN, H4, H6, Per., Oth., Wiv.*, The Spanish tragedy, Edward 2, and An humourous day's mirth.

Rev: H. B. Charlton Manchester Guardian 28 Ag '36:174; sir C. M. Bowra Spect 28 Ag '36:353–4; M. E. N. Cornhill Mag 154:381 '36; Q R 267:371 '36; Lond Merc 34:471 '36; TLS 19 D '36:1053; J. S[mart] Oxford Mag 55:232–3 '36; G. Connes Études Angl 1:96 '37; W. Empson Life & Letters 15:210–11 '37; J. B. Martin Dalhousie R 17:126 '37; M. Priess Eng Studien 71:402–7 '37; W. Keller Sh Jahrb 74:182–4 '38.

1201 **Handelman, Celia** and **R. W. Babcock.** One part wisdom, and ever two parts ——? Sh Assn Bull 11n04:191–225 Oc '36. diagr., tables.

'. . . in Q2 and F1 we have two accidentally printed texts of two transitional theatrical versions of a play in the process of being cut down from an unprinted two-part original (written in the late 1590's) to an acting version compressed for production in two hours.' (p.225)

1202 **Nosworthy, James M.** Dram of eale. TLS 21 Mr '36:244; sir W. W. Greg *ib.* 28 Mr '36:278; J. M. Nosworthy 25 Ap '36:356.

Reads 'So heauens candle' for 'To his own scandal' at 1.4.38.

1203 **Tannenbaum, Samuel Aaron.** That monster custom, an emendation of Hamlet, III,iv,161. Philol Q 15n04:401–5 Oc '36.

Reads 'doth ease / Of habits evil'.

1204 **Gray, Henry David.** The Hamlet first quarto pirate. Philol Q 16n04:394–401 Oc '37.

Argues against Cairncross's view in no.1200.

1205 **Parrott, Thomas Marc.** An emendation of the text of Hamlet. Sh Assn Bull 12n01:44–8 Ja '37.

Reads 'braves' for 'browes' at 3.3.5–7; *see also* no.1208.

1206 **Pyles, Thomas.** Rejected Q2 readings in the New Shakespeare Hamlet. Eng Lit Hist 4no2:114–46 Je '37. tables.

Q2 spellings, misreadings, and misprints . . . which are properly normalised, modernised, or corrected.—Rejected Q2 readings not involving meaning . . . some of which are worth preserving in a scholarly text based on Q2.—Rejected Q2 variants which nevertheless make sense.—Unnecessary emendations of Q2.—Q2 readings adopted by Wilson.—Totals of departures from Q2.—Summary and conclusion.

Examination of Dover Wilson's use of Q2 as copytext in the New Cambridge ed., concluding '1. Mr. Wilson has not been very faithful to his chosen text; 2. His edition is much more eclectic, much less revolutionary, than he leads us to believe; 3. Q2 is a much better text than even Mr. Wilson thinks it is'. (p.146)

1207 **Scott, Inez.** A Hamlet emendation. TLS 4 S '37:640.

Reads 'crack the ring' for 'crack the wind' at 1.3.108.

1208 **Tannenbaum, Samuel Aaron.** A Hamlet emendation. Sh Assn Bull 12no1: 64–6 Ja '37.

Supports superiority of F text without emendation, against Parrott; *see* no.1205.

1209 **Cripps, A. R.** A difficult line in Hamlet. TLS 8 Ja '38:28.

Emends 1.3.73–4 to 'And they of France of the chiefe rancke and station, / Are of all most select and generous in that'.

1210 **Tannenbaum, Samuel Aaron.** A Hamlet facsimile. Sh Assn Bull 13no2: 125–6 Ap '38.

A note on the Huntington library facsim. of *Ham.* Q2.

1211 **Lawrence, William John.** The folio text of Hamlet. (Bibliographical notes) TLS 30 D '39:760; C. L. Stainer *ib.* 6 Ja '39:7.

For country acting.—Act-divisions.

'. . . the Folio text . . . was fashioned by Shakespeare's company wholly and solely for their country acting.'

1212 **McManaway, James Gilmer** and **W. B. van Lennep.** A Hamlet emendation. Mod Lang R 34no1:68–70 Ja '39.

Readings in three playhouse copies of *Ham.* support Pope's emendation to 'Ouzle', a misreading of 'Wozell' at 3.2.396–7.

1213 **Kirschbaum, Leo.** The sequence of scenes in Hamlet. Mod Lang N 55no5: 382–7 My '40.

Arrangement of scenes in Q1 arises from memorial reconstruction.

1214 **Tannenbaum, Samuel Aaron.** Hamlet's sect and force. Sh Assn Bull 15no2: 125–6 Ap '40.

Supports F 'sect and force' at 1.3.26.

1215 —— Meddling with Shakspere's text. Sh Assn Bull 15no1:62–4 Ja '40.

On 'Comrade/courage' at 1.3.65.

1216 **Allen, N. B.** A note on Wilson's Hamlet. Sh Assn Bull 16no3:154–65 Jl '41.

The application of the conclusions of Dover Wilson's The manuscript of Shakespeare's Hamlet (no.1197) fails to produce a good text because the links in his chain of reasoning are 'pure conjecture', and his theory did not enable him to select the correct readings.

1217 **Duthie, George Ian.** The bad quarto of Hamlet, a critical study. Cambridge, C.U.P., 1941. xi,279p. 18cm. (Shakespeare problems, VI)

Foreword by W. W. Greg.—Introduction.—1. The external evidence for a pre-Shakespearian Hamlet.—2. The external evidence for a Shakespearian first draft.—3. The first quarto of Hamlet: the main controversy.—4. Blank verse peculiar to Q1.—5. The Marcellus theory.—6. The composite nature of the copy of Q1.—7. What stage of the Hamlet text-history underlies Q1?—8. Der bestrafte Brudermord.—9. The first quarto: conclusions.

Rev: TLS 22 F '41:94; N&Q 180:215–16 '41; C. J. Sisson Mod Lang R 36:404–7 '41; H. Spencer Mod Lang N 57:223–5 '42.

1218 **Shapin, Betty.** An experiment in memorial reconstruction. Mod Lang R 39no1:9–17 Ja '44.

An experimental reconstruction of a modern play supports Duthie's endorsement of the Marcellus reporter theory.

1219 **Smith, Robert Metcalf.** Hamlet said Pajock. J Eng Germ Philol 44no3: 292–5 Jl '45.

Rejoinder to Tannenbaum; *see* no.1191.

1220 **Tannenbaum, Samuel Aaron.** Claudius not a patchcock. Sh Assn Bull 20no3:156–9 Jl '45.

Defends his 'puttock' against Smith's 'pajock' and 'patchcock' at 3.2.295.

1221 **Gordon, R. G.** The crux in Hamlet. TLS 11 D '48:697; R. W. Cruttwell *ib.* 18 D '48:713; sir W. W. Greg 1 Ja '49:9.

Reads 'Doth all the substance of a noble doubt' at 1.4.37.

1222 **Jones, Harold Whitmore.** Hamlet, I.i.60–63. N&Q 194:535 D '49.

Supports the 'pollax' of Q2 at 1.1.63.

1223 **McManaway, James Gilmer.** The two earliest prompt books of Hamlet. Pa Bib Soc Am 43:288–320 '49. facsims.

Copies of 1676 Q and 1683 Q annotated by John Ward shortly after 1740.

1224 **Altman, George J.** Good advice from the bad Hamlet quarto. Educ Theat J 2:308–18 D '50. (Not seen)

1225 **Danks, Kenneth B.** An implication of bibliographical links. N&Q 195:73–4 F '50.

'Q2 is related to Q1 by bibliographical links. Therefore the Q2 text is related to the Q1 copy.' (p.74)

1226 **Nosworthy, James M.** Hamlet and the player who could not keep counsel. Sh Surv 3:74–82 '50.

Q1 pirated by actor who played Marcellus, Lucianus, and an attendant lord.

1227 **Savage, Derek S.** Hamlet & the pirates; an exercise in literary detection. London, Eyre & Spottiswoode [1950] 115p. 21cm.

1. The riddle of Fortinbras.—2. Thieves of mercy.—3. Shakespeare's manuscript.—4. Shakespeare as playwright and Shakespeare as man of letters.—5. Pirates and piracy.—6. Hamlet personified.—7. Two crafts directly meet.—8. A prologue to my brains.—9. Summary and conclusion.—Some additional notes.

Sh. arranged for the piracy of Q1, and added the pirate episode to the ms. for Q2.

Rev: B. Raymund Arizona Q 7:177–8 '50; TLS 15 D '50:796; 5 Ja '51:7; *rf*. D. S. Savage *ib*. 22 D '50:815; J. I. M. Stewart New Statesm 30 D '50:683.

1228 **Walker, Alice.** The textual problem of Hamlet, a reconsideration. R Eng
Stud new ser 2no8:328–38 Oc '51.

Q1, the bad quarto, 1603, and Q2, 1604-5.—Q2 and F1.

'... Q2 was printed (so far as was practicable) from a corrected copy of Q1, and ... F1,
in its turn, was printed from a corrected copy of Q2.' (p.328)

1229 **Danks, Kenneth B.** Hamlet: the problem of copyright. N&Q 197:47–8
F '52.

1230 **Bowers, Fredson Thayer.** A note on Hamlet, I.v.33 and II.ii.181. Sh Q
4no1:51–6 Ja '53.

'... a critic ... should follow either Q2 in *good-rootes*, or Warburton and F1 in *god-rots*'
(p.56). The Q2 reading is better.

1231 **Parsons, Howard.** The dram of eale. N&Q 200:409 S '55; D. Hart *ib.* 200:
500 N '55.

Reads 'the dram of ill / Doth all the noble substance oft divert / To his own scandal.' at
1.4.36-8.

1232 **Bowers, Fredson Thayer.** The printing of Hamlet Q2. Stud Bib 7:41–50 '55;
'addendum' 8:267–9 '56.

Running-title evidence confirming Brown's compositor attributions shows that Q2 was
ptd. on two presses.

1233 **Brown, John Russell.** The compositors of Hamlet Q2 and The merchant of
Venice. Stud Bib 7:17–40 '55.

Distinguishes the two Roberts compositors of *MV* (1600) in *Ham.*, and examines their
work in other books ptd. by Roberts around the same time.

1234 **Jenkins, Harold.** The relation between the second quarto and the Folio
text of Hamlet. Stud Bib 7:69–83 '55.

Rejects A. Walker's view that F was ptd. from a corrected copy of Q for theory that F
was ptd. from ms. copy prepared with some reference to Q.

1235 **Walker, Alice.** Collateral substantive texts, with special reference to
Hamlet. Stud Bib 7:51–67 '55.

Collateral texts must be edited eclectically. Gives tables of errors in *MV* and part of
Ham. as basis for general discussion of the problems of editing collateral texts.

1236 **Bowers, Fredson Thayer.** The textual relation of Q2 to Q1 Hamlet (I).
Stud Bib 8:39–66 '56. tables.

1237 —— Hamlet's sullied or solid flesh: a bibliographical case-history.
Sh Surv 9:44–8 '56.

Q1 'sallied' at 1.2.129 is a variant of 'sullied'; F 'solid' is a corruption.

1238 **Bronson, Bertrand Harris.** Costly thy habit, &c. Sh Q 7no2:280–1 '56.

For Q2 'chiefe' at 1.3.74 reads 'chive' or 'chieve', 'to prosper; flourish'.

1239 **Leech, Clifford.** Studies in Hamlet, 1901–1955. Sh Surv 9:1–15 '56.

'The text' (p.4–7)

1240 **Murphy, Mallie John.** Hamlet's sledded Polack. N&Q 201:509 D '56.

Reads 'studded pollax' at 1.1.63.

1241 **French, Joseph N.** Hamlet, an emendation. TLS 21 Je '57:381; sir W. W. Greg *ib.* 28 Je '57:397.

Reads 'diest' for 'didst' at 4.7.58.

1242 **Nowottny, Winifred M. T.** The application of textual theory to Hamlet's dying words. Mod Lang R 52no2:161–7 Ap '57.

At 5.2.355–6 reads 'O God, Horatio, what a wounded name / (Things standing thus unknown) shall't leave behind me!' with interesting reflections on the applicability of a textual theory to literary emendation.

1243 **Rockwell, K. A.** Hamlet I.iii.74: Of a most select. N&Q 202:84 F '57; *ib.* 202:148 Ap '57 [the same]

Reads 'Are of all most select'.

1244 **Cairncross, Andrew S.** Two notes on Hamlet. Sh Q 9no4:586–8 '58.

On 3.4.169, where Q2 'And either the devil' has an antithetical basis, and 5.2.218–36, where a marginal insertion is improperly placed.

1245 **David, R. W.** Sullied flesh. TLS 14 N '58:657.

1246 **Kökeritz, Helge.** This sullied solid flesh. Studia Neophilol 30no1:3–10 '58.

'It is either *solid* or *sullied*' (p. 4) against Bowers's 'sallied' at 1.2.129.

1247 **Jenkins, Harold.** Two readings in Hamlet: IV.v.152–3; IV.vii.58. Mod Lang R 54no3:391–5 Jl '59.

In sc. 5, the Q2 SP *Laer.* should precede 'How now . . .'; in sc. 7, reads 'diest' for 'didst'.

1248 **Byrne, Muriel St. Clare.** The earliest Hamlet prompt book in an English library. Theat Notebk 15no1:21–31 '60. facsims.

1782 ed. used for performance in Chester, 1785.

1249 **Chwalewik, Witold.** Hamlet, Q2, w zbiorach Biblioteki Uniwersyteckiej we Wrocławiu. Kwartalnik Neofilologiczny 7:102 '60.

Copy of *Ham.* Q2 formerly in Wrocław Municipal library has been deposited in the University of Wrocław library.

1250 **Flatter, Richard.** Solid or sullied and another query. Sh Q 11no4:490–3 '60.

Supports 'solid' at 1.2.129.

1251 **Jenkins, Harold.** Playhouse interpolations in the Folio text of Hamlet. Stud Bib 13:31–47 '60. tables.

F has some of the characteristics of a reported text, the superfluous interjections and exclamations in F being less likely omissions by the two Q compositors than memorial errors.

1252 **A new copy of Hamlet Q2.** Sh Q 11no4:497 '60.

Report of copy now in University of Warsaw [sic] library; *see* no.1249.

1253 **Ware, Malcolm.** Hamlet's sullied/solid flesh. Sh Q 11no4:490 '60.

Tennyson in 1883 originated the preference for the 'solid' reading at 1.2.129.

1254 **Weiner, Albert B.** Two Hamlet emendations. N&Q 207:143–5 Ap '62.

At 2.2.626, reads 'bleach' for 'blench'; at 3.1.150 reads 'fidge' for 'jig'.

1255 **Weiner, Albert B.** Evidence of a stray sheet in the Q1 Hamlet manuscript. AUMLA 19:88–92 My '63.

'. . . the Q1 scene containing the soliloquy and the Nunnery scene was interpolated, merely jammed into an alien spot.' (p.90)

1256 **Nosworthy, James M.** The death of Ophelia. Sh Q 15n04:345–8 '64.

Sh. 'inserted a last-minute addition in his foul papers' at 4.7.167–84; Q2 appears to offer a first draft, F was set from a marked copy of Q2.

1257 **Clayton, Thomas S.** A crux and no crux in Hamlet I.iii: safety: sanctity (21) and beguide : beguile (131). Sh Stud 3:42–50 '67.

Reads 'surety', and supports F 'beguile'.

1258 **Crawford, Jane.** Hamlet III.ii.146. R Eng Stud new ser 18n069:40–5 F '67.

Reads 'munching malice' for 'munching Mallico' at 3.2.147.

1259 **Torczon, Vern.** Paperback editions of Hamlet: the limits of editorial eclecticism. Coll Eng 28n07:519–24 Ap '67.

Demonstrates uniformity amongst recent 'new' ed., and suggests students would profit from use of an old-spelling ed.

INDIVIDUAL TEXTS—1 HENRY 4

1270 **Taylor, George Coffin.** Notes and comments on Henry IV, part I, Variorum edition. Sh Assn Bull 12n03:159–67 Jl '37.

Addenda and corrigenda.

1271 **Crundell, H. W.** The text of 1 Henry IV. N&Q 177:347–9 N '39.

Comparisons of the punctuation in Q1, Q5, and F1 'show the Folio reviser amending his copy with ideas of elocution in mind'.

1272 **Osborn, E. H. Douglas-.** Danke as a Dog. TLS 25 F '39:122.

Reads 'Bog' at 2.1.9–10.

1273 **Shaaber, Matthias A.** A textual dilemma in 1 Henry IV. Mod Lang N 54n04:276–8 Ap '39.

Reads 'bulky' for 'busky' at 5.1.2 in Q1.

1274 **Babcock, Robert Witbeck.** Mr. Wilson's Henry IV, parts I and II. Sh Assn Bull 22n02:69–80 Ap '47.

Review article on the New Cambridge ed.

1275 **Evans, Gwynne Blakemore.** Laying a Shakespearian ghost: 1 Henry IV, II.iv.225. Sh Q 5n04:427 '54.

Q1 'elfskin' is 'elsskin'.

1276 **Walker, Alice.** The Folio text of 1 Henry IV. Stud Bib 6:45–59 '54. tables.

Although F corrects 26 errors in Q5, it carries over about 200 from Q2–5. 'The tell-tale list of literal errors in B's pages is . . . suggestive of habitual carelessness and the suspicion that compositor B was unusually prone to take liberties with his copy is confirmed by an examination of the stage directions.' (p.55)

1277 **Evans, Gwynne Blakemore.** The Dering MS of Shakespeare's Henry IV and sir Edward Dering. J Eng Germ Philol 54n04:498–503 Oc '55.

1278 —— [Same]: *in* University of Illinois studies by members of the English department in memory of John Jay Parry. Urbana, Ill., 1955. p.38–43.

On the implications of Dering's manuscript of the first page of the ms.

1279 **Craig, Hardin.** The Dering version of Shakespeare's Henry IV. Philol Q 35n02:218–19 Ap '56.

Speculation that the ms., rather than deriving from Q5 (1613), reflects an older textual tradition.

INDIVIDUAL TEXTS—2 HENRY 4

1285 **A curious** piece of quarto typography. Shakespeariana 8n02:114–16 Ap '91; *rf.* E. E. Baker *ib.* 9n03:189–90 Jl '92. facsim.

Correspondence by T. L. De Vinne, E. R. Collins, and E. E. Baker on marks in Halliwell-Phillipps's copy of the 1600 Q.

1286 **Bayfield, M. A.** Elizabethan printing, an instructive blunder. TLS 23 S '20: 618–19; J. D. Wilson *ib.* 30 S '20:636; M. A. Bayfield 14 Oc '20:667–8.

The forms of the reset sheet E in *2H4* Q show that the ptr. 'regarded both spelling and abbreviation as largely a matter of indifference'.

1287 **Pollard, Alfred William.** The variant settings in 2 Henry IV, and their spelling. TLS 21 Oc '20:680; M. A. Bayfield *ib.* 11 N '20:738; A. W. Pollard 9 D '20:838; M. A. Bayfield 16 D '20:858; A. W. Pollard 23 D '20:877.

Detailed analysis of the ptg. of sheet E, further to the previous correspondence.

1288 **Schücking, Levin Ludwig.** The quarto of King Henry IV, part II. TLS 25 S '30:752.

The text was cut for political reasons, rather than shortened for performance.

1289 **McManaway, James Gilmer.** 'The cancel in the quarto of 2 Henry IV' *in* Prouty, Charles T. Studies in honor of A. H. R. Fairchild. Columbia [Miss.] 1946. p.67–80.

'. . . the cancel sheet E3–6 was not printed until after the completion of the rest of the play; . . . in Simmes's shop within a short time after the original publication; and . . . it was set by the compositor who set the rest of the quarto.' (p.80)

1290 **Maxwell, James C.** 2 Henry IV, II.iv.91ff. Mod Lang R 42no4:485 Oc '47.
For Q '& your ancient swaggrer' reads 'and [if] your ancient swagger, a [he]'.

1291 **Walker, Alice.** Quarto copy and the 1623 Folio: 2 Henry IV. R Eng Stud new ser 2no7:217–25 Jl '51. tables.
'. . . a manuscript was collated with a copy of Q in order to provide Jaggard with printed copy and . . . this manuscript was a fair copy of the foul papers (represented by Q).' (p.225)

1292 —— The cancelled lines in 2 Henry IV, IV.1.93, 95. Library ser5 6no2: 115–16 S '51.
The two lines were removed from F4ᵛ in Q1 mistakenly for two others in the following speech; F was therefore ptd. from a copy of Q with the erroneously corrected outer forme of sheet F.

1293 **Shaaber, Matthias A.** The Folio text of 2 Henry IV. Sh Q 6no2:135–44 '55.
Examines A. Walker's theory of annotated Q copy for F, and supports his suggestion of ms. copy with spelling evidence.

1294 **Phialas, Peter G.** Coleville of the Dale. Sh Q 9no1:86–8 '58.
At 4.3.10 'dale' is 'de'il' for 'devil'.

1295 **Ferguson, W. Craig.** The compositors of Henry IV, part 2, Much ado about nothing, The shoemaker's holiday, and The first part of the contention. Stud Bib 13:19–29 '60. tables.
The same Simmes compositor set the whole of 2H4 Q and Ado. Q and shared Q2 Contention and Holiday.

1296 **Humphreys, Arthur R.** A note on 2 Henry IV, II.iv.362–3. N&Q 208:98 Mr '63.
Reads 'attends' for Q 'blinds', F 'outbids' at 2.4.363.

1297 —— Two notes on 2 Henry IV. Mod Lang R 59no2:171–2 Ap '64.
At 4.3.45–6 reads 'three wordes' for Q 'there cosin'.

1298 **Smith, John Hazel.** The cancel in the quarto of 2 Henry IV revisited. Sh Q 15no3:173–8 '64.
Type concurrence during the ptg. of Q Ado. by Simmes shows that the cancel was ptd. after sheet G of Ado. The cancel inserts omitted matter.

1299 **Fusillo, Robert J.** Enter Prince John, quarto or Folio? Sh Q 14no2:179–82 '63.
Discusses the possibility of scene-change at 'Enter Prince John . . .' (4.3.26SD) and the authority of F: 'If it must be assumed that one text or the other is in error, then it really amounts to a toss-up.'

INDIVIDUAL TEXTS—HENRY 5

1310 **Bradley, Henry.** Table of green fields. Acad 45:331 Ap '94.
Reads 'and' as 'on' at 2.3.17.

1311 **Pollard, Alfred William** and **J. D. Wilson.** The stolne and surreptitious
Shakespearian texts. Henry V (1600). TLS 13 Mr '19:134.

1312 **Price, Hereward Thimbleby.** The text of Henry V. Newcastle-under-Lyme.
Mandley & Unett [1920] 55p. tables. 18cm.
1. Introduction.—2. History of the controversy.—3. The quarto text.—4. The Folio
text.—Textus receptus.
Rev: A. W. Pollard Mod Lang R 16:339–40 '21; H. M. Flasdieck Angl Beibl 34:230–2
'23; L. L. Schücking Eng Studien 57:300–2 '23.

1313 **Craig, Hardin.** The relation of the first quarto version to the First folio
version of Shakespeare's Henry V. Philol Q 6no3:225–34 Jl '27.
F represents a revised version of Q, which was ptd. from a 'genuine manuscript of the
play'.

1314 **Albright, Evelyn May.** The Folio version of Henry V in relation to Shakespeare's times. Pub Mod Lang Assn 43no3:722–56 S '28.
'. . . careful comparison of the texts shows a purposive cutting of materials in Quarto 1
as compared with Folio 1, stripping the play of its most significant personal and political
references.' (p.756)

1315 **Simison, Barbara Damon.** Stage-directions; a test for the playhouse origin
of the first quarto Henry V. Philol Q 11no1:39–56 Ja '32.
Comparison of the first quarto directions with the Folio directions.—Comparison of the
first quarto directions with directions in extant plots.—Comparison of the first quarto
directions with the directions of extant prompt-books.
Stage-direction evidence confirms the legitimacy of the copy for Q1, which represents an
authorized abridgement for performance, against H. Craig, no.1313.

1316 **Price, Hereward Thimbleby.** The quarto and Folio texts of Henry V.
Philol Q 12no1:24–32 Ja '33.
Maintains the superiority of the SD in F, against Simison, no.1315.

1317 **Okerlund, Gerda.** The quarto version of Henry V as a stage adaptation.
Pub Mod Lang Assn 49no3:810–34 S '34. tables.
Supports W. J. Lawrence's view that the bad Q are 'nothing more than unauthorized
stage adaptations made directly from the full theatre ms. by pirates who then performed
the plays in the provinces'. (p.80)

1318 **Walter, J. H.** With Sir John in it. Mod Lang R 41no2:237–45 Jl '46.
On textual evidence for revision in scenes in which Pistol and Fluellen appear.

1319 **Maxwell, James C.** Henry V, II.ii.103–104. N&Q 199:195 My '54.
Reads 'black on white' for F 'black and white' at 2.2.104.

1320 **Cairncross, Andrew S.** Quarto copy for Folio Henry V. Stud Bib 8:67–93
'56. facsims., tables.
F was set up from one or more corrected exemplars of the bad Q, and 'two editions of
the quarto, Q2 and Q3, were used as the basis for F'. (p.68)

1321 **Hulme, Hilda E.** Falstaff's death: Shakespeare or Theobald. N&Q 201: 283–7 Jl '56.

Supports F at 2.3.17.

1322 **Walker, Alice.** Some editorial principles, with special reference to Henry V. Stud Bib 8:95–111 '56. tables.

Shows 'what the analysis of compositors' errors in Henry V suggests about the kinds of error we must expect to find and where the greater concentration of errors is likely to be; and . . . how the basis of enquiry can be broadened by considering the evidence of the immediately antecedent text set by the same compositors'. (p.107)

1323 **Fogel, Ephim G.** A table of green fields: a defense of the Folio reading. Sh Q 9no4:485–92 '58.

1324 **Gittings, Robert William V.** Falstaff and sir Richard Grenville. TLS 9 My '58:255; L. Hotson; sir E. M. W. Tillyard; J. C. Maxwell *ib.* 16 My '58:269; N. Young; R. Walker 23 My '58:283; L. Hotson; C. H. Davidson 30 My '58:297; R. W. V. Gittings; A. L. Rowse; H. R. Williamson 9 Je '58:329; E. G. Coulson 20 Je '58:345; H. R. Williamson 27 Je '58:361.

On 2.3.17 and 'babled'.

1325 **Johnson, S. F.** A table of green fields once more. Sh Q 10no3:450–1 '59.

Notes 'table/talke' misprint in Ford's Loves sacrifice (2.1) in support of 'a' talke' or 'a' talkt'.

1326 **Nathan, Norman.** A Table of green fields. N&Q 204:92–4 Mr '59.

Supports F at 2.3.17.

1327 **Duthie, George Ian.** 'The quarto of Shakespeare's Henry V' *in* Papers mainly Shakespearian, collected by G. I. Duthie. Edinburgh [1964] p.106–30.

'. . . Q depends ultimately on F; . . . Q is full of memorial corruption—too extensive and too serious to be explained as due to mere scribal and compositorial error; and . . . Q cannot be a stenographic report.' (p.117)

INDIVIDUAL TEXTS—I HENRY 6

1335 **Evans, Gwynne Blakemore.** Rough notes on editions collated for I Henry VI. Sh Res Opp 2:41–8 '66.

Annotated checklist with summary of ed. for complete and partial collation.

1340 **Pollard, Alfred William.** The York and Lancaster plays in the Folio Shakespeare. TLS 19 S '18:438; 26 S '18:452.

Consideration of the problems of *H6* arising from examination of the relationship of F and Q *R3*.

1341 **Alexander, Peter.** Shakespeare's Henry VI and Richard III, with an introduction by Alfred W. Pollard. Cambridge, C.U.P., 1929. viii,229p. 18cm. (Shakespeare problems, III)

Introduction, by Alfred W. Pollard. 1. More bad quartos.—2. Shakespeare's earliest work.—3. Shakespeare a Queen's man.—4. Had Shakespeare a collaborator?—5. Verse tests.—The argument. 1. Greene's quotation from 3 Henry VI.—The bad quartos of 2 and 3 Henry VI.—3. The early plays of the schoolmaster from the country.—4. The alternative to Heminge and Condell.—5. The first period.

Revs: TLS 12 D '29:1053; P. Alexander *ib.* 19 D '29:1081; Eng R 49:641 '29; N&Q 157:269 '29; H. D. Sykes R Eng Stud 6:323–9 '30; W. Keller Sh Jahrb 66:220–2 '30; E. Eckhardt Deutsche Literaturzeitung 51:1849–51 '30; E. Groth Angl Beibl 41:97–102 '30; F. C. Danchin R Anglo-Am 547–8 '30; E. H. C. Oliphant Mod Lang N 45:543–6 '30; C. F. T. Brooke J Eng Germ Philol 29:442–6 '30; Spectator 4 Ja '30:24.

1342 **Greer, Clayton Alvis.** More about the revision date of 1 Henry VI. N&Q 195:112 Mr '50.

Location of an early source for the Talbot epitaph supports his previously suggested early revision date.

INDIVIDUAL TEXTS—2 HENRY 6

1350 **Alexander, Peter.** II Henry VI and the copy for The contention, 1594. TLS 9 Oc '24:629–30.

'. . . the notion that The contention is an early draft of II Henry VI is demonstrably unsound: and to support the view that it is an imperfect version of that play by establishing by a comparison of the texts (1) that the greater part of The contention is derived from reports supplied by two of the actors . . . (2) that in places, however, it was printed from a fragmentary transcript of II Henry VI.' (p.629)

1351 **Pollard, Alfred William.** The quartos of The contention and Richard duke of York. TLS 27 N '24:797.

Alexander's conclusions make it probable that the bad Q of *Ham.* and *Wiv.* were also memorially reconstructed by actors.

1352 **Baldwin, Thomas Whitfield.** Texts and prompt copies. TLS 19 Ap '28:290.

Chambers's notice of an actor's name in F *2H6* indicates that it was ptd. from prompt copy.

1353 **Doran, Madeleine.** Actors' names in The contention and 2 Henry VI. Philol Q 7no4:399–400 Oc '28.

'The circumstances of actors' names in the Contention points to that play's being a prompt-copy rather than a pirated version of 2 Henry VI, as Mr. Alexander suggests.' (p.400)

1354 **Doran, Madeleine.** Henry VI, parts II and III, their relation to The contention and The true tragedy. Iowa City, University of Iowa, 1928. 88p. table. 23cm. (Iowa. University. Humanistic studies 4no4)

1. The Contention and the True tragedy.—2. 2 and 3 Henry VI.—3. The relation of the quartos to the Folio: a bibliographical examination.—4. The relation of the quartos to the Folio: a comparison of matter.—5. Conclusions.—Appendix: a comparison . . . on the basis of their sources.

The Q are adapted or reported versions of the F plays.

Rev: W. Keller Sh Jahrb 66:222–3 '30.

1355 **Brooke, Charles Frederick Tucker.** Elizabethan proof corrections in The first part of the contention, 1600. Huntington Lib Bull 2:87–9 N '31. facsims., table.

Ms. corrections in sheet B in the Bridgewater copy of Q2.

1356 —— Elizabethan proof corrections. Mod Lang N 47no3:144 Mr '32.

Corrects his former assumption that the outer forme of sig. B of The contention was ptd. before the inner.

1357 **Greer, Clayton Alvis.** The York and Lancaster quarto–folio sequence. Pub Mod Lang Assn 48no3:655–704 S '33. tables.

Supports Tucker Brooke's view that 'there is a lost text from which the Contention and the True tragedy, the Whole contention, and the Folio all came separately or independently'. (p.655)

1358 **McKerrow, Ronald Brunlees.** A note on Henry VI, part II, and The contention of York and Lancaster. R Eng Stud 9no34:157–69 Ap '33.

A memorial reconstruction of the Contention, based on the 1577 ed. of Holinshed was ptd. in 1594 and 1600; a copy of the 1594 ed. with some improvements was used for the ed. of 1619; for F some revision from the Holinshed ed. of 1587 was made to the prompt-book.

1359 —— 2 Henry VI and The contention, a correction. R Eng Stud 9no35: 315–16 Jl '33.

1360 **Everett, A. L.** A note on Shakspere's Henry VI. Sh Assn Bull 10no2: 106–8 Ap '35.

Supports view of The contention as a piracy of 2 and 3 *H6*.

1361 **Greg, sir Walter Wilson.** Henry VI and the Contention plays. Pub Mod Lang Assn 50no3:919–20 S '35.

Comments on Greer; *see* no.1357.

1362 **Knickerbocker, William S.** Shakespeare excursion: who wrote 2 and 3 Henry VI? Sewanee R 45no3:328–42 Jl/S '37.

Survey of modern scholarship, particularly C. F. T. Brooke's The authorship of the second and third part of king Henry VI. Connecticut Acad Arts & Sci Trans 17:141–211 Jl '12.

1363 **McKerrow, Ronald Brunlees.** A note on the bad quartos of 2 and 3 Henry VI and the Folio text. R Eng Stud 13no49:64–72 Ja '37.

Marked similarities between passages of the Q and F texts can be explained by the F editor's use of Q to make up defective matter.

1364 **Jordan, John E.** The reporter of Henry VI, part 2. Pub Mod Lang Assn 64n04:1089–1113 D '49. tables.

'. . . there could have been an important bit player who took the parts of Armourer–Spirit–Mayor–Vaux–Scales, and he could have reported the play.' (p.1113)

1365 **Prouty, Charles Tyler.** The Contention and Shakespeare's 2 Henry VI. New Haven, Yale U.P.; London, G. Cumberlege, O.U.P., 1954. ix,157p. 21cm.

1. The problem.—2. Variations in playing.—3. Style.—4. Character and structure.—5. Memorial reconstruction.—6. Revision.—7. Conclusions.—Appendix: Parallel passages cited in the text.

'. . . the sources point inevitably to the fact that Q cannot have been derived from F. The variations in playing enforce this conclusion, while the style of the unique material in the Folio proves that we have to do with revision, for no theory of memory, even abetted by abridgment, can explain the absence of this material from the Quarto text. . . . If Q is not then derived from the Folio and is an independent text, it can no longer be regarded as a version of a play written by Shakespeare.' (p.120)

Rev: G. B. Harrison Sat R 25 S '54:22; G. B. Evans J Eng Germ Philol 53:628–37 '54; U.S. Q Bk R 10:333 '54; C. G. Thayer Bks Abroad 29:349 '55; W. T. Hastings Sh Q 6:119–21 '55; H. T. Price Mod Lang N 70:527–9 '55; J. Crow Sh Q 7:420–31 '56; H. Heuer Sh Jahrb 92:391–3 '56; G. I. Duthie Mod Philol 53:200–4 '56; J. G. McManaway Sh Surv 9:153–4 '56; G. Lambin Langues Modernes 49:463 '56; J. P. Brockbank R Eng Stud new ser 8:60–3 '57.

1366 **Greer, Clayton Alvis.** The quarto–Folio relationship in 2 and 3 Henry VI once again. N&Q 201:420–1 Oc '56.

1367 —— More about the actor-reporter theory in The contention and The true tragedy. N&Q 202:52–3 F '57.

The coincidence and number of SD tells against the actor-reporter theory.

1368 **McManaway, James Gilmer.** 'The Contention and 2 Henry VI' *in* Korninger, Siegfried, *ed.* Studies in English language and literature presented to professor dr. Karl Brunner. Wein-Stuttgart, 1957. p.143–54.

'The purpose of this paper will be to show by examination of the verse, the stage directions, and the speech headings that The contention is not a substantive play, . . . and that the manuscript from which it was printed in 1594 was neither an author's foul sheets nor a prompt book.' (p.143–4)

1369 **Jackson, Macdonald P.** Langbaine and the memorial versions of Henry VI, parts II and III. N&Q 209:134 Ap '64.

Gerard Langbaine, New catalogue, 1688, records derivation of The contention and The true tragedy from 2 and 3 *H6*.

1370 **Hibbard, George R.** An emendation in 2 Henry VI, I.iv. N&Q 210:332 S '65.

At 1.4.74–5 reads '. . . these oracles are hard, / Hardly attain'd and hardly understood'.

1380 **Alexander, Peter.** 3 Henry VI and Richard, duke of York. TLS 13 N '24:730.

'... in the Folio we have the earlier and original text of which the Quarto gives only a stolen or surreptitious copy.'

1385 **Rossiter, A. P.** A passage in Henry VIII. TLS 15 Jl '49:459.

'No emendations are required' at 1.1.72f.

1386 **Foakes, R. A.** On the First folio text of Henry VIII. Stud Bib 11:55–60 '58. tables.

Copy for F was a carefully prepared ms. based on foul papers, by one hand, and had not been used in the theatre.

1387 **Clayton, Thomas S.** Internal evidence and Elizabethan dramatic authorship, an essay in literary history and method: review article. Sh Stud 4:350–76 '68.

'The "ye/you" test and the authorship and composition of Henry VIII' (p.365–74): detailed examination of compositorial influence on the distribution of 'ye' and 'you' taken as a sign of Fletcher's share in *H8*. Contextual, rhetorical considerations have not been given proper weight.

1395 **Bartlett, Henrietta Collins.** Quarto editions of Julius Caesar. Library ser3 4no14:122–32 Ap '13.

TP transcrs., collations, and bibliogr. discussion for six ed., 1684–91.

———

1398 **Madan, Falconer.** A Shakespeare emendation. TLS 23 Ap '25:284; H. Cuningham; P. Chare *ib*. 30 Ap '25:300; A. C. R. Carter 14 My '25:335.

Reads 'milice' for 'malice' at 3.1.174.

1399 **Tannenbaum, Samuel Aaron.** An emendation to Julius Caesar. Sh R 1no5:322–3 S '28.

Reads 'puts', i.e. 'put'st' for 'path' at 2.1.83.

1400 —— Adding a word to Shakspere's vocabulary. Sh Assn Bull 11n02:120–1 Ap '36.

Reads 'arms, unstrength'd' at 3.1.174 for 'Armes in strength'.

1401 **Rossiter, A. P.** Line-division in Julius Caesar. TLS 29 Jl '39:453–4; R. B. McKerrow *ib.* 19 Ag '39:492.

Division of long lines which, left undivided, would not have resulted in turn-overs, was not compositorial as McKerrow had suggested, but probably dramatic in intention.

1402 **Evans, Gwynne Blakemore.** Shakespeare's Julius Caesar, a seventeenth century manuscript. J Eng Germ Philol 41n04:101–17 Oc '42.

Descr. and collation of a ms. copy derived from F2, around 1665.

1404 **Goldstein, Malcolm.** Pope, Sheffield, and Shakespeare's Julius Caesar. Mod Lang N 71n01:8–10 Ja '56.

Pope's ed. influenced by Sheffield's adaptation, The tragedy of Julius Caesar.

1405 **Stirling, Brents.** Julius Caesar in revision. Sh Q 13n02:187–205 '62.

Variant SP at 2.1.86–228 and 4.3.129–66 provide evidence of revision.

1406 **Velz, John W.** The text of Julius Caesar in the second folio: two notes. Sh Q 20n01:95–8 '69. tables.

1. Sophistication in the Methuen facsimile.—2. Press-correction in the second folio.

1407 —— Pirate Hills and the quartos of Julius Caesar. Pa Bib Soc Am 63:177–93 '69.

Discussion of ptg. of six restoration Q listed by Bartlett, with textual notes. 'Appendix: Original readings in QU4.' (p.193)

INDIVIDUAL TEXTS—KING JOHN

1415 **Maxwell, James C.** Notes on King John. N&Q 195:75–6 F '50.

1416 —— King John: textual notes. N&Q 195:473–4 Oc '50.

1417 **Price, George Rennie.** Compositors' methods with two quartos reprinted by Augustine Matthewes. Pa Bib Soc Am 44:269–74 '50.

Ptg. analysis of The first and second part of the troublesome raigne, 1622.

INDIVIDUAL TEXTS—KING LEAR

1425 **Tannenbaum, Samuel Aaron.** Shakspere's King Lear, a concise bibliography. New York, 1940. (Repr. Port Washington, N.Y., Kennikat pr. [1967]) x,101p. 23cm. (Elizabethan bibliographies, no.16)

1428 **Law, Robert Adger.** On the date of King Lear. Pub Mod Lang Assn 21no2:462–77 '06.
Survey of the publishing history of *Lr.* and Leir.

1429 **Cunnington, R. H.** The revision of King Lear. Mod Lang R 5no4:445–53 Oc '10.
F represents a text revised from Q, to which it adds substantial matter.

1430 **Jespersen, Otto.** 'A marginal note on Shakespeare's language and a textual crux in King Lear' *in* Gollancz, sir Israel, *ed.* A book of homage to Shakespeare. [Oxford, 1916] p.481–3.
Reads 'like—a better way' at 4.3.21.

1431 **Doran, Madeleine.** The text of King Lear. Stanford university, Calif., Stanford U.P.; London, H. Milford, O.U.P., 1931. 148p. tables. 25cm. (Stanford university publications. University ser. Lang & Lit 4no2)
1. History of the problem.—2. The relation of Q2 to Q1.—3. The First folio version of the play.—4. The copy for the Folio.—5. The first quarto.
Rev: TLS 31 Mr '32:227; E. Eckhardt Eng Studien 67:272–4 '32; R. M. Smith J Eng Germ Philol 31:296–9 Ap '32; G. Tillotson Mod Lang R 38:251–2 Ap '33; W. Wokatsch Archiv 163:269–70 '33; B. A. P. Van Dam Eng Stud 15:99–105 '33; P. Alexander R Eng Stud 10:353–6 '34; W. Keller Zeitschrift für französischen und englischen Unterricht 33:210 '34.

1432 **Rendall, Vernon.** A point in King Lear. TLS 28 My '31:427; P. Simpson *ib.* 4 Je '31:447; J. A. H. Coates 11 Je '31:467.
Reads 'Ye jewels' at 1.1.271 for 'The jewels', from an incorrect expansion of ye for ẛ.

1433 **Adams, Joseph Quincy.** The quarto of King Lear and shorthand. Mod Philol 31no1:135–63 N '33.
Q was a shorthand report, using Bright's Charactery.

1434 **Doran, Madeleine.** Elements in the composition of King Lear. Stud Philol 30no1:34–58 Ja '33.
Theory of revision to explain textual irregularities.—Sources of the play as structural elements.—Minor additions and alterations.—Revisions in the minor plot.—Textual irregularity in reflective passages.—Sources of reflective passages.—Revision in the part of Lear.—The case for revision.

Exposition of a theory of composition founded on her theory that Q1 was set from a revised first draft of the play; irregular printing of verse and prose reflects similar irregularity in ms. and is evidence of a revised ms.

1435 **Greg, sir Walter Wilson.** The function of bibliography in literary criticism illustrated in a study of the text of King Lear. Neophilol 18:241–62 '33.
2. The order of the early quartos.—The variants between copies of the first quarto.—The source of the quarto text.—The source of the Folio text.—The relation of the texts.
'. . . we reach the remarkable conclusion that the testimony of Quarto and Folio together is of appreciably less authority than that of the Folio alone' (p.262). Repr. in no.147.

1436 —— Some textual notes on Lear. TLS 9 N '33:771.

1437 **Doran, Madeleine.** The quarto of King Lear and Bright's shorthand. Mod Philol 33no2:139–57 N '35.

Shows, against Adams, that Q cannot be explained by use of Charactery, which was in any case inadequate.

1438 **Hubler, Edward.** 'The verse lining of the first quarto of King Lear' *in* Craig, Hardin, *ed.* Essays in dramatic literature: the Parrott presentation volume. Princeton, 1935. p.421–41.

Mislineations by compositor attempting to save space.

1439 **Van Dam, Bastiaan Adriaan P.** The text of Shakespeare's Lear. Louvain, Librairie universitaire, C. Uystpruyst, 1935. 110p. tables. 25cm. (Materials for the study of old English drama. New ser 10)

1. The first quarto of King Lear.—2. The Jaggard quarto.—3. The folio text.—4. Our approach to the first scene.—Appendix: Dr. Greg's views.

The 1608 Q was ptd. from a prompt-book prepared from Sh. holograph; F is 'a blending, partly reprinted from the Jaggard quarto [of 1619], partly set up from the prompt-book of 1623, and "overseen" by Heminge (and Condell)'. (p.76)

Rev: R. W. Zandvoort Eng Stud 18:48 '35; W. Keller Sh Jahrb 72:148–9 '36; M. Doran Mod Philol 34:430–3 '37; R. A. Law J Eng Germ Philol 36:275–6 '37; H. Craig Mod Lang N 53:204–7 '38.

1440 **Greg, sir Walter Wilson.** King Lear, mislineation and stenography. Library ser4 17no2:172–83 S '36.

Incorrect line-division does not indicate a stenographer; the persistent mislining in Q 'suggests that the compositor was dealing with undivided copy' (p.179). Lr. was reported and 'it was based on a shorthand report'. (p.180)

1441 **Cuningham, Henry.** King Lear, III.7.65. TLS 19 Mr '38:188.

Reads 'cruel'st' for 'cruels'.

1442 **Kirschbaum, Leo.** How Jane Bell came to print the third quarto of Shakespeare's King Lear. Philol Q 17no3:308–11 Jl '38.

'. . . on the basis of an assignment of Leir, Jane Bell printed and published Q3 of Shakespeare's King Lear. She did violate Flesher's copyright . . . unwittingly.' (p.311)

1443 **Greg, sir Walter Wilson.** The variants in the first quarto of King Lear, a bibliographical and critical inquiry. London, Ptd. for the Bibliographical society at the O.U.P., 1940. (Repr. New York, Haskell house, 1966) 192p. tables. 21cm. (Bib Soc Trans. Supplement no.15)

Part one — Bibliographical. 1. Introduction.—2. The copies and their formes.—3. The variants. Table of variants.—4. Bibliographical analysis.—Appendix 1: Errors in the Praetorius facsimile.—Appendix 2: Misprints in the original.—Appendix 3: Doubtful readings.—Appendix 4: Early manuscript corrections.—Table of lines and pages.—Part two — Critical.—Postscript.

Rev: TLS 16 N '40:584; M. Doran R Eng Stud 17:468–74 '41; L. Kirschbaum Mod Lang N 56:624–6 '41; J. G. McManaway Mod Lang R 37:86–8 '42.

1444 **Kirschbaum, Leo.** The true text of King Lear. Sh Assn Bull 16no3:140–53 Jl '41.

Shows from the 1865 Globe, 1901 Arden, and 1940 Kittredge ed. how the memorially reconstructed Q has corrupted the received text.

1445 **Tannenbaum, Samuel Aaron.** An emendation in King Lear. Sh Assn Bull 16no1:58–9 Ja '41.

Reads 'toe th'' for F 'to'th' at 1.2.21.

1446 **Kirschbaum, Leo.** The true text of King Lear. Baltimore, Johns Hopkins pr., 1945. ix,81p. 21cm.

Introduction.—Table of passages analyzed.—Textual analyses.—Epilogue.

F was ptd. from a memorially reconstructed Q later corrected from a playhouse transcript.

Rev: TLS 13 Oc '45:488; Duke Univ J 37:32 '45; B. Maxwell Philol Q 24:280–1 '45; S. A. Small Mod Lang N 61:68–70 '46; M. Doran J Eng Germ Philol 47:227–30 '46; G. I. Duthie Mod R 41:326–30 '46; R. H. Perkinson Mod Lang Q 7:503–4 '46; J. M. Nosworthy Library ser5 1:77–9 '46; sir W. W. Greg R Eng Stud 22:230–4 '46; H. B. Charlton Manchester Guardian Wkly 54:151 '46; J. B. Fort Langues Modernes 44:415–16 '50.

1447 **Greg, sir Walter Wilson.** The staging of King Lear. R Eng Stud 22no87: 229 Jl '46.

Accepts view that F act and scene division may be work of F editor (*rf.* R Eng Stud 16:300–3 Jl '40)

1448 **Small, Samuel Asa.** The King Lear quarto. Sh Assn Bull 21no4:177–80 Oc '46.

Review article on Kirschbaum, no.1446.

1449 **Bowers, Fredson Thayer.** An examination of the method of proof correction in Lear. Library ser5 2no1:20–44 Je '47. table.

Analysis of Greg's hypothesis in light of evidence from headlines indicating three-skeleton ptg.

1450 **Williams, Philip.** The compositor of the Pied Bull Lear. Stud Bib 1:61–8 '48. tables.

Okes's 1608 Q was set, from spelling evidence, by the compositor B of Webster's The white devil (Q1 1612) and Robert Armin's The history of the two maids of More-clacke (Q1 1609)

1451 **Duthie, George Ian.** Elizabethan shorthand and the first quarto of King Lear. Oxford, B. Blackwell, 1949. 82p. diagrs., tables. 22cm.

'I do not believe that any of the shorthand systems known to have been available for use in 1608 was sufficiently practicable to have been able to convey from performance a report of the standard found in Q Lear.' (p.2)

Rev: TLS 12 My '50:290; N&Q 195:308 '50; J. G. McManaway Sh Q 2:85–6 '51; W. Matthews Mod Lang R 16:263–5 '51; R. Flatter Sh Jahrb 88:223–4 '52.

1452 **Muir, Kenneth.** King Lear, IV.i.10. TLS 3 Je '49:365; W. Bliss *ib.* 24 Je '49:413; R. Flatter 22 Jl '49:473.

Suggests 'poorly 'rayd?' for 'poorly led?'

1453 **Owen, W. J. B.** A dogge, so bade in office. N&Q 194:141–2 Ap '49.

A misreading rather than mishearing, at 4.6.163.

1454 **Williams, George Walton.** A note on King Lear, III.ii.1–3. Stud Bib 2:175–82 '49.

In Q, a comma after 'blow' was mistakenly dropped to the end of the next line.

1455 **Muir, Kenneth.** King Lear, II.iv.170. N&Q 196:170 Ap '51.

Reads 'blister her' for F 'blister'.

1456 **Walker, Alice.** King Lear; the 1608 quarto. Mod Lang R 47no3:376–8 Jl '52.

'Owing to the peculiarities of the quarto's transmission, the Folio is, of course, our best authority, but Q and the Folio between them may preserve a better text of Lear than is generally supposed.' (p.378)

1457 **Cauthen, Irby B.** Compositor determination in the First folio King Lear. Stud Bib 5:73–80 '52/3.

'. . . Lear was set by one compositor, B, of the Folio.' (p.80)

1458 **Parrott, Thomas Marc.** God's or gods in King Lear, V.iii.17. Sh Q 4no4: 427–32 Oc '53.

Surveys capitalization and the use of the apostrophe with the genitive singular in early ed. and concludes '. . . the original "Gods" of line 17 should be modernised "gods"'. (p.432)

1459 **Williams, Philip.** Two problems in the Folio text of King Lear. Sh Q 4no4:451–60 Oc '53.

Divides the text between compositor B and another on spelling evidence, and shows that B was not setting directly from a corrected copy of Q but from ms. copy. 'In 1623, the prompt-book of King Lear was a conflation of "good" pages from QI supplemented by inserted manuscript leaves to replace corrupt passages of QI. Reluctant to let the official prompt-book leave their possession, the company permitted a scribe to make a transcript of this conflated text to serve as copy for the First folio.' (p.460)

1460 **Anderson, D. M.** A conjecture in King Lear, IV.ii.57. N&Q 199:331 Ag '54.

Discussion of proof variants of passage in Q not in F, and reads 'With plumed helm his state begins thy rout(e)'.

1461 **Jazayery, Mohammad Ali** and **R. A. Law.** Three texts of King Lear, their differences. Univ Texas Stud Eng 32:14–24 '54.

Assessments of the Globe, Neilson, and Kittredge ed.

1462 **Cairncross, Andrew S.** The quartos and the Folio text of King Lear. R Eng Stud new ser 6no23:252–8 Jl '55. tables.

'. . . both quartos of Lear, after correction from an authoritative manuscript, were in fact used as copy, or basis, for F.' (p.258)

1463 **Musgrove, S.** King Lear I.i.170. R Eng Stud new ser 8no30:170–2 My '57.

Notes variant in Grey copy of F which suggests 'sentences' as the correct reading at 1.1.173.

1464 **Kahn, Sholom J.** Enter Lear mad. Sh Q 8no3:311–29 '57.

Incidental evaluation of Q/F references to Lear's madness suggests that 'the same editor who deleted the words "mad" and "running" from the stage directions may also have sought the occasions . . . for smoothing some of the prose speeches into iambic pentameters' (p.320) and for making cuts.

1465 **Bolton, Joseph S. G.** Wear and tear as factors in the textual history of the quarto version of King Lear. Sh Q 11n04:428–38 '60.

Offers a 'new explanation for many . . . single-word variants between Q and F' and suggests F was ptd. from Sh. ms. used as a prompt-book.

1466 **Ringler, William.** Exit Kent. Sh Q 11n03:312–17 '60.

Q 2.4.289 SD is incorrect; at 2.4.135 'a stage direction has been omitted in both the Quarto and the Folio'. (p.312)

1467 **Craig, Hardin.** The composition of King Lear. Renaiss Pa 1961:56–61 '62.

Q1 was ptd. from foul papers; F from a transcript of a revised prompt-book.

1468 **Hogan, J. J.** Cutting his text according to his measure: a note on the Folio Lear. Philol Q 42n01:72–81 Ja '62.

Some variations between Q and F may be explained by the F compositor's tampering with the text to fit it to the width of his measure.

1469 **Smidt, Kristian.** The quarto and the Folio Lear; another look at the theories of textual derivation. Eng Stud 45n02:149–62 Ap '64.

The diversity and incompatibility of the theories explaining Q as a memorially reconstructed text, and the relative goodness of Q, make it unlikely that Q is a bad text.

1470 **Honigmann, Ernst Anselm Joachim.** Spelling tests and the first quarto of King Lear. Library ser5 20n04:310–15 D '65. tables.

1471 **Ingham, Patricia.** A note on the aural errors in the first quarto of King Lear. Sh Stud 3:81–4 '67.

Reclassification of the 'aural errors' shows 'that those unmistakably aural are fewer than generally supposed, and that whoever was responsible for them used an advanced or vulgar form of speech'. (p.84)

1472 **McNeir, Waldo Forest.** The last lines of King Lear, V.iii.320–327. Eng Lang N 4n03:183–8 Mr '67.

The final speech, assigned to Albany in Q2, Edgar in F, should be divided between the two.

INDIVIDUAL TEXTS—LOVE'S LABOUR'S LOST

1480 **Jonas, Maurice.** Love's labour's lost. N&Q ser9 2:85 Jl '98.

On the Kean copy, in his collection.

1481 **Charlton, H. B.** A disputed passage in Love's labour's lost. Mod Lang R 12n03:279–85 Jl '17.

Against Theobald's assignation of 'The party is gone' to Costard, at 5.2.678.

1482 —— A textual note on Love's labour's lost. Library ser3 8no32:355–70 Oc '17.

Inconsistencies of nomenclature at 2.1.115–27 and 2.1.195 derive from Sh. manuscript and not from ptg. error. F was set from Q.

1483 **Fort, J. A.** Love's labour's lost. TLS 21 Ag '24:513; C. H. Herford; J. D. Wilson *ib.* 28 Ag '24:525; J. A. Fort [and addenda] 4 S '24:540.

1484 **Dunstan, W. R.** Perttaunt. TLS 3 Oc '36:791; H. Cuningham *ib.* 20 Oc '36:815; W. R. Dunstan 17 Oc '36:839; J. D. Wilson 24 Oc '36:863; W. R. Dunstan 31 Oc '36:887; J. D. Wilson 7 N '36:908.

Discussion of Dunstan's suggestion, 'forteune', at 5.2.67.

1485 **Kirschbaum, Leo.** Is the Spanish tragedy a leading case? Did a bad quarto of Love's labour's lost ever exist? J Eng Germ Philol 37no3:501–12 Oc '38.

A survey of contemporary TP formulas leads to conclusion that 'there is almost no probability that a bad quarto preceded' Burby's *LLL*.

1486 **Strathmann, Ernest A.** The textual evidence for The school of night. Mod Lang N 56no3:176–86 Mr '41.

'. . . there is no independent evidence . . . to establish the Q reading "Schoole of night" as an allusion to Ralegh and his associates' (p.186): 4.3.255.

1487 **Carter, Albert Howard.** On the use of details of spelling, punctuation, and typography to determine the dependence of editions. Stud Philol 44no3: 497–503 Jl '47. tables.

On the relationship of Ling's text of 'The passionate shepherd's song' in England's Helicon to that of *LLL* and *PP*.

1488 **Danks, Kenneth B.** L.L.L. N&Q 193:545 D '48; R. L. Eagle *ib.* 194:64 F '49.

On the bibliographical warrant for the customary orthography of the title.

1489 **Babcock, Weston.** Fools, fowls, and perttaunt-like in Love's labour's lost. Sh Q 2no3:211–19 Jl '51.

Reads 'partlet-like' at 5.2.67, after Kellner.

1490 **Allen, E. G.** Cruxes in Love's labour's lost. N&Q 200:287 Jl '55; I. A. Shapiro *ib.* 200:287–8 Jl '55.

At 4.3.177, reads 'With men of like inconstancy', and 'style' for 'Schoole' at 4.3.255.

1491 **Pafford, John Henry P.** Schoole of night. N&Q 202:143 Ap '57.

Reads 'shield' at 4.3.255; gives a comprehensive survey of previous suggestions.

1492 **Lambrechts, Guy.** The brief and tedious of it; note sur le texte de Love's labour's lost. Études Angl 17:269–83 Juin/S '64.

'Nous nous proposons de montrer que l'hypothèse d'un abrégement . . . permet de rendre compte de l'état des textes, dont plusieurs passages sont embarrassants.' (p.269)

INDIVIDUAL TEXTS—MACBETH

1500 **Tannenbaum, Samuel Aaron.** Shakspere's Macbeth, a concise bibliography. New York, 1939. (Repr. Port Washington, N.Y., Kennikat pr. [1967]) x,165p. 23cm. (Elizabethan bibliographies, no.9)

1505 **Jonas, Maurice.** Macbeth, 1673. N&Q ser8 4:386 N '93.

1506 **Cuningham, Henry.** Macbeth, IV.iii.34. TLS 26 F '25:128; N. W. H. ib. 5 Mr '25:156.
Reads 'assured' for 'affear'd'.

1507 **Spencer, Hazelton.** D'Avenant's Macbeth and Shakespeare's. Pub Mod Lang Assn 40no3:619–44 S '25.
Bibliogr. and textual discussion of restoration texts, with analysis of D'Avenant's 1674 version.

1508 **Bald, Robert Cecil.** Macbeth and the short plays. R Eng Stud 4no16:429–30 Oc '28.
Stage directions, and comparison with other short plays, support Pollard's thesis of a class of short plays given at private performances and theatrically distinct from longer texts.

1509 **Dunlap, A. R.** What purgative drug? Mod Lang N 54no2:92–4 F '39.
Reads 'Tyme' (thyme) for 'Cyme' at 5.3.55.

1510 **Sullivan, Frank.** Cyme, a purgative drug. Mod Lang N 56no4:263–4 Ap '41.
'. . . the line in question . . . was printed correctly in the First Folio.' (p.264)

1511 **Eliason, Norman E.** Shakespeare's purgative drug Cyme. Mod Lang N 57no8:663–5 D '42.
Reads 'cumin' (cymen) for 'Cyme' at 5.3.55.

1512 **Smith, Robert Metcalf.** Macbeth's Cyme once more. Mod Lang N 60no1: 33–8 Ja '45.
Reads 'ocyme' after Seager.

1513 **Nosworthy, James M.** Macbeth at the Globe. Library ser5 2no2/3:108–18 S/D '47.
F Mac., ptd. from an abridged prompt-book, shows from comparison with Forman's account 'no omission of whole scenes or incidents. . . . Macbeth was never anything but a short play' (p.115). 'Appendix II. The authenticity of the Forman MS.' (p.117–18)

1514 **Donner, Henry Wolfgang.** Rebellious dead. TLS 28 S '49:617; J. D. Wilson ib. 30 S '49:633.
Supports F reading at 4.1.97.

1515 **Flatter, Richard.** The latest edition of Macbeth. Mod Philol 49no2:124–32 N '51.
Notes on the line division, apostrophes, glossary, and SD of the New Cambridge ed. See no.1517.

1516 **Parsons, Howard.** Macbeth, some emendations. N&Q 197:403 S '52.

1517 **Wilson, John Dover.** Letter to the editor. Mod Philol 49n04:274–5 My '52.
Reply to Flatter: *see* no.1515.

1518 **Maxwell, James C.** The punctuation of Macbeth, I.i.1–2. R Eng Stud new
ser 4n016:356–8 Oc '53.

1519 **Parsons, Howard.** Macbeth, some further conjectures. N&Q 198:54–5,
464–6 F '53.

1520 —— Macbeth: emendations. N&Q 199:331–3 Ag '54.

1521 **Maxwell, James C.** Macbeth IV,iii,107. Mod Lang R 51n01:73 Ja '56.
Reads 'accurs'd' for F 'accust' as 'accus'd' is unsupported in Sh. orthography.

1522 **Danks, Kenneth B.** Is F1 Macbeth a reconstructed text? N&Q 202:516–19
D '57.
Application of the methods used by H. R. Hoppe in his study of *Rom.* suggests that
Mac. too is a reconstructed text.

1523 **Amnéus, Daniel A.** A missing scene in Macbeth. J Eng Germ Philol
60n03:435–40 Jl '61.
Survey of the arguments for the authenticity of Forman's Book of plays suggests from
'Forman's eyewitness testimony that at least some cut material was preserved and re-
inserted in the play'. (p.440)

INDIVIDUAL TEXTS—MEASURE FOR MEASURE

1530 **Skeat, Walter William.** The prenzie Angelo. Acad 49:285 Ap '96; M.
Liddell *ib.* 49:325 Ap '96; W. W. Skeat; W. Worrall 49:346–7 Ap '96;
M. Liddell 49:385 My '96.
Misprint of 'preuzie' (worthy) at 3.1.94.

1531 **Skeat, Walter William.** Shakespeare Measure for measure, II,i,39. Mod
Lang R 5n02:197–8 Ap '10.
Reads 'Some run through brakes o'fire'.

1532 **Praz, Mario.** All-bridling law. TLS 13 F '37:111.

1533 **Stevenson, David L.** On restoring two Folio readings in Measure for measure. Sh Q 7n04:450–3 '56.
Maintains F readings at 1.2.135 and 2.1.39.

1534 **Holland, Norman N.** Do or die in Measure for measure, I.iii.43. N&Q 202: 52 F '57.

Reads 'to die in slander' for 'To do . . .'.

1535 **Drew, Philip.** A suggested reading in Measure for measure. Sh Q 9no2: 202–4 '58.

Suggests 'puisne' (puny) for 'prenzie' at 3.1.94, 97.

INDIVIDUAL TEXTS—MERCHANT OF VENICE

1542 **Tannenbaum, Samuel Aaron.** Shakspere's The merchant of Venice, a concise bibliography. New York, 1941. (Repr. Port Washington, N.Y., Kennikat pr. [1967]) x,140p. 23cm. (Elizabethan bibliographies, no.17)

1545 **Joicey, G.** Merchant of Venice, III.v.82. N&Q ser8 2:445 D '92.

Q 'meane' a misreading of ms. 'winne'.

1546 **Van Dam, Bastiaan Adriaan P.** The text of The merchant of Venice. Neophilol 13:33–51 S '27.

Detailed examination in light of theory that Q was ptd. from a prompt-book made from Shakespeare's ms. 'which had been cut, interpolated and slightly changed by an experienced actor'. (p.46)

1547 **A Shakespeare** quarto. (Notes on sales) TLS 28 Jl '32:548.

A Pavier quarto, 1600 (1619)

1548 **Flatter, Richard.** The wooing of Nerissa. TLS 9 D '49:809; J. L. Nevinson *ib*.30 D '49:857; H. D. Gray 3 F '50:73; J. D. Wilson 17 F '50:105.

Flatter's support for 'rough' (ruff) at 3.2.206 countered by Gray's 'tongue' and Wilson's 'roofe'.

1549 **Danks, Kenneth B.** A notable copyright award. N&Q 201:283 Jl '56.

1550 **Galloway, David.** Alcides and his rage: a note on The merchant of Venice. N&Q 201:330–1 Ag '56.

Reads 'rag' for 'rage' at 2.1.35.

1551 **McKenzie, Donald Francis.** Compositor B's role in The merchant of Venice Q2, 1619. Stud Bib 12:75–90 '59. table.

Jaggard's compositor setting from Q1 1600.

1552 —— Shakespearian punctuation, a new beginning. R Eng Stud new ser 10no40:361–70 N '59.

Comparison of compositor B's work in Q1 and 2 shows 'that many of the most disturbing features of the Folio punctuation are in fact compositorial'. (p.369)

INDIVIDUAL TEXTS—MERRY WIVES OF WINDSOR

1560 **Joicey, G.** Merry wives of Windsor, I.iii,111. N&Q ser8 8:324 Oc '95.

Reads 'Nim' for 'mine'.

1561 **Jonas, Maurice.** Merry wives of Windsor. N&Q ser8 9:122 F '96.

Reports possession of 1619 Q.

1562 **Perring, Philip.** Merry wives of Windsor, II.i.197: An-heires. N&Q ser10 8:302–3 Oc '07.

Misreading of 'mine Ares' at 2.1.228.

1563 **Chambers, sir Edmund Kerchever.** Merry wives of Windsor, I.iii,93. Mod Lang R 4no1:88 Oc '08.

In the Cambridge ed., 'skirted page' is incorrect rendering of F 'skirted *Page*'.

1564 **Friedrich, Paul.** Studien zur englischen Stenographie im Zeitalter Shakespeares: Timothe Brights Characterie entwicklungsgeschichtlich und kritisch betrachtet; mit einem Anhang: neue Gesichtspunkte für stenographische Untersuchungen von Shakespeare-Quartos, dargelegt an der ersten Quarto der Merry wives of Windsor, 1602. Leipzig, K. F. Koehler, 1914. 94p. illus., tables. 24cm.

1. Bright's Stellung in der Geschichte der Stenographie. — 2. Die Entwicklung der Brightschen Kurzschrift. — 3. Kritische Betrachtungen. — 4. Neue Gesichtspunkte für stenographische Untersuchungen von Shakespeare-Quartos, dargelegt an der ersten Quarto der Merry Wives of Windsor, 1602.

1565 **Pollard, Alfred William** and **J. D. Wilson.** The stolne and surreptitious Shakespearian texts. Merry wives of Windsor (1602). TLS 7 Ag '19:420.

1566 **Schücking, Levin Ludwig.** The fairy scene in The merry wives in Folio and quarto. Mod Lang R 19no3:338–40 Jl '24.

Q is superior to F at 5.5.

1567 **Collins, Douglas Cecil.** The 1602 quarto of Shakespeare's Merry wives of Windsor. J South-west Essex Technical Coll 1no1:23–7 D '41.

Q1 is 'a redaction from the prompt copy' prepared for a touring company.

1568 **Ogburn, Vincent H.** The Merry wives quarto, a farce interlude. Pub Mod Lang Assn 57no3:654–60 S '42.

Q1 represents a revision in interlude style.

1569 **Hoppe, Harry Reno.** Borrowings from Romeo and Juliet in the bad quarto of The merry wives of Windsor. R Eng Stud 20no78:156–8 Ap '44.

At 511–12, 578, and 1108, in the numbering of Greg's 1910 ed.

1570 **E., S. Y.** A Shakespeare MS? N&Q 189:193 N '45; W. Jaggard *ib.* 189: 263 D '45; J. G. McManaway 189:284 D '45; W. Jaggard 190:65 F '46; S. Y. E. 191:85 Ag '46; 192:218 My '47; 193:388 S '48; J. G. McManaway 193:525 N '48; S. Y. E. 193:547 D '48; 194:19 Ja '49.

Ms. of prompt-book of c.1660 formerly owned by Halliwell-Phillipps, now Folger ms. 617.1.

1571 **Bracy, William.** The Merry wives of Windsor, the history and transmission of Shakespeare's text. Columbia, Miss., University of Missouri, 1952. 156p. 26cm. (University of Missouri studies, 25no1)

Includes: 1. Early history and criticism.—2. Quarto first-sketch and shorthand theories. —3. Pirate actors and printers.—4. Reconstruction of the text.—5. The reductio ad absurdum of memorial construction.—6. Play abridgment.—7. The textual evidence of abridgment in the quarto.—8. Abridgment in later stage versions of the play.— 12. Transmission of the quarto text.—13. Transmission of the Folio text.—14. Concluding statement.

Rev: Sir W. W. Greg Sh Q 4:77–9 '53; C. Leech Mod Lang R 48:333–5 '53; H. Craig Sh Q 4:119 '53; J. G. McManaway Sh Surv 6:169 '53; H. Heuer Sh Jahrb 89:220 '53.

1572 **Long, John H.** Another masque for The merry wives of Windsor. Sh Q 3no1:39–43 Ja '52.

Sh. wrote two versions of the masque in 5.5; although the F version is a better masque the text of the Q version is superior.

1573 **Greer, Clayton Alvis.** An actor-reporter in The merry wives of Windsor. N&Q 201:192–4 My '56.

Q1 is an adaptation of a lost play, The jealous comedy, rather than a report.

INDIVIDUAL TEXTS—MIDSUMMER NIGHT'S DREAM

1580 **Jonas, Maurice.** Printer's marks. N&Q ser9 1:504 Je '98.

Device in Q1.

1581 **Cuningham, Henry.** Hot ice and wondrous strange snow. TLS 24 Je '20:402.

Reads 'stranger' for 'strange' at 5.1.59.

1582 —— That is, hot ice, and wondrous strange snow. TLS 12 Je '24:371–2; A. H. F. S. *ib.* 19 Je '24:388; H. Cuningham 26 Je '24:404; B. A. P. Van Dam 3 Jl '24:420.

Reiteration of his 'stranger' reading.

1583 **Spencer, Hazelton.** A note on cutting and slashing. Mod Lang R 31no3: 393–5 Jl '36. table.

Mislined passages derive from cuts, against Dover Wilson's revision theory.

1584 **Allen, N. B.** An insertion in A midsummer-night's dream. Sh Assn Bull 13no2:121–2 Ap '38.

Amends New Cambridge ed. account of insertion and mislineation at 5.1.4–16.

1585 **Alexander, Peter.** Two notes on the text of Shakespeare. Edinburgh Bib Soc Trans 2pt4:409–13 '46.

F 'thou not' at 2.1.77 should not be preferred to Q 'not thou'; in *Wiv.* 2.2. the opening lines should be rearranged to compensate for compositorial line-skipping in both Q and F.

1586 **Babler, Otto František.** Shakespeare's Midsummer night's dream in Czech and Slovakian. N&Q 202:151–3 Ap '57.

Discursive checklist of trans., 1866–1943.

1587 **Turner, Robert Kean.** Printing methods and textual problems in A midsummer night's dream Q1. Stud Bib 15:33–55 '62. diagrs., tables.

Analysis of composition and type distribution. 'The bibliographical evidence seems . . . to point toward the kind of heavily revised manuscript described by Professor [Dover] Wilson as copy.' (p.55)

INDIVIDUAL TEXTS—MUCH ADO ABOUT NOTHING

1595 **Haworth, Peter.** A textual puzzle in Much ado. TLS 12 F '25:104.

Reads 'swagge' (suage) in 'and sorrow, wagge' at 5.1.16.

1596 **Brereton, J. LeGay.** Much adoe about nothing, IV.i.145–160. R Eng Stud 4no13:84–6 Ja '28.

In Q1 the Friar's speech is in prose to allow room for insertion above. Repr. in his Writings on Elizabethan drama, comp. by R. G. Howarth. Melbourne, 1948. p.96–8.

1597 **Tannenbaum, Samuel Aaron.** A crux in Much ado and its solution. Mod Lang N 46no8:512–14 D '31. illus.

Read 'Bid sorrow trudge' at 5.1.16.

1598 **Smith, John Hazel.** The composition of the quarto of Much ado about nothing. Stud Bib 16:9–26 '63. table.

Miscalculations in casting-off, and printing practices, are responsible for features which earlier critics have taken as evidence of earlier (revised?) states of the text.

INDIVIDUAL TEXTS—OTHELLO

1605 **Tannenbaum, Samuel Aaron.** Shakspere's Othello, a concise bibliography. New York, 1943. (Repr. Port Washington, N.Y., Kennikat pr. [1967]) x,132p. illus. 23cm. (Elizabethan bibliographies, no.28)

1610 **Greg, sir Walter Wilson.** A fellow almost damn'd in a fair wife. Mod Lang Q 5no2:71 Jl '02.

Reads 'A fellow al miss daub'd in a fair wise' at 1.1.21.

1611 **Cuningham, Henry.** A fellow almost damn'd in a faire wife. TLS 19 Je '19:337; R. G. Bury ib. 26 Je '19:350; T; W. J. M. Starkie 3 Jl '19:364; A. Gray 10 Jl '19:377; N. Moller 7 Ag '19:425.

Reads 'life' for 'wife'.

1612 —— Othello III.3,453–456. TLS 22 S '27:647.

Reads 'seekes' for 'keepes' at 3.3.455.

1613 **Cameron, Kenneth Walter.** Othello, quarto 1, reconsidered. Pub Mod Lang Assn 47no3:671–83 S '32. tables.

Oth. Q1, together with other King's company texts pub. by Walkley in 1619–22, 'furnish uniformly good texts, generally unsophisticated, with the original oaths, with act and scene divisions, and the stage directions of the theatre . . . all point to a prompt-book origin'. (p.682)

1614 —— The text of Othello, an analysis. Pub Mod Lang Assn 49no3:762–96 S '34. tables.

Supplies 'complete classification of the variants between' Q and F. Q, which 'as a whole, is in no way inferior to the F . . . probably represents the actual playhouse version'. (p.794–5)

1615 **Cuningham, Henry.** The Ponticke sea. TLS 31 My '34:392.

Reads 'seekes' for 'keepes' at 3.3.455: *see* no.1612.

1616 **Hart, Alfred.** The date of Othello. TLS 10 Oc '35:631; A. S. Cairncross ib. 24 Oc '35:671; R. Noble 14 D '35:859.

An earlier date (1602) is supported by textual links with *Ham.* Q1.

1617 **Tannenbaum, Samuel Aaron.** Cassio's hopes. Philol Q 18no3:316–18 Jl '39.

Reads 'forfeited' for 'surfetted' at 2.1.50.

1618 **Hinman, Charlton J. K.** 'The copy for the second quarto of Othello, 1630' *in* McManaway, James G., G. E. Dawson, and E. E. Willoughby, *ed.* Joseph Quincy Adams memorial studies. Washington, 1948. p.373–89.

Q2 was set up from an exemplum of Q1 with additions transcribed from F1; the readings show that it has no textual authority.

1619 —— Nether and Neither in the seventeenth century. Mod Lang N 63no5: 333–5 My '48.

Reproduction in Q2 (1630) of 'neither' from copy of F1 with uncorrected state of forme vv3:4ᵛ.

1620 **Walker, Alice.** The 1622 quarto and the First folio texts of Othello. Sh Surv 5:16–24 '52.

F was ptd. from a corrected copy of Q which was memorially contaminated; discussion of bibliogr. evidence, common errors, orthographical evidence, and variant readings.

1621 **Muir, Kenneth.** Folio sophistications in Othello. N&Q 197:335–6 Ag '52.

1622 **Dorsch, T. S.** This poor trash of Venice. Sh Q 6n03:359–61 '55.

Supports F 'trace' at 2.1.312.

1623 **Ivy, Geoffrey S.** Othello and the rose-lip'd cherubin: an old reading restored. Sh Q 9n02:208–12 '58.

Reads 'I' (pronoun) for 'I' (ay!) at 4.2.64.

1624 **Bowers, Fredson Thayer.** 'The copy for the Folio Othello' *in* Bibliography and textual criticism. Oxford, 1964. p.158–201.

1. Printer's copy: problems in the transmission of texts.—2. The example of Richard III. —3. Compositorial spellings as bibliographical evidence.—4. Compositor E and the Folio Othello.
Partial analysis of compositor E's influence in F *Oth.* supports A. Walker's view that F was ptd. from Q copy.

1625 **Coghill, Nevill Henry K.** 'Revision after performance' *in* Shakespeare's professional skills. Cambridge, 1964. p.164–202.

'. . . a dramaturgical analysis of certain passages in the 1623 Folio text of Othello which diverge from the 1622 Quarto text. . . . These divergences can only be explained on the supposition that, in this play at least, Folio embodies a Shakespearean revision of the play that appears in Quarto.' (p.164)

1626 **Muir, Kenneth.** The text of Othello. Sh Stud 1:227–39 '65. tables.

After preliminary examination of the relationship of Q and F, a survey of the cruxes suggests that 'a reasoned and controlled eclecticism should be the basis of a modern text.' (p.239)

1627 **Williams, William P.** The F1 Othello copy-text. Pa Bib Soc Am 63:23–5 '69.

The thesis that F copy was an annotated copy of Q best explains the kind and amount of F proofreading.

INDIVIDUAL TEXTS—PERICLES

1635 **Lee, sir Sidney,** *ed.* 'Census of copies' *in* Shakespeare's Pericles, being a reproduction in facsimile of the first edition. . . . Oxford, 1905. p.35–48.

'The history of the publication and text.' (p.20–35)

———

1638 **Jonas, Maurice.** Pericles. N&Q ser8 4:84 Jl '93.

Reports ownership of 1611 Q.

1639 **Roberts, William.** Shakespeare quartos in Switzerland in 1857. N&Q ser11 2:288 Oc '10; W. Jaggard; Scotus *ib.* ser11 2:353 Oc '10.

Early report of discovery of Sh. Q proves ill-founded, although the Zurich State library possesses copy of Q1 *Per.*

1640 **Trent, William Peterfield.** 'Some textual notes on Pericles' *in* Matthews, Brander and A. H. Thorndike, *ed.* Shaksperian studies by members of the department of English and comparative literature in Columbia university. New York, 1916. p.[43]–57.

1641 **Hastings, William T.** Exit George Wilkins? Sh Assn Bull 11no2:67–83 Ap '36.

1. Wilkins and Pericles; the Wilkins canon.—2. The play and the novel.—3. The type of Pericles.—4. The manner of Pericles.—5. The argument from versification.—6. The argument from parallels.—7. Conclusion.

Twine's Painful adventures, Wilkins's Pericles, and the pirated 1609 Q are 'evidence of three successive attempts to profit by the success of a play . . .' probably produced c.1606/7.

1642 **Tannenbaum, Samuel Aaron.** A passage in Pericles. Sh Assn Bull 12no3: 190–1 Jl '37.

Reads 'love, become enflam'd' for 'love bosome, enflame' at 4.1.5.

1643 **Hastings, William T.** Shakspere's part in Pericles. Sh Assn Bull 14no1:67–85 Ja '39.

Pericles not wholly Shakspere's.—Pericles the result of Shakspere's revision of a previous play.—What part of the play is by Shakspere?—Tentative classification on literary grounds.

1644 **Parrott, Thomas Marc.** Pericles, the play and the novel. Sh Assn Bull 23no3:105–13 '48.

1645 **Edwards, Philip.** An approach to the problem of Pericles. Sh Surv 5:25–49 '52.

Per. was not by two authors; copy for Q derives from two reporters of disparate ability; the Q was ptd. by three compositors. 'Appendix: the compositors.' (p.47–9)

INDIVIDUAL TEXTS—RICHARD 2

1650 **Eichhoff, Theodor.** Richard II in der Clarendon-Press-Ausgabe. Angl 35:80–100 Jl '11.

1651 **Some** literary rarities. (Notes on sales) TLS 31 D '31:1056.

Includes W. G. Damper copy of *R2*, 1608, the first issue of the 4th ed.

1652 **Greer, Clayton Alvis.** The deposition scene of Richard II. N&Q 197:492–3 N '52.

A cut for political reasons.

1653 **Hasker, Richard E.** The copy for the First folio Richard II. Stud Bib 5:53–72 '52/3.

F copy was 'an exemplum of Q3 containing some leaves from a copy of Q5'. (p.53)
Rev: H. T. Price Sh Q 5:119–20 '54.

1654 **Greer, Clayton Alvis.** More about the deposition scene of Richard II. N&Q 198:49–50 F '53.

Lawe, the publisher of Q3, ptd. the scene from an original, authorized source.

1655 **Danks, Kenneth B.** King Richard II: the deposition scene in Q4. N&Q 200:473–4 N '55.

Copy for this scene was not the result of piracy.

1656 **Maxwell, James C.** Blackstone on Richard II. Sh Q 9n04:595 '58.

Supplies source of M. W. Black's references to Blackstone's emendations, in his Problems in the editing of Shakespeare: interpretation. Eng Inst Essays 1947:117–36 '48.

1657 **Ryan, Pat M.** Facsimiles, fakes, and forgeries: punctuation in Shakespeare's King Richard II. Speech Monographs 27:323–7 N '60. (Not seen)

1658 **Griffin, William J.** Conjectures on a missing line in Richard II. Tennessee Stud Lit 7:105–11 '62.

At 2.1.277–82.

1659 **McManaway, James Gilmer.** Richard II at Covent Garden. Sh Q 15n02: 161–75 '64. illus., facsims.

Descr. of F2 prepared as prompt-book for 1738 revival by John Roberts, and now in Folger library.

INDIVIDUAL TEXTS—RICHARD 3

1665 **Smidt, Kristian,** *ed.* 'Extant quartos and press variants: descriptive catalogue' *in* The tragedy of king Richard the third; parallel texts. . . . Oslo; New York [1969] p.14–28.

1670 **Pape, Richard Otto.** Die erste Quarto von Shakespeare's Richard III, ein stenographischer Raubdruck. Archiv für Stenographie 57n08:242–3 '06.

Q1 pirated with Bright's stenography.

1671 **Pape, Richard Otto.** Über die Entstehung der ersten Quarto von Shakespeare's Richard III. Berlin, G. Reimer, 1906. 49p. diagrs., tables. 24cm.

1672 **Babcock, Robert Witbeck.** An introduction to the study of the text of Richard III. Stud Philol 24no2:243–60 Ap '27.

Includes comprehensive survey of early views.

1673 **Van Dam, Bastiaan Adriaan P.** Shakespeare problems nearing solution: Henry VI and Richard III. Eng Stud 12no3:81–97 Je '30.

R3 was ptd. from a stenographic report, against Alexander, no.1341.

1674 **Patrick, David Lyall.** The textual history of Richard III. Stanford university, Calif., Stanford U.P.; London, H. Milford, O.U.P., 1936. 153p. tables. 25cm. (Stanford university publications. Univ ser. Lang & Lit 6no1)

1. An introduction to the problem.—2. The quarto an acting version.—3. The quarto an actors' version.—4. Errors of memory—shifting.—5. Errors of memory—substitutions.—6. Matter in the Folio but not in the quarto.—7. Matter in the quarto but not in the Folio.—8. Conclusion.

Q1 is a report of an abridged acting version.

Rev: N&Q 172:270 '37; S. A. Tannenbaum Sh Assn Bull 12:192 '37; sir W. W. Greg Library ser4 19:118–20 '38; A. Walker R Eng Stud 14:468–9 '38; O. J. Campbell Mod Lang N 53:391–4 '38; H. T. Price J Eng Germ Philol 37:428–31 '38; A. Brandl Archiv 172:249 '38.

1675 **Greg, sir Walter Wilson.** Richard III—Q5, 1612. Library ser4 17no1: 88–97 Je '36. tables.

Sheets A,B,D were ptd. from Q4, 1605, sheets C,E–M from Q3, 1602.

1676 **Griffin, William J.** An omission in the Folio text of Richard III. R Eng Stud 13no51:329–32 Jl '37; *rf.* H. Spencer *ib.* 14no54:205 Ap '38.

4.2.102–21 was deleted from F to avoid reference to Villiers.

1677 **Maas, Paul.** Two passages in Richard III. R Eng Stud 18no71:315–17 Jl '42.

1. An actor's interpolation in Q2 of Richard III [1.1.101–2].—2. Richard III, 1.1.32.

Urges retention of Q1–2 inductions against Q3+ inductions.

1678 **Wilson, John Dover.** Shakespeare's Richard III and The true tragedy of Richard the third, 1594. Sh Q 3no4:299–306 Oc '52.

'T.T. cannot be a Bad Quarto of Richard III . . . Shakespeare must himself have borrowed either from T.T. or from the old play it misrepresents.' (p.306)

1679 **Parsons, Howard.** Shakespeare emendations, Richard III. N&Q 200: 288–9 Jl '55.

1680 **Walton, James Kirkwood.** The copy for the Folio text of Richard III, with a note on the copy for the Folio text of King Lear. [Auckland] Auckland university college, 1955. 164p. tables. 21cm. (Auckland university college. Monograph series, no.1)

Section one ['a general probability that F was throughout printed from an exemplum of Q3'].—Section two ['F was in fact throughout printed from an exemplum of Q3'].—Section three ['why there are so few Q and F variants in III.i.1–166 and V.iii.48, et sequ.'].—The copy for the Folio text of King Lear.—Appendix: an examination of a recent theory of the copy for the Folio text of King Lear [that of P. Williams: *see* no.1459]

Rev: I. B. Cauthen J Eng Germ Philol 55:503–15 '55; TLS 9 D '55:750; sir W. W. Greg Library ser5 11:125–9 '56; R. Davril Études Angl 11:51 '58; H. Heuer Sh Jahrb 94:294 '58; F. T. Bowers Sh Q 10:91–6 '59.

1681 **Cairncross, Andrew S.** Coincidental variants in Richard III. Library ser5 12no3:187–90 S '57.

Indifferent variants show F to be dependent on Q6 copy as well as on Q3. *See* no.1684.

1682 —— The quartos and the Folio text of Richard III. R Eng Stud new ser 8no31:225–33 Ag '57. tables.

'The F text, set up by the *two* compositors, A and B, was printed from *three* of the six quartos then available—Q1, Q3, and Q6—used in some sort of rotation, and corrected with varying degrees of accuracy from an authentic manuscript.' (p.225)

1683 **Gerevini, Silvano.** Il testo del Riccardo III di Shakespeare; saggio critico. Pavia, R. Cortina, 1957. 101p. tables. 23cm.

1. Le condizioni del testo.—II. Storia della critica.—III. Il problema degli in-quarto e la formazione dell'in-folio.—Errata.

1684 **Walton, James Kirkwood.** Coincidental variants in Richard III. Library ser5 13no2:139–40 Je '58.

Coincidence of indifferent variants is normal and *Ham.* Q6, rather than being a typical example, as Cairncross claimed (*see* no.1681), is unique.

1685 **Oyama, Toshikazu.** 'The folio copy of Richard III' *in* Araki, Kazuo [and others] *ed.* Studies in English grammar and linguistics, a miscellany in honour of Takanobu Ōtsuka. Tokyo, 1958. p.369–78. (Not seen)

1686 **Bowers, Fredson Thayer.** The copy for the Folio Richard III. Sh Q 10no4: 541–4 '59.

Withdraws earlier endorsement of Walton's views on Q3 copy (*see* no.1680 reviews); re-examination shows 'the evidence for Q6 cannot be explained away entirely'. (p.544)

1687 **Walton, James Kirkwood** [and] **A. S. Cairncross.** The quarto copy for the Folio Richard III. R Eng Stud new ser 10no38:127–40 My '59. tables.

Rebuttal of Cairncross (see above) with comments by Cairncross (p.139–40)

1688 **Smidt, Kristian.** Iniurious imposters and Richard III. [Oslo] Norwegian U.P.; New York, Humanities pr. [1964] 213p. 21cm. (Norwegian studies in English, no.12)

Shakespeare's bad quartos.—The quarto an acting version?—Transposition.—Anticipation and recollection (repetition).—Substitution.—Omission.—Rebuttal of the bad quarto theory.—The copy for the Folio Richard III.—Shakespeare at work.—Appendices: Substantive agreement of Q1 and F1 against Q3 and Q6 in act I.—Substantive agreements Q3/F, Q6/F and Q3/Q6/F against Q1.—Substantive agreements Q1/Q3/F against Q6 in act I.—Use of parentheses.—Formes and stints in the composition of the Folio Richard III.—Q6 p. C4^r with corrections to make it conform with the Folio.—Possible distribution of named and speaking parts for a minimum number of actors.—Variants in Middleton's A game at chesse.—Substantive differences between the MS and the Folio of Fletcher's Bonduca.

Rev: W. C. McAvoy Sh Q 16:126 '65; G. W. Williams Mod Philol 63:265–7 '66; F. B. Williams Eng Stud 47:225–6 '66; J. K. Walton R Eng Stud new ser 17:81–3 '66; J. A. Barish Stud Eng Lit 6:366–7 '66; W. Riehle Angl 84:445–8 '66; J. B. Fort Études Angl 19:183 '66; G. B. Evans Sh Stud 2:365–6 '66.

1689 **Honigmann, Ernst Anselm Joachim.** The text of Richard III. Theat Res 7no1/2:48–55 '65.

'Since Q sometimes transmits the very words of Shakespeare's source . . . , where F prints a variant word or words, the editor should not only accept those Q readings vouched for by the source but should, in addition, recognise that F's margin of superiority over Q is by no means . . . large.' (p.48)

INDIVIDUAL TEXTS—ROMEO AND JULIET

1700 **Tannenbaum, Samuel Aaron** and **Dorothy R. Tannenbaum.** Shakspere's Romeo and Juliet, a concise bibliography. New York, 1950. (Repr. Port Washington, N.Y., Kennikat pr. [1967]) ii,133 l. 28cm. (Elizabethan bibliographies, no.41) (Duplicated typescript)

1703 **Reynolds, W.** Run-awayes eyes. Shakespeariana 7no3:171–8 Jl '90.

Survey and appraisal of readings at 3.2.6.

1704 **Henderson, W. A.** Runawayes eyes. N&Q ser8 3:285 Ap '93; W. W. Skeat *ib.* 4:84 Jl '93.

Reports Zachariah Jackson's emendation 'unawayres' (unawares) from A few concise examples, 1818.

1705 **Cutter, W. P.** Garrick's version of Romeo and Juliet. N&Q ser11 2:47 Jl '10; W. Norman *ib.* 2:95 Jl '10.

Seeks 1748 ed.

1706 **Macaulay, George Campbell.** Shakespeare, Romeo and Juliet, II,ii,38ff. Mod Lang R 10no2:223–4 Ap '15.

Disarrangement of F lines accompanying additions to the Q text.

1707 **Cuningham, Henry.** Runaway's eyes. TLS 23 Ja '19:44; R. Harris *ib.* 30 Ja '19:56; H. Cuningham 6 F '19:69; R. L. Eagle 13 F '19:84.

Supports Dyce's reading of 'rude day's' at 3.2.6.

1708 **Wilson, John Dover** and **A. W. Pollard.** The stolne and surreptitious Shakespearian texts; Romeo and Juliet, 1597. TLS 14 Ag '19:434; W. J. Lawrence *ib.* 21 Ag '19:449; A. W. Pollard; sir W. W. Greg 28 Ag '19:461; Janet Spens 18 S '19:500.

1709 **Hoskins, Edgar.** Runaways eyes. Sh Q (Sydney) 3no3:36 Jl '24.

Reads 'wideawakes' at 3.2.6.

1710 **Hjort, Greta.** The good and bad quartos of Romeo and Juliet and Love's labour's lost. Mod Lang R 21no2:140–6 Ap '26.

Suggests that there was a bad Q for *LLL* similar to Q1 *Rom.*; the good texts were ptd. from the bad Q corrected from prompt-books.

1711 **Van Dam, Bastiaan Adriaan P.** Did Shakespeare revise Romeo and Juliet? Angl neue Folge 51:39–62 Ja '27.

Denies Pollard and Wilson's suggestion in no.1708 that Q1 is a revised pre-Sh. play.

1712 **Babcock, Robert Weston.** Romeo and Juliet, I.iv,86: an emendation. Philol Q 8no4:407–8 Oc '29; S. A. Tannenbaum *ib.* 9no1:72–3 Ja '30; E. P. Kuhl 9no3:307–8 Jl '30.

Reads 'deaths' for 'healths' at 1.4.85.

1713 **Cuningham, Henry.** Skaines mates. TLS 17 Oc '29:822.

At 2.4.162 reads 'queane/s'.

1714 **Camp, G. C.** The printing of Romeo and Juliet. TLS 27 Je '36:544; R. B. McKerrow *ib.* 4 Jl '36:564.

Camp's notice that Danter's ptg. of Q1 was interrupted shown to be familiar.

1715 **Eich, Louis M.** A previous adaptation of Romeo and Juliet. Q J Speech 23:589–94 D '37. (Not seen)

1716 **Hoppe, Harry Reno.** Runaways' eyes in Romeo and Juliet, III.ii.6. N&Q 173:171–2 S '37.

Reads 'That runaways' ends may work' at 3.2.6.

1717 —— An approximate printing date for the first quarto of Romeo and Juliet. Library ser4 18no4:447–55 Mr '38.

Typographical evidence showing that sigs. E–K were not ptd. by John Danter, and historical evidence, suggest that Q1 was in print between 9 F and 17 Mr 1596/7.

1718 —— The first quarto version of Romeo and Juliet, II.vi and IV.v.43ff. R Eng Stud 14no55:271–84 Jl '38.

These passages 'can be explained as an actor-reporter's attempt to reconstruct a text for parts of the play that he was not immediately familiar with'. (p.271)

1719 **Allen, N. B.** Romeo and Juliet further restored. Mod Lang N 54no2:85–92 F '39.

Discusses and objects to the preference of Q1 readings in modern ed.

1720 **Hoppe, Harry Reno.** The bad quarto of Romeo and Juliet, a bibliographical and textual study. Ithaca, N.Y., Cornell U.P., 1948. viii,230p. tables. 20cm. (Cornell studies in English, XXXVI)

1. The printing of the first quarto.—2. The relation of Q1 to Q2: editorial views.—3. The case for memorial reconstruction: external evidence.—4. . . . : internal evidence.—5. The reporters of Romeo and Juliet.

Rev: TLS 5 Mr '49:159; M. Doran J Eng Germ Philol 49:112–14 '50; C. J. K. Hinman Mod Lang N 65:66–8 '50; sir W. W. Greg R Eng Stud new ser 1:64–6 '50; G. I. Duthie Mod Lang R 45:375–7 '50; R. Flatter Sh Jahrb 88:232–3 '52.

1721 **Thomas, Sidney.** The bibliographical links between the first two quartos of Romeo and Juliet. R Eng Stud 25no98:110–14 Ap '49.

Q2 was ptd. from ms. except for 1.2.46–3.36 which were ptd. from Q1.

1722 —— Henry Chettle and the first quarto of Romeo and Juliet. R Eng Stud new ser 1no1:8–16 Ja '50.

The un-Sh. passages in Q1 'are the work of an editor, commissioned by John Danter, the printer-publisher of Q1, to tidy up the manuscript supplied by the reporter and to fill in gaps' (p. 11); the ed. was Chettle.

1723 **Maxwell, James C.** Juliet's days, hours, and minutes. R Eng Stud new ser 2no7:262 Jl '51.

3.5.44–5 Q1 as evidence of reporting.

1724 **Duthie, George Ian.** The text of Shakespeare's Romeo and Juliet. Stud Bib 4:3–29 '51/2.

Q2 was set up from 'three different types of copy—(i) Q1 unaltered, (ii) Q1 edited by comparison with a Shakespearian manuscript, and (iii) direct transcription of that Shakespearian manuscript' (p.18). Reference to both Q1 and Q2 must be made in editing the text.

1725 **Hosley, Richard.** A stage direction in Romeo & Juliet. TLS 13 Je '52:391.

Reference to the bad Q corrects a modern emendation at 4.5.95 derived from Q4.

1727 —— The corrupting influence of the bad quarto on the received text of Romeo and Juliet. Sh Q 4no1:11–33 Ja '53.

'. . . editorial reliance on Q1 is the source of a number of errors in the received text' (p.11). 'Q1 has influenced the received text . . . in two different ways: through the Q2 compositor's use of Q1 as auxiliary copy for Q2, and through subsequent editors' reliance on the authority of Q1 where Q2 is corrupt' (p.21). *See also* no.1729.

1728 **Boyce, Benjamin.** Pope's yews in Shakespeare's graveyard. N&Q 199:287 Je '54.

Notes conventional adoption of Pope's sophistication, 'yew trees' for 'young trees' at 5.3.3.

1729 **Leech, Clifford.** Notes on dr. Richard Hosley's suggestions concerning the received text of Romeo and Juliet. Sh Q 5no1:94–5 Ja '54.

Questions the application of Hosley's principles (no.1727) to 3.1.1–4, 2.2.187–8, the end of 2.2 and the beginning of 2.3; and 3.5.173–5. *See also* no.1731.

1730 **Hinman, Charlton J. K.** The proof-reading of the First folio text of Romeo and Juliet. Stud Bib 6:61–70 '54.

Examination of a proofsheet of ff1ᵛ:6ʳ (p.62,71) suggests 'a particular *attitude* toward the Romeo text would seem to have prevailed in the printing-house'. (p.70)

1731 **Hosley, Richard.** The Good night, good night sequence in Romeo and Juliet. Sh Q 5no1:96–8 Ja '54.

Agrees with Leech (no.1729) on 3.5.173–5 and modifies his position on the reassignment of speeches at 2.2.185–8.

1732 **Culliford, Stanley George.** Romeo and Juliet, II.i.38. N&Q 200:475 N '55.

Reads '&c' for Q2 'or'.

1733 **Wilson, John Dover.** The new way with Shakespeare's texts II: Recent work on the text of Romeo and Juliet. Sh Surv 8:81–99 '55.

Account of the problems of *Rom.* and their treatment by Wilson and Duthie in their ed.

1734 **Culliford, Stanley George.** Scholarship and the university, a demonstration of deficiencies in a recent edition of Romeo and Juliet. N.Z. Univ J 4no1: 28–33 '56.

General note on the New Cambridge ed.

1735 **Cantrell, Paul L.** and **G. W. Williams.** The printing of the second quarto of Romeo and Juliet, 1599. Stud Bib 9:107–28 '57. diagrs., tables.

Distinguishes two compositors; evidence of SP's seems 'to point quite clearly to an independent manuscript as copy'. (p.127)

1736 **Hosley, Richard.** Quarto copy for Q2 Romeo and Juliet. Stud Bib 9:129–41 '57. table.

'. . . combined influence of quarto and manuscript copy on the text of Q2 could only have resulted from compositor's consultation of an exemplar of Q1 during the process of typesetting Q2 directly from the manuscript.' (p.136)

1737 **Titherley, A. W.** The two hours traffic of our stage. Sh Authorship R 3:3–4 '60.

'. . . it is possible that the pirated Q1 of Danter, which is much shorter than Q2, substantially reproduces what was performed.' (p.4)

1738 **Williams, George Walton.** A new line of dialogue in Romeo and Juliet. Sh Q 11no1:84–7 '60.

Analysis of compositorial practice suggests Q2 '*Away* Tibalt' at 3.1.93 is not SD but a speech for the mute Petruchio.

1739 —— The printer and date of Romeo and Juliet, Q4. Stud Bib 18:253–4 '65. table.

William Stansby is identified as the ptr. from the presence of the tailpiece in other books ptd. by him; the date is before N 1622.

1740 **Henning, Standish.** The printer of Romeo and Juliet, Q1. Pa Bib Soc Am 60:363–4 '66. table.

H. R. Hoppe's identification of Allde confirmed by types common to Allde's books.

INDIVIDUAL TEXTS—TAMING OF THE SHREW

1750 **Ashton, Florence Huber.** The revision of the Folio text of The taming of the shrew. Philol Q 6no2:151–60 Ap '27.

Marginal or paginal insertion of new material, confused speech headings, and the deletion of old material prove *Shr.* to be the reworking of an old play.

1751 **Van Dam, Bastiaan Adriaan P.** The taming of a shrew. Eng Stud 10no3:97–106 Je '28.

A Shrew a stenographic report of a play 'purloined from Shakespeare'.

1752 —— The taming of the shrew. Eng Stud 10no6:161–77 D '28.

Discussion of hitherto unremarked textual corruption.

1753 **Gray, Henry David.** 'The taming of a shrew' *in* Maxwell, Baldwin [and others] *ed.* Renaissance studies in honor of Hardin Craig. Stanford university, Calif.; London [1941] p.325–33.

Repr. from Philol Q 20no3:325–33 Jl '41. 'A Shrew is a bad quarto based upon The Shrew before it underwent revision.' (p.327)

1754 **Houk, Raymond A.** The evolution of The taming of the shrew. Pub Mod Lang Assn 57no3:1009–38 S '42. table.

'A comparative chart' (p.1013). A shrew and The shrew derive from a common source.

1755 **Duthie, George Ian.** The taming of a shrew and The taming of the shrew. R Eng Stud 19no76:337–56 Oc '43.

A Shrew is a memorial reconstruction of an early Shrew play of which *Shr.* is a reworking.

1756 **Danks, Kenneth B.** A shrew & The shrew. N&Q 200:331–2 Ag '55.

Although Alexander's view that A Shrew was an actor piracy of The shrew is correct, bibliogr. evidence shows that 'the correct title of this play is A Shrew (short-title)'.

1757 **Shroeder, John W.** The taming of a shrew and The taming of the shrew: a case reopened. J Eng Germ Philol 57no3:424–43 Jl '58.

'A Shrew is simply a text, admittedly imperfect, of an old play which Shakespeare used as one of the sources for his own comedy.' (p.425)

INDIVIDUAL TEXTS—THE TEMPEST

1765 **Dey, Edward Merton.** Tempest, I.ii.175. N&Q ser10 8:503–4 D '07; W. S. Brassington *ib.* 9:264 Ap '08; J. E. Norcross 9:505–6 Je '08.

'Heuen' for 'Heuens' at l.285 in the Lee facsim.

1766 **Macaulay, George Campbell.** Shakespeare, Tempest, act I, sc. II, l. 269. Mod Lang R 10no1:75 Ja '16.

Reads 'blear ey'd' for 'blew ey'd' at 3.1.15.

1767 **Trench, W. F.** Most busie lest, when I doe it. TLS 28 Jl '21:484.

Supports F reading at 3.1.15.

1768 **Chambers, sir Edmund Kerchever.** The integrity of The tempest. R Eng Stud 1no2:129–50 Ap '25.

Defends the text against disintegrators, with observations on its length, mute and semi-mute characters, broken lines, mis-divisions, incoherencies and obscurities.

1769 **Tannenbaum, Samuel Aaron.** How not to edit Shakspere, a review. Philol
Q 10no2:97–137 Ap '31.
Extensive examination of the New Cambridge ed.

1770 —— Textual difficulties in The tempest, old and new. Sh Assn Bull 6no4:
148–60 Oc '31.

1771 **Fairchild, Hoxie Neale** [and] **S. A. Tannenbaum.** Emending the text of The
tempest, a friendly remonstrance. Sh Assn Bull 7no4:186–91 Oc '32.

1772 **Garvin, Katharine.** Most busy lest. TLS 25 Ap '36:356.
Medieval scribes' confusion over apposition of 'most/lest' and 'lest/least' spellings
related to *Tmp.* reading at 3.1.15.

1773 **Parsons, Howard.** Shakespeare's Tempest, an emendation. N&Q 194:
121–2 Mr '49.
Reads for 'into truth, by telling of it' at 1.2.100, 'acted truth by telling oft'.

1774 **Jones, Harold Whitmore.** The Tempest, III.i.13–17. N&Q 195:293–4 Jl '50.
Reads 'Most busilyest' at 3.1.15.

1775 **Parsons, Howard.** Shakespeare's Tempest, a further emendation. N&Q
194:424 Oc '49.
Reads 'I fatigate, / But these sweet thoughts do e'er refresh my labours, / Most busiest
when I do need it most' at 3.1.13–15.

1776 —— Further emendations in The tempest. N&Q 195:74–5,294–5 F '50;
J. B. Whitmore *ib.* 195:195 Ap '50; H. Parsons 195:261,369 Je,Ag '50;
196:54–5 F '51.

1777 **Cairncross, Andrew S.** The Tempest, III.i.15, and Romeo and Juliet,
I.i.121–128. Sh Q 7no4:448–50 '56.
Reads 'Most busiest when idlest' in *Tmp.*, and suggests rearrangement of line-order
in *Rom.*

1778 **Kermode, Frank.** A crux in The tempest. TLS 29 N '57:728; H. W. Jones
ib. 6 D '57:739.
Reads 'Most busilest' at 3.1.15.

INDIVIDUAL TEXTS—TIMON OF ATHENS

1785 **Joicey, G.** Timon of Athens, III.iv.112. N&Q ser8 3:102 F '93.
'Vllorxa' is a misreading of 'Villaines'.

1786 **Littledale, Harold.** On Vllorxa in Timon of Athens, III.iv.112. Athenæum 3839:672 Je '01; H. Cuningham; F. J. Payne *ib.* 3846:71–2 Jl '01; H. Littledale; A. Dillon 3848:136 Jl '01; F. J. Payne 3851:231–2 Ag '01; H. Cuningham 3854:327–8 S '01; F. J. Payne 3857:424 S '01.

Ms. read 'VII or Xa' therefore ed. should read 'and Sempronius: / seven or ten other: All!'.

1787 **Adams, Joseph Quincy.** Timon of Athens and the irregularities in the First folio. J Eng Germ Philol 7n01:53–63 '07.

The irregularities associated with the ptg. of *Tro.* have no bearing on the authorship of *Tim.*

1788 **MacNaghten, Hugh.** Timon, an emendation. TLS 28 F '24:128; C. R. Haines *ib.* 6 Mr '24:144; H. Cuningham 13 Mr '24:160.

Reads 'all hawks, all' for 'Vllorxa' at a 3.4.112, a mishearing.

1789 **Tannenbaum, Samuel Aaron.** Farewell to Vllorxa. Sh Assn Bull 11n01:41–5 Ja '36.

Reads 'all or ha' at 3.4.112.

1790 **Pyle, Fitzroy.** Hostilius: Timon of Athens, III.ii.70. N&Q 197:48–9 F '52.

A compositorial misunderstanding.

INDIVIDUAL TEXTS—TITUS ANDRONICUS

1800 **Discovery** of the lost first quarto of the Titus Andronicus. New Shakespeareana 4n02:70–2 Ap '05.

1801 **Ljunggren, Evald.** A unique copy of the first edition of Shakspeare's earliest tragedy. Athenæum 4030:91–2 Ja '05.

Discovery of Q1, 1594.

1802 **Chambers, sir Edmund Kerchever.** The first illustration to Shakespeare. Library ser4 5n04:324–30 Mr '25. facsims.

Repr. in his Shakespearian gleanings. [Oxford] 1944. p.57–60.

Discussion, transcript and facsim. of Henry Peacham's drawing of scenes from *Tit.*

1803 **Bolton, Joseph S. G.** The authentic text of Titus Andronicus. Pub Mod Lang Assn 44n03:765–88 S '29. tables.

'. . . the poet was neither directly nor indirectly concerned with any of the modifications subsequent to 1594' (p.765). Q1 is therefore the only substantive text.

1804 —— Two notes on Titus Andronicus. Mod Lang N 45no3:139–41 Mr '30. table.

> 1. The stage direction before I.i.18.—2. The speech-headings before I.i.358, 360, 368, 369, and 371.

1805 **McKerrow, Ronald Brunlees.** A note on Titus Andronicus. Library 15no1: 49–53 Je '34.

> Q2, 1600, was ptd. from a copy of Q1, 1594, defective at the foot of the last two leaves.

1806 **Price, Hereward Thimbleby.** The first quarto of Titus Andronicus. Eng Inst Essays 1947:137–68 '48.

> Sh. metrical and orthographic practices revealed by the spellings in Q1.

1807 **Munro, John.** Titus Andronicus. TLS 10 Je '49:385; J. D. Wilson *ib.* Je 24 '49:413; J. Munro; A. J. Perrett 1 Jl '49:429.

> Argument on Munro's view 'that the artist added lines from the play, or had them added, in order that his picture [Peacham's drawing] should be readily interpreted'.

1808 **Parrott, Thomas Marc.** Further observations on Titus Andronicus. Sh Q 1no1:22–9 Ja '50. illus.

> Agrees with Dover Wilson on the Peacham drawing that 'the appended text in the manuscript was written later by a scribe who . . . transcribed from a printed text lines that he thought would explain the picture'. (p.27)

1809 **Greg, sir Walter Wilson.** Alteration in act I of Titus Andronicus. Mod Lang R 48no4:439–40 Oc '53.

> Although there is enough evidence to make probable the theory that the sacrifice of Alarbus (1.1.33f.) was inserted, the basis of J. D. Wilson's original theory 'proves to be nothing but a misunderstanding'.

1810 **Cantrell, Paul L.** and **G. W. Williams.** Roberts' compositors in Titus Andronicus Q2. Stud Bib 8:27–38 '56. tables.

> Identifies the stints of compositors X and Y and adds to J. R Brown's analysis of their characteristics in *Ham.* Q2 and *MV* Q1.

1811 **Price, Hereward Thimbleby.** Author, compositor, and metre: copy-spelling in Titus Andronicus and other Elizabethan printings. Pa Bib Soc Am 53:160–87 '59.

> Some metrical spellings in *Tit.* briefly considered in light of Harington's Orlando ms.
>
> *Rev*: H. Heuer Sh Jahrb 97:266–7 '61.

1812 **Adams, John Cranford.** Shakespeare's revisions in Titus Andronicus. Sh Q 15no2:177–90 '64.

> 'Differences, omissions, contradictions, additions, redundancies . . . indicate a full-scale revision of an old play before . . . 1594.' (p.190)

1815 **Tannenbaum, Samuel Aaron** and **Dorothy R. Tannenbaum.** Shakspere's Troilus & Cressida, a concise bibliography. New York, 1943. (Repr. Port Washington, N.Y., Kennikat pr. [1967]) ix,44p. 23cm. (Elizabethan bibliographies, no.29)

1820 **Lee, sir Sidney.** Some bibliographical problems connected with the Elizabethan drama. Bib Soc Trans 4:148–50 '98.

Report of paper read on the Burdett Coutts-Sheldon F1 and the *Tro.* cancel.

1821 **Haworth, Peter.** A misprint in Troilus. TLS 21 My '25:352; sir W. W. Greg *ib.* 28 My '25:368; P. Haworth 4 Je '25:384.

'On examining a reduced facsimile of the First Folio which corrects many blunders in the 1609 Quartos, I find that the crucial word [at 3.3.3] . . . is not "sight" at all but "fight" ', but in fact it is 'sight'.

1822 **Alexander, Peter.** Troilus and Cressida, 1609. Library ser4 9no3:267–86 D '28.

Comparison of Q and F leads to conclusions 'I. The copy for the 1623 version . . . consisted of a Quarto text corrected from a manuscript in the possession of Heminge and Condell' (p.269); 'II. The Quarto gives a later draft of the play than that in the possession of Heminge and Condell from which it was corrected'. (p.274)

1823 **Tannenbaum, Samuel Aaron.** Notes on Troilus and Cressida. Sh Assn Bull 7no2:72–81 Ap '32.

1824 —— A critique of the text of Troilus and Cressida. Sh Assn Bull 9nos2–4: 55–74,125–44,198–214 Jl–Oc '34. tables.

1. The quarto text.—2. The Folio text.—Postscript[s] [on handwriting and *STM*]
Detailed analysis of textual features of Q and F which were set up from independently prepared transcripts of holograph, with no prompt-book influence.

1825 **Baldwin, Thomas Whitfield.** Shakespeare facsimile. TLS 6 My '39:265.

Blemish in the Methuen facsim. affecting text of *Tro.*

1826 **Rossiter, A. P.** Troilus and Cressida. TLS 8 My '48:261.

Suggests rearrangement of Hector's speeches at 2.2, and at 5.7.11 reads 'double-horned Spartan' for Q 'double-hen'd Spartan'.

1827 **Williams, Philip.** The second issue of Shakespeare's Troilus and Cressida, 1609. Stud Bib 2:25–33 '49. diagr.

The half-sheet signed ¶ was 'very probably printed along with the final half-sheet M of the text as a pre-publication cancellans'. (p.27)

1828 **Walker, Alice.** The textual problem of Troilus and Cressida. Mod Lang R 45no4:459–64 Oc '50. tables.

The copy for the first three pages of F, which was set from a corrected copy of Q, 'differed from that which was available when work on the play was resumed'.

1829 **Williams, Philip.** Shakespeare's Troilus and Cressida; the relation of quarto and Folio. Stud Bib 3:131–43 '51.

F was set from a copy of Q.

1830 **Greg, sir Walter Wilson.** The printing of Shakespeare's Troilus and Cressida in the First folio. Pa Bib Soc Am 45:273–82 '57. tables.

Repr. in no.147. Endorsement of A. Walker's findings (*see* no.1828) with some account of the copyright problem.

1831 **Alexander, Peter.** Troilus and Cressida. TLS 18 Mr '65:220; J. C. Maxwell *ib.* 25 Mr '65:240; N. Coghill 19 Ja '67:52; P. Alexander 16 F '67:136; W. Empson 2 Mr '67:167; I. R. W. Cook 9 Mr '67:202; F. T. Bowers 16 Mr '67:226; N. Coghill 30 Mr '67:274; W. Empson; J. C. Maxwell; I. R. W. Cook 6 Ap '67:296; P. Alexander; W. Empson 20 Ap '67:340; N. Coghill; I. R. W. Cook 4 My '67:384.

On the circumstances of publication in light of the TP and prefatory epistle.

INDIVIDUAL TEXTS—TWELFTH NIGHT

1840 **Tannenbaum, Samuel Aaron.** Sound or soughe in Twelfth night, I.i.8. Sh Assn Bull 5n04:189–91 Oc '30. illus.

Ms. 'souue' (soughe) misread as 'sound' at 1.1.5.

1841 —— 'Comments on Twelfth night' *in* Shaksperian scraps and other Elizabethan fragments. New York, 1933. p.118–28.

Comments on the textual commentary in the New Cambridge ed.

1842 **Chapman, Raymond.** Twelfth night and the Swan theatre. N&Q 196: 468–70 Oc '51.

Composition and revision of *TN* in light of de Witt's sketch of the Swan theatre.

INDIVIDUAL TEXTS—TWO GENTLEMEN OF VERONA

1850 **Tannenbaum, Samuel Aaron.** The New Cambridge Shakspere and The two gentlemen of Verona. Sh Assn Bull 13n03:151–72 Jl '38; 13n04: 208–23 Oc '38.

Detailed examination of the text.

1851 **Tannenbaum, Samuel Aaron.** [Same]: New York [Tenny pr.] 1939. 68p. 25cm. Covertitle. (Shakspere studies, no.4)

'Reprinted, with large additions and some corrections, from the Shakespeare Association Bulletin.'

INDIVIDUAL TEXTS—WINTER'S TALE

1860 **Tannenbaum, Samuel Aaron.** Textual and other notes on The winter's tale. Philol Q 7no4:358–67 Oc '28.

Eighteen, mainly palæographically based, notes; F copy was holograph.

1861 —— 'Ralph Crane and The winter's tale' *in* Shaksperian scraps and other Elizabethan fragments. New York, 1933. p.75–86.

Disagrees with J. D. Wilson that *WT* was set from a Crane transcript as F copy was holographic.

1862 **Pafford, John Henry P.** The Winter's tale: typographical peculiarities in the Folio text. N&Q 206:172–8 My '61. tables.

Detailed survey of orthographical features.

1863 **Hill, Trevor Howard Howard-.** Knight, Crane, and the copy for the Folio Winter's tale. N&Q 211:139–40 Ap '66.

Disputes suggestion of J. H. P. Pafford that Knight influenced copy for *WT*, which may have been a transcript by Crane of his transcript of the prompt-book.

APOCRYPHA

1875 **Brooke, Charles Frederick Tucker,** *ed.* 'Bibliography' *in* The Shakespeare apocrypha. Oxford, 1908. (Repr. 1967) p.438–[56]

Classified checklist of works and criticism.

1876 **Tannenbaum, Samuel Aaron.** Anthony Mundy, including the play of Sir Thomas Moore, a concise bibliography. New York, 1942. (Repr. Port Washington, N.Y., Kennikat pr. [1967]) viii,36p. 23cm. (Elizabethan bibliographies, no.27)

'Sir Thomas Moore' (p.[23]–30)

1877 **[Erdman, David V.** and **E. G. Fogel]** *ed.* 'Shakespeare' *in* Evidence for authorship; essays on problems of attribution, with an annotated bibliography of selected readings. Ithaca, N.Y. [1966] p.432–94.

Classified annotated checklist of works on the Sh. canon and *H6, Tit., Shr., H8, Ed3, STM, Per.* and *TNK* in particular.

1880 **Schücking, Levin Ludwig.** Das Datum des pseudo-Shakespeareschen Sir Thomas Moore. Eng Studien 46n02:228–51 Je '13.

1. Die Ausgaben des Stücks. — 2. Der Inhalt des Stücks. — 3. Meinungen über die Verfasserschaft. — 4. Meinungen über die Entstehungszeit. — 5. Das Problem. — 6. Sir Thomas Moore und Julius Caesar. — 7. Die Redeszene des Sir Thomas Moore und ihre Quelle. — 8. Sir Thomas Moore und Hamlet. — 9. Die Hamletszene des Sir Thomas Moore und die Quelle. — 10. Sir Thomas Moore und andre Shakespearesche Stücke. — 11. Sir Thomas Moore und der Tamer tamed. — 12. Sir Thomas Moore und Thomas lord Cromwell. — 13. Sir Thomas Moore und das Rührstück. — 14. Schlußfolgerungen. — 15. Das Moore-Thema. — 16. Ergebniße.

1881 **Simpson, Percy.** The play of Sir Thomas More and Shakespeare's hand in it. Library ser3 8n029:79–96 Ja '17.

Largely a review article on Maunde Thompson's Shakespeare's handwriting, no.1009.

1882 **Shakespeare's** hand in the play of Sir Thomas More. TLS 24 Ap '19:222; A. D. Wilde *ib.* 1 My '19:237; J. D. Wilson 8 My '19:251; M. A. Bayfield 15 My '19:265; A. W. Pollard; A. D. Wilde 22 My '19:279; J. D. Wilson; M. A. Bayfield; R. R. Steele; Charlotte C. Stopes 29 My '19:295–6; M. A. Bayfield; A. D. Wilde 5 Je '19:312; sir W. W. Greg 6 N '19:630.

General account of the problem favourable to Sh. authorship of the addition by hand D.

1883 **Greenwood, sir Granville George.** Shakspere's handwriting. London, J. Lane, Bodley head, 1920. 36p. 18cm.

Denies Maunde Thompson's identification of Sh. hand in *STM.*

Rev: TLS 27 My '20:326; sir G. G. Greenwood *ib.* 10 Je '20:368, J. P. Gilson 17 Je '20:384; sir G. G. Greenwood 24 Je '20:403; K. E. T. Wilkinson 1 Jl '20:424; sir G. G. Greenwood 8 Jl '20:441.

1884 **Bayfield, M. A.** Shakespeare's handwriting. TLS 30 Je '21:418; sir E. M. Thompson *ib.* 4 Ag '21:499–500; M. A. Bayfield 18 Ag '21:533.

Comparison with the signatures shows that hand D is not Shakespeare's.

1885 **Greenwood, sir Granville George.** Shakespeare's signatures and Sir Thomas More. TLS 7 Jl '21:436–7.

1886 **Pollard, Alfred William,** *ed.* Shakespeare's hand in The play of Sir Thomas More; papers by Alfred W. Pollard, W. W. Greg, E. Maunde Thompson, J. Dover Wilson & R. W. Chambers, with the text of the Ill May day scenes edited by W. W. Greg. Cambridge, C.U.P., 1923. (Repr. 1939) vi,229[14]p. facsims. 17cm. (Shakespeare problems, II)

1. Introduction, by A. W. Pollard.—2. The handwritings of the manuscript, by W. W. Greg.—3. The handwriting of the three pages attributed to Shakespeare compared with his signatures, by sir E. Maunde Thompson.—4. Bibliographical links between the three pages and the good quartos, by J. Dover Wilson.—5. The expression of ideas, particularly political ideas, in the three pages and in Shakespeare, by R. W. Chambers.— 6. Ill May day scenes from the play of Sir Thomas More: text edited by W. W. Greg.— 7. Special transcript of the three pages, by W. W. Greg.

'The object of this book is to strengthen the evidence of the existence (in the Harleian MS. 7368 at the British museum) of three pages written by Shakespeare in his own hand as part of the play of Sir Thomas More.' (p.[v])

Rev: Month 142:568 '23; Lond Merc 9:1–4 '23; R. B. McKerrow Library ser4 4:238–42 '23; V. Rendall Nation–Athenæum 34:283–4 '23; N&Q 145:339–40 '23; TLS 18 Oc '23: 687; T. S. Graves Stud Philol 21:435–6 '24; S. C. Chew Nation 119:219–20 '24; B. Fehr Angl Beibl 35:97–102 '24; P. Aronstein Eng Studien 59:445–50 '25.

1887 **Greenwood, sir Granville George.** The Shakspere signatures and Sir Thomas More. [London] C. Palmer [1924] xvii,112p. facsims. 17cm.

Denies the identification of Sh. hand in *STM*; Sh. of Stratford and Sh. the player were separate individuals.

Rev: TLS 30 Oc '24:682; sir G. G. Greenwood *ib.* 6 N '24:710.

1888 **Kenyon, sir Frederic George.** An autograph of Shakespeare. Discovery 5no51:60–3 Mr '24.

A play by many writers.—The nature of the evidence.—The importance of the discovery.

1889 **Wilson, John Dover.** Shakespearian elisions in Sir Thomas More. TLS 25 S '24:596; C. H. Herford; J. A. Fort *ib.* 9 Oc '24:631; J. D. Wilson 16 Oc '24:651.

On the occurrence and significance of elisions in Sh. early ptd. texts.

1890 **Schücking, Levin Ludwig.** Shakespeare and Sir Thomas More. R Eng Stud 1no1:40–59 Ja '25.

1. The supposed Shakespearian flavour.—2. Shakespearian in feeling?—3. The position of the play in the development of the drama.—4. The date.—5. The authorship of the scene.

'. . . the final judgment must needs be that Shakespeare's authorship of the "147 lines" is more than doubtful.' (p.59)

1891 **Tannenbaum, Samuel Aaron.** Shakspere's unquestioned autographs and the addition to Sir Thomas Moore. Stud Philol 22no2:133–60 Ap '25. facsims.

'. . . on the basis of the six unquestioned signatures the weight of the evidence is overwhelmingly against the theory that in . . . Moore we have a Shakspere holograph.' (p.156)

1892 —— The booke of Sir Thomas Moore, a bibliotic study. New York, Tenny pr. [1927] 135p. facsims. 24cm.

1. The number of penmen in Sir Thomas Moore.—2. The authors of the play.—3. Conjectural dates of composition.—4. Anthony Mundy's authorship.—5. Thomas Kyd and his share in the play.—6. Henry Chettle's (A's) hand in the play.—7. Thomas Heywood's (B's) hand in the play.—8. D's (Shakspere's?) hand in the play.—9. When was the play revised?—10. Chettle's contribution to the play.—11. Kyd's contribution to the play.—12. Thomas Dekker's contribution to the play.—13. When the play was written.—Appendix . . . D. Transcripts of facsimiles. . . .

Rev: Sir W. W. Greg Library ser4 9:202–11 S '28; R. B. McKerrow R Eng Stud 4:237–41 '28; C. J. Sisson Mod Lang R 23:231–4 '28; C. F. T. Brooke Yale R 17:406–10 '28; T. W. Baldwin Mod Lang N 43:327–32 '28; M. Praz Eng Stud 11:73–4 '29; E. Ekwall Angl Beibl 40:362–4 '29; E. Eckhardt Eng Studien 63:428–9 '29; R. A. Law J Eng Germ Philol 28:555–7 '29.

1893 **Golding, S. R.** Further notes on Robert Wilson and Sir Thomas More. N&Q 155:237–40 Oc '28.

Additional support on palæographical grounds for his attribution of the Sh. lines to Wilson.

1894 **Marschall, Wilhelm.** Das Sir Thomas Moore Manuskript und die englische commedia dell'arte. Angl 52:193–241 S '28.

General summary of current position.

1895 **Tannenbaum, Samuel Aaron.** More about the Booke of Sir Thomas Moore. Pub Mod Lang Assn 13no3:767–78 S '28. facsim.

Further argument against Sh. association with *STM*, with notes on the ms. in general.

1896 —— Shakspere and Sir Thomas Moore. New York, Tenny pr.; London, T. W. Laurie, 1929. 64p. illus., facsims. 23cm.

Rev: M. Praz Eng Stud 12:228–31 '30; W. Keller Sh Jahrb 66:224–5 '30; R. S. Forsythe Mod Lang N 46:192–4 '31; E. Eckhardt Eng Studien 66:121–2 '31.

1897 **Bald, Robert Cecil.** Addition III of Sir Thomas More. R Eng Stud 7no25: 67–9 Ja '31.

Suggests that Addition III by Hand C was written by Sh.

1898 **Acheson, Arthur.** 'Shakespeare, Chapman, and Sir Thomas More' *in* Shakespeare, Chapman, and Sir Thomas More, providing a more definite basis for biography and criticism. London, 1931. p.99–134.

Hand D's portion 'a full and free revision of a portion of the play originally written by George Chapman'. (p.105)

1899 —— 'Peele's hand in Sir Thomas More' *in* Shakespeare, Chapman, and Sir Thomas More. London, 1931. p.265–73. fold.facsims.

Identifies Hand C as Peele.

1900 **Law, Robert Adger.** Is Heywood's hand in Sir Thomas More? Univ Texas Stud Eng 11:24–31 S '31. table.

The orthography and literary style do not support the identification of Heywood as Hand B, whereas the handwriting similarities are not conclusive.

1901 **Tannenbaum, Samuel Aaron.** An object lesson in Shaksperian research. New York [Tenny pr.] 1931. 23p. facsims. Covertitle. (Shakspere studies, no.2)

Introductory.—Controversy re-opened.—Inexpert testimony.—Expert testimony.—Script re-examined.

On the 'Goodal' notation in *STM*.

1902 **Crundell, H. W.** Shakespeare and the play of More. TLS 20 My '39:297–8; R. W. Chambers *ib*. 3 Je '39:327.

1903 **Cadwalader, John.** Theobald's alleged Shakespeare manuscript. Mod Lang N 55no2:108–9 F '40.

Notes a ms. reference by Theobald to his introduction of 'an original play of Shakespeare'.

1904 **Deutschberger, Paul.** Shakspere and Sir Thomas More. Sh Assn Bull 18nos2–4:75–91,99–108,156–7 Ap–Oc '43.

Examines 'the present status of the question' and concludes against Sh. hand in Addition IV.

1905 **Beaumont, Comyns.** Shakespeare's handwriting. Baconiana 32no128: 156–60 Jl '48.

Anti-Stratfordian comment on Sh. hand in *STM*.

1906 **Jenkins, Harold.** Readings in the manuscript of Sir Thomas More. Mod Lang R 43no3:512–14 Oc '48.

At f.11ᵃ, c.647–58, reads 'hange chefely' for 'hange the foly', and at f.11ᵇ, 722, for 'acts' reads 'arts'.

1907 **Bald, Robert Cecil.** The booke of Sir Thomas More and its problems. Sh Surv 2:44–65 '49. facsims.

The manuscript.—Company and date.—The handwriting and spelling of the three pages.—Style, thought and imagery.

Detailed examination of the problems which endorses the most general view in favour of Sh. association with the ms. 'The Shakespearian additions . . . Addition II, c' (p.62–5): a transcript.

1908 **Parks, Edd Winfeld.** 'Simms's edition of the Shakespeare apocrypha' *in* Matthews, Arthur D. and C. M. Emery, *ed.* Studies in Shakespeare. Coral Gables, Fla., 1953. p.30–9.

1909 **Nosworthy, James M.** Shakespeare and Sir Thomas More. R Eng Stud new ser 6no21:12–25 Ja '55.

The authorship and date of the original play.—The date of Addition II (hand D).—The authorship and date of Addition III.

'. . . Munday, Chettle, and Dekker wrote Sir Thomas More round about 1600, . . . Shakespeare wrote his section of Addition II c.1601–2, . . . he also wrote Addition III and at the same time.' (p.24–5)

1910 —— Hand B in Sir Thomas More. Library ser5 11no1:47–50 Mr '56.

Comparison of Heywood's The captives and Hand B does not conclusively identify Heywood as a co-author.

1911 **Lane, Ralph H.** Shakespearean spelling. Sh Newsl 8no4:28 S '58.

Shakespeare's preference.—Shakespeare's hand not in Sir Thos. More.

1912 **Waller, Frederick O.** Printer's copy for The two noble kinsmen. Stud Bib 11:61–84 '58. table.

Copy was the collaborators' foul papers, incompletely revised by Fletcher.

1913 **Huber, R. A.** 'On looking over Shakespeare's secretarie' *in* Jackson B. A. W., *ed.* Stratford papers on Shakespeare. Toronto [1961] p.[52]–77 facsims.

The problem.—The complications.—The work to date.—Some fundamentals.—The evidence.—In summary.—Other problems.—Postscript, by C. J. Sisson.

Comparison of Hand D in *STM* with the signatures by the Canadian (police) Examiner of questioned documents. '. . . the evidence is not sufficiently strong to justify a positive identification of the poet.' (p.66)

1914 **Jenkins, Harold.** 'A supplement to sir Walter Greg's edition of Sir Thomas More' *in* Malone society. Collections, volume VI. [London] 1961. p.177–92. table.

Repr. of the supplement added to the 1961 repr. of Greg's 1911 ed.; a fresh assessment.

1915 **Hoy, Cyrus.** The shares of Fletcher and his collaborators in the Beaumont and Fletcher canon, VII. Stud Bib 15:72–90 '62. tables.

'The Two noble kinsmen' (p.72–6): linguistic evidence is compatible with collaboration, on evidence drawn from Sh. later plays. The copy appears to have been a scribal transcript of foul papers. 'Henry VIII' (p.76–85): divides between Sh. and Fletcher, with Fletcherian interpolations in Sh. scenes.

1916 **Bertram, Paul Benjamin.** 'The manuscript' *in* Shakespeare and The two noble kinsmen. New Brunswick, N.J. [1965] p.58–123.

'Checklist of editions' (p.297–9)

1917 **Clayton, Thomas S.** A computer-produced aid to the study of Shakespeare's spelling and handwriting. Sh Newsl 16no1:6 F '66.

Concordance of the Sh. portion of *STM*, designed to aid palæographical study.

POEMS

1930 **Lee, sir Sidney,** *ed.* 'Census of extant copies [and bibliography]' *in* Shakespeare's Lucrece, being a reproduction in facsimile of the first edition. . . . Oxford, 1905. p.37–56.

1931 —— [Bibliographical notes and census of copies] *in* The passionate pilgrim, being a reproduction in facsimile of the first edition. . . . Oxford, 1905. p.45–57.

1932 —— [A census of copies] *in* Shakespeare's Venus and Adonis, being a reproduction in facsimile of the first edition. . . . Oxford, 1905. p.54–75. facsim.

'The history of the publication' and 'The history of the text'. (p.39–53)

1935 **Lee, sir Sidney.** Shakespeare's Poems and Pericles. TLS 9 Oc '03:289.

Request for material for his facsim. ed.

1936 **Evans, H. A.** Early ms. mention of Shakespeare. N&Q ser10 1:310 Ap '04.

Inquiry about location of ms. diary containing note of purchase of *Ven.* in 1593, cited in Malone's Inquiry.

1937 **Jonas, Maurice.** The Passionate pilgrim. N&Q ser11 12:259 Oc '15.

On whereabouts of copies of 1599 ed.

1938 **Alden, Raymond Macdonald.** The 1710 and 1714 texts of Shakespeare's poems. Mod Lang N 31no5:268–74 My '16.
> 1. Corrections made in 1714.—2. Erroneous or unique readings of 1714.—3. Readings of 1714 in doubtful passages.
> Gildon's ed. of 1710 and 1714, published by Curll.

1939 **Keynes, sir Geoffrey Langdon.** A note on Shakespearian end-papers. Library ser4 6no3:280–1 D '25.
> Sheet of Poems, 1640, bound in Fuller's Holy war, 1639.

1940 **Swan, Marshall W. S.** Shakespeare's Poems, the first three Boston editions. Pa Bib Soc Am 36:27–36 '42.
> Account of the history of ed. by Munroe and Francis, 1808.

1941 **Farr, Harry.** The Longner Hall Venus and Adonis. TLS 26 F '20:144.
> This copy is of an 'unknown and hitherto unrecorded edition'.

1942 —— Notes on Shakespeare's printers and publishers, with special reference to the poems and Hamlet. Library ser4 3no4:225–60 Mr '23. facsims.
> Discussion of ed. of *Ven.* published by William Leake, and others; early ed. of *Luc.*, *PP*, *Son.*, the Poems, and 17th-century ed. of *Ham.*

1943 **Partridge, Astley Cooper.** Shakespeare's orthography in Venus and Adonis and some early quartos. Sh Surv 7:35–47 '54.
> General survey under spelling, syncope and elision, possessive genitive, punctuation, capitals, and contractions.

1944 **Cutts, John P.** Venus and Adonis in an early seventeenth-century song-book. N&Q 208:302–3 Ag '63.
> A version of stanza 87 (A thousand kisses) in BM Add. ms. 24665, c.1615, prepared for music.

1945 **Commonplace-book** from the time of Shakespeare. Brit Mus Q News Supp 12:6–7 Ap/Je '65.
> Report of acquisition of BM Add. ms. 52585, containing ms. extract from *Luc.*, l. 764–1036.

SONNETS

1960 **Lee, sir Sidney,** *ed.* 'Census of copies' *in* Shakespeare's Sonnets, being a reproduction in facsimile of the first edition. . . . Oxford, 1905. p.62–71. facsim.
> 'The history of the publication' and 'The state of the text' (p.26–50); 'Early manuscript copies and reprints'. (p.51–62)

1961 **Alden, Raymond Macdonald,** *ed.* 'Bibliography' *in* The Sonnets of Shakespeare. Boston, Houghton, Mifflin, 1916. p.[485]–530.

1962 **Tannenbaum, Samuel Aaron.** Shakspere's Sonnets, a concise bibliography. New York, 1940. (Repr. Port Washington, N.Y., Kennikat pr. [1967]) xii,68p. 24cm. (Elizabethan bibliographies, no.10)

1970 **Alden, Raymond Macdonald.** The 1640 text of Shakespeare's Sonnets. Mod Philol 14no1:17–30 My '16. tables.
Benson's 1640 ed. was ptd. from 1609 Q copy and has no independent authority.

1971 **Richmond, Oliffe.** Shakespeare's Sonnets, a reading. TLS 26 D '18:657; W. D. Sargeaunt *ib.* 2 Ja '19:10; H. Cuningham 9 Ja '19:21; W. D. Sargeaunt 16 Ja '19:34; C. Creighton 23 Ja '19:46.
'Rescribe' for 'reserve' in 85.

1972 **Whorlow, H.** Shakespeare's Sonnets, a reading. TLS 16 Ja '19:34.
'Tells' for 'kills' in 44.

1973 **Tannenbaum, Samuel Aaron.** The copy for Shakespeare's Sonnets. Philol Q 10no4:393–5 Oc '31.
Palæographical examination of certain textual errors in Sh. shows that *Son.* were ptd. from copy in secretary hand.

1974 **Evans, Willa McClung.** Lawes' version of Shakespeare's sonnet CXVI. Pub Mod Lang Assn 51no1:120–2 Mr '36. facsim.
In John Gamble's commonplace book, now in N.Y. Public library Drexel collection.

1975 **Eagle, Roderick L.** The headpiece on Shakespeare's Sonnets, 1609. N&Q 192:38 Ja '47.
Occurrence of ornamental woodcut in books ptd. by Simmes and Eld.

1976 **Hayward, John Davy.** Shakespeare's Sonnets, 1609. (Note no.16) Bk Coll 1no4:266 '52.
Corrects provenance of Bodmer copy from sir George Holford to the earl of Caledon: *see* no.308.

1977 **Shield, H. A.** Links with Shakespeare, X. N&Q 197:387–9 Ag '52.
Thomas Thorpe as publisher of *Son.* and also, perhaps, as mayor of Chester.

1978 **Rostenberg, Leona.** Thomas Thorpe, publisher of Shake-Speares Sonnets. Pa Bib Soc Am 54:16–37 '60.

1979 **Landry, Hilton.** Malone as editor of Shakespeare's Sonnets. N.Y. Pub Lib Bull 67no7:435–42 S '63.

1980 **Nosworthy, James M.** Shakespeare and mr. W. H. Library ser5 18no4:294–8 D '63.
'W. H.' a misprint for 'W. SH.' or 'W. S.'?

1981 **Bennett, Josephine Waters.** Benson's alleged piracy of Shake-Speares Sonnets and of some of Jonson's works. Stud Bib 21:235–48 '68.

INDEX

THE Index records the names of authors, compilers, editors, and publishers of the items listed in the Bibliography, together with subjects, in a single alphabetical sequence. Name references and the references pertaining to them are in roman type. Subject entries are in SMALL CAPITALS. Under the main subject headings, the numbers printed in **bold** face refer to the entries under the same heading in the main arrangement of the Bibliography. Prefixes such as 'bp., sir, ld.' have been ignored in the filing order. Titles of books and periodicals are in *italics*, or *ITALIC SMALL CAPITALS* if they are the subjects of entries in the Bibliography.

Items dealing with a particular textual point have been listed in act and scene order after the subheading 'Text' under the title of the respective work. The number in brackets is the Folio through-line number given in the Oxford Old-Spelling Concordances and the Norton facsimile.

A., H. 1043
ABBEY, Edwin A.—Bibliogr. 58
Abbott, G. F. 848
Aberystwyth. National library of Wales *see* Wales. National Library, Aberystwyth.
ABERYSTWYTH. University college *see* WALES. University. University college, Aberystwyth.
Abrahams, Aleck. 536 671 710
Acheson, Arthur. 1898–9
ACT AND SCENE DIVISION. 582 614 862 864–5 1211 1447
Adams, Herbert Mayow. 304
Adams, John Cranford. 1812
Adams, Joseph Quincy. 286 294 868 1038 1432 1787
ADAPTATIONS—Bibliogr. 205–6 213 217
ADAPTATIONS FOR CHILDREN—Bibliogr. 232
Adee, Alvey A. 695 713
Adout, Jacques. 116
Aguiar, Thereza da Silva. 104 144
Aitken, George Atherton. 717
Akrigg, G. P. V. 601
Albert, Gábor. 117
Albright, Evelyn May. 1314
Alden, John Eliot. 329
Alden, Raymond Macdonald. 1938 1961 1970
ALDENHAM, Henry Hucks Gibbs, baron, 1819–1907 *see* GIBBS, Henry Hucks, baron Aldenham.
Alexander, Peter. 118 739 869 891 905 1198 1341 1350 1380 1585 1822 1831
ALLDE, Edward, c.1583–1624. 1740
Allen, Don Cameron. 926
Allen, E. G. 1490
Allen, Edward A. 1153
Allen, N. B. 1216 1584 1719
Allen, Percy. 1199
ALL'S WELL THAT ENDS WELL—Text. **1080–5**

— — 2.1.110 (715). 1067
— — 3.2.113 (1519). 1081
— — 4.2.38 (2063). 1080–1 1083–5
Altman, George J. 1224
American art association, New York. 289
American library association. 40
Amnéus, Daniel A. 1523
And, Metin. 119
Anderson, D. M. 1460
Anderson galleries, New York. 203
Andhra university. 952
Ann Arbor, Mich. University microfilms *see* University microfilms, Ann Arbor, Mich.
ANTISHAKESPEARIANA *see also* BACONIANA; EDWARD DE VERE. 79
ANTONY AND CLEOPATRA—Text. 923 943 **1090–7**
— — 1.1.58–9 (70–1). 1090
— — 1.5.48 (578). 1092–3
— — 3.10.28–9 (2010–12). 1094
— — 3.13.75 (2242). 1097
— — 4.15 1095–6
APOCRYPHA. 205 **1875–917**
— Bibliogr. 1875–7
ARDEN SHAKESPEARE. 1444
ARGENTINA *see* WORKS IN ARGENTINA.
ARMIN, Robert, d.1615. 1450
Armstrong college, Newcastle-upon-Tyne *see* Durham. University. Armstrong college, Newcastle-upon-Tyne.
ARMY AND SHAKESPEARE—Bibliogr. 100
Ashe, Geoffrey. 1045
Ashton, Florence Huber. 1750
ASPLEY, William, d.1640. 1031
ASSEMBLED TEXTS. 850 853 856 886
AS YOU LIKE IT. 371
— Text. 1070 **1105–10**
— — 2.1.5. (611). 1105
— — 2.7.73 (1047). 1106 1108
— — 4.2.13 (2139). 1110

INDEX TO BRITISH LITERARY
BIBLIOGRAPHY

I
Bibliography of British literary bibliographies

SUPPLEMENT

PREFACE

PUBLICATION of the second volume of the *Index to British Literary Biblio-graphy* makes it possible to bring the first volume to the same terminal date, by the addition of bibliographies which were published by the end of 1969. I have also been able to supply revised entries for many items which earlier were marked 'Not seen'. There is a larger number of additional items. For some of these I am indebted to friends and correspondents, but most were gathered as I worked through the principal English and bibliographical periodicals volume by volume for the third volume of the *Index*.

The full table of contents identifies the subject-headings which appear for the first time in the Supplement so that owners of the first volume may insert cross-references if they desire. It has been necessary to renumber a few items in order to accommodate new entries. Such renumbered items have been printed again in the Supplement, and the index takes account of the new numbers given to them here. Further, some entries, such as those for Mandeville and Richard de Bury, have been moved, and for some headings the entries have been rearranged: the heading 'Keats' gives an example of this.

The index includes corrections brought over from the first volume, and also shows that index entries starting with 'De', 'New', and similar particles have been properly arranged. Readers will notice that the index is disproportionately large for the extent of the Supplement which comprises only about eight hundred items. This is because when an entry in the Supplement has added a number to a reference already in the index, the whole revised entry has been printed in the index to the Supplement. Hence, one will find on account of 2613a, the excerpt of the Bunyan portion of the British Museum catalogue, that the whole index entry for 'British Museum. Dept. of printed books' has been reprinted: the index reference in the Supplement incorporates references to both the Supplement and the parent volume. Similarly, the index entry for 'Bunyan' in this case refers to the whole sequence of Bunyan entries, not just the bibliographies listed in the Supplement. It follows therefore that readers should commence their researches in the Supplement index. (The references under 'British books printed abroad' have been broken down by country.)

The great increase in the number of bibliographies which are reprinted year by year makes it uneconomical to alter the entries of the first volume just to take account of the reprints. Accordingly, reprints that I have noticed are listed separately at the end of the Supplement in the order of their appearance in the first volume. However, if the reprint contained substantial new material it has been listed in the main sequence as a separate item. As libraries already possess-ing the original books rarely need to obtain the reprints, I have seen very few of the reprints listed here and in some cases, because reprint publishers often omit to note the date of the reprint, my entries may be incorrect. However, readers may obtain some assistance from such general guides as Diaz, A. J., *ed.* *Guide to reprints, 1967– .* Washington, D.C., Microcard editions, 1967– , and *Bibliographia anastatica,* Amsterdam, 1964– .

Through an oversight for which I hasten to apologize, I omitted to mention my appreciation of the help given by my friend and colleague, J. E. Traue, with the entries for Katharine Mansfield. I am happy also to record the laborious kindness of John Simmons and Simon Nowell-Smith who gave me detailed lists of corrections and additions. I am further indebted to John Simmons for the use I have been able to make of *Bibliography in Britain,* and for his kindness in reading the revises. Other helpers and correspondents have been B. Hutchison, editor, *Book Collecting and Library Monthly;* James Thompson, Librarian, University of Reading; R. C. Johnson, Newberry Library, Chicago; Professor W. M. Smith, Trinity Evangelical Divinity School, Deerfield, Illinois; Dr. J. D. Fleeman, Pembroke College, Oxford; Dr. Keith Walker, University College, London; G. Wakeman, Loughborough, Leics.; J. S. Cox, St. Peter Port, Guernsey; and Miss Kathleen I. Garrett, Guildhall Library, London. I am grateful for their assistance, and would be pleased to learn of corrections and additions to the Supplement.   T. H. H.

'Trevenny', Noke, Oxford
December 1969

CONTENTS

Asterisked headings appear for the first time in the Supplement

TABLE OF ABBREVIATIONS

Ag	August
Ala.	Alabama
Am	America/n
Ann	Annual
Ap	April
Assn	Association
B.C.	British Columbia
Bib	Bibliographical/y
bibliogr.	bibliographical/y
Biblioth	Bibliotheck
Bk	Book
Bull	Bulletin
c.	*circa*
Calif.	California
Cath	Catholic
Cent	Century
Chron	Chronicle
chronol.	chronological
Circ	Circular
cm.	centimetre/s
col.	coloured; column/s
Coll	Collector/'s; College
comp.	compiled; compiler/s
Conn.	Connecticut
contrib/s.	contribution/s
C.U.P.	Cambridge University Press
D	December
Dept.	Department
diagr/s.	diagram/s
ed.	edited; edition/s; editor/s
Eng	English
F	February
facsim/s.	facsimile/s
Fict	Fiction
fl.	*floruit* (flourished)
fold.	folded
Gaz	Gazette
Geol	Geological
Germ	Germanic
Guildh	Guildhall
Hist	Historical; History
H.M.S.O.	His (or Her) Majesty's Stationery Office
ib.	*ibidem* (in the same place)
Ill.	Illinois
illus.	illustration/s; illustrated
Ind.	Indiana

Inst	Institute
Ital	Italian
J	Journal
Ja	January
Je	June
Jl	July
l.	leaf, leaves; line/s
Lang	Language
Leics.	Leicestershire
Lib	Library
Lit	Literary; Literature
Mag	Magazine
Mass.	Massachusetts
Misc	Miscellany
Miss.	Mississippi
M.I.T.	Massachusetts institute of Technology
Mod	Modern
Mr	March
ms/s.	manuscript/s
Mthly	Monthly
Mus	Music
My	May
N	Note/s; November
N&Q	Notes and Queries
Nat	National; Natural
n.d.	no date
Neb.	Nebraska
Neophilol	Neophilologus
Newsl	Newsletter
no/s.	number/s
N.J.	New Jersey
N.Y.	New York
Oc	October
Opp	Opportunities
O.U.P.	Oxford University Press
p.	page/s
Pa	Paper/s
Pa.	Pennsylvania
Philobib	Philobiblon
Philol	Philological; Philology
Philos	Philosophical; Philosophy
port/s.	portrait/s
pr.	press
Priv	Private
Proc	Proceedings
pseud.	pseudonym
pt/s.	part/s
ptd.	printed
ptr.	printer
Pub	Public; Publications; Publisher/s'; published
Q	Quarterly
quasifacsim.	quasifacsimile

R	Review
Rec	Record
refs.	references
Renaiss.	Renaissance
repr.	reprint/ed
Res	Research
Restor	Restoration
rev.	revised
R.I.	Rhode Island
Roy	Royal
S	September
ser	series
Sevent	Seventeenth
Sh	Shakespeare
Soc	Society; Societies
STC	Short-title catalogue, comp. by Pollard and Redgrave
Stud	Studies; Study; Studien
Tech	Technical
Theat	Theatre; Theatrical
TLS	Times Literary Supplement
TP	title-page
Trans	Transactions
transcr/s.	transcription/s
Transit	Transition
Twent	Twentieth
Univ	University
U.P.	University Press
v.	volume/s
Va.	Virginia

GENERAL BIBLIOGRAPHIES OF
AND GUIDES TO
BRITISH LITERATURE

ENGLISH LITERATURE — GENERAL GUIDES

1 **Dobrée, Bonamy,** *ed.* Introductions to English literature. Rev. ed. London, Cresset pr., 1950–8. (First pub. 1938–40). 5v. 21cm.
Contents: 1. Renwick, William L. and H. Orton. The beginnings of English literature to Skelton. (1952).—2. Pinto, Vivian de S. The English renaissance, 1510–1688. (3d ed., rev. 1966).—3. Dyson, Henry and J. Butt. Augustans and romantics, 1689–1830. (3d ed., rev. 1961).—4. Batho, Edith C. and B. Dobrée. The Victorians and after, 1830–1914. (1950).—5. Daiches, David. The present age, after 1920. (1958). (Replaces Muir, Edwin. The present age from 1914. (1939))

2 **National book league,** LONDON. Writers and their work; general ed. T. O. Beachcroft. [1-] London, Longmans, 1950– . v. 21cm. (Formerly Bibliographical supplements to British book news)
Monographs devoted largely to lives and works of British authors, with select bibliogrs.

3 **Saul, George Brandon.** 'An introductory bibliography in Anglo-Irish literature' *in* Stephens, Yeats, and other Irish concerns. New York, 1954. p.12–18.
Repr. from N.Y. Pub Lib Bull 57:429–25 S '54.

4 **Kennedy, Arthur Garfield** and **D. B. Sands.** A concise bibliography for students of English. 4th ed. Stanford, Calif., Stanford U.P. [1960]. (First pub. 1940). xi,567p. 22cm.
'Journalistic art, periodical and newspaper bibliographies, and publication rights' (p.304–23); 'Printing, the book trade, and library science' (p.324–46); 'General bibliographical guides' (p.347–92).

5 **Watson, George Grimes,** *ed.* The concise Cambridge bibliography of English literature, 600–1950. 2d ed. Cambridge, C.U.P., 1965. (First pub. 1958). xi,269p. 21cm.
See CBEL: no.349.

6 **Altick, Richard Daniel** and **A. Wright.** Selective bibliography for the study of English and American literature. 3d ed. New York, Macmillan [1967]. (First pub. [1960]). xii,152p. 21cm.

7 **Bateson, Frederick Wilse.** A guide to English literature. 2d ed. London, Longmans, 1967; Garden City, N.Y., Anchor books, 1968. (First pub. [1965]). xi,261p. 18cm.

7a **McNamee, Lawrence F.** Dissertations in English and American literature: theses accepted by American, British and German universities, 1865–1964. New York, R. R. Bowker, 1968. xi, 1124p. 25cm. (Supplement, 1969 not seen).

ENGLISH LITERATURE — SERIAL BIBLIOGRAPHIES

22 **Gerstenberger, Donna Lorine** and **G. Hendrick.** Second directory of periodicals publishing articles in English and American literature and language. Denver, A. Swallow [1965]. (First pub. [1959]). 151p. 23cm.

SERIAL BIBLIOGRAPHIES ARRANGED BY PERIOD COVERED — PERIOD

31a 'Restoration and 18th century theatre research bibliography for 1961– ' *in* **Restoration and 18th century theatre research.** 1– . Chicago, Loyola university, 1962– .
Formerly titled 17th and 18th Century theatre research. Annually, N 1962– .

33 'The romantic movement, a selective and critical bibliography for 1949[–63]' *in* **Philological quarterly,** a journal. . . . 1– . Iowa City, Iowa, University of Iowa, 1922– .
Annually, v.19–42, 1950–64.

33a 'The romantic movement, a selected and critical bibliography for 1964– ' *in* **English language notes.** 3n01– . Boulder, Col., University of Colorado, 1965– .
From Philol Q 43n04 Oc '64.

BIBLIOGRAPHY—BIBLIOGRAPHIES

56 **[Esdaile, Arundell James Kennedy]** *comp.* 'Bibliographies' *in* Bateson, Frederick W., *ed.* Cambridge bibliography of English literature. Cambridge, 1940–57. V.1(1940), p.3–9; 5(1957), p.[3]–5, by Catherine M. Ing.

57 **[Pollard, Graham]** *comp.* 'Book production and distribution' *in* Bateson, Frederick W., *ed.* Cambridge bibliography of English literature. Cambridge, 1940–57. V.1, p.345–62; 2, p.82–107; 3, p.70–106; 5(1957), p.183–9, by sir Frank C. Francis; p.533–41, by F. Plaat; p.382–8, by Cyprian Blagden.
See also no.249a.

68 **London. University. School of librarianship and archives.** Bibliographies, calendars, and theses. . . . London, 1968. 14p. 21cm. (Occasional publications, no.14)

89a **Britton, M. C.** An outline bibliography of the publications of Bonamy Dobrée to 1962. 1963.

83a **Cambridge, David G.** English music printing, 1601–1629: bibliography. 1966.

102a **Cowan, Patricia M.** Ronald Knox. 1964.

105a **Cutter, Eric.** Sir Archibald Geikie, a bibliography. 1964.

105b **Czigány, M. M.** Hungarian literature in Great Britain, 1830–1963, a bibliography of English translations published in Great Britain. 1964.

108a **De la Mare, Judith.** The published musical works of Ralph Vaughan Williams in the library of the British museum up to 1st May, 1949. 1949.

115a **Easton, Judith M.** An amateur bibliography of the works of John Webster, the dramatist, with brief miscellaneous notes on the title pages, and an index. 1937.

119a **Farrand, Nancy.** Twentieth century study of Keats, a bibliography. 1939.

121a **Fernie, G. Elaine.** English editions of The Spanish tragedy. 1939.

123a **Flew, G. S. M.** C. V. Wedgwood. 1957.

123b **Fowler, J. E. H.** A bibliography of sir Charles Oman. 1954.

144a **Hully, P. M.** The writings of John Holland Rose. 1955.

147a **Jones, B. P.** Fielding in France, a bibliography of editions and critical references, 1733–1847. 1962.

148a **Jones, Winstan M.** Writings on J. M. Barrie appearing up to the end of 1960: bibliography. 1964.

148b **Judson, S.** Biographical and descriptive works on the rev. John Wesley: bibliography. 1963.

149a **Kennedy, M. J. O.** George Hawkins, bookseller at Milton's head, betwixt the Temple gates, an essay. (Includes 'A chronological list of Hawkins' publications'.) 1948.

153a **Kinsey, J. M.** Writings of York minster clergy holding office, 1660–1700. 1966.

154a **Langstadt, E.** A bibliography of G. G. Coulton. 1946.

155a **Lea, J.** A bibliography of works by sir Frederick George Kenyon. 1954.

165a **Madden, John L.** Joseph Henry Shorthouse and Charlotte Mary Yonge, biographical and critical studies: bibliographies. 1964.

167a **Mathews, Alison M.** The Court and city register, 1742–1813, a bibliography. 1939.

178a **Parry, V. T. H.** An interim bibliography of the writings of Holbrook Jackson. 1953.

179a **Partington, E.** Herbert Butterfield; bibliography. 1963.

179b **Passey, J. M. D.** Bibliography of the works of Hannah Glasse. 1955.

179c **Patry, Madeleine.** A bibliography of the works of Gilbert Murray. 1950.

189b **Raphael, Sandra.** The Folio society, 1947–1962. 1963. (*See* no.1323a)

189c **Rattenbury, S. K.** Peter Warlock (Philip Heseltine): a bibliography of his published works, both literary and musical, with a section on biography and criticism. 1959.

189d **Rees, Margaret J.** Sir Ronald Ross, 1857–1932: bibliography. 1966.

192a **Roper, I. A.** Bibliography of Thomas Love Peacock. 1956.

201a **Smith, Helen R.** The published works of David Garrick, a bibliography. 1966.

210a **Stevenson, C. L.** Sir Joseph Paxton, architect and gardener, a bibliography. 1961.

221a **Thomson, Myra.** Thomas Mann in England. 1950.

232a **Williams, F. H. B.** A bibliography of the writings of dr. Terrot Reaveley Glover, 1869–1943. 1952.

237a **Wood, J. R.** Rainer Maria Rilke, a bibliography of translations and criticism of his works published in Great Britain since 1930. 1946.

237b **Woolven, G. B.** Publications of the Independent labour party, 1893–1932. 1966.

249 **Cook, D. F.** and **A. N. Ricketts.** Kenneth Povey, 1898–1965. (Obituary notice.) Library ser5 23:51–6 Mr '68.
Checklist of his writings, 1926–65 (p.53–6)

249a **[Mosley, James]** *comp.* 'II. Book production and distribution' *in* Watson. George G., *ed.* The new Cambridge bibliography of English literature, Cambridge, 1969. V.3, col. 25–90.

BIBLIOGRAPHY — SERIAL BIBLIOGRAPHIES

253 **Bibliography** in the Republic of Ireland, 1963– . Irish Bk 3no1– , '64– .
Comp. by M. Hewson and Mary Pollard.

BIBLIOGRAPHY — PRINCIPAL CUMULATED INDEXES

260a **Colophon.** Index: the Colophon, 1930–1935, volumes I, II, III, IV, V with a history of the quarterly by John T. Winterich. . . . New York, 1935. (Repr. Metuchen, N.J., Scarecrow pr., 1935) 47[136]p. 24cm.

260b **Keller, Dean H.** An index to The colophon, new series; The colophon. new graphic series, and The new colophon. Metuchen, N.J., Scarecrow pr., 1968. 139p. (Not seen)

BIBLIOGRAPHY — PERIODICALS

282 Black art. 1no1–3no4, 1962–5. London, 1962–5.

284a Book collecting & library monthly. 1– , 1968– . London, 1968– .

293a The dolphin, a journal of the making of books. 1–4pt3, 1933–41. New York, Limited editions club, 1933–41.

294 Durham philobiblon. 1–2, 1949–69. Durham, Durham university library, 1949–69. (Index in last part)

298 Glasgow bibliographical society. Records. 1–14, 1912–39. Glasgow, 1912–39.

301 Irish book. 1– , 1959– . Dublin, Bibliographical society of Ireland, 1959– . (Apparently defunct; nothing seen after 3no1 '64)

312 Printing and graphic arts. 1–10, 1953–65. Lunenburg, Vt., 1953–65. (Formerly Notes on printing and the graphic arts, 1. 1953)

313 Private library. 1–8, 1957–67; ser2 1– , 1968– . North Harrow, Private libraries association, 1957– . (Formerly Private libraries association quarterly, 1no1–5, 1957–8)

313a Private printer & private press. 1– , 1968– . Oxford, 1968– .

GENERAL AND PERIOD
BIBLIOGRAPHIES

PERIOD DIVISIONS (entries arranged by date of publication)

1475–   [general catalogues]
1475–1500 [incunabula only]
1475–1640 [STC period]
1475–1700 [STC and Wing books; 'early' books]
1641–1700 [Wing period]
1701–1800
1801–1900
1901–

See also period divisions under *Drama, Fiction, Newspapers and periodicals, Pamphlets* and *Poetry*. The heading BOOKS in the Index gives period divisions for other subjects.
See also Regional bibliographies.

BOOKS — 1475–

325a **Tennant, sir Charles.** Catalogue of the library collected. . . . London, Privately ptd. at the Chiswick pr., 1896. 334p. 25cm.
Comp. by C. J. Toovey.

337a **[Watney, O. V.]** Catalogue of the library at Cornbury, March 1917. Oxford, 1917. 374p. 27cm.

343a **Brotherton, sir Edward Allen.** Roundhay Hall, the library of . . . . [2d ed.] Leeds, 1926. 170p. illus. (part col.), ports., facsims. 28cm.
Discursive accounts of some of the principal books; 'English literature' (p.37–[126])

348 **Annals** of English literature, 1475–1950. Oxford, 1935.
Comp. by J. C. Ghosh and E. G. Withycombe. *See* no.364.

359a **India. National library,** CALCUTTA. The Carey exhibition of early printing and fine printing. Calcutta, Government of India pr., 1955. [3]41p. illus., facsims. (1 fold., col.) 27cm.

367a **Gordan, John Dozier.** New in the Berg collection. N.Y. Pub Lib Bull 67:625–38 D '63; 68:6–12,73–82 Ja, F '64.
See also no.375.

368a **Gordan, John Dozier.** Doctors as men of letters; English and American writers of medical background, an exhibition in the Berg collection. New York, New York public library, 1964. 32p. 26cm.
Repr. from N.Y. Pub Lib Bull 68:574–601 N '64.

372 **Liverpool. Cathedral. Radcliffe library.** Short title catalogue of books printed before 1801. Liverpool, 1968. 60p. 21cm.

Comp. by David Cook.

Rev: P. Morgan Library ser5 12:163–4 '69.

373 **Wallington Hall,** NORTHUMBERLAND. **Library.** Catalogue of the library at Wallington Hall, Northumberland. Comp. by Christopher John Hunt. Newcastle upon Tyne, 1968. 136p. 30cm. (Newcastle upon Tyne. University. Library. Publications, extra ser 9) (Duplicated typescript)

Short-title catalogue of library with many books used by Macaulay and members of the Trevelyan family.

374 **Dove, Jack.** 123, a catalogue of rare and valuable books in the Hove public library, including incunabula, facsimiles, books from modern fine printing presses and fine bindings. Hove, Public library and museum committee, 1969. 45p. facsims. 20cm.

375 **Szladits, Lola L.** New in the Berg collection, 1962–1964. N.Y. Pub Lib Bull 73:227–52 Ap '69.

376 **Watson, George Grimes,** *ed.* The new Cambridge bibliography of English literature. Cambridge, C.U.P., 1969– . (First pub. 1940–57). v. 25cm.

Contents: 3. 1800–1900. (1969)—

BOOKS — 1475–1500 — BIBLIOGRAPHIES

410a **Tucker, Lena Lucile** and **A. R. Benham.** A bibliography of fifteenth century literature, with special reference to the history of English culture. Seattle, Washington, University of Washington pr., 1928. 162p. 26cm. (Univ Washington Pub Lang & Lit 2no3)

'Bibliography' (p.9–11); 'Literature' (p.68–146)

410b **[Juchhoff, Rudolf]** *comp.* 'Der Buchdruck Englands und der nordischen Länder im fünfzehnten Jahrhundert' *in* [Rath, Erich von] *ed.* Der Buchdruck des 15. Jahrhunderts, eine bibliographische Übersicht. Herausgegeben von der Wiegendruck-Gesellschaft. Berlin, 1930. p.[71]–92.

'England' (p.73–84)

413 **Berkowitz, David Sandler.** Bibliotheca bibliographica incunabula, a manual of bibliographical guides to inventories of printing, of holdings, and of reference aids. Waltham, Mass., 1967. vi,336l. 29cm. (Not seen)

414 **Heilbronner, Walter L.** Printing and the book in fifteenth-century England, a bibliographical survey. Charlottesville, Published for the Bibliographical society of the University of Virginia [by] the University pr. of Virginia [1967] xiv,105p. 23cm.

'Part I. Catalogs and checklists' (p.[1]–9); 'Part II. Survey of works dealing with fifteenth-century English printing' (p.[11]–81)

Rev: TLS 18 Ap '68:405.

BOOKS — 1475–1500

444a **Esposito, M.** Incunabula in Irish libraries. N&Q ser12 2:247–8 S '16.
List of 4 items in Royal Irish academy library, with bibliogr. notes and refs.

456a **White, Newport Benjamin.** Cashel incunabula in Dublin. TLS 12 My '27:472.
Checklist of 14 items in Marsh's library, Dublin, formerly in Cashel cathedral library, with bibliogr. refs.

485 **Bath. Public library.** Catalogue of incunabula. Bath [1966] 26p. 20cm. Covertitle. (Duplicated typescript)
Comp. by V. J. Kite.

486 **Mellon, Paul.** Fifty-five books printed before 1525 representing the works of England's first printers; an exhibition from the collection of Paul Mellon, January 17–March 3, 1968. [New York] Grolier club, 1968. xiii,62p.+6 plates. illus., facsims. 26cm.
Comp. by Joan Crane.
Rev: TLS 18 Ap '68:405; Pa Bib Soc Am 62:482 '68.

487 **Mitchell, William Smith.** Catalogue of the incunabula in Aberdeen university library. Edinburgh, Published for the University of Aberdeen [by] Oliver and Boyd, 1968. 107p. illus., facsims. 22cm.
Revision of no.454; 230 items in Proctor order, with bibliogr. notes and refs.; 'Index of provenance' (p.[100]–5); 'Concordance of numbers in 1925 List and this catalogue' (p.[106]–7)
Rev: R. Donaldson Biblioth 5:178–9 '69; D. E. Rhodes Library ser5 25:62–3 '70.

BOOKS — 1475–1640

490 **[Craig, Hardin]** *comp.* 'Bibliographies . . .' *in* Bateson, Frederick W., *ed.* Cambridge bibliography of English literature. Cambridge, 1940–57. V.1 (1940), p.317–19; 5(1957), p.[171]

490a **Lievsay, John Leon.** The sixteenth century: Skelton through Hooker. New York, Appleton-Century-Crofts [1968] xi,132p. 24cm. (Goldentree bibliographies) (Not seen)

524 **Morrison, Paul Guerrant,** *comp.* Index . . . Pollard and Redgrave, 'A short-title catalogue . . .'. 2d impression offset from the Secretary's copy, with a few corrections written in by hand. Charlottesville, Va., Bibliographical society of the University of Virginia, 1961. 82p. 27cm. (Duplicated typescript)

532a **Williams, Franklin Burleigh.** Corrections to The short-title catalogue. TLS 12 S '35:565.
See no.521.

554a **Mitchell, William Smith.** A list of the post-incunabula in the University library, Newcastle upon Tyne. Newcastle upon Tyne, 1965. 70p. 26cm. Covertitle. (Duplicated typescript)
Alphabetical STC with some notes of provenance.

554b **Bath. Public library.** Printed books, 1476–1640: catalogue. Bath, 1968. 93p. 20cm. Covertitle. (Duplicated typescript)
Author checklist, with STC nos., comp. by V. J. Kite.

BOOKS — 1475–1700

588 **Great Britain. Foreign office. Library.** A short title catalogue of books printed before 1701 in the Foreign office library, compiled by Colin L. Robertson. London, H.M.S.O., 1966. vii,176p. 25cm.

590 **London. Guildhall library.** A list of books printed in the British Isles and of English books printed abroad before 1701 in Guildhall library. London, Corporation of London, 1966–7. 2 pts. (iv,222p.) 28cm.
Comp. by Kathleen I. Garrett.
Rev: Pa Bib Soc Am 61:153 '67; *ib.* 62:481 '68; P. Morgan Library ser5 23:358–9 '68; TLS 1 Ag '68:832.

591 —— **[Same]**: Additions. Guildh Misc 3:85–9 Oc '69.

BOOKS — 1701–1800

627 **[Bernbaum, Ernest]** *comp.* 'Bibliographies . . .' *in* Bateson, Frederick W., *ed.* Cambridge bibliography of English literature. Cambridge, 1940–57. V.2(1940), p.3–4; 5(1957), p.[361], by A. Ward.

628a **Cordasco, Francesco G. M.** Eighteenth century bibliographies; handlists of critical studies relating to Smollett, Richardson, Sterne, Fielding, Dibdin, 18th century medicine, the 18th century novel, Godwin, Gibbon, Young and Burke, to which is added John P. Anderson's bibliography of Smollett. Metuchen, N.J., Scarecrow pr., 1970. 230p. 19cm.

633a **Gordan, John Dozier** and **Adelaide M. Smith.** The age of queen Anne, 1702–1714. N.Y. Pub Lib Bull 56:431–45,395–410 Jl,Ag '52.

BOOKS — 1801–1900

654 **[Templeman, William Darby]** *comp.* 'Bibliographies . . .' *in* Bateson, Frederick W., *ed.* Cambridge bibliography of English literature. Cambridge, 1940–57. V.3(1940), p.3–4; 5(1957), p.[520], by D. H. Malone and W. P. Friederich.
See also no.657c.

657c **Watson, George Grimes,** *ed.* 'I. General works. (1) Bibliographies' *in* The new Cambridge bibliography of English literature. Cambridge, 1969. V.3, col. 1–4.

667 **Muir, Percival Horace.** Points, 1874–1930; being extracts from a bibliographer's note-book. London, Constable, 1931. xvii,167p. illus., facsims. 23cm. ([Bibliographia, no.5])
Includes checklists and bibliogr. discussion of numerous modern authors.

670 **Muir, Percival Horace.** Points, second series, 1866–1934. London, Constable; New York, R. R. Bowker, 1934. xiv,155p. illus., facsims. 23cm. ([Bibliographia, no.8])

Includes checklists and bibliogr. discussion of E. C. Blunden, J. Bridie, baron Corvo, D. Garnett, J. C. Powys, L. P. Smith, and G. L. Strachey.

672a **Hogan, Francis Joseph.** The romantics, 1801–1820; an exhibition of books and autograph letters, from the collection of Frank J. Hogan. Los Angeles, 1938. 16p. facsims. 27cm.

Comp. by Ward Ritchie.

675 **Hayden, John O.** 'Reviews of romantic literature' *in* The romantic reviewers, 1802–1824. London [1969] p.270–98.

Author and title checklist by name of author reviewed; 'British reviewing periodicals, 1802–24' (p.261–9)

BOOKS — 1901–

678 **Temple, Ruth (Zabriskie)** and **M. Tucker.** 'Bibliography' *in* A library of literary criticism: modern British literature. New York [1966] V.3, p.403–37.

Checklists.

679 **Temple, Ruth (Zabriskie).** Twentieth century British literature, a reference guide and bibliography compiled and edited by Ruth Z. Temple with the assistance for the author bibliographies of Martin Tucker. New York, F. Ungar [1968] x,261p. 24cm. (Not seen)

Rev: Pa Bib Soc Am 63:225 '69.

BOOKS — SCOTLAND — 1701–1800

719b **Chambers, Charles Edward Steuart.** Mr. Terry's bibliography of the '45. Athenæum 3823:145 F '01.

Checklist of 15 mss. and other addenda to no.719c.

719c **Terry, Charles Sanford.** 'A bibliography of Jacobite history, 1689–1788' *in* The rising of 1745. . . . New ed. London, 1903. (First pub. 1900.) p.[227]–335.

Classified and indexed checklist of early material.

GENERAL AND PERIOD BIBLIOGRAPHIES — BRITISH BOOKS PUBLISHED ABROAD

743a **Price, Lawrence Marsden.** 'Bibliography' *in* English > German literary influences: bibliography and survey. Berkeley, Calif., 1920. p.1–111.

See no.752a.

752a **Price, Lawrence Marsden.** 'Bibliography' *in* English literature in Germany. Berkeley, Calif., 1953. p.[387]–516.

Expansion of no.743a.

763 [**Hutchison, B.**] Tauchnitz edition: centenary catalogue, 1837–1937. Leipzig, B. Tauchnitz. Bk Coll & Lib Mthly 17:163 S '69.

Checklist of editions and corrections.

764 —— Tauchnitz of Leipzig: the first 100. Bk Coll & Lib Mthly 19:230–1 N '69; the second hundred *ib*. 20:256–7 D '69.

Supersedes no. 763.

765 —— Tauchnitz, of Leipzig, 199–400. Bk Coll & Lib Mthly 22:332–4 F '70.

Further notes on p.320–1.

GENERAL AND PERIOD BIBLIOGRAPHIES — FOREIGN BOOKS PUB-
LISHED IN ENGLISH IN BRITAIN

770a **Farrar, Clarissa Palmer** and **A. P. Evans.** Bibliography of English translations from medieval sources. New York, 1946. xiii,534p. 23cm. (Records
of civilization. Sources and studies, XXXIX)

Checklist, with some bibliogr. notes, arranged by names of the medieval authors.

—— CLASSICAL. GREEK. HOMER

776a **Bush, Douglas.** English translations of Homer. Pub Mod Lang Assn
41:335–41 Je '26.

Annotated chronol. checklist, supplementing Foster (no.776)

—— —— —— MUSAEUS

801a **Bush, Douglas.** Musaeus in English verse. Mod Lang N 43:101–4 F '28.

Checklist of 30 English versions, 1589–1926.

—— FRANCE. ALEXANDRE VILLEDIEU

807a **Rhodes, Dennis Everard.** The early London editions of the Doctrinale of
Alexander grammaticus, with a [note on Duff 224. Library ser5 24:232–4
S '69.

—— —— CAMUS

808a **Hoy, Peter.** Camus in English, an annotated bibliography of Albert
Camus's contributions to English and American periodicals and newspapers.
Wymondham [Leics.] Brewhouse pr., 1968. 31p. illus., port. 26cm.

Annotated checklist of contribs. in English, and French, with 'A note on some private
press editions of Camus's work in English' (p.[25]–6)

—— —— D'OUTRE-MEUSE

See under Authors—Mandeville, sir John, fl.1350.

—— —— VERNE

815a **[Hutchison, B.]** Jules Verne, 1828–1905. Bk Coll & Lib Mthly 15:72–8 Jl '69.
Title checklist of British issues.

—— GERMANY. BÜRGER

821a **Greg, sir Walter Wilson.** English translations of Lenore, a contribution to the history of the literary relations of the romantic revival. Mod Q Lang Lit 2:13–28 Ag '99.
'Index of translations' (p.28): chronol. checklist of 21 English ed., 1796–1870.

—— —— GOETHE

821b **Carré, Jean-Marie.** Bibliographie de Gœthe en Angleterre. Paris, Plon-Nourrit, 1920. [8]176p. 23cm.
See extensive additions in review by A. E. Turner Mod Lang R 16:364–70 '21.

—— —— LESSING

822a **Kenwood, Sydney H.** Lessing in England. Mod Lang R 9:344–58 Jl '14.
'Bibliography' (p.355–8): chronol. checklist of 46 translations and notices, 1773–1899.

—— —— MANN

822b **English, David John,** 1966: no.118a.

822c **Thomson, Myra,** 1950: no.221a.

—— —— RILKE

822d **Wood, J. R.,** 1946: no.237a.

—— HOLLAND. ERASMUS

826a **Devereux, E. James.** A checklist of English translations of Erasmus to 1700. Oxford, Oxford bibliographical society, Bodleian library, 1968. viii,40p. 25cm. (Oxford bibliographical society. Occasional pub. 3)
Title checklist of about 88 items, with bibliogr. refs., locations of copies and some bibliogr. notes.
Rev: TLS 19 Je '69:668; R. R. Allen Library ser5 25:164–6 '70.

—— ITALY

826d **Gerber, A.** All of the five fictitious Italian editions of writings of Machiavelli and three of those of Pietro Aretino printed by John Wolfe of London, 1584–1588. II. Mod Lang N 22:129–35 My '07.
Checklist of Italian books ptd. by Wolfe (p.134–5)

—— ITALY — DANTE

831a **Cunningham, Gilbert Farm.** The Divine comedy in English, a critical bibliography, 1901–1966. Edinburgh, Oliver and Boyd [1966] xi,290p. 23cm.

Rev: J. H. Whitfield Ital Stud 20:104–5 '66.

—— —— PETRARCH

833a **Watson, George Grimes.** The English Petrarchans, a critical bibliography of the Canzoniere. London, Warburg institute, 1967. 47p. illus. 24cm. (Warburg institute surveys, 3)

Rev: C. Fahy Library ser5 24:59 '69; F. Marenco N&Q 214:119–20 '69.

—— RUSSIA. STEPNIAK-KRAVCHINSKY

838a **[Hutchison, B.]** Dangerous books. Stepniak, 1852–95. Bk Coll & Lib Mthly 5:4–5 S '68.

—— UNITED STATES. ELLIS

845b **[Hutchison, B.]** American collectors, your last chance! The British editions of Edward S. Ellis, 1840–1916. Bk Coll & Lib Mthly 16:108–13 Ag '69.

—— —— LONDON

848g **[Hutchison, B.]** Jack London, 1876–1916: the British first, and early editions, and Tauchnitz issues. Bk Coll & Lib Mthly 19:216–19 N '69.

REGIONAL BIBLIOGRAPHIES

REGIONAL BIBLIOGRAPHIES — ENGLAND

—— BEDFORDSHIRE

872a **Conisbee, Lewis Ralph.** A Bedfordshire bibliography: 1967 supplement. [Luton] Bedfordshire historical record society [1967] 85p. 24cm.

—— GLOUCESTERSHIRE

895a **Gloucester. Public library.** The Dancey gift; catalogue of manuscripts, books, pamphlets and prints relating to the city and county of Gloucester and other works of general literature deposited. . . . [Gloucester, J. Jennings, ptr.] 1911. viii,55p. 26cm.
Ed. by Roland Austin.

895b —— Painswick House collection: catalogue of books, tracts, broadsides, leaflets, election squibs, and newspaper cuttings relating to the county of Gloucester and the city of Bristol, presented by Francis Adams Hyett. . . . [Gloucester, J. Bellows, ptr.] 1916. x,185p. 25cm.
Introduction by Roland Austin.

—— HUNTINGDONSHIRE

899a **Norris, Herbert Ellis.** Huntingdonshire almanacs. N&Q ser12 1:5–8 Ja '16.
Chronol. checklist of 28 items, 1782–1905, with some bibliogr. notes.

899b —— The witches of Warboys: bibliographical note. N&Q ser12 1:283–4, 304–5 Ap '16; W. B. H. *ib.* 1:414 My '16.
Chronol. checklist of 28 items, 1589–1891, with some bibliogr. notes.

—— LANCASHIRE

901a **Tupling, George Henry.** Lancashire directories, 1684–1957. Rev., enl. and ed. by Sidney Horrocks. Manchester, Central library, Joint Committee on the Lancashire bibliography, 1968. x,78p. 24cm. (Lancashire bibliography, pt.1)

—— LONDON

915a **Kahl, William Frederick.** The development of London livery companies, an historical essay and a select bibliography. Boston, Mass., Baker library, Harvard graduate school of business administration, 1960. viii,104p. 26cm.
'A select list of books, pamphlets and broadsides on the London livery companies' (p.33–104); 'Stationers' (p.85–91); not indexed.

915b **Kahl, William Frederick.** A checklist of books, pamphlets, and broadsides on the London livery companies. Guildh Misc 2:99–126 Ap '62.

Classified alphabetical checklist, with some locations of copies, supplementing no.915a. 'Stationers' (p.113–16)

916c **Calamities,** wonders, and topics of the town, 1603–1902: some aspects of popular taste as reflected in a list of items in Guildhall library. Guildh Misc 2:463–82 Oc '68.

916d **Rubinstein, Stanley Jack.** 'Bibliography' *in* Historians of London, an account of the many surveys, histories, perambulations, maps and engravings made about the city. . . . London; Hamden, Conn., 1968. p.219–26.

———— —— CAMDEN SOCIETY

916f **Hall, Hubert,** *ed.* List and index of the publications of the Royal historical society, 1871–1924, and of the Camden society, 1840–1897. London, Offices of the [Royal historical] society, 1925. xvii,110p. 22cm.

'List of the publications of the Camden society and of the Camden series of the Royal historical society' (p.[27]–43)

916g **Milne, Alexander Taylor.** A centenary guide to the publications of the Royal historical society, 1868–1968, and of the former Camden society, 1838–1897. London, Royal historical society, 1968. xi,249p. 24cm. (Royal historical society. Guides and handbooks, 9)

'Camden society' (p.1–80)

———— —— CHEAPSIDE CROSS

917a **Abraham, Aleck.** Cheapside cross, its bibliography. N&Q ser10 9:445 Je '08.

———— —— ST. PAUL'S CATHEDRAL

920a **Duff, Edward Gordon.** The stationers at the sign of the trinity in st.Paul's churchyard. Bibliographica 1:93–113,175–93 '95; [addenda] 2:499 '96.

—— MAN, ISLE OF

922a **Black, George Fraser.** List of works in the New York public library relating to the Isle of Man. N.Y. Pub Lib Bull 15:756–68 D '11.

—— NORTHUMBERLAND. NEWCASTLE

927a **Leake, L. A.** The typographical society of Newcastle upon Tyne. Priv Lib ser2 1no3:86–98 '68. facsims.

Includes a chronol. checklist, 1817–64.

—— OXFORDSHIRE

934a **Honnold library for the Associated colleges,** Claremont, Calif. The William W. Clary Oxford collection, a supplementary catalogue, ed. by Catharine K. Firmin. Claremont, Calif., Ptd. for the Honnold library of the Claremont colleges by V. Ridler, O.U.P., 1965. xiv,324p. 23cm.

—— —— OXFORD. UNIVERSITY

937a **Cordeaux, Edward Harold** and **D. H. Merry.** A bibliography of printed works relating to the University of Oxford. Oxford, Clarendon pr., 1968. xxvii,809p. 23cm.

Classified subject list, with Bodleian shelfmarks.

Rev: TLS 19 S '68:1061; A.N.O. Priv Lib ser2 1:186–7 '68.

—— SOMERSET. BATH

940 **Bath. Public library.** Bath guides, directories and newspapers. Bath, 1962. [17]p. 20cm. Covertitle. (Duplicated typescript)

940a —— [**Same**]: Rev. ed. Bath, 1967. [19]p. 20cm. Covertitle. (Duplicated typescript)

—— YORKSHIRE

947a **Yorkshire cobook group of libraries.** Some novels set in Yorkshire. [Leeds, 1967] 20p. illus. 23cm. Covertitle.

REGIONAL BIBLIOGRAPHIES — WALES

—— ANGLESEY

961 **Jones, Thomas Llechid.** Bye-paths in Anglesey bibliography. Welsh Bib Soc J 3:125–65 D '27.

REGIONAL BIBLIOGRAPHIES — SCOTLAND

—— LANARKSHIRE. GLASGOW

1002a **Mitchell library,** Glasgow. Catalogue of the Andrew Bain memorial collection. . . . Glasgow, Privately ptd., 1924. vii,180p. ports. 26cm.

Short-title catalogue ed. by S. A. Pitt. Includes collection of books from Bell and Bain pr., and a Burns collection.

—— PERTHSHIRE. PERTH

1005a **Couper, William James.** The rebel press at Perth in 1715. Glasgow Bib Soc Rec 8:44–56 '30.

'Bibliography' (p.52–6): checklist of 24 items, with some bibliogr. notes and locations of copies.

REGIONAL BIBLIOGRAPHIES — IRELAND

—— ARMAGH. TANDRAGEE

1039 **McClelland, Aiken.** Provincial printing: Tandragee. Irish Bk 1n04:98–100 '62.

Checklist, 1843–51, with some bibliogr. notes.

PRESSES AND PRINTING

PRINTING IN ANGLO-SAXON

1173a **Smith, M. Morton-.** Books printed with Anglo-Saxon types. . . . Crediton, 1965. 66p. facsims. 23cm. (His Catalogue no.21, pt.1) (Not seen)

PRIVATELY PRINTED BOOKS

1186a **Roxburghe** club publications; the following prices were obtained at Sotheby's on 9 October. Bk Coll & Lib Mthly 8:248–9 D '68.

TYPOGRAPHY — GENERAL

1189 **Williamson, Hugh Albert Fordyce.** Book typography, a handlist for book designers. London, Published for the National book league by the C.U.P., 1955. 15p. 19cm. (The book, no.1)

1189a **Oxford university press.** John Johnson collection. Select subject lists. Oxford [1964] various pagings. 37cm. (Duplicated typescript)

A. Penmanship.—B. Announcements.—C. Early book sale catalogues.—D. Booksellers' auctions.—E. Book almanacks.—F. Booksellers' and publishers' lists before 1800. —G. Education books.—H. Prospectuses to journals.—I. Proposals for English books before 1800.—K. Proposals, after 1800.—L. Circulating library labels (London).—M. Circulating library labels (provincial)

The collection is now in the Bodleian library, Oxford.

TYPOGRAPHY—MANUALS

1193 **Gaskell, Philip, G. Barber** and **Georgina Warrilow.** An annotated list of printers' manuals to 1850. J Ptg Hist Soc 4:11–31 '68.

'Manuals in English' (p.13–19): chronol. checklist of 23 items, 1683–1846, with some locations of copies.

TYPOGRAPHY — PROPOSALS

1197 **[Simmons, John Simon Gabriel]** *comp.* 'Fell's announcements and proposals' *in* Morison, Stanley and H. G. Carter. John Fell, the University press and the Fell types. . . . Oxford, 1967. p.[253]

TYPOGRAPHY — SPECIMENS

1200a **Grolier club,** NEW YORK. Type specimen books and broadsides printed before 1900 exhibited. . . . [New York, 1926] [10]p. 18cm. Covertitle.

'Great Britain' (nos.80–106)

1211 **[Simmons, John Simon Gabriel]** *comp.* 'The Fell type specimens' *in* Morison, Stanley and H. G. Carter. John Fell, the University press and the Fell types. . . . Oxford, 1967. p.[229]–32.

PRESSES — GENERAL

1233 **Manchester. Public libraries.** Reference library. Subject catalogue: section 094: Private press books. Edited by Sidney Horrocks. Manchester, Libraries committee, 1959–60. 2v. 24cm.

Alphabetical by press, with typographical and bibliogr. notes, and indexes.

1237 **Graham, Rigby.** Books from the private presses. Priv Ptr & Priv Pr 1– . Oxford, 1968– .

1238 **Lincoln, David,** *comp.* 'Select bibliography of private presses with some recent auction room prices' *in* Franklin, Colin. The private presses. London [1969] p.[183]–237.

Checklists of the Daniel, Kelmscott, Ashendene, Essex house, Vale, Eragny, Caradoc, Doves, Gregynog, Golden cockerel, and Shakespeare head presses.

1239 **Mills, Stuart.** Concrete poetry. Priv Lib ser2 2no3:95–106 '69.

Checklists for the Wild hawthorn, Openings, and Writers forum presses.

PRESSES — ACKERMANN, RUDOLPH, 1764–1834

1240a **Burke, William Jeremiah.** Rudolph Ackermann, promoter of the arts and sciences, with a selected list of his publications in the New York public library. New York, New York public library, 1935. 36p. facsim. 25cm.

Repr. from N.Y. Pub Lib Bull 38:807–26,939–53 Oc–N '34. 'Ackermann's publications' (p.34–6): selected author checklist.

PRESSES — ACKERS, CHARLES, 1702?–1759

1240c **McKenzie, Donald Francis** and **J. F. Ross,** *ed.* 'Appendix I: list of books' *in* A ledger of Charles Ackers. . . . [Oxford] 1968. p.[233]–303.

Author checklist of 441 items, with collations and some bibliogr. notes. 'Appendix II Chronological list of books printed by Ackers in the years covered by his extant ledger, 1732–1748' (p.[305]–16); 'Addenda' (p.[317]). Note corrections and additions in rev. by D. F. Foxon, Library ser5 25:65–73 '70.

PRESSES — ART SOCIETY PRESS

1240g **Chambers, David.** The Art society press. Priv Lib ser2 2no3:107–17 '69.

'Check-list of books printed at the Art society press' (p.115–17): 28 items ptd. at King's college school, Wimbledon.

PRESSES — BALLANTYNE, JAMES, 1772–1833

1248 **Johnston, George P.** The first book printed by James Ballantyne, being An apology for Tales of terror, with notes on Tales of wonder and Tales of terror. Edinburgh Bib Soc Pub 1pt4:1–16 [i.e. 21–36] Oc '94.

'Appendix' (p.[11]–13): checklist, with bibliogr. descrs. of 10 items, and TP facsims.

1266a **Cordasco, Francesco G. M.** The Bohn libraries, a history and a checklist. New York, B. Franklin, 1951. 11p. port. 21cm. (Burt Franklin bibliogr. ser., no.5)

Classified checklist of 'libraries', with some bibliogr. notes. 'Appendix II: A checklist of original writings by Henry G. Bohn' (p.103–4)

See also Thomas, Thomas, 1553–1588.

1281a **Moore, Samuel.** Caxton reproductions, a bibliography. Mod Lang N 25:165–7 Je '10.

Checklist of facsimiles and reprints, in Blades order.

1298g **Graham, Rigby.** A Juliet Standing checklist. Priv Ptr & Priv Pr 1:19–20 F '68.

Chronol. checklist, 1964–8, of works privately ptd. by Juliet Standing.

1302g **Lavin, J. A.** John Danter's ornament stock. Stud Bib 23:21–44 '70.

'Additions to the Danter canon' (p.39–40): chronol. checklist, 1591–7.

1304 **Isaac, Peter Charles Gerald.** 'Handlist of Davison's caricatures' *in* Some Alnwick caricatures, a note and a handlist. Wylam, 1965. p.10–12.

1304b —— William Davison of Alnwick, pharmacist and printer. Library ser5 24:1–32 Mr '69.

'Checklist of books printed by Davison' (p.18–32): title list of 111 items, with some bibliogr. notes, and locations of copies.

1311g **Dolmen press.** Books and booklets published by the Dolmen press, Dublin, August MCMLI—August MCMLXVI. Dublin, 1966. [22]p. illus. 24cm.

Covertitle: The Dolmen press . . . a checklist.

1322a **Cotton, John.** The Fantasy poets. Priv Lib ser2 2no1:3–13 '69.

'Checklist' (p.10–13): classified checklists of Fantasy poets pamphlet series; New poems; Oxford poetry; other books and pamphlets ptd. by Oscar Mellor.

PRESSES — FOLIO SOCIETY

1323a **Folio society,** LONDON. Folio 21, a bibliography of the Folio society, 1947–1967. London, Folio pr., 1968. 207p. illus., facsims. (part col.) 28cm.

Annotated, chronol. checklist of 243 items comp. by Sandra Raphael, based on her no.189b.

Rev: TLS 24 Oc '68:1208; D. Chambers Priv Lib ser2 2:39–40 '69.

1323b **[Hutchison, B.]** The Folio society. Bk Coll & Lib Mthly 10:295–301 F '69.

PRESSES — GED, WILLIAM, 1690–1749

1329 **Gibb, John S.** Notes on William Ged & the invention of stereotyping. . . . Edinburgh Bib Soc Pub 1pt2:1–6 [i.e. 9–14] Oc '92; Supplement *ib.* 1pt5:1–2 [i.e. 15–16] F '96.

Discussion and short descrs. of 4 items, 1739–44.

PRESSES — HAWKINS, GEORGE, fl.1741–1780

1341g **Kennedy, M. J. O.,** 1948: no.149a.

PRESSES — HOTTEN, JOHN CAMDEN, 1832–1873

See under Authors.

PRESSES — HOURS PRESS

1344a **Ford, Hugh,** *ed,* 'Bibliography of Hours press publications' *in* Cunard, Nancy. These were the hours; memories of my Hours press, Réanville and Paris, 1928–1931. Carbondale, Ill.; London, 1969. p.209–12.

Checklist, with some bibliogr. notes.

PRESSES — JONES, WILLIAM, fl.1587–1626

1347a **Curtis, Mark H.** William Jones, puritan printer and propagandist. Library ser5 19:38–66 '64.

Checklist of 16 works ptd. by Jones, 1605–8 (p.47–8); checklist of puritan pubs. 'A. Printed by Richard Schilders of Middleburg' (p.62–3) and 'B. Works for which the printer is uncertain' (p.63): 10 items.

PRESSES — KELMSCOTT PRESS

1347c **[Cockerell, sir Sidney Carlyle]** *comp.* 'An annotated list of all the books printed at the Kelmscott press in the order in which they were issued' *in* Morris, William. A note by William Morris on his aims in founding the Kelmscott press together with a short description of the press by S. C. Cockerell. . . . [London, 1898] (Repr. Shannon, Irish U.P., 1969) p.21–65.

PRESSES — LIMITED EDITIONS CLUB

1359 **Warde, Beatrice.** George Macy and the Limited editions club. Penrose Ann 48:35–9 '54.

'A short list of Limited editions club books illustrated and designed, and mostly printed in Great Britain, from the British museum catalogue' (p.38–9). Fuller bibliogr. notes on these books may be found in Limited editions club, New York. Quarto-millenary; the first 250 publications. . . . New York, 1959.

PRESSES — MINERVA PRESS

1368a **Summers, Alphonse Montague Joseph-Mary Augustus.** The Minerva press. TLS 17 Oc '42:516.

Seven additions to Blakey.

PRESSES — MORES, EDWARD ROWE, 1731–1778

See under Authors.

PRESSES — OXFORD UNIVERSITY PRESS

See under Authors—Fell, bp. John, 1625–1686.

PRESSES — PICKERING, WILLIAM, 1796–1854

1382 **Keynes, sir Geoffrey Langdon.** 'William Pickering: list of publications, 1820–1854' *in* William Pickering, a memoir and a check-list of his publications. Rev. ed. [London, 1969] (First pub. 1924) p.47–121.

Author checklist, with some bibliogr. notes and TP facsims.

PRESSES — RAIKES, ROBERT, 1735–1811

1388b **Gloucester. Public library.** Raikes centenary, April 5, 1911: an exhibition of books, prints, and miscellaneous objects in commemoration of the centenary of the death of Robert Raikes. . . . [Gloucester, Chance & Bland, Offices of the Gloucester journal, 1911] [7]p. port. 25cm. Covertitle.

Comp. by Roland Austin.

PRESSES — STANBROOK ABBEY PRESS

1401b **Times bookshop,** LONDON. Books from Stanbrook abbey press and the Vine press, introduced by J. G. Dreyfus. London [1965] 12p. 21cm. Covertitle.

1401c **Ward, Philip.** Stanbrook abbey press. Priv Lib 4:13–15 Ja '62.

Check-list of Stanbrook abbey press books printed since 1945' (p.14–15)

PRESSES — STOURTON PRESS

1401g **Hall, Fairfax.** The Stourton press from 1930–1935. Priv Lib ser2 2no2: 54–62 '69.

'Check-list of books printed at the Stourton press' (p.61–2): chronol. list of 23 items.

PRESSES — THOMAS, THOMAS, 1553–1588

1406c **Morris, John.** Thomas Thomas, printer to the University of Cambridge, 1583–8. Part II: some account of his materials and bookbindings, with a short-title list of his printing. Cambridge Bib Soc Trans 4pt5:339–62 '68.

'Appendix B: A short-title list of items printed by Thomas Thomas, 1583–8' (p.356–62): chronol. checklist, with collations, locations of copies, and bibliogr. refs.

PRESSES — TONSON, JACOB, 1656–1736

1406s **Papali, George Francis.** 'Publications of the Tonson house' *in* Jacob Tonson, publisher, his life and work, 1656–1736. [Onehunga, Auckland] N.Z., 1968. p.[144]–213.

Chronol. checklist, 1675–1767, with some bibliogr. notes.

PRESSES — TULLIS PRESS

1408b **Mackay, Æneas James George.** 'The Cupar press of R. and G. S. Tullis, from 1803 to 1859; and of A. Westwood and A. Westwood & son, from 1862 to 1895' *in* A list of books relating to Fife and Kinross. Edinburgh Bib Soc Pub 3pt1:1–30 Oc '97. p.25–9.

Repr. from A history of Fife and Kinross. Edinburgh, 1896, p.361–90.

1408c **Doughty, Dennis William.** The Tullis press, Cupar, 1803–1849. Dundee, Abertay historical society, 1967. vi,74p. illus., facsims. 22cm.

'Lists and indexes' (p.23–74): classified checklist of 127 items, with quasifacsim. TP transcrs., and some bibliogr. notes.

PRESSES — WALSH, JOHN, d.1736

1414a **Smith, William Charles** and **C. Humphries.** A bibliography of the musical works published by the firm of John Walsh during the years 1721–1766. London, Bibliographical society, 1968. xx,351p. facsim. 21cm.

Author checklist of 1564 items, with some bibliogr. notes and refs., and locations of copies; no index.

Rev: TLS 20 Mr '69:300 G. Heard Priv Lib ser2 2:118–21 '69; M. Dawney Bk Coll 19:115–16 '70.

PRESSES — WILSON, JOHN, c.1759–1821

1419b **Thomson, Frances Mary.** John Wilson, an Ayrshire printer, publisher and bookseller. Biblioth 5no2:41–61 '67.

'Books printed and published by Wilson and his partners' (p.52–61): chronol. checklist, 1783–1820, with collations and locations of copies.

PRESSES — WREITTOUN, JOHN, fl.1624–1639

1421a **Beattie, William.** John Wreittoun. TLS 13 Ag '38:536.

Checklist of 11 items.

FORMS AND GENRES

ALMANACS AND PROGNOSTICATIONS

1428a **Thornton, Richard H.** Early Punch almanacs. N&Q 147:405–6,463 D '24.
Chronol. checklist, 1842–61.

ANONYMA AND PSEUDONYMA

1442a **Keith, Sara.** Nineteenth-century anonyma, some identifications. N&Q 204:210–12 Je '59.

AUCTION AND SALE CATALOGUES

1457 **Isaac, Peter Charles Gerald.** Three sale catalogues. Durham Philobib 2pt9/10:67 '69.
Addenda to the British museum list, no.1448.

1458 **Maggs brothers, ltd.,** LONDON. A catalogue of Maggs catalogues, 1918–1968. London, Ptd. for Maggs bros. by the Courier pr., Leamington Spa, 1969. 59p.+18 plates. illus., facsims., ports. 22cm. (Maggs catalogues, no.918)
Comp. by Clare Lightfoot.

BALLADS

1462a **Trenery, Grace R.** Ballad collections of the eighteenth century. Mod Lang R 10:283–303 Jl '15.
'Bibliography. (i) Collections' (p.302–3): author checklist of 10 items.

1464a **Hamer, Douglas.** Parodies of Chevy chase, 1690–1847. N&Q 164:434–8 Je '33; F. T. Wood ib. 165:8 Jl '33.

1464b —— References to Chevy chase, 1548–1765. N&Q 154:308–13, 327–32, 344–6 My '33; C. R. Beard ib. 164:392 Je '33; D. Hamer 164:427–8 Je '33.

1468 **Simpson, Claude M.** The British broadside ballad and its music. New Brunswick, N.J., Rutgers U.P. [1966] xxxiii,922p. facsim., music. 25cm.
Title checklist with extensive discursive bibliogr. notes. 'Index of authors, composers, publishers, and collectors of ballads and ballad tunes' (p.815–23); 'Index of titles, first lines, tune names, and refrains of ballads' (p.825–919)

BIBLE

1499 **Darlow, Thomas Herbert** and **H. F. Moule.** Historical catalogue of printed editions of the English bible, 1525–1961. Rev. and expanded . . . by A. S Herbert. London, British and foreign bible society; New York, American bible society [1968] xxxi,549p. 25cm.
Chronol. catalogue of 2331 items, with TP transcrs., bibliogr. notes and locations of copies. Rev. from v.1 of no.1471.
Rev: TLS 5 D '68:1392.

BIBLE, WELSH

1507a **Wales. National library,** ABERYSTWYTH. The fourth centenary of the Welsh New testament [a list and annotations of the contents of an exhibition to celebrate the fourth centenary of the translation of the New testament into Welsh in 1567] [Aberystwyth, 1967] 23p. facsims. 25cm.

CHAPBOOKS

1541a **Humphreys, Arthur Lee.** The highwayman and his chap-book. N&Q 178: 308–12,326–30,347–50,368–72,383–6,402–4 My,Je '40.
Annotated chronol. checklist, 1597–1831, with bibliogr. notes.

1547 **Neuberg, Victor Edward Reuben Parvincio.** 'Bibliography' *in* The penny histories, a study of chapbooks for young readers over two centuries. London, 1968. p.208–20.
Checklist of collections and works relating to.

1548 **Newcastle-upon-Tyne. Library.** Newcastle chapbooks in Newcastle upon Tyne university library [a catalogue by] Frances M. Thomson. Newcastle-upon-Tyne, Oriel pr., 1969. 109p. illus. 21cm. (Not seen)
Rev: TLS 10 Jl '69:760; D. S. Mack Biblioth 5:179–80 '69; P. C. G. Isaac Library ser5 25:83–4 '70.

CHARACTERS

1549 **Baldwin, Edward Chauncey.** The relation of the seventeenth century character to the periodical essay. Pub Mod Lang Assn 19:75–114 '04.
'Bibliography [a chronological list of Character-books . . .]' (p.104–14)

1550a **Sloane, William.** Some notes on character-writing. Mod Lang N 53:113–16 F '38.
Discursive supplement to Murphy, no.1550.

CHILDREN'S LITERATURE

1556a **Weiss, Harry Bischoff.** American editions of Sir Richard Whittington and his cat. N.Y. Pub Lib Bull 42:477–85 Je '38.
'Preliminary check list of American editions of Dick Whittington and his cat' (p.484–5): chronol. checklist, 1788–1937, with location of copy seen.

1559a **Partridge, Charles.** Evangelical children's books, 1828–1859. N&Q 195:56–8 F '50.
Checklist of 63 items.

1572a **Connecticut. Southern Connecticut state college,** NEW HAVEN. **Library.** The Carolyn Sherwin Bailey historical collection of children's books, a catalogue. Researched, compiled, and edited by Dorothy R. Davis. [New Haven] Southern Connecticut state college, 1966. 232p. illus., facsims. 23cm.
Not indexed.

1573c **Harris public library**, PRESTON. A catalogue of the Spencer collection of early children's books and chapbooks presented to the Harris public library. . . . Comp. by David Good. Preston, 1967. ix,307p. 22cm.

Classified subject lists, with 'Books bound together in collections' (p.[229]–33); 'Chronological list of editions up to 1800' (p.[235]–8); 'List of illustrators and engravers' (p.[239]–58)

Rev: R. A. Brimmell Bk Coll 17:366–7,370 '68; Pa Bib Soc Am 62:642–3 '68.

1573d **National book league**, LONDON. British children's books. 3d ed. London, 1967. 98p. 22cm.

See also nos.1559, 1569.

1573e **Bishop Lonsdale college of education**, DERBY. **Library**. Catalogue of the collection of early children's books, together with books of special educational interest in the library. . . . Comp. by C. E. Saunders. [Mickleover, Derby] 1968. 29p. 26cm. Covertitle. (Duplicated typescript)

1573f **British museum**. An exhibition of early English children's books. [London, 1968] 32p. 24cm. (Duplicated typescript)

CONCORDANCES

1574 **Cooper, Lane.** Concordances of English authors. N&Q ser11 10:461–2 D '14.

DRAMA — 1475–

1586a **Loewenberg, Alfred.** The theatre of the British Isles, excluding London: a bibliography. London, Society for theatre research, 1950. ix,75p. 22cm.

1587b **Hamilton, Walter.** 'Theatrical burlesques and travesties' *in* Parodies of the works of English and American authors collected and annotated. London, 1884–9. (Repr. New York, B. Franklin, 1967) V.6 (1889), p.[331]–44.

Title checklist of about 800 entries.

1587d **Catalogue** of the Becks collection of prompt books in the New York public library. N.Y. Pub Lib Bull 10:100–48 F '06.

Title checklist, with some bibliogr. notes, and index.

1589a **Coleman, Edward Davidson.** The bible in English drama, an annotated list of plays including translations from other languages. New York, New York public library, 1931. iv,212p. 26cm.

Repr. from N.Y. Pub Lib Bull 34:695–714,785–817,839–82 Oc–D '30; 35:31–50,103–27, 163–80 Ja–Mr '31.

DRAMA — 1475–1640

1601a **Mares, Francis Hugh.** The origin of the figure called 'the Vice' in Tudor drama. Huntington Lib Q 22:11–29 N '58.

'Plays containing Vices' (p.12)

1601b **Yamada, Akihiro.** A checklist of English printed drama before 1641 at the library of the University of Illinois. Res Opp Renaiss Drama 9:31–53 '68.

Author checklist of about 332 entries with some bibliogr. notes and refs.; indexed.

1601c **Young, Steven C.** A check list of Tudor and Stuart induction plays. Philol Q 48:131–4 Ja '69.

DRAMA — 1475–1700

1611a **Ribner, Irving.** 'A chronological list of extant English history plays, 1519–1653' *in* The English history play in the age of Shakespeare. Princeton, N.J.; London, 1957. p.319–27.

1611b —— [Same]: [Rev. ed.] London [1965] p.313–20.

1616 **Langhans, Edward A.** Restoration manuscript notes in seventeenth century plays. Restor & 18th Cent Theat Res 5:30–9 My '66; 5:2–17 N '66.
Annotated checklist of 252 items.

1617 **Silvette, Herbert.** 'Bibliography' *in* The doctor on the stage: medicine and medical men in seventeenth-century England. Ed. by Francelia Butler. Knoxville [1967] p.279–82. (Not seen)

1618 **English** renaissance plays in the University of London library. Res Opp Renaiss Drama 9:65–72 '68.
'Dramatic works published in England before 1640' (p.66–70); 'Dramatic works published in England, 1641–c.1660' (p.70–2): author checklists of 150 items, with bibliogr. refs.

1619 **Omans, Stuart.** Newberry library: English renaissance drama from the Silver collection. Res Opp Renaiss Drama 9:59–63 '68.
Author checklist of 97 items to 1660 with Greg nos.

DRAMA—1641–1700

1621a **Noyes, Robert Gale.** Contemporary musical settings of the songs in restoration drama. Eng Lit Hist 1:325–44 D '34.
Checklist in first-line order, with some bibliogr. notes.

1623a **Noyes, Robert Gale.** Songs from restoration drama in contemporary and eighteenth-century poetical miscellanies. Eng Lit Hist 3:291–316 D '36.
Checklist in first-line order, with some bibliogr. notes.

DRAMA — 1701–1800

1630 **Stratman, Carl Joseph.** Theses and dissertations in restoration and 18th century theatre. Restor & 18th Cent Theat Res 2:20–45 N '63.
'Addenda' (p.45)

1630a **Vernon, P. F.** Theses and dissertations in restoration and 18th century theatre: addenda. Restor & 18th Cent Theat Res 6:55–6 My '67.

1630b **Perrin, Michel P.** Theses and dissertations in restoration and 18th century theatre: further addenda. Restor & 18th Cent Theat Res 7:1–6 My '68.

1630c **Stratman, Carl Joseph,** *ed.* Restoration and 18th century theatre research bibliography, 1961–1968, compiled by Edmund Napieralski and Jean E. Westbrook. Troy, N.Y., Whitston pub. co., 1969. ii,241p. 23cm.

1631a **Wray, Edith.** English adaptations of French drama between 1780 and 1815. Mod Lang N 43:87–90 F '28.
Chronol. checklist, with note of French original.

1633a **Wood, Frederick Thomas.** The attack on the stage in the XVIII century. N&Q 173:218–22 S '37.
Chronol. checklist from Collier (1698) to the end of the 18th century, on the morality of the stage.

1636 **Jackson, Allan S.** Bibliography of 17th & 18th century play editions in the rare book room of the Ohio State university library. Restor & 18th Cent Theat Res 8:30–58 My '69.
Author checklist of 284 items.

DRAMA — IRELAND — 1900–

1653 **French, Frances-Jane.** The Abbey theatre series of plays, a bibliography. [Dublin] Dolmen pr. [1969] 53p. facsims., diagrs. 26cm.
Quasifacsim. TP transcrs., collations and bibliogr. notes and refs. on 24 items; no index.
Rev: J. Cotton Priv Lib ser2 2:131–2 '69.

ENCYCLOPEDIAS

1656g **Walsh, S. Padraig.** Anglo-American general encyclopedias, a historical bibliography, 1703–1967. New York, R. R. Bowker, 1968. xix,270p. 24cm.
Annotated alphabetical checklist.
Rev: G. G. Freeman Pa Bib Soc Am 63:56–9 '69.

FICTION — 1475–

1659 **Bell, Inglis F.** and **D. Baird.** The English novel, 1578–1956, a checklist of twentieth-century criticisms. Denver, A. Swallow [1958] xii,169p. 21cm.

1664a **Boyce, Benjamin.** News from hell; satiric communications with the nether world in English writing of the seventeenth and eighteenth centuries. Pub Mod Lang Assn 58:402–37 Je '43.
'Bibliography' (p.427–37): chronol. checklist of 201 items, 1590–1939.

1664b **Bolitho, T. G. G.** Some utopias. N&Q 193:522 N '48.

1669a **Duke university,** DURHAM, N. C. **Library.** Utopia collection of the Duke university library [by] Glenn R. Negley. Durham, Friends of the Duke university library, 1965. iii,83p. 29cm. (Duplicated typescript) (Not seen)

FICTION — 1601–1700

1686d **Begley, Walter,** *ed.* 'Bibliography of the only two companions in England (1600–50) of Nova solyma . . . [i.e. Mundus alter et idem, and Godwin's The man in the moon]' *in* Nova solyma, the ideal city. London, 1902. V.2, p.388–96.

1689 **Mish, Charles Carroll.** English prose fiction, 1600–1700, a chronological checklist. [2d ed.] Charlottesville, Va., Bibliographical society of the University of Virginia, 1967. (First pub. 1952) 110p. 23cm.

FICTION — 1801–

1721 **Harris, Wendell V.** Fiction in the English experimental periodicals of the 1890's. Bull Bib 25:111–18 Ja/Ap '68.
Albemarle; Anglo-Saxon review; Butterfly; Dome; Evergreen; Pageant; Quarto; Savoy; Venture; Yellow book.

1722 —— John Lane's Keynote series and the fiction of the 1890's. Pub Mod Lang Assn 83:1407–15 Oc '68.
'Bibliographic note' (p.1412–15) includes checklist of 31 items.

FICTION — 1901–

1723 **Goetsch, Paul** and **H. Kosok,** *comp.* 'Literatur zum modernen englischen Roman: eine ausgewählte Bibliographie' *in* Oppel, Horst, *ed.* Der moderne englische Roman: Interpretationen. Berlin, 1965. p.417–28.

1724 **Gerber, Richard.** 'Appendix: an annotated list of English utopian fantasies, 1901–1951' *in* Utopian fantasy, a study of English utopian fiction since the end of the nineteenth century. London [1955] p.143–57.

1724a **Rabinovitz, Rubin.** 'Bibliography' *in* The reaction against experiment in the English novel, 1950–1960. New York, 1967. p.173–221.
Checklists of works by and about Kingsley Amis, Angus Wilson, C. P. Snow, and 'Selected general critical works' (p.212–21)

GRAMMARS

1726a **Carr, Charles T.** German grammars in England in the nineteenth century. Mod Lang R 30:481–501 Jl '35.
Chronol. checklist of 14 items, 1774–1836 (p.481–2)

1726b **Spink, J. S.** The teaching of French pronunciation in England in the eighteenth century. . . . Mod Lang R 41:155–63 Ap '46.
'Bibliographical note: French grammars and dictionaries, 1694–1800' (p.161–3)

ILLUSTRATED BOOKS

1754a **Rainbird, George.** The making of colour plate books. Priv Lib 5:47–9 Jl '64.
'A checklist of colour plate books produced by Rainbird McLean ltd. and George Rainbird ltd.' (p.48–9)

JESTBOOKS

1757 **Schulz, Ernst,** *ed.* 'Bibliographie der englischen Schwankbücher' *in* Die englischen Schwankbücher bis herab zu Dobsons drie bobs, 1607. Berlin, 1912. (Palaestra, CXVII) p.18–23.

1758 **Wilson, Frank Percy.** The English jestbooks of the sixteenth and early seventeenth centuries. Huntington Lib Q 2:121–58 Ja '39.

'Bibliographical notes' (p.147–58): checklist, with some bibliogr. notes and refs., of 17 'Collections of detached jests'; 13 'Jest-biographies', and 3 'Collections of comic novelle'.

1758a —— [Same]: Repr. in Shakespearian and other essays. Ed. by Helen Gardner. Oxford, 1969. p.[284]–324.

'Bibliographical notes' (p.313–24)

1759 **Zall, Paul M.** English prose jestbooks in the Huntington library, a chronological checklist, 1535?–1799. Sh Res Opp 4:78–91 '68/9.

With index and checklist of facsims., etc.

LETTER-WRITERS

1760 **Hornbeak, Katherine Gee.** 'A bibliography of the English letter-writer, 1568–1800' *in* The complete letter-writer in English, 1568–1800. Northampton [Mass., 1934] p.128–45.

1760a **Robertson, Jean.** 'A bibliography of complete letter-writers', 1568–1700' *in* The art of letter writing; an essay on the handbooks published in England during the sixteenth and seventeenth centuries. [Liverpool] 1942. p.67–80.

Author checklist.

LIBRARY CATALOGUES

1760d **Jayne, Sears Reynolds.** 'Inventory' *in* Library catalogues of the English renaissance. Berkeley, Calif., 1956. p.[57]–172.

Classified annotated checklists of catalogues of private and institutional libraries. 'Appendix 1: Miscellaneous book lists, 1500–1640' (p.175–82)

1760e **Kaufman, Paul.** The community library, a chapter in English social history. Philadelphia, American philosophical society, 1967. 67p. facsims., tables. 30cm. (American Philos Soc Trans new ser 57pt7)

Includes 'Descriptive outline of circulating library catalogues' (p.11–13); 'A descriptive census of subscription library catalogues' (p.26–8); 'Check list of circulating libraries in England to 1800' (p.50–3); 'Checklist of subscription libraries in England' (p.53–4); 'Bibliography' (p.63–5)

1760f **McDonald, William R.** Circulating libraries in the north-east of Scotland in the eighteenth century. Biblioth 5no4:119–37 '68.

Includes checklists of 'extant catalogues', with collations, location of copy seen, and some bibliogr. notes.

MAPS — GENERAL

1771 **London. Public record office.** Maps and atlases in the Public record office. 1. British Isles, c.1410–1860. London, 1967. xv,648p. 26cm.

MAPS — DURHAM

1781a **Benedikz, Phyllis Mary.** Durham topographical prints up to 1800, an annotated bibliography. Durham, G. Bailes for the University library,

1968. xii,88p. facsims. 21cm. (Durham. University. Library. Publications, no.6)

Rev: P. C. G. Isaac Library ser5 24:356 '69.

MAPS — HUNTINGDONSHIRE

1790d **Dickinson, Philip George M.** Maps in the County record office, Huntingdon. [Huntingdon, I. L. Norie and Wilson] 1968. viii,72p. maps. 21cm.

'Maps of Huntingdonshire' (p.1–37)

MAPS — LONDON

1795 **Darlington, Ida** and **J. Howgego.** Printed maps of London circa 1553–1850. London, G. Philip, 1964. ix,257p. facsims. 25cm.

Chronol. list of 421 items, with descriptive notes and locations of copies.

Rev: TLS 19 N '64:1048; Pa Bib Soc Am 60:133 '66; P. D. A. Harvey J Soc Archiv 13:148–9 '66.

MAPS — WALES

1813 **Evans, Olwen Caradoc.** Maps of Wales and Welsh cartographers. London, Map collectors' circle, 1964. 22p.+20 plates. maps. 25cm.

'List of printed maps of Wales' (p.14–22)

MAPS — SCOTLAND

1813d **Bartholomew, John George.** 'The cartography of Scotland from earliest times to the present date' *in* Royal Scottish geographical society. Atlas of Scotland. [Edinburgh] 1895. p.[16]–18.

MUSIC — GENERAL

1826a **Ford, Wyn Kelson.** Music in England before 1800, a selected bibliography. London, Library association, 1967. xiv,128p. 23cm. ([Library association bibliographies, no.7])

1837a **Tilmouth, Michael.** A calendar of references to music in newspapers published in London and the provinces, 1660–1719. Roy Mus Assn Res Chron 1:i–vii,1–107 '61; Errata and general index *ib.* 2:1–15 '62.

1839a **London. Guildhall library.** Gresham music library, a catalogue of the printed books and manuscripts deposited in Guildhall library. London, Ptd. . . . on behalf of the Gresham committee, 1965. ii,92p. 21cm.

'Printed works' (p.1–71) mainly of the 18th century.

1841 **Reid, Douglas J.** and **B. Pritchard.** Some festival programmes of the eighteenth and nineteenth centuries. 1. Salisbury and Winchester. Roy Mus Assn Res Chron 5:51–79 '65; 2. Cambridge and Oxford *ib.* 6:3–23 '66.

1841a **Simpson, Adrienne.** A short-title list of printed English instrumental tutors up to 1800, held in British libraries. Roy Mus Assn Res Chron 6:24–50 '66.

Chronol. checklist, 1574–1800, with locations of copies.

1842 **Harman, Richard Alexander.** A catalogue of the printed music and books on music in Durham cathedral library. London, O.U.P., 1968. xv,136p. 21cm.

Classified checklist to 1825.

Rev: TLS 27 Je '68:688.

NEWSPAPERS AND PERIODICALS — 1601–

1847a **Catalogue** of literary annuals and gift books in the New York public library, N.Y. Pub Lib Bull 6:270–5 Jl '02.

1853a **Stark, Lewis M.** Lonsdale collection of English newspapers. N.Y. Pub Lib Bull 52:35–6 Ja '48.

'Checklist of the papers in the Lonsdale collection' (p.35–6)

NEWSPAPERS AND PERIODICALS — 1601–1700

1873b **Williams, J. B.,** *pseud.* The first English newspaper. N&Q ser11 9:341–2 My '14.

Checklist of 24 corantos in BM.

1873c **Shaaber, Matthias A.** The history of the first English newspaper. Stud Philol 29:551–87 Oc '32.

'Nicholas Bourne and Thomas Archer' (p.557–8): a checklist of 19 items issued by them, with bibliogr. refs. 'Nathaniel Butter' (p.558–9); 'William Sheffard, Nathaniel Newbery, Bartholomew Downes' (p.559)

1875a **Collins, Douglas Cecil.** A handlist of newspamphlets, 1590–1610. London, South-west Essex technical college, 1943. xix,129p. 23cm.

Annotated chronol. checklist, with indexes.

Rev: L. W. Hanson Library ser4 26:203–4 '45.

1880 **Frank, Joseph.** 'A chronological list of English newspapers from November 1641 through May 1642' *in* The beginnings of the English newspaper, 1620–1660. Cambridge, Mass., 1961. p.[278]–80.

'A chronol. list of the various issues of A perfect diurnall of the passages in Parliament from June through December 1642' (p.[281]–2; 'A chronological list of English newspapers between September, 1647 and the end of 1648 that lasted fewer than five numbers' (p.[283]–4)

1881 **Thomas, Peter William.** 'Appendix II. Mercurius Aulicus: Supplements' *in* Sir John Berkenhead, 1617–1679, a royalist career in politics and polemics. Oxford, 1969. p.[245]–8.

Note also 'Delays in the publication of Mercurius Aulicus' (p.[238]–44)

NEWSPAPERS AND PERIODICALS — 1801–1900

1915a **The annuals** of sixty years ago. Pub Circ 54no1280:680 Je '91.

'The annuals, 1823 to 1853': chronol. checklist.

1921a **Mineka, Francis Edward.** 'Appendix: identification of authorship' *in* The dissidence of dissent; the Monthly repository, 1806–1838. Chapel Hill, 1944. p.[394]–428.

First series, 1806–1826.—Second series, 1827–1837.

1927c **Madden, Lionel.** Victorian periodicals in Leicester. [Leicester] University of Leicester, Victorian studies centre, 1969. 2v.(37l.) 26cm. Covertitle. (Victorian studies handlist, 1) (Duplicated typescript)

NEWSPAPERS AND PERIODICALS — SCOTLAND — 1801–1900

1938a **Strout, Alan Lang.** Contributors to Blackwood's magazine. N&Q 194:541–3 D '49; 195:70–2 F '50; J. C. Corson *ib*. 195:63 F '50.

1940a —— The first twenty-three numbers of the Noctes ambrosianae; excerpts from the Blackwood papers in the National library of Scotland. Library ser5 12:108–18 Je '57.

'Authorship of the Noctes ambrosianae, I–XXIII' (p.118)

POETRY — 1475–

1981 **Havens, Raymond Dexter.** [Appendices] *in* The influence of Milton on English poetry. New Haven, 1922. (Repr. New York, Russell and Russell, 1961) p.625–97.

'Poems in non-Miltonic blank verse [1680–1750]' (p.625–6); 'Loco-descriptive poems not known to be Miltonic [1642–1828]' (p.627–31); 'Rimed technical treatises [1673–1819]' (p.632–3); 'Bibliography I: Poems influenced by Paradise lost [1685–1915]' (p. 637–68); 'Bibliography II: Poems influenced by L'Allegro and Il penseroso [1647–1832]' (p.669–79); 'Bibliography III: Poems influenced by the remaining works of Milton' (p.680–4); 'Bibliography IV: Eighteenth-century sonnets' (p.695–97)

1981b **Bush, Douglas.** 'Appendix [Chronological list of mythological poems, 1681–1935]' *in* Mythology and the romantic tradition in English poetry. Cambridge, Mass., 1937. (Repr. 1969) p.[539]–77.

1982a **Weiss, Harry Bischoff.** English and American valentine writers. N.Y. Pub Lib Bull 43:71–86 F '39.

'Preliminary checklist of valentine writers' (p.77–86): title checklist of 153 items, with location of copy seen.

POETRY — 1475–1700

1998a **Frank, Joseph.** Hobbled Pegasus, a checklist of minor English poetry, 1641–1660. Alberquerque, University of New Mexico pr. [1968] 482p. 25cm. (Not seen)

Rev: TLS 26 Je '69:712.

POETRY — 1701–1800

1999d **Bleackley, Horace W.** Cryptographic satires of the eighteenth century. N&Q ser11 12:413–14 N '15.

2003a **Aubin, Robert Arnold.** A note on the eighteenth-century progress pieces. Mod Lang N 49:405–7 '34.

Supplement to Griffith, no.631.

2007a **Boys, Richard Charles.** The English poetical miscellany in colonial America. Stud Philol 42:114–30 Ja '45.

'References to miscellanies in colonial America' (p.119–30): title checklist based on Case.

2017a **Faverty, Frederic Everett,** *ed.* The Victorian poets; a guide to research. 2d ed. Cambridge, Mass., Harvard U.P.; London, O.U.P., 1968. (First pub. 1956) 433p. 24cm.

Bibliogr. essays by various hands on 'general materials'; Tennyson; Browning; E. B. Browning; FitzGerald; Clough; Arnold; Swinburne; the pre-Raphaelites; Hopkins; and the later Victorian poets.

2022 **Ewing, James Cameron.** Brash and Reid, booksellers in Glasgow and their collection of Poetry original and selected. Glasgow Bib Soc Rec 12:1–20 '36.

Discursive collations and contents.

PRESENTATION BOOKS

2035b **Heltzel, Virgil Barney.** Sir Thomas Egerton as patron. Huntington Lib Q 11:105–27 F '48.

'Authors and works' (p.124–7): author checklist of works dedicated to Egerton, with some bibliogr. notes.

2035c **Rosenberg, Eleanor.** 'A chronological list of works dedicated to the earl of Leicester' *in* Leicester, patron of letters. New York, 1955. p.[355]–62.

Checklist of 94 items, 1559–88.

SERMONS

2063 **MacLure, Millar.** 'A register of sermons preached at Paul's cross, 1534–1642' *in* The Paul's cross sermons, 1534–1642. [Toronto; London, 1958] p.[184]–256.

2064 **ó Súilleabháin, Pádraig.** Catholic sermon books printed in Ireland, 1700–1850. Irish Ecclesiastical Rec ser5 99:31–6 Ja '63.

In the Franciscan library, Killiney, co. Dublin.

TRANSLATIONS

See Foreign books published in English in Britain.

SUBJECTS

AESTHETICS

2087 **Draper, John William.** Eighteenth century English aesthetics, a bibliography. Heidelberg, C. Winters, 1931. 140p. 23cm. (Anglistische forschungen, 71)
Classified checklist of contemporary literature of aesthetics, architecture and gardening, pictorial and plastic arts, literature and drama, and music including opera.

2088 **Babcock, Robert Witbeck.** The idea of taste in the eighteenth century. Pub Mod Lang Assn 50:922–6 S '35.
Chronol. checklist, 1712–99, of sources for study of the subject.

2089 —— Benevolence, sensibility and sentiment in some eighteenth-century periodicals. Mod Lang N 62:394–7 Je '47.

2089a —— A note on genius, imagination and enthusiasm in some late eighteenth century periodicals. N&Q 192:93–5 Mr '47.
Chronol. checklists of contemporary discussions of these terms.

AGRICULTURE
See also Botany; Gardening.

ARCTIC

2104 **Corley, N. T.** Bibliography of books printed before 1800. Arctic 19:78–98 Mr '66. (Not seen)

ASTROLOGY

2108 **Parr, Johnston.** 'Sources of the renaissance Englishman's knowledge of astrology, a bibliographical survey and a bibliography' *in* Tamburlaine's malady and other essays on astrology in Elizabethan drama. University, Ala., 1953. p.[112]–50.
Author checklist (p.132–50) with anonyma at end.

BALLET

2110d **Forrester, Felicitée Sheila.** Ballet in England, a bibliography and survey, c.1700–June, 1966. [London] Library association, 1968. 224p. illus., facsims. 22cm. (Library association. Bibliographies, no.9)
'Ballet in England to 1830' (p.65–70)

BIRDS

2118 **National book league,** LONDON. British birds and their books; catalogue of an exhibition . . . arranged by Raymond Irwin. London, Published for the National book league by the C.U.P. [1952] 38p. illus. 19cm.
'Part III (items 164–181) a collection of children's bird books, mostly of the nineteenth century' (p.34–6)

2121 **Newcastle-upon-Tyne. University. Library.** An exhibition of fine bird books, 1555–1900, from the library of the Natural history society of Northumberland, Durham and Newcastle upon Tyne. Newcastle upon Tyne, 1966. 5p. 30cm. (Newcastle-upon-Tyne. University. Library. Publications, extra ser., no.5) (Not seen)

BOTANY

2130 **Scotland. National library,** EDINBURGH. Botanical illustration, a loan exhibition. Edinburgh, 1964. 39p. illus. 24cm.

'BOUNTY', MUTINY ON THE

2133 **Houston, Neal B.** The mutiny on the Bounty: a historical and literary bibliography. Bull Bib 26:37–41 Ap/Je '69.
Classified checklist.

COOKERY

2141d **Pennell, Elizabeth Robins.** 'Bibliography' *in* My cookery books. Boston, 1903. p.[107]–71.

2144 **Oxford, Arnold Whitaker.** English cookery books: bibliography. N&Q 147:367 N '24 153:4–5 Jl '27; 160:436–7 Je '31; H. Askew *ib.* 161:16 Jl '31.

2144a **Stark, Lewis M.** The Whitney cookery collection. N.Y. Pub Lib Bull 50:103–23 F '46.
Chronol. checklist of 218 items, 1558–1932, with bibliogr. refs.; and mss., largely English.

COURTESY

2150 **Wilkinson, David Robert McIntyre.** 'Bibliography of seventeenth-century courtesy books cited, with information on the numbers of reprints' *in* The comedy of habit, an essay on the use of courtesy literature in a study of restoration comic drama. Leiden, 1964. p.171–4.

ECONOMICS

2171 **Harvard university. Graduate school of business administration. Baker library. Kress library of business and economics.** . . . Catalogue supplement, 1473–1848, giving data also upon cognate items in other Harvard libraries. Boston, Mass., Baker library, Harvard graduate school, 1967. (Not seen)

EDUCATION

2174 **Hart, H. Raven-** and **Marjorie Johnston.** Bibliography of the registers, printed, of the universities, inns of court, colleges, and schools of Great Britain and Ireland. Bull Inst Hist Res 9:19–30,65–83,154–70 Je '31–F '32; 10:109–13 N '32.

ESTHETICS

See Aesthetics.

GARDENING

2187a **Royal horticultural society. Lindley library.** The Lindley library catalogue of books, pamphlets, manuscripts and drawings. London, 1927. viii,487p. 26cm.

Comp. by H. R. Hutchinson.

JEWS

2198a **Roth, Cecil.** 'The Jew in English literature' *in* Magna bibliotheca . . . Anglo-judaica, a bibliographical guide to Anglo-Jewish history. New ed., rev. and enl. London, 1937. (First pub. 1887) p.172–6, 399–406.
See also no.2199b.

2199b **Lehmann, Ruth Pauline.** 'The Jew in English literature' *in* Nova bibliotheca Anglo-judaica, a bibliographical guide to Anglo-jewish history, 1937–1960. London, 1961. p.137–40.

LANGUAGE

2203 **Alston, Robin Carfrae.** A bibliography of the English language from the invention of printing to the year 1800. Leeds, Ptd. for the author by E. J. Arnold [1965–   ]   v. 27cm.

Contents: 1. English grammars written in English and English grammars written in Latin by native speakers. ([1965]).—2. Polyglot dictionaries and grammars: treatises on English written for speakers of French, German, Dutch, Danish, Swedish, Portuguese, Spanish, Italian, Hungarian, Persian, Bengali and Russian. ([1967]).—3pt1. Old English, Middle English, Early modern English, miscellaneous works, vocabulary. [1970].— 4. Spelling-books ([1967]).—5. The English dictionary. ([1966]).—6. Rhetoric, style, elocution, prosody, rhyme, pronunciation, spelling reform. ([1969]).—7. Logic, philosophy, epistemology, universal language. ([1967]).—8. Treatises on shorthand. ([1966])

LAW

2209 **Putnam, Bertha Haven.** 'Appendix I. A bibliography of printed treatises for justices of the peace, 1506–1599' *in* Early treatises on the practice of the justices of the peace in the fifteenth and sixteenth centuries. Oxford, 1924. p.[224]–37.
Checklist of 32 items, with some locations of copies.

MEDICINE

2230a **Liverpool. Medical institution. Library.** Catalogue of the books . . . to the end of the nineteenth century. Liverpool, 1968. 569p. illus. 23cm.

2230b **Royal college of obstetricians and gynaecologists. Library.** Short-title catalogue of books printed before 1851. . . . 2d ed., illustrated. London, 1968. (First pub. 1956) 90p. facsims. 21cm.
Ed. by John L. Thornton.

MILITARY BOOKS

2236a **Webb, Henry J.** English military books. . . . Philol Q 23:116–28 Ap '44.

2240a **Schwoerer, Lois G.** Chronology and authorship of the Standing army tracts, 1697–1699. N&Q 211:382–90 Oc '66.
Chronol. checklist of 37 pamphlets, Oc 1697–1700 (p.384–90)

MUTINY ON THE 'BOUNTY'

See 'Bounty', Mutiny on the.

NAVAL BOOKS

See Military books.

PARLIAMENT

2245 **Great Britain. Parliament. House of commons. Library.** A bibliography of parliamentary debates of Great Britain. London, H.M.S.O., 1956. 62p. 2 col.diagrs. 25cm. Covertitle. (House of commons. Library. Document, no.2)

Classified annotated checklist of debates, diaries, and proceedings, with index.

PIRATES

2245d **Gosse, Philip Henry G.** My pirate library. London, Dulau, 1926. (Repr. New York, B. Franklin, 1967) 75p. facsims. 21cm.

Dictionary catalogue; the collection is now in the National maritime museum, Greenwich.

RAILWAYS

2249 **Cotterell, Samuel.** A handbook to various publications, documents, and charts connected with . . . the railway system chiefly in Great Britain and Ireland . . . to be sold by mr. Edward Baker . . . Birmingham. [Birmingham, E. Baker] 1893. (Repr. Newton Abbot, David & Charles, 1969) 128p. illus. 15cm. Covertitle.

2249a —— **[Same]**: Supplement. Birmingham [1895] (Repr. Newton Abbot, David & Charles, 1969) 92p. 17cm. Covertitle.

Includes index to the Handbook.

2249b **National liberal club,** LONDON. **Gladstone library.** Early railway pamphlets, 1825–1900. London, 1938. 60p. facsim. 22cm. (Gladstone library pamphlet collection. Subject lists, no.1)

RELIGION

2250a **Smith, Wilbur Moorehead.** A bibliography of biblical, ecclesiastical and theological dictionaries and encyclopaedias published in Great Britain and America. Fuller Lib Bull 20/3:3–30 Oc '53/S '54.

Annotated author checklist, 1612–1850, with some bibliogr. notes. 'Chronological arrangement of biblical and theological dictionaries, 1612–1850' (p.3)

—— CATHOLIC BOOKS — JESUIT

2266a **Clancy, Thomas H.** 'Chronological list of political writings of the Allen-Persons party, 1572–1613' *in* Papist pamphleteers. . . . Chicago, 1964. p.235–43.

—— METHODIST BOOKS

2270d **Wesleyan methodist conference,** LONDON. **Library.** A catalogue of manuscripts and relics, engravings and photographs, medals, books and pamphlets. . . . London, Methodist publishing house [1921] vii,217p. illus., facsims. 23 cm.

Classified short-title dictionary catalogue of pubs. by the Wesleys, Methodist and anti-Methodist literature. Comp. by J. Alfred Sharp.

—— NONCONFORMIST BOOKS

2272a **Dr. Williams's library,** LONDON. Early nonconformity, 1566–1800: a catalogue of books. Boston, Mass., G. K. Hall, 1968. 12v. 33cm.

Introduction by Kenneth Twinn.

—— OXFORD MOVEMENT

2273 **Johnston, John Octavius,** *ed.* 'Appendix: The tracts for the times' *in* Liddon, Henry P. Life of Edward Bouverie Pusey. London, 1893–7. V.3 (1894), p.[473]–80.

2273a **Doubleday, W. E.** The Oxford movement and the church crisis. (Bibliographies of questions of the day.) Lib Assn Rec 1:324–30 My '99.

RHETORIC

2276a **Alston, Robin Carfrae** [1965–]: no.2203.

SHORTHAND

2279d **Institute of shorthand writers,** LONDON. **Library.** Catalogue of the books in the library. . . . by Matthias Levy. London, 1900. 93p. 22cm.

Briefer lists pub. in 1892, 1895.

2281 **Matthews, William.** 'Bibliography' *in* English pronunciation and shorthand in the early modern period. Berkeley [Calif.] 1943. p.209–13.

STYLE

2286c **Alston, Robin Carfae** [1965–]: no.2203.

2286d **Milic, Louis T.** Style and stylistics. New York, Free pr.; London, Collier-Macmillan [1967] 199p. 22cm.

2286e **Bailey, Richard W.** and **Dolores M. Burton.** English stylistics, a bibliography. Cambridge, Mass., M.I.T. pr. [1968] xxii,198p. 24cm.

TRAVEL BOOKS

See also Regional bibliographies—Topography.

2289d **Brown, Wallace Cable.** The popularity of English travel books about the near east, 1775–1825. Philol Q 15:70–80 Ja '36.

Author checklist of the 15 most popular near east travel books (p.78–9)

2289e **Parker, John.** 'Bibliography' *in* Books to build an empire, a bibliographical history of English overseas interests to 1620. Amsterdam, 1965. p.[243]–65.
Chronol. checklist with some bibliogr. notes and refs.

2289f **National maritime museum,** GREENWICH. **Library.** Voyages & travels. London, H.M.S.O., 1968. xi,403+2 fold.maps. 25cm. (Its Catalogue, v.1)

2289g **Naylor, Bernard.** Accounts of nineteenth-century South America; an annotated checklist of works by British and United States observers. London, University of London, Pub. for the Institute of Latin American studies [by] Athlone pr., 1969. 80p. 23cm.

VETERINARY SCIENCE

See Medicine.

VOYAGES

See Travel books.

AUTHORS

2300 **Christophers, Richard Albert.** George Abbot, archbishop of Canterbury, 1562–1633, a bibliography. Charlottesville, Published for the Bibliographical society of the University of Virginia [by] University pr. of Virginia [1966] xxiv,211p. 24cm. (Duplicated typescript)

Quasifacsim. TP transcrs., collations, bibliogr. notes and refs. for works; letters; sermons and speeches; archiespiscopal business; Abbot's will; works attrib. to; and ana. Based on London university School of librarianship and archives thesis: no.97.

Rev: TLS 3 N '66:1009; J. Horden Library ser5 23:168–70 '68.

ABERCROMBIE, LASCELLES, 1881–1938

2303a **Cooper, Jeffrey.** A bibliography and notes on the works of Lascelles Abercrombie. London, Kaye & Ward [1969] 166p. illus., port., facsims. 21cm.

Quasifacsim. TP transcrs., collations and bibliogr. notes on works; contribs. to books; contribs. to periodicals and newspapers; broadcasts; with a chronol. table.

ACHELLEY, THOMAS, fl.1568–1595

2303g **Freeman, Arthur.** The writings of Thomas Achelley. Library ser5 25:40–2 Mr '70.

'Works by Thomas Achelley' (p.40–2): quasifacsim. TP transcrs., collations, bibliogr. notes and refs., and locations of copies for 6 items, c.1571–1600.

Æ., *pseud. of* GEORGE WILLIAM RUSSELL, 1867–1935

2311 **Denson, Alan.** Printed writings of George W. Russell (Æ): a bibliography with notes on his pictures and portraits. London, Northwestern U.P., 1961; Evanston, Ill., Northwestern U.P., 1962. 255p. port. 23cm.

Classified, part chronol., part alphabetical arrangement of works, mss., ephemera, ana, etc., with discursive collations, locations of copies, and bibliogr. notes.

Rev: TLS 9 N '62:864; Pa Bib Soc Am 56:513 '62.

2312 —— 'Additions and corrections to this compiler's bibliography of G. W. Russell . . .' *in* James H. Cousins . . . a bio-bibliographical survey. Kendal, 1967. p.304–32,344,349–50.

AINSWORTH, WILLIAM HARRISON, 1805–1882

2315a **[Hutchison, B.]** William Harrison Ainsworth, 1805–82. Bk Coll & Lib Mthly 17:144–7 S '69.

ALKEN, HENRY THOMAS, 1785–1851

2320c **Van Devanter, Willis,** *comp.* 'A checklist of books illustrated by Henry Alken' *in* Haupt, Hellmut Lehmann-, *ed.* Homage to a bookman; essays on

manuscripts, books and printing written for Hans P. Kraus. . . . Berlin [1967] p.245–[61]
Alphabetical checklist of 89 items, with some bibliogr. notes.

AMIS, KINGSLEY, 1922–

2323d **Rabinovitz, Rubin,** 1967: no.1724a.

ANDERTON, LAWRENCE, 1575–1643

2323g **Sparke, Archibald.** Andertons of Lostock and Horwich. N&Q ser 11:21–2 Ja '15; R. S. B.; J. B. Wainewright *ib.* 11:75 Ja '15.
Alphabetical checklist of 18 items (p.21–2)

ARNOLD, MATTHEW, 1822–1888

2335 **Faverty, Frederic Everett,** *ed.,* 1968: no.2017a.

2336a **Brown, Edward Killoran.** 'Bibliography' *in* Studies in the text of Matthew Arnold's prose works. Paris, 1935. p.[132]–5.
Checklist of prose works of which more than one version appeared in his lifetime.

2337a **Super, Robert Henry.** Arnold's Oxford lectures on poetry. Mod Lang N 70:581–4 D '55.
Chronol. checklist, 1857–67 (p.581–2)

2338a —— Arnold's notebooks and Arnold bibliography. Mod Philol 56:268–9 My '59.
Four further contribs. to periodicals.

ARTHUR, LEGENDARY KING OF BRITAIN, fl.520

2348c **Northup, Clark Sutherland** and **J. J. Parry.** The Arthurian legends: modern retellings of the old stories, an annotated bibliography. J Eng Germ Philol 43:173–221 Ap '44.
Classified annotated checklist.

2348d —— Supplement, by Paul A. Brown [and] J. J. Parry. *ib.* 49:208–16 Ap '50.

2349a **Roberts, Bryn F.** 'Supplementary bibliography' *in* Chambers, sir Edmund K. Arthur of Britain. Cambridge; New York [1964] (First pub. 1927) p.301–20.

ASCHAM, ROGER, 1515–1568

2351a **Johnson, Robert Carl.** Minor Elizabethans: Roger Ascham, 1946–1966; George Gascoigne, 1941–1966; John Heywood, 1944–1966; Thomas Kyd, 1940–1966; Anthony Munday, 1941–1966. London, Nether pr., 1968. 51p. 22cm. (Elizabethan bibliographies supplements, IX)
Chronol. checklists supplementing the Elizabethan bibliographies of S. A. Tannenbaum.

ASTELL, MARY, 1666?–1731

2352a **Fawcett, J. W.** Mary Astell, 1668–1731: bibliography. N&Q 166:117–18
F '34; H. Askew *ib.* 166:178 Mr '34; M. H. Dodds 166:211 Mr '34.
Checklist of ana.

AUNGERVILLE, RICHARD (RICHARD DE BURY), 1287–1342?
See Richard de Bury.

AUSTEN, JANE, 1775–1817

2366a —— [**Same**]: Errata leaf. London, Nonesuch pr., 1931. il. 19cm.

AUSTIN, JOHN LANGSHAW, 1911–1960

2369g **Fann, K. T.,** *ed.* 'Bibliography' *in* Symposium on J. L. Austin. London
[1969] p.469–82.
Checklist of works and ana.

BACON, FRANCIS, BARON VERULAM AND VISCOUNT ST. ALBAN,
1561–1626

2373a **Houk, J. Kemp.** Francis Bacon, 1926–1966. London, Nether pr., 1968.
72p. 22cm. (Elizabethan bibliographies supplements, XV)
Chronol. checklist of works and ana.

BALLANTYNE, ROBERT MICHAEL, 1825–1894

2385d [**Hutchison, B.**] The first editions of R. M. Ballantyne, 1825–94: a provisional list. Bk Coll & Lib Mthly 1:17–19 My '68.

2385e **Quayle, Eric.** R. M. Ballantyne, a bibliography of first editions. London,
Dawsons, 1968. 128p. illus., facsims. 22cm.
Quasifacsim. TP transcrs., bibliogr. notes of works, with a select list of newspaper and
periodical contribs.
Rev: Pa Bib Soc Am 62:484 '68; R. Stokes Priv Lib ser2 1:189–90 '68; Bk Coll & Lib
Mthly 3:15 '68; R. A. Brimmell Bk Coll 18:252,255–6 '69.

BARNES, WILLIAM, 1801–1886

2394a **Hearl, Trevor W.** 'Select bibliography of the works of William Barnes' *in*
William Barnes, 1801–1886, the schoolmaster. Dorset, 1966. p.333–41.

BARRIE, SIR JAMES MATHEW, 1860–1937

2399a **Jones, Winston M.,** 1964: no.148a.

BEAUMONT, FRANCIS, 1584–1616, AND JOHN FLETCHER, 1579–
1625

2413a **Pennel, Charles A.** and **W. P. Williams.** Francis Beaumont—John
Fletcher—Philip Massinger, 1937–1965; John Ford, 1940–1965; James
Shirley, 1945–1965. London, Nether pr., 1968. 52p. 22cm. (Elizabethan
bibliographies supplements, VIII)
Chronol. checklists supplementing S. A. Tannenbaum's Elizabethan bibliographies.

BECKETT, SAMUEL BARCLAY, 1906–

2414 **Cohn, Ruby.** 'Bibliography' *in* Samuel Beckett, the comic gamut. New Brunswick, N.J. [1962] p.[328]–40.

2414a **Marissel, André.** 'Bibliographie' *in* Samuel Beckett. Paris [1963] p.[111]–22.

2414b **Bryer, Jackson R.,** *comp.* 'Critique de Samuel Beckett: sélection bibliographique' *in* [Friedman, Melvin J.] *ed.* Samuel Beckett. Paris, 1964. p.[169]–84.

2414c **Fletcher, John Walter J.** 'Bibliography' *in* The novels of Samuel Beckett. London, 1964. p.[234]–51.
Checklist of works and ana, 1929–60, with some bibliogr. notes.

2414d **Scott, Nathan Alexander.** 'A selected bibliography' *in* Samuel Beckett. London [1965] p.135–[41]

2414e **Davis, Robin J.,** 1966: no.106a.

BECKFORD, WILLIAM, 1759–1844

2414h **Gemmett, Robert J.** William Beckford, bibliographical addenda. Bull Bib 25:62–4 My/Ag '67.

2418 **[Bishop, Philippa]** *comp.* 'William Beckford exhibition' *in* [Summers, Peter] William Beckford: some notes on his life in Bath, 1822–1844, and a catalogue of the exhibition in the Holburne of Menstrie museum. [Bath] 1966. p.16–31.

BENNETT, ENOCH ARNOLD, 1867–1931

2444a **Emery, Norman.** Arnold Bennett, 1867–1931, a bibliography. Stoke-on-Trent, Central library, 1967. iii,66p. 25cm. (Horace Barks reference library. Bibliographical series, no.3) (Duplicated typescript)
Classified checklist.

2444b **Gordan, John Dozier.** Arnold Bennett, the centenary of his birth; an exhibition in the Berg collection. N.Y. Pub Lib Bull 72:72–122 F '68.

2444c **Tillier, Louis.** 'L'œuvre d'Arnold Bennett' *in* Arnold Bennett et ses romans réalistes. Paris [1968] p.[333]–51
Classified checklist of works and ana.

BENNETT, HENRY STANLEY, 1899–

2444h **[Brewer, Derek Stanley]** A list of his writings presented to H. S. Bennett on his eightieth birthday, 15th January, 1969. Cambridge, 1969. 15p. ports. 21cm.
Chronol. checklist, 1922–66.
Rev: TLS 8 My '69:496.

BENTLEY, RICHARD, 1854–1936

2449a **B., L. R.** Richard Bentley's literary work. N&Q 171:154 Ag '36.
Checklist, 1892–1927.

BERKENHEAD, SIR JOHN, 1617–1679

2454g **Thomas, Peter William.** 'Berkenhead's works' *in* Sir John Berkenhead, 1617–1679, a royalist career in politics and polemics. Oxford, 1969. p.[267]–71.
Checklist of newsbooks; pamphlets; prefaces by; and verses.

BISHOP, EDMUND, 1846–1917

2463d **Abercrombie, N. J.** Bibliography of Edmund Bishop. TLS 6 Je '52:384; 13 Je '52:396.
Chronol. checklist of 188 items, 1870–1952.

BLACKMORE, RICHARD DODDRIDGE, 1825–1900

2465a **Dunn, Waldo Hilary.** 'Bibliography of Blackmore's writings' *in* R. D. Blackmore, the author of Lorna Doone, a biography. London [1956] p.292–3.
Checklist.

BLADES, WILLIAM, 1824–1890

2467 **Reed, Talbot Baines,** *comp.* 'List of published works by William Blades' *in* Blades, William. The pentateuch of printing. London, 1891. p.xix–xxiv.
Chronol. checklist, 1858–91.

2467a **St. Bride foundation institute,** LONDON. Catalogue of an exhibition in commemoration of the centenary of William Blades . . . compiled by William Turner Berry. [London, Ptd. by Blades and Blades, 1924] 39p. 22cm.
Annotated checklist, with quasifacsim. TP transcrs.

BLAKE, WILLIAM, 1757–1827

2479a **Keynes, sir Geoffrey Langdon** and **R. Todd.** William Blake's catalogue, a new discovery. TLS 12 S '42:456.
'A census': details of 18 copies.

2484a **Adams, Hazard.** 'Bibliographical appendix' *in* William Blake, a reading of the shorter poems. Seattle, 1963. p.299–332.
'. . . commentaries of all kinds upon Blake's shorter poems.'

2486a **William Blake trust.** An exhibition of the illuminated books of William Blake, poet, printer, prophet, arranged by the William Blake trust: a commemorative handbook with a study by Geoffrey Keynes and a foreword by Lessing J. Rosenwald. [Clairvaux, Trianon pr., 1964] 56p. facsims. (part col.) 30cm.
Ed. by Arnold Fawcus. 'The illuminated books, by Geoffrey Keynes' (p.11–[55])

2488 **Keynes, sir Geoffrey Langdon.** Blake's Little Tom the sailor. Bk Coll 17n04:421–7 '68.

Bibliogr. descr., with census of 8 copies; bibliogr. notes and locations of copies.

2489 **Westminster. City libraries.** William Blake: catalogue for the Preston Blake library presented by Kerrison Preston in 1967. [London] 1969. [127]p. 26cm.

Comp. by Phyllis Goff.

BLISS, PHILIP, 1787–1857

2491 —— [Same]: Additions and corrections. *ib.* 3pt3:367–8 '33; Oxford Bib Soc Pub new ser 1pt1:40–2 '47.

BODKIN, THOMAS PATRICK, 1887–1961

2500b —— 'Some corrections . . .' *in* James H. Cousins . . . a bio-bibliographical survey. Kendal, 1967. p.302–3,349–50.

BOHN, HENRY GEORGE, 1796–1884

See under Presses and printing.

BOSWELL, JAMES, 1740–1795

2508a **McKinlay, Robert.** Boswell's fugitive pieces. Glasgow Bib Soc Rec 8:64–80 '30.

'Bibliography' (p.78–80): checklist, 1761–91.

2508b **Brown, Anthony E.** Boswellian studies. Cairo Stud Eng 1963/6:1–75 '66.

Indexed classified checklist of 674 entries: editions; biographies of Boswell; the Boswell papers; general studies; theses and dissertations.

BOTTOMLEY, GORDON, 1874–1948

2508h **[Muir, Percival Horace** and **M. T. H. Sadleir]** *comp.* 'Gordon Bottomley, a check list' *in* Muir, Percival H. Points, 1874–1930. . . . London, 1931. p.93–8.

Chronol. checklist, 1896–1930, with some bibliogr. notes.

BRADDON, MARY ELIZABETH (MRS. JOHN MAXWELL), 1837–1915

2519c **[Hutchison, B.]** Miss M. E. Braddon, 1837–1915. Bk Coll & Lib Mthly 20:251–3 '69.

BRADLEY, ANDREW CECIL, 1851–1935

2519h **Blish, Mary.** A. C. Bradley, a summary account. Bk Coll 62:607–12 '68.

'A bibliography of the works of Andrew Cecil Bradley' (p.609–12): chronol. checklist of works; essays and notes; works ed., introduced or trans. by; and mss.

BRAMAH, ERNEST, *pseud. of* ERNEST BRAMAH SMITH, 1868–1942

2522a **White, William.** Two Bramah variants. Pa Bib Soc Am 62:254–6 '68.

BRETON, NICHOLAS, 1545?–1626?

2524a **Robertson, Jean,** *ed.* 'Canon' *in* Poems by Nicholas Breton not hitherto printed. Liverpool, 1952. (Repr. 1969) p.xxxii–cliii.
Annotated checklist of 66 works and doubtful and attrib. works, with some bibliogr. notes and locations of copies.

BRIDGES, ROBERT SEYMOUR, 1844–1930

2529a **Kable, William S.** The Ewelme collection of Robert Bridges, a catalogue. [Columbia, S. C.] University of Carolina, 1967. 35p. 23cm. (University of South Carolina. Dept. of English. Bibliographical series, no.2)
Rev: TLS 6 Je '68:602; S. Nowell-Smith Bk Coll 17:370–1 '68.

BRONTË, EMILY, 1818–1848

2532d **Graham, Rigby.** Wuthering heights, and the illustrator. Priv Lib ser2 1no3:99–108 '68; 1no4:145–82 '68.
'List of illustrated editions' (p.157–82): annotated chronol. checklist, from 1872/3 with bibliogr. notes.

BROOKE, FRANCES (MOORE), 1723–1789

2544 **Poole, E. Phillips,** *ed.* 'Bibliographical list of mrs. Brooke's published writings' *in* Lady Julia Mandeville, by Frances Brooke. London, 1930. p.39–40.
Chronol. checklist of 12 items, 1755–90.

BROWN, JOHN ALEXANDER HARVIE, 1844–1916

2556 [**Scott, Walter**] Bibliography of the writings of J. A. Harvie-Brown . . . arranged . . . in chronological order. [Stirling] Privately ptd. [1897] ii,32,iip. 28cm.
Chronol. checklist of 199 items, 1864–96, with some bibliogr. notes.

BROWNE, SIR THOMAS, 1605–1682

2566a **Donovan, Dennis G.** Sir Thomas Browne, 1924–1966; Robert Burton, 1924–1966. London, Nether pr., 1968. 50p. 22cm. (Elizabethan bibliographies supplements, X)
Chronol. checklist supplementing Keynes, no.2564 and Jordan-Smith, no.2655.

2566b **Keynes, sir Geoffrey Langdon.** A bibliography of sir Thomas Browne, kt., MD. 2d ed., rev. and augmented. Oxford, Clarendon pr., 1968. (First pub. 1924) 293p. illus., facsims., ports. 26cm.
Omits 'Works of dr. Edward Browne'.
Rev: TLS 20 Je '68:660; Pa Bib Soc Am 63:220 '69; J. Horden Library ser5 24:350–2 '69.

BROWNING, ELIZABETH (BARRETT), 1806–1861

2568a **Joyce, Hewette Elwell.** Mrs. Browning's contributions to American periodicals. Mod Lang N 35:402–5 N '20.
Checklist of 26 periodical contribs.

2572 **Barnes, Warner.** A bibliography of Elizabeth Barrett Browning. [Austin, Tex.] University of Texas & Baylor university [1967] 179p. facsims. 24cm.

Bibliogr. of primary entries; fugitive printings and forgeries; contributions; letters; and reprints. The indexes include 'Index of textual variants' (p.151–66)

Rev: TLS 31 Jl '69:864; Pa Bib Soc Am 63:59–60 '69; J. W. Carter Bk Coll 19:101–4 '70.

BROWNING, ROBERT, 1812–1889

2577a **McElderry, B. R.** The ring and the book. TLS 22 My '37:400.

Checklist of 8 contemporary reviews, hitherto unnoticed.

2582a **Faverty, Frederic Everett,** *ed.*, 1968: no.2017a.

2582b **Leudecke, Margaret Ann.** A bibliography of the Brownings, 1965–1968. Browning Newsl 2:13–24 Ap '69.

2582c —— A checklist of publications, June 1968–December 1968. Browning Newsl 2:48–51 '69.

2582h **Anderson, John Parker,** *comp.* 'Bibliography' *in* Sharp, William. Life of Robert Browning. London, 1890. p.[i]–xxii at end.

2582i **[Campbell, James Dykes]** *comp.* 'A chronological bibliography of Browning's works' *in* Orr, mrs. Alexandra S. A handbook to the works of Robert Browning. [6th ed.] London, 1892. (Repr. 1895, 1899, 1902) p.[365]–409.

2587a **British museum. Dept. of printed books.** Robert Browning, an excerpt from the General catalogue of printed books. London, W. Clowes, 1939. 28col. 33cm. Covertitle.

2590 **Barnes, Warner.** Catalogue of the Browning collection, the University of Texas. [Austin, Tex., Humanities research center, University of Texas, 1966] 120p. facsims. 25cm.

Rev: TLS 16 My '68:512; W. Whitta N&Q 214:239–40 '69; E. C. McAleer Browning Newsl 2:46–7 '69.

BUCHANAN, GEORGE, 1506–1582

2604 **Murray, David.** Catalogue of printed books, manuscripts, charters and other documents relating to George Buchanan or illustrative of his life . . . exhibited in the library of the University of Glasgow. [Proof under revision] Glasgow, J. Maclehose, 1906. 102,6p. 23cm.

At head of title: Commemoration at Glasgow of the quatercentary of the birth of George Buchanan.

BUNYAN, JOHN, 1628–1688

2611a **McCombs, Charles F.** The pilgrim's progress: John Bunyan, his life and times, 1628–1928. N.Y. Pub Lib Bull 32:786–809 D '28.

2613a **British museum. Dept. of printed books.** John Bunyan, an excerpt from the General catalogue of printed books. . . . London, W. Clowes, 1939. 74col. 33cm.

2634a **Ewing, James Cameron.** Robert Burns's Letters addressed to Clarinda: a history of its publication and interdiction, with a bibliography. Edinburgh Bib Soc Pub 11pt2:87–112 Oc '21.

'Bibliography' (p.107–12): TP transcrs. and facsims., collations, some bibliogr. notes and locations of copies for 20 items, 1802–1907; and ana.

BURTON, ROBERT, 1557–1640

2651a **Donovan, Dennis G.** . . . Robert Burton. . . . London, Nether pr., 1968. *See* no.2566a.

2657 **Heventhal, Charles.** Robert Burton's Anatomy of melancholy in early America. Pa Bib Soc Am 63:157–75 '69.

'A check list of seventeenth-century quarto and folio editions of the Anatomy of melancholy available in the United States in the year 1964' (p.174–5)

BURY, JOHN BAGNELL, 1861–1927

2658 **Baynes, Norman Hepburn.** A bibliography of the works of J. B. Bury, compiled with a memoir. Cambridge, C.U.P., 1929. 183p. 22cm.

'Bibliography' (p.125–70): chronol. checklist, 1887–1909.

Rev: N&Q 158:143–4 '30.

BUTLER, SAMUEL, 1612–1680

2661 **Chew, Beverly C.** 'Some notes on the three parts of Hudibras' *in* Essays and verses about books. New York, 1926. p.65–97.

Repr. from Bibliographer 1no4:123–38 Ap '02. TP facsims., collations, and bibliogr. notes.

BUTT, JOHN EVERETT, 1906–1965

2671d **Carnall, G. D.,** *comp.* 'A list of the published writings of John Butt' *in* Mack, Maynard and I. Gregor, *ed.* Imagined worlds: essays on some English novels and novelists in honour of John Butt. London [1968] p.477–[86]

Chronol. checklist of books and pamphlets; words ed. or trans. by; contribs. to books and periodicals; and reviews.

BUTTERFIELD, SIR HERBERT, 1900–

2671h **Partington, E.,** 1963; no.179a.

BYRON, GEORGE GORDON, BARON BYRON, 1788–1824

2690a **British museum. Dept. of printed books.** Byron, an excerpt from the General catalogue of printed books . . . London, W. Clowes, 1939. 78col. 33cm.

CARROLL, LEWIS, *pseud.* of CHARLES LUTWIDGE DODGSON, 1832–1898

2736 **[Smith, Robert Dennis Hilton]** Alice one hundred, being a catalogue in celebration of the 100th birthday of Alice's adventures in Wonderland. Victoria, B.C., Adelphi book shop, 1966. 77p. facsims. 23cm.

The collection is now in the library of the University of British Columbia.

CARY, ARTHUR JOYCE LUNEL, 1888–1957

2742 **Reed, Peter J.** Joyce Cary, a selected checklist of criticism. Bull Bib 25:133–4,151 My/Ag '68.

CHAPMAN, GEORGE, 1559?–1634

2761a **Ray, George W.** George Chapman, a checklist of editions, biography, and criticism, 1946–1965. Res Opp Renaiss Drama 9:55–8 '68.

Additions to Yamada, no.2761.

CHARLES I, KING OF GREAT BRITAIN AND IRELAND, 1660–1649

2762a **Whiting, G. W.** On the authorship of Eikon basilike, a supplementary list. N&Q 162:134–5 F '32.

CHAUCER, GEOFFREY, 1340?–1400

2779a **Alderson, William L.** A check-list of supplements to Spurgeon's Chaucer allusions. Philol Q 32:418–27 Oc '53.

2781a **British museum. Dept. of printed books.** Chaucer, an excerpt from the General catalogue of printed books. . . . London, W. Clowes, 1943. 46col. 33cm.

2782a **Hetherington, John Rowland.** Chaucer. . . . Reissued 1967 with appendix to 1687 & corrections. Birmingham, 1967. 24p. facsims. 33cm. (Duplicated typescript)

CHESTERTON, GILBERT KEITH, 1874–1936

2787a **Sullivan, John.** Chesterton continued, a bibliographical supplement. [London] University of London pr. [1968] xiv,120p. facsims. 23cm.

Rev: Bk Coll & Lib Mthly 1:22 '68; B. C. Bloomfield Library ser5 24:355 '69.

CHETTLE, HENRY, d.1607?

2787d **Jenkins, Harold.** 'Bibliography' *in* The life and work of Henry Chettle. London, 1934. p.262–8.

Quasifacsim. TP transcrs., collations, locations of copies and some bibliogr. notes on plays; non-dramatic works; letters; and modern editions.

CHUBB, THOMAS, 1679–1747

2792d **Bushell, Thomas L.** 'Bibliography' *in* The sage of Salisbury: Thomas Chubb, 1679–1747. [London] 1968. p.151–6.

Checklist of works and ana.

CHURCHILL, SIR WINSTON LEONARD SPENCER, 1874–1965

2800 **Woods, Frederick W.** A bibliography of the works of sir Winston Churchill. [2d ed., rev.] London, Kaye & Ward [1969] 398p. illus., port., facsims. 22cm.

See no.2799.

CIBBER, COLLEY, 1671–1757

2806a **Ashley, Leonard R. N.** Colley Cibber, a bibliography. Restor & 18th Cent Theat Res 6:14–27,51–7 My,N '67; Addenda *ib.* 7:17 My '68.

Classified checklist of works and ana.

2806b **Kalson, Albert E.** Eighteenth-century editions of Colley Cibber's Richard III. Restor & 18th Cent Theat Res 7:7–17 My '68.

Quasifacsim. TP transcrs. and some bibliogr. notes.

CLARE, JOHN, 1793–1864

2809a **Northampton. Public library.** Catalogue of the John Clare collection . . . with indexes to the poems in manuscript. Northampton, 1964. 72p. illus., facsims., port. 21cm.

Comp. by D. Powell.

Rev: L. Haddakin Mod Lang R 61:295–7 '66.

CLOUGH, ARTHUR HUGH, 1819–1861

2817 **Faverty, Frederic Everett,** *ed.,* 1968: no.2017a.

2819 **Gollin, Richard M., W. E. Houghton,** and **M. Timko.** Arthur Hugh Clough, a descriptive catalogue; poetry, prose, biography, and criticism. [New York] New York public library [1967] 117p. port. 26cm.

Repr. from N.Y. Pub Lib Bull 70:554–85 N '66; 71:55–8,173–99 Ja,Mr '67.

Rev: W. V. Harris Eng Lang N 6:222–3 '69; J. Bertram N&Q 214:230–2 '69.

COCKER, EDWARD, 1631–1675

2823a **Heal, sir Ambrose.** Cocker's Arithmetick. N&Q 162:318–19 Ap '32.

Addenda to previous list, based on the George Potter collection now at University of Michigan.

COLERIDGE, SAMUEL TAYLOR, 1772–1834

2826a **Hall, Thomas.** Coleridge criticism. Bull Bib 25:124–31 Ja/Ap '68; 25:153–6 My/Ag '68; 25:175–182,172 S/D '68.

COLLINS, WILLIAM, 1721–1759

2844a **Woodhouse, A. S. P.** Imitations of the Ode to evening. TLS 30 My '29:436; D. Cook *ib.* 6 Je '29:454.

Supplements Havens, no.1981.

COLLINS, WILLIAM WILKIE, 1824–1889

2852 [Hutchison, B.] Books by and about Wilkie Collins. Bk Coll & Lib Mthly 5:15–19 S '68.

COMBE, WILLIAM, 1742–1823

2855h Hamilton, Harlan W. 'Bibliography' in Doctor Syntax, a silhouette of William Combe, esq. . . . London, 1969. p.303–34.
Classified checklist of works; words ed., trans., or with contribs. by; newspaper and periodical contribs.; and unpublished mss., with some bibliogr. notes.

CONRAD, JOSEPH, pseud. of TEODOR JÓZEF KONRAD KORZENIOWSKI, 1857–1924

2855m Curle, Richard Henry Parnell. A handlist of the various books, pamphlets, prefaces . . . written about Joseph Conrad by Richard Curle, 1911–1931. Brookville, Pa., 1932. 23p. 24cm.

2873 Ehrsam, Theodore George. A bibliography of Joseph Conrad. Metuchen, N.J., Scarecrow pr., 1969. 448p. 22cm. (Not seen)
Rev: Pa Bib Soc Am 63:221 '69; ib. 63:350 '69; TLS 25 Je '70:674.

COOK, JAMES, 1728–1779

2878a Du Rietz, Rolf. Captain James Cook, a bibliography of literature printed in Sweden before 1819. Upsala [Ptd. by Almqvist & Wiksells] 1960. 27p. illus. 21cm.

COOPER, JOHN GILBERT, 1723–1769

2880d Ryskamp, Charles. John Gilbert Cooper and Dodsley's Museum. N&Q 203:210–11 My '58.
'. . . list of Cooper's contributions to the Museum, or the literary and historical register . . .' (p.211): checklist of 22 items, 10 My 1746–23 My '47.

COPLAND, ROBERT, fl.1508–1547

2880h Heseltine, George Coulehan, ed. 'English editions of the Kalendar of shepherds' in The Kalendar of shepherds. London, 1931. p.176.
Chronol. checklist of 19 items, 1503–1892.

COULTON, GEORGE GORDON, 1858–1947

2886d Langstadt, E., 1946: no.154a.

COUSINS, JAMES HENRY SPROULL, 1873–1956

2887d Denson, Alan. James H. Cousins, 1873–1956, and Margaret E. Cousins, 1878–1954; a bio-bibliographical survey. Kendal, 1967. 350p. 35cm. (Duplicated typescript)
Discursive extensively indexed checklist.

COUSINS, MARGARET E. (GILLESPIE), 1878-1954

See Cousins, James Henry Sproull, 1873-1956.

CRAIG, EDWARD GORDON, 1872-1966

2912d **Fletcher, Ifan Kyrle.** Edward Gordon Craig, a check-list. Theat Arts Mthly 19no4:293-304 '35.

2912e **Fletcher, Ifan Kyrle** and **A. Rood.** Edward Gordon Craig, a bibliography. London, Society for theatre research, 1967. 117p. port. 21cm.

Classified chronol. checklist of works; works contrib. to; books illustr. by; texts of plays produced by; periodicals ed. by; periodicals contrib. to; exhibitions; and programmes of plays, with bibliogr. notes.

Rev: TLS 19 S '68:1053; Pa Bib Soc Am 62:647 '68.

2912f **Rood, Arnold.** Edward Gordon Craig, artist of the theatre, 1872-1966, a memorial exhibition in the Amsterdam gallery. . . . Introduction by Donald Oenslager. New York, New York public library, 1967. 57p. illus. 26cm.

Repr. from N.Y. Pub Lib Bull 71:445-68,524-41 S,Oc '67.

CROMWELL, OLIVER, 1599-1658

2920d **Swann, John Hibbert.** Oliver Cromwell. (Bibliographies of questions of the day). Lib Assn Rec 1no8:528-34 Ag '99.

CUDWORTH, RALPH, 1617-1688

2940a **Guffey, George Robert,** 1969: no.4976g.

CULVERWEL, NATHANIEL, d.1651 ?

2940h **Guffey, George Robert,** 1969: no.4976g.

CUMBERLAND, GEORGE, 1754-1848

2940m **Keynes, sir Geoffrey Langdon.** Some uncollected authors, XLIV. George Cumberland, 1734-1848. Bk Coll 19no1:31-65 '70.

'Works by George Cumberland' (p.57-65): quasifacsim. TP transcrs., collations and bibliogr. notes on 15 items, 1793-1829.

DANIEL, SAMUEL, 1562-1619

2948a **Guffey, George Robert.** Samuel Daniel, 1942-1965; Michael Drayton, 1941-1965; sir Philip Sidney, 1941-1965. London, Nether pr., 1967. 52p. 22cm. (Elizabethan bibliographies supplements, VII)

Chronol. checklist supplementing S. A. Tannenbaum's Elizabethan bibliographies.

2948b **Spriet, Pierre.** 'Bibliographe' *in* Samuel Daniel, 1563-1619, sa vie, son œuvre. [Paris] 1968. (Not seen)

DAY-LEWIS, CECIL, 1904-

See Lewis, Cecil Day-.

DE BURY, RICHARD (RICHARD AUNGERVILLE), 1287–1342?
See Richard de Bury.

DEFOE, DANIEL, 1661?–1731

2976b **Staverman, Werner Henrik.** 'Bibliografie' *in* Robinson Crusoe in Neder-
land, een bijdrage tot de geschiedenis van den roman in de XVIII⁰ eeuw.
Groningen, 1907. p.[145]–82.

2990 **Boston. Public library.** A catalogue of the Defoe collection . . . with a preface
by John Alden. Boston, Mass., G. K. Hall, 1966. vi,200p. 25cm. (Duplicated typescript)

DEKKER, THOMAS, 1570?–1641

2996a **Donovan, Dennis G.** Thomas Dekker, 1945–1965; Thomas Heywood,
1938–1965; Cyril Tourneur, 1945–1965. London, Nether pr. [1967] 56p.
22cm. (Elizabethan bibliographies supplements, II)
Chronol. checklists supplementing S. A. Tannenbaum's Elizabethan bibliographies.

DENHAM, SIR JAMES, formerly STEUART, 1712–1780

3010d **Skinner, Andrew S.,** *ed.* 'Published writings of sir James Steuart' *in*
Steuart, sir James D. An inquiry into the principles of political œconomy.
Edinburgh [1966] V.2, p.740–1.
Chronol. checklist, 1757–1810.

DENHAM, SIR JOHN, 1615–1669

3011a **Aubin, Robert Arnold.** Materials for a study of the influence of Cooper's
Hill. Eng Lit Hist 1:197–204 S '34.

DIBDIN, THOMAS FROGNALL, 1776–1847

3031a **O'Dwyer, Edward John.** 'A check-list of T. F. Dibdin's bibliographical
works' *in* Thomas Frognall Dibdin, bibliographer & bibliomaniac extraordinary, 1776–1847. Pinner, 1967. p.43–4.

DICKENS, CHARLES JOHN HUFFAM, 1817–1870

3095b **Weitenkampf, Frank.** Illustrator in masquerade, a short chapter in
Dickens bibliography. N.Y. Pub Lib Bull 49:423–6 Je '45.
'The list' (p.424–6): title checklist of American illus. ed., with notes on the illus.

3102 **Tillotson, Kathleen Mary,** *ed.* 'Descriptive list of editions, 1838–1867' *in*
Dickens, Charles. Oliver Twist. Oxford, 1966. p.[xlviii]–lvi.

3103 **Carr, sr. Mary Callista.** A catalogue of the VanderPoel Dickens collec-
tion at the University of Texas. Compiled by sister Lucile Carr. Austin,
Tex. [University of Texas, Humanities research center, 1968] xi,274p.
facsims. 25cm.
Rev. ed. of no.3099.
Rev: TLS 26 F '70:232; S. N. Nowell-Smith Library ser5 25:170 '70.

3104 **Collins, Philip Arthur William.** A Dickens bibliography; an extract from the third volume of the New Cambridge bibliography of English literature. [London] Published by the Dickens fellowship, 1970. cols. 779–850. 24cm.

D'ISRAELI, ISAAC, 1766–1848

3149d **Ogden, James.** 'Bibliography' *in* Isaac D'Israeli. Oxford, 1969. p.[210]–20.

Checklist of works, articles and reviews, and ana.

DOBRÉE, BONAMY, 1891–1969

3150d **Britton, M. C.,** 1963: no.89a.

DOWSON, ERNEST CHRISTOPHER, 1867–1900

3179a **Longaker, John Mark.** 'A chronology of Dowson's works' *in* Ernest Dowson. [3d ed.] Philadelphia [1967] (First pub. 1944) p.299–301.

Chronol. checklist of works, 1886–1934, with ana.

DRAYTON, MICHAEL, 1563–1631

3188a **Guffey, George Robert.** . . . Michael Drayton. . . . London, Nether pr., 1967. *See* no.2948a.

3189a **Jensen, Bent Juel-.** Fine and large-paper copies of S.T.C. books, and particularly of Drayton's Poems, 1619, and The battaile of Agincourt, 1627. Library ser5 19:226–30 '64.

Checklist of large-paper copies (p.229–30)

DRYDEN, JOHN, 1590–1680

3196a **Gatto, Louis C.** An annotated bibliography of critical thought concerning Dryden's Essay of dramatic poesy. Restor & 18th Cent Theat Res 5:18–29 My '66.

DU MAURIER, GEORGE LOUIS PALMELLA BUSSON, 1834–1896

3216a **Ormonde, Leonée.** 'Appendix' *in* George du Maurier. London, 1969. p.[499]–501.

Chronol. checklist of works and ana.

DURRELL, LAWRENCE GEORGE, 1912–

3223d **Beebe, Maurice.** Criticism of Lawrence Durrell, a selected checklist. Mod Fict Stud 13no3:417–21 '67.

3228 **Thomas, Alan G.,** *comp.* 'Bibliography' *in* Fraser, G. S. Lawrence Durrell, a study. London [1968] p.200–50.

Classified checklist of books; translations; prefaces; some contribs. to books; ana; periodical contribs.; gramophone records and musical settings, etc., with some bibliogr. notes.

Rev: R. J. Roberts Bk Coll 18:389–90 '69.

ELIOT, GEORGE, *pseud. of* MARY ANN (EVANS) CROSS, 1819–1880

3246a **Marshall, William H.** A selective bibliography of writings about George Eliot to 1965. Bull Bib 25:70–2,88–94 My/Ag,S/D '67.

ELIOT, THOMAS STEARNS, 1888–1965

3260 **Malawsky, Beryl York.** T. S. Eliot, a check-list, 1952–1964. Bull Bib 25:59–61,69 My/Ag '67.
Classified checklist of works and ana, supplementing Gallup, no.3257.

3261 **Gallup, Donald Clifford.** T. S. Eliot, a bibliography. London, Faber & Faber [1969] (First pub. 1952) 414p. 22cm.
See no.3257.
Rev: TLS 5 Mr '70:264.

EVELYN, JOHN, 1655–1699

3276a **Keynes, sir Geoffrey Langdon.** John Evelyn, a study in bibliophily & a bibliography of his writings. [2d ed.] Oxford, Clarendon pr., 1968. (First pub. 1937) xvii,313p. illus., ports., facsims. 26cm.
Rev: N. H. H. Russell R Eng Stud new ser 20:346–7 '69; TLS 30 Ja '69:116; J. Horden Library ser5 25:64–5 '70.

FAIRBANK, ALFRED JOHN, 1895–

3280p **McClean, Ruari,** *comp.* 'Catalogue of Alfred Fairbank's works' *in* Osley, Arthur S., *ed.* Calligraphy and palaeography: essays presented to Alfred Fairbank. . . . [London] 1965. p.20–8.
Chronol. checklist of manuscript books and published works.

FARNOL, JOHN JEFFERY, 1878–1952

3282p **[Hutchison, B.]** Jeffrey Farnol. Bk Coll & Lib Mthly 18:180–2 Oc '69.
Title checklist.

FARQUHAR, GEORGE, 1678–1707

3282d **Gibb, I. P.,** 1952: no.126.

FARRAR, FREDERICK WILLIAM, 1831–1903

3283 **Farrar, Reginald.** 'Bibliography' *in* The life of Frederick William Farrar, sometime dean of Canterbury. London, 1904. p.xiii–xxii.
Chronol. checklist, 1857–1901, of works; and editions published in the United States.

FEARN, JOHN RUSSELL, 1908–1960

3283b **Harbottle, Philip James.** The multi-man, a biographic and bibliographic study of John Russell Fearn, 1908–60. Wallsend, 1968. 69p. illus. 24cm. (Not seen)

FELL, BP. JOHN, 1625–1686

3283g **Morison, Stanley** and **H. G. Carter.** John Fell, the University press and the Fell types. . . . Oxford, Clarendon pr., 1967. xvi,278p. illus., port., facsims. 39cm.

'List of the published writings of John Fell' (p.[215]–26): chronol. checklist, 1638–1868, with varying descrs., bibliogr. notes and refs., comp. by J. S. G. Simmons. 'The Fell type specimens' (p.[229]–32) and 'Fell's announcements and proposals' (p.[251]–2), comp. by J. S. G. Simmons. 'Books in Fell type published by the University of Oxford from 1902 to 1927' (p.[253]), comp. by H. G. Carter.

FENN, GEORGE MANVILLE, 1831–1909

3283k **[Hutchison, B.]** George Manville Fenn, 1831–1909. Bk Coll & Lib Mthly 9:260–6 Ja '69.

Title checklist.

FIELDING, HENRY, 1707–1754

3299a **A Fielding** bibliography. Academy 72:166 F '07; A. J. Barnouw *ib.* 72:220 Mr '07.

3306 **Jones, B. P.,** 1962: no.147a.

FIELDING, SARAH, 1710–1768

3311a **Grey, Jill Elizabeth,** *ed.* 'Bibliography' *in* Sarah Fielding: The governess or Little female academy, a facsimile reproduction . . . with an introduction and bibliography. London, 1968. p.349–69.

Chronol. checklist of works, 1744–62; 'Sarah Fielding, a publishing history of her The governess' (p.353–60); and imitators, etc.

FITZGERALD, EDWARD, 1809–1883

3320 **Faverty, Frederic Everett,** *ed.*, 1968: no.2017a.

FLAXMAN, JOHN, 1755–1826

3330 **Bentley, Gerald Eades, jr.** Notes on the early editions of Flaxman's classical designs. New York, New York public library, 1964. 63p. illus., facsims. 26cm.

Repr. from N.Y. Pub Lib Bull 68:277–307,361–80 My,Je '64.

Quasifacsim. TP transcrs., collations, locations of copies, and bibliogr. notes on early ed.

FORD, FORD MADDOX, 1873–1939

3342 **Ludwig, Richard M.** 'A list of Ford's books' *in* Letters of Ford Maddox Ford. Princeton, N.J.; London, 1965. p[xiii]–xvi.

FORD, JOHN, fl.1639

3345a **Pennel, Charles A.** and **W. P. Williams.** . . . John Ford. . . . London, Nether pr., 1968. *See* no.2413a.

FRASER, CLAUD LOVAT, 1890–1921

3360a **Hull. University.**

FREEMAN, RICHARD AUSTIN, 1862–1943

3364a **[Hutchison, B.]** Dilemma for detective fiction collectors: R. Austin Freeman, 1862–1943. Bk Coll & Lib Mthly 3:10–11 Jl '68.
'The British first editions of R. Austin Freeman' (p.10–11)

FRY, CHRISTOPHER, 1907–

3365d **Schear, Bernice Larson** and **E. G. Prater.** A bibliography on Christopher Fry. Tulane Drama R 4:88–98 Mr '60.
Classified checklist of works and ana.

GALSWORTHY, JOHN, 1867–1933

3385 **[Birmingham. University. Library]** Galsworthy centenary exhibition: catalogue. [Birmingham, 1967] 16p. 25cm. Covertitle. (Duplicated typescript)

3386 **Birmingham. University. Library.** John Galsworthy; catalogue of the collection. . . . [Birmingham] 1967. 88p. facsim. 26cm.
Comp. by D. Wyn Evans.

GARNETT, RICHARD, 1835–1906

3397a **Prance, Claude Annett.** 'Notes on Richard Garnett's writings' *in* Peppercorn papers, a miscellany on books and book-collecting. Cambridge, 1964 [i.e. 1965] p.153–73.

GARRICK, DAVID, 1717–1779

3399a **Smith, Helen R.,** 1966: no.201a.

GASCOIGNE, GEORGE, 1525 ?–1577

3401a **Johnson, Robert Carl.** Minor Elizabethans . . . George Gascoigne . . . London, Nether pr., 1968. *See* no.2351a.

3401b **Price, John Edward.** A secondary bibliography of George Gascoigne, with an introduction summarizing the trend of Gascoigne scholarship. Bull Bib 25:138–40 My/Ag '68.

GEIKIE, SIR ARCHIBALD, 1835–1924

3416g **Cutter, Eric,** 1964: no.105a.

GIBBON, LEWIS GRASSIC, *pseud. of* JAMES LESLIE MITCHELL, 1901–1935

3425a **Young, Douglas F.** James Leslie Mitchell/Lewis Grassic Gibbon, a chronological checklist. Additions 1. Biblioth 5no5:169–73 '69.

3425b —— Additions II, by James Kidd. *ib.* 5n05:174-7 '69.

GIBBON, WILLIAM MONK, 1896-

3425d **Denson, Alan.** Monk Gibbon, a checklist of his publications. Dublin Mag 5n03/4:17-22 '66.

Classified checklist of books and pamphlets; contribs. to books; trans.; periodicals contrib. to.

GILBERT, WILLIAM, 1804-1890

3429d **Bulloch, John Malcolm.** W. S. Gilbert's father. N&Q 171:435-9 D '36.

Chronol. checklist, 1857-82, with some bibliogr. notes.

GILBERT, SIR WILLIAM SCHWENCK, 1836-1911

3432a **Bulloch, John Malcolm.** The anatomy of the Bab ballads. N&Q 171:344-8,385 N '36.

'. . . a list of the Ballads which appeared serially in Fun . . .' (p.346-8): chronol. checklist, with some bibliogr. notes.

3432b —— The Bab ballads by titles. N&Q 172:362-7,387 My,N '37.

Alphabetical arrangement of the previous list, with the incorporation of 43 additional titles.

3434 **Jones, John Bush.** W. S. Gilbert's contributions to Fun, 1865-1874. N.Y. Pub Lib Bull 73:253-66 Ap '69.

Annotated chronol. checklist.

GLADSTONE, WILLIAM EWART, 1809-1898

3457a **Bassett, Arthur Tilney.** 'Bibliography' *in* Gladstone's speeches: descriptive index and bibliography. London, 1916. p.91-105.

Chronol. checklist, 1827-98, with 'Gladstone's speeches' (p.6-90): table of date, subject, place and ptd. length.

GLASSE, HANNAH, fl.1747

3458d **Passey, J. M. D.,** 1955: no.179b.

GLOVER, TERROT REAVELEY, 1869-1943

3458g **Williams, F. H. B.,** 1952: no. 232a.

GODWIN, WILLIAM, 1756-1836

3461a **Pollin, Burton Ralph.** Godwin criticism, a synoptic bibliography. Toronto, University of Toronto pr. [1967]; London, O.U.P., 1969. xlvi,659p. 23cm.

'Index XI. The writings of William Godwin, 1756-1836, a list of books and pamphlets in successive editions, reprints and translations' (p.655-9)

Rev: L. T. Milic Computer Stud Humanities & Verbal Behavior 1:156 '68; D. H. Reiman J Eng Germ Philol 67:715-17 '68; TLS 20 Mr '69:290; J. W. Marken Keats-Sh J 18:117-20 '69.

GOLDING, ARTHUR, 1536?–1605?

3463d **Wallace, Malcolm William,** ed. [Checklist of Golding's works] in A tragedy of Abrahams's sacrifice . . . translated by Arthur Golding. . . . [Toronto] 1906. p.xxxii–xxxvii.

3463e **Golding, Louis Thorn.** 'His published works' in An Elizabethan puritan; Arthur Golding, the translator of Ovid's Metamorphoses and also of John Calvin's Sermons. New York, 1937. p.149–63.
Chronol. checklist, 1562–1608.

GOLDING, WILLIAM GERALD, 1911–

3463k **Hodson, Leighton.** 'Bibliography' in William Golding. Edinburgh, 1969. p.[110]–16.
Checklist of poems; novels; drama; miscellaneous; essays and articles; and criticism.

GORDON, THOMAS, 1692?–1750

3477a **Séguin, J. A. R.** A bibliography of Thomas Gordon, ca.1692–1750. . . . Jersey City, R. Paxton, 1965. 71p. 25cm. (Not seen)

GOSSE, SIR EDMUND WILLIAM, 1849–1928

3477g **Woolf, James D.** Sir Edmund Gosse, an annotated bibliography of writings about him. Eng Lit Transit 11no3:126–72 '68.

GRAVES, ROBERT RANKE, 1895–

3500 **Kirkham, Michael.** 'Bibliography of Robert Graves, 1916–1968' in The poetry of Robert Graves. [London] 1969. p.275–8.

GRAY, THOMAS, 1716–1771

3501a **Starr, Herbert Wilmarth.** Spanish translations of Gray's Elegy written in a country churchyard. N&Q 196:206–9 My '51.

3503 **Basden, E. B.** Thomas Gray in Buckinghamshire, a supplementary bibliography. N&Q 207:249–61,283–96,336–49 Jl–S '62.
Author checklist of 154 items, with some bibliogr. notes, supplementing Northup, and Starr.

GREENAWAY, CATHERINE ('KATE'), 1846–1901

3510a **[Hutchison, B.]** Kate Greenaway; prices at Sotheby's sale of 24 February, 1969. Bk Coll & Lib Mthly 13:17–18 My '69.

GREENE, ROBERT, 1560?–1592

3521a **Johnson, Robert Carl.** Robert Greene, 1945–1965; Thomas Lodge, 1939–1965; John Lyly, 1935–1965; Thomas Nashe, 1941–1965; George Peele, 1939–1965. London, Nether pr., 1968. 69p. 22cm. (Elizabethan bibliographies, V)
Chronol. checklists supplementing S. A. Tannenbaum's Elizabethan bibliographies.

GREG, SIR WALTER WILSON, 1875–1959

3527g **Francis, sir Frank Chalton,** 1945: no.60.

3527h **McKenzie, Donald Francis,** 1960: no.245a.

GRIERSON, SIR HERBERT JOHN CLIFFORD, 1866–1960

3531g **A list** of sir Herbert Grierson's publications, 1906–1937' *in* Seventeenth century studies presented to sir Herbert Grierson. Oxford, 1938. (Repr. New York, Octagon books, 1967) p.[395]–403.

HALLEY, EDMOND, 1656–1742

3552h **Lang, W. J.** Edmond Halley. N&Q 166:340 My '34.

HARDY, THOMAS, 1840–1928

3603 **Carter, Kenneth.** Thomas Hardy catalogue; a list of the books by and about Thomas Hardy, O.M., 1840–1928, in Dorset county library. [Dorchester, Dorset] Dorset county council, 1968. 37p. illus., port. 25cm. (Duplicated typescript)

HART, JOHN, d.1574

3613h **Danielsson, Bror,** *ed.* 'Bibliographical introduction' *in* John Hart's works on English orthography and pronounciation. Stockholm, 1955. p.87–106.
Quasifacsim. TP transcrs., collations, bibliogr. notes and locations of copies.

HAWKESWORTH, JOHN, 1715 ?–1773

3621d **Eddy, Donald D.** John Hawkesworth, book reviewer in the Gentleman's magazine. Philol Q 43:223–8 Ap '64
'Books reviewed by John Hawkesworth in the Monthly review and by X in the Gentleman's magazine' (p.236–8)

HAWKINS, SIR JOHN, 1719–1789

3621k **Scholes, Percy Alfred.** 'Books and articles by Hawkins and his family' *in* The life and activities of sir John Hawkins, musician, magistrate and friend of Johnson. London, 1953. p.[231]–7.
Classified checklist of books, pamphlets and other writings, with some bibliogr. notes.

HAWORTH, ADRIAN HARDY, 1768–1833

3621p **Stearn, William Thomas,** *ed.* 'List of Haworth's publications' *in* Haworth, Adrian H. Complete works on succulent plants. [London] Gregg pr., 1965. V.I, p.27–39.
Chronol. checklist of 60 items, 1794–1834, with some bibliogr. notes.

HERRICK, ROBERT, 1591–1674

3650a **Guffey, George Robert.** Robert Herrick, 1949–1965; Ben Jonson, 1947–1965; Thomas Randolph, 1949–1965. London, Nether pr., 1968. 53p. 23cm. (Elizabethan bibliographies supplements, III)
Chronol. checklists supplementing S. A. Tannenbaum's Elizabethan bibliographies.

HESELTINE, PHILIP ARNOLD, 1894–1930
See Warlock, Peter, pseud.

HEYWOOD, JOHN, 1497?–1580?

3657a **Johnson, Robert Carl.** Minor Elizabethans . . . John Heywood. . . . London, Nether pr., 1968. *See* no.2351a.

HEYWOOD, THOMAS, 1514?–1641

3659a **Donovan, Dennis G.** . . . Thomas Heywood. . . . London, Nether pr., [1967] *See* no.2996a.

HILL, THOMAS, fl.1590

3664d **Johnson, Francis Rarick.** Thomas Hill, an Elizabethan Huxley. Huntington Lib Q 7:329–51 Ag '44.
'A bibliographical list of Thomas Hill's works' (p.341–7): checklist of 15 works, 1556–99, with later ed.; some bibliogr. notes and refs. 'Hill's list of his own writings, 1571' (p.347–51)

HOGARTH, WILLIAM, 1697–1764

3675a **Read, Stanley E.** Bibliography of Hogarth books and studies, 1900–1940. . . . Chicago, DePaul university, 1941. iii,32p. 28cm. (DePaul university, Chicago. Graduate school. Publications) (Duplicated typescript) (Not seen)

3675b —— Some observations on William Hogarth's Analysis of beauty: a bibliographical study. Huntington Lib Q 5:360–73 Ap '42.
'Separate English editions' (p.363–8): quasifacsim. TP transcrs., collations, and bibliogr. notes on 6 items, 1753–1909, with notes on foreign ed., and ed. in Hogarth's collected works.

HOGG, JAMES, 1770–1835

3682a **Strout, Alan Lang.** James Hogg's The spy, 1810–1811. N&Q 180:272–6 Ap '41.
Checklist of contribs. to.

HOPKINS, GERARD MANLEY, 1844–1889

3704 **Cohen, Edward H.** A comprehensive Hopkins bibliography, 1863–1918. Bull Bib 25:79–81 S/D '67.
Chronol. checklist of works and ana.

HOUSMAN, LAURENCE, 1865–1959

3733 **Kemp, Ivor.** Laurence Housman, 1865–1959: a brief catalogue of the collection of books, manuscripts and drawings presented to the Street library. . . . Street, Somerset county library, Street branch, 1967. 17p. facsims.(part col.), port. 22cm. Covertitle.

HUISH, ROBERT, 1777–1850

3755d **Summers, Alphonse Montague Joseph-Mary Augustus.** Robert Huish. N&Q 176:102–3 F '39.
Chronol. checklist of 36 items, 1795–1850.

HULME, THOMAS ERNEST, 1883–1917

3755h **Hynes, Sam.** 'Appendix C: a bibliography of Hulme's writings' *in* Further speculations, by T. E. Hulme. Minneapolis [1955] p.221–4.
Chronol. checklist, 1908–38, with criticism.

3755i **Jones, Alun Richard.** 'A bibliography of T. E. Hulme's published writings' *in* The life and opinions of Thomas Ernest Hulme. London, 1960. p.221–4.

3755j **Martin, W.** T. E. Hulme, a bibliographical note. N&Q 207:307 Ag '62.

HUTTON, RICHARD HOLT, 1826–1897

3773d **LeRoy, Gaylord C.** Richard Holt Hutton. Pub Mod Lang Assn 56:809–40 Je '41.
'Bibliographical note' (p.838–40): discursive checklist.

HUXLEY, THOMAS HENRY, 1825–1895

3779 **Huxley, Leonard.** 'Appendix III: list of essays, books, and scientific memoirs, by T. H. Huxley' *in* Life and letters of Thomas Henry Huxley. [2d ed.] London, 1903. (First pub. 1900) V.3, p.436–61.

3779a **Davis, James Richard Ainsworth.** 'B. List of published works' *in* Thomas H. Huxley. London; New York, 1907. p.256–76.

3779b **Bibby, Harold Cyril.** 'Select list of Huxley's publications' *in* T. H. Huxley, scientist, humanist and educator. London; New York [1959] p.260–6.
Chronol. checklist, 1845–1935.

INNES, COSMO, 1798–1874

3783d **Weir, J. L.** Cosmo Innes, a bibliography. N&Q 178:128–31,206–7 F,Mr '40.
Classified checklist of separate works, works ed. for Bannatyne, Maitland, and Spaulding clubs, and miscellanea.

IRELAND, WILLIAM HENRY, 1777–1835

3783h **Libbis, G. Hilder.** William Henry Ireland . . . catalogue of works. N&Q
162:347–50 My '32.
Chronol. checklist, 1795–1826.

JACKSON, HOLBROOK, 1874–1948

3785d **Parry, V. T. H.,** 1953: no.178a.

JAMES, HENRY, 1843–1916

3801a **Beebe, Maurice** and **W. T. Stafford.** Criticism of Henry James, a selected
checklist with an index to studies of separate works. Mod Fict Stud
3no1:73–96 '57.

3801b —— [**Same**]: *ib.* 12no1:117–77 '66.
Rev. and enlarged.

3804a **Reid, Forrest.** A chronological list of the novels and stories of Henry
James. TLS 12 Ag '20:520; A. Wade *ib.* 19 Ag '20:537; F. Reid 2 S '20:569.

3810 **Hagemann, E. R.** Life buffets (and comforts) Henry James, 1883–1916: an
introduction and an annotated checklist. Pa Bib Soc Am 62:207–25 '68.
'Annotated check list of Jamesiana in Life, 1883–1916' (p.211–25)

JAMES, MONTAGUE RHODES, 1862–1936

3816a **Cox, J. Randolph.** Montague Rhodes James, an annotated bibliography
of writings about him. Eng Lit Transit 12no4:203–10 '69.

JAMES, THOMAS, 1573?–1629

3816m **Wheeler, George William.** List of the works of Thomas James, S.T.P.
Bod Q Rec 4no42:138–41 Jl '24.
Chronol. checklist, 1598–1627.

JEFFERIES, JOHN RICHARD, 1848–1887

3820a **Looker, Samuel Joseph,** *comp.* 'Bibliographical check-list' *in* Looker,
Samuel J. and C. Porteous. Richard Jefferies, man of the fields; a biography and letters. London [1965] p.244–58.

JOHANNES PECHAM, fl.1279–1292
See Pecham, John.

JOHNSON, SAMUEL, 1709–1784

3841a **McKinlay, Robert.** Some notes on dr. Johnson's Journey to the western
islands. Glasgow Bib Soc Rec 8:144–50 '30.
'Unauthorized editions of dr. Johnson's Journey to the western islands of Scotland,
1775–1800'; 'Scottish editions of the Journey' (p.149–50): checklists, with some bibliogr.
notes.

3841b **Philadelphia. Free library.** An exhibition of original manuscripts, autograph letters and books of and relating to dr. Samuel Johnson, 1709–1784 ... from the collection of dr. A. S. W. Rosenbach. [Philadelphia] 1934. [6]p. 17cm. Covertitle.

3845b **Bloom, Edward Alan.** 'The journalistic canon' *in* Samuel Johnson in Grub street. Princeton, R.I., 1957. p.[263]–70.
Alphabetical checklist by title of journal contrib. to.

3851 **Harvard university. Library. Houghton library.** An exhibit of books and manuscripts from the Johnsonian collection formed by mr. and mrs. Donald F. Hyde at Four Oaks farm. Cambridge [Mass.] 1966. vi,39p. port., facsims. 23cm.
Comp. by Sidney Ives.

JONSON, BENJAMIN, 1573?–1637

3867 **Guffey, George Robert.** . . . Jonson. . . . London, Nether pr., 1968. *See* no.3650a.

JOYCE, JAMES AUGUSTINE, 1882–1941

3879a **Beebe, Maurice, P. F. Herring** and **W. Litz.** Criticism of James Joyce, a selected checklist. Mod Fict Stud 15no1:105–82 '69.

JUNIUS, *pseud.*

3900a **Cordasco, Francesco G. M.** Additions to the Junius bibliography. Bull Bib 26no2:41 Ap/Je '69.

KAVANAGH, PATRICK JOSEPH GREGORY, 1931–

3900d **Sealy, Douglas.** The writings of Patrick Kavanagh. Dublin Mag 4no3/4: 5–23 '65.
'The works of Patrick Kavanagh, a check list' (p.22–3)

KEATS, JOHN, 1795–1821

3904 **Forman, Harry Buxton,** *ed.* 'List of principal works consulted' *in* The complete works of John Keats. Glasgow, 1900. V.1, p.[xvii]-xxii.

3905 **English association,** 1912: no.650.

3905a **Marsh, George L.** and **N. I. White.** Keats and the periodicals of his time. Mod Philol 32:37–53 Ag '34.
Annotated checklist, 1816–21, of notices of Keats's works.

3906 **[Forman, Maurice Buxton]** *comp.* 'List of principal works concerning Keats' *in* Forman, Harry B., *ed.* The poetical works and other writings of John Keats. Rev. with add. by Maurice Buxton Forman. Hampstead ed. New York, 1938. V.1, p.xcix–cxxviii.

3906a **Farrand, Nancy,** 1939: no.119a.

3907 **MacGillivray, James Robertson.** Keats, a bibliography and reference guide, with an essay on Keats' reputation. [Toronto] University of Toronto pr., 1949. lxxxii,210p. 24cm.

Classified list of books; collected ed.; periodical contribs.; and ana.

Rev: N&Q 195:395 '50; G. L. Marsh Mod Philol 48:134–6 '50; C. D. Thorpe Philol Q 29:122 '50; G. H. Ford Mod Lang Q 13:310–11 '50; Dalhousie R 29:464–5 '50; TLS 24 F '50:120; F. Page R Eng Stud new ser 2:404 '51.

3907a **Raysor, Thomas Middleton,** *ed.*, 1956: no.2015.

KENYON, SIR FREDERICK GEORGE, 1863–1952

3923d **Lea, J.,** 1954: no.155a.

KER, WILLIAM PATON, 1855–1923

3923h **Pafford, John Henry P.** W. P. Ker, 1855–1923, a bibliography. London, University of London pr., 1950. 72p. ports., facsim. 23cm.

Chronol. checklist of works and ana.

Rev: TLS 9 F '51:92; H. W. Husbands Mod Lang R 46:298–9 '51.

KINGSTON, WILLIAM HENRY GILES, 1814–1880

3933 **[Hutchison, B.]** W. H. G. Kingston, 1814–1880. Bk Coll & Lib Mthly 3:18–23 Jl '68.

Title checklist.

KINSELLA, THOMAS, fl.1954

3933d **Freyer, Michael G.** The books of Thomas Kinsella, a checklist compiled from his Dolmen press bibliography. Dublin Mag 5no2:79–81 '66.

Chronol. checklist of 13 items, 1952–66.

KIPLING, RUDYARD, 1865–1936

3952a **Something** of Rudyard Kipling and his works, with an index to the volumes published by Macmillan & co. ltd. [Edinburgh, Ptd. by R. & R. Clark, n.d., 1938?] 63p. port. 18cm. Covertitle.

Index, p.[27]–63.

3961 **Rao, Kanatur Bhaskara.** 'Published works by Kipling written in India, 1882–1889' *in* Rudyard Kipling's India. Norman, Oklahoma, 1967. p.166–7.

3962 **Young, William Arthur** and **J. H. McGivering.** 'Bibliography' *in* Kipling dictionary. Rev. ed. London; New York, 1967. (First ed. 1911) p.213–30. (Not seen)

KIRBY, ELIZABETH, 1823–1873

3964 **E., L. E.** Mary and Elizabeth Kirby. N&Q 150:371 My '26; A. S. Lewis; A. Sparke *ib.* 150:430 Je '26.

Chronol. checklist of joint and separate pubs. (p.430)

KIRBY, MARY (MRS. H. GREGG), 1817–1893

3964d **E., L. E.**, 1926: no.3964a.

KNIGHT, GEORGE WILSON, 1897–

3966d **Van Domelen, John E.** 'A select list of the published writings of George Wilson Knight' *in* Jefferson, D. W., *ed.* The morality of art; essays presented to G. Wilson Knight. . . . London [1969] p.222–31.
Chronol. checklist of 109 items, 1926–68.

KNOX, RONALD ARBUTHNOTT, 1888–1957

3968a **Cowan Patricia M.**, 1964: no.102a.

3968b **Matzek, Richard.** Ronald Arbuthnott Knox, 1888–1957, a bibliography. Cath Lib World 38:305–7,437–8 Mr '67.
Checklist of Knox collection at Sacred heart university, Bridgeport, Connecticut.

KORZENIOWSKI, TEODOR JÓZEF KONRAD, 1857–1924
See Conrad, Joseph, pseud.

KOTELIANSKY, SAMUEL SOLOMONOVICH, 1882–1955

3968m **Zytaruk, George J.** S. S. Koteliansky's translations of Russian works into English. Bull Bib 25:65–6 My/Ag '67.

KYD, THOMAS, 1557?–1595?

3968z **Fernie, G. E.**, 1939: no.121a.

3969a **Johnson, Robert Carl.** Minor Elizabethans . . . Thomas Kyd. . . . London, Nether pr., 1968. *See* no.2351a.

LANDOR, WALTER SAVAGE, 1775–1864

3993a **Wheeler, Stephen.** Bibliography of Walter Savage Landor. Athenæum 3898:64 Jl '02.
Additional items 20–44 to his no.3993.

3993b —— Bibliography of Walter Savage Landor. Athenæum 3892:692–3 My '02.
Checklist of 19 items pub. in the Athenæum, 1834–62

3993c —— Landor bibliography: poems in The examiner. N&Q ser11 3:364–5 My '11.

LASSELS, RICHARD, 1603?–1668

4006g **De Beer, Esmond S.** Richard Lassel's Voyage of Italy. N&Q 160:292–3 Ap '31.
Checklist of 5 ed., 1670–1705, with bibliogr. notes.

LAVIN, MARY (MRS. WILLIAM WALSH), 1912–

4008q **Doyle, Paul A.** Mary Lavin, a checklist. Pa Bib Soc Am 63:317–21 '69.

Checklist of books; poems; short stories pub. separately; novel serialized; essay; book review; and principal critical and general material about.

LAWRENCE, DAVID HERBERT, 1885–1930

4023 **Edwards, Lucy I.** D. H. Lawrence, a finding list and holdings in the city, county and university libraries of Nottingham. Nottingham [Nottingham county library] 1969. 125p. illus., facsims. 23cm.

Rev: TLS 22 My '69:566.

LEDELH, JACOBUS, fl.1481–1495

4030d **Beattie, William.** Two notes on fifteenth century printing. I. Jacobus Ledelh. Edinburgh Bib Soc Trans 3ptl:75–7 '52.

Descrs. of 3 items, with locations of copies and bibliogr. refs.

LEFANU, JOSEPH SHERIDAN, 1814–1873

4040a **[Hutchison, B.]** Joseph Sheridan LeFanu, 1814–73. Bk Coll & Lib Mthly 9:276–8 Ja '69.

itle checklist.

LE GALLIENNE, RICHARD, 1866–1947

4042 **Lingel, Robert J.** A bibliographical checklist of the writings of Richard Le Gallienne. Metuchen, N.J., 1926. 95p. port. 25cm.

Chronol. checklist of 91 first ed., 1887–1925, with quasifacsim. TP transcrs. and some bibliogr. notes.

LENTON, FRANCIS, fl.1630–1640

4045d **Willis, Leota Snider.** 'Bibliography' *in* Francis Lenton, queen's poet. Philadelphia, 1931. p.94–8.

Checklist of ms. and ptd. works, and ana.

LEWIS, CECIL DAY-, 1904–

4048d **Taylor, Geoffrey Handley-** and **T. d'Arch Smith.** Cecil Day-Lewis, the poet laureate; a bibliography. Chicago, St. James pr., 1968. xii,42p. illus., ports.(1 col.), facsim. 24cm.

Checklist of books and pamphlets; contribs. to books; and detective stories under the pseud. of Nicholas Blake, with some bibliogr. notes.

Rev: TLS 9 Ja '69:44; A. Rota Bk Coll 18:542,545–6 '69.

LOCKE, JOHN, 1632–1704

4069a **Kelly, Patrick.** A note on Locke's pamphlets on money. Cambridge Bib Soc Trans 5ptl:61–73 '69.

'The list of pamphlet editions and variants' (p.70–2): quasifacsim. TP transcrs., collations and some bibliogr. notes.

LODGE, THOMAS, 1558?–1625

4074a **Johnson, Robert Carl.** . . . Thomas Lodge. . . . London, Nether pr., 1968.
See no.3521a.

LOWRY, CLARENCE MALCOLM, 1909–1957

4077d **Woolmer, J. Howard, ltd.,** NEW YORK. 'Catalogue' *in* A Malcolm Lowry
catalogue, with essays by Perle Epstein and Richard Hauer Costa. New
York, 1968. p.45–65.

LYLY, JOHN, 1554?–1606

4082a **Johnson, Robert Carl.** . . . John Lyly. . . . London, Nether pr., 1968. *See*
no.3521a.

MACDIARMID, HUGH, *pseud. of* CHRISTOPHER MURRAY GRIEVE, 1892–

4092a **Glen, Duncan.** 'Hugh MacDiarmid . . . a chronological bibliography' *in*
Hugh MacDiarmid and the Scottish renaissance. Edinburgh [1964]
p.[245]–62.

Classified checklist of books; poems and very small ed.; translations; selections; books
ed.; periodicals ed.; contribs. to books; introductions; anthologies with contribs.;
uncollected prose contribs. to periodicals.

MACDONALD, GEORGE, 1824–1905

4094a **[Hutchison, B.]** George MacDonald, 1824–1905. Bk Coll & Lib Mthly
12:364–9 Ap '69.

Classified checklist based on BM catalogue.

MACHEN, ARTHUR LLEWELYN JONES, 1863–1947

4096x **Sweetser, Wesley D.** Arthur Machen, a bibliography of writings about
him. Eng Lit Transit 11no1:1–33 '68.

4098a **[Hutchison, B.]** The British first editions of Arthur Machen, 1863–1947.
Bk Coll & Lib Mthly 2:18 Je '68.

MACKENZIE, HENRY, 1745–1831

4101d **Thompson, Harold William.** 'Appendix I. Mackenzie's principal works
and the chief biographical accounts' *in* A Scottish man of feeling, some
account of Henry Mackenzie, esq., of Edinburgh. . . . London, 1931.
p.[417]–23.

MCKERROW, RONALD BRUNLEES, 1872–1940

4101m **Francis, sir Frank Chalton,** 1940/1: no.58.

MADAN, JUDITH (COWPER), 1702-1781

4109d **Madan, Falconer.** 'A bibliography of poems and other pieces by Judith Madan' *in* The Madan family and Maddens of Ireland and England, a historical account. Oxford, 1933. p.[264]-72.

Chronol. checklist of 45 items, 1717-81, with some bibliogr. notes.

MADAN, MARTIN, 1725-1790

4109f **Madan, Falconer.** 'A bibliography of the printed pieces written by the rev. Martin Madan' *in* The Madan family and Maddens of Ireland and England, a historical account. Oxford, 1933. p.[273]-302.

Chronol. checklist, 1758-89, with some bibliogr. notes.

MANDEVILLE, SIR JOHN, fl.1350.

4116a **Cordier, Jean.** Jean de Mandeville. Leide, E. J. Brill, 1891. 38p. 25cm.

Classified chronol. checklist of English and foreign ed., with some bibliogr. notes. Repr. from T'oung-Pao, v.3.

4116b **Letts, Malcolm Henry Ikin.** 'Bibliography II: printed editions, mainly before 1600' *in* Sir John Mandeville, the man and his book. London, 1949. p.177-81.

4116c **Bennett, Josephine Waters.** 'Appendix II. The editions' *in* The rediscovery of sir John Mandeville. New York, 1954. p.335-85.

'English editions' (p.[346]-59): chronol. checklist of 59 items, 1496-1953, with short collations, locations of copies, and bibliogr. notes and refs.

MARLOWE, CHRISTOPHER, 1564-1593

4124a **Johnson, Robert Carl.** Christopher Marlowe, 1946-1965. London, Nether pr., 1967. 45p. 22cm. (Elizabethan bibliographies supplements, VI)

Classified checklist supplementing S. A. Tannenbaum's Elizabethan bibliographies.

4124m **Ingram, John Henry.** 'The bibliography of Christopher Marlowe' *in* Christopher Marlowe and his associates. London, 1904. p.280-98.

MARVELL, ANDREW, 1621-1678

4147a **Donovan, Dennis G.** Andrew Marvell, 1927-1967. London, Nether pr., 1969. 50p. 23cm. (Elizabethan bibliographies supplements, XII)

Chronol. checklist supplementing Legouis, no.4146.

MASSINGER, PHILIP, 1583-1640

4169a **Bennett, A. L.** The early editions of Philip Massinger's plays. Pa Lang Lit 1no2:177-81 '65.

Checklist of 14 items, with some bibliogr. notes and locations of copies.

4169b **Pennel, Charles A.** and **W. P. Williams.** Francis Beaumont—John Fletcher—Philip Massinger. . . . London, Nether pr., 1968. *See* no.2413a.

MATHIAS, THOMAS JAMES, 1754?-1835

4170d **Brack, O. M.** Thomas James Mathias' The pursuits of literature. Pa Bib
Soc Am 62:123–7 '68.
'Short-title list of editions' (p.124–7)

MAUGHAM, WILLIAM SOMERSET, 1874–1965

4179 **Henry, William H.** A French bibliography of W. Somerset Maugham.
Charlottesville, Va., University of Virginia Bibliographical society, 1967.
(Not seen)

MAY, EDWARD, fl.1633

4183 **Hudson, Hoyt H.** Edward May's borrowings from Timothe Kendall and
others. Huntington Lib Bull 11:23–58 Ap '37.
'Tabulation [one hundred and sixty-five of May's two hundred and one poems and . . .
the location of the sources whence he drew them]' (p.51–8)

MIDDLETON, THOMAS, 1570?-1627

4216a **Donovan, Dennis G.** Thomas Middleton, 1939–1965; John Webster,
1940–1965. London, Nether pr., 1967. 61p. 22cm. (Elizabethan bibliographies supplements, I)
Chronol. checklists supplementing S. A. Tannenbaum's Elizabethan bibliographies.

MILLER, THOMAS, 1807-1874

4217d **Gainsborough. Public library.** Thomas Miller, a list of his works and books
about him, in the local collection. Comp. and introduced by J. S. English.
Gainsborough, 1966. iii,4p. 26cm. Covertitle. (Local history handbook,
no.1) (Duplicated typescript)
Title checklist of 49 items.

MILNE, ALAN ALEXANDER, 1882-1956

4217m **[Hutchison, B.]** Christopher Robin, Pooh and Piglet; prices at Sotheby's
sale of 24 February, 1969. Bk Coll & Lib Mthly 13:20–1 My '69.

MILTON, JOHN, 1608-1674

4218a **Stratman, Carl Joseph.** Milton's Samson agonistes: a checklist of criticism. Restor & 18th Cent Theat Res 4:2–10 N '65.

4218b **Low, Anthony.** Addenda to a checklist of criticism of Samson agonistes.
Restor & 18th Cent Theat Res 7:53–4 My '68.

4219a **Hanford, James Holly** and **C. W. Crupi.** Milton. New York, Appleton-
Century-Crofts [1966] viii,63p. 24cm. (Goldentree bibliographies)

4247 **Riffe, Nancy Lee.** Milton's minor poetry in British periodicals before 1740.
N&Q 210:453–4 D '65.

4248 **Williams college,** WILLIAMSTOWN, MASS. **Chapin library.** John Milton
through three centuries. 1967. (Not seen)

4249 **Parker, William Riley.** 'Appendix 1. Milton's publications, 1628–1700, in the order of their appearance, and with the number of surviving copies located in public, institutional, or private libraries' *in* Milton, a biography. Oxford, 1968. p.[1205]-8.

'Appendix 2. Surviving copies of seventeenth-century editions of Milton located in public or institutional libraries' (p.[1209]–13)

4249a **Indiana. University. Lilly library.** An exhibit of seventeenth-century editions of writings by John Milton. Bloomington, Ind., 1969. [24]p. port. 28cm.

4249b **Huckabay, Calvin.** John Milton, an annotated bibliography, 1929–1968. Pittsburgh, Duquesne U.P., 1970. (Not seen)

Rev. ed. of no.4244.

MINTO, WILLIAM, 1845–1893

4250b **Macdonald, Kenneth I.** William Minto, 1845–1893: a checklist. Biblioth 5n05:152–64 '64.

Classified checklist of articles in periodicals and corporate works; separately pub. works; works ed. by; and letters.

MINTON, FRANCIS JOHN, 1917–1957

4250d **Graham, Rigby.** John Minton as a book illustrator. Priv Lib ser2 1n01:7–36 '68.

'Summary of illustrated books' (p.36): chronol. checklist, 1947–64.

MOORE, DUGALD, 1805–1841

4263d **Sinclair, William.** Bibliography of Dugald Moore, poet and bookseller, 1805–1841. Glasgow Bib Soc Rec 3pt2:109–14 '15.

'Bibliography' (p.113–14): TP transcrs., short collations, and some bibliogr. notes on 6 items, 1829–39.

MOORE, EDWARD, 1712–1757

4263m **Caskey, John Homer.** 'Bibliography' *in* The life and works of Edward Moore. New Haven; London, 1927. p.[168]–89.

Classified checklist of works; translations, adaptations and imitations; songs; collections; mss.; and ana.

MORE, HANNAH, 1745–1833

4274d **Weiss, Harry Bischoff.** Hannah More's Cheap repository tracts in America. New York, New York public library, 1946. 21p. 26cm.

Repr. from N.Y. Pub Lib Bull 50:539–49 Jl '46; 50:634–41 Ag '46.

'A preliminary check-list of Cheap repository tracts published in America, 1797–1826' (p.14–21)

MORE HENRY, 1614–1687

4275a **Guffey, George Robert,** 1969: no.49769.

MORRIS, WILLIAM, 1834–1896

4302a **Fenn, Louie M.** A William Morris bibliography. J South-West Essex Tech Coll 2no4:276–7 D '48.

MUIR, EDWIN, 1887–1959

4314 **Mellown, Elgin W.** A checklist of critical writings about Edwin Muir. Bull Bib 25:157–60 My/Ag '68; 25:173–5 S/D '68.

4314b **Hoy, Peter.** Edwin Muir, a preliminary checklist of addenda to Mellown's bibliography. Serif 6:27–32 Je '69.

4314m **Duval, K. D., bksllr.** [1961]: no.726.

MUNDAY, ANTHONY, 1553–1633

4317 **Turner, Julia Celeste.** 'A list of the works of Anthony Mundy' *in* Anthony Mundy, an Elizabethan man of letters. Berkeley, Calif., 1928. p.[201]–15.
Chronol. checklist, 1577–1633, with some locations of copies.

4317a **Tannenbaum, Samuel Aaron.** Anthony Mundy, including the play of Sir Thomas Moore, a concise bibliography. New York, 1942. viii,36p. 23cm. (Elizabethan bibliographies, no.27)
Classified checklist of works and ana; 394 items; 'Sir Thomas Moore' (p.[23]–30)

4317b **Johnson, Robert Carl.** Minor Elizabethans . . . Anthony Munday. . . . London, Nether pr., 1968. *See* no.2351a.

MURDOCH, JEAN IRIS (MRS. J. O. BAYLEY), 1919–

4317m **Widmann, R. L.** An Iris Murdoch checklist. Critique 10no1:17–29 '67. (Not seen)

MURRAY, GEORGE GILBERT AIMÉ, 1866–1957

4319a **Patry, Madeleine,** 1950: no.179c.

NASHE, THOMAS, 1567–1601

4325a **Johnson, Robert Carl.** . . . Thomas Nashe. . . . London, Nether pr., 1968. *See* no.3521a.

NEWMAN, CARD. JOHN HENRY, 1801–1890

4334a **Läpple, Alfred,** *comp.* 'Chronologie der Schriften Newmans' *in* Fries, Heinrich and W. Becker, *ed.* Newman-Studien. Nürnberg, 1948–57. V.1 (1948), p.287–94.

4334b —— [Same]: [Supplement] by Norbert Schiffers and W. Becker. V.2 (1954), p.325.

4334c —— [Same]: [Supplement] by Werner Becker and G. Biemer. V.3 (1957), p.286–92.

NEWTON, SIR ISAAC, 1642–1727

4339a **Babson institute**, BABSON PARK, MASS. **Library.** A supplement to the catalogue of the Grace K. Babson collection . . . by Henry P. Macomber. [Babson Park, Mass.] 1955. viii,91p. 26cm.

NORRIS, JOHN 1657–1711

4352h **Guffey, George Robert,** 1969: no.4976g.

NORTH, CHRISTOPHER, *pseud. of* JOHN WILSON, 1785–1854

4353a **Strout, Alan Lang.** The Recreations of Christopher North, 1842. N&Q 182:314–15 Je '42; 183:69–71 Ag '42.

Checklist of items in Recreations corresponding to compositions in Blackwood's magazine.

4353b **Wadimar,** *pseud.* Wilson's Penny plain, two pence coloured. N&Q 189:50–2 Ag '45.

Index to illus., from ms. by Charles D. Williams.

O'CONNOR, FRANK, *pseud. of* MICHAEL O'DONOVAN, 1903–1966

4356d **Sheehy, Maurice,** *ed.* 'Towards a bibliography of Frank O'Connor's writing' *in* Michael/Frank; studies on Frank O'Connor. . . . London [1969] p.[168]–99.

Classified checklist of books; translations; articles; short stories; and ana, etc.

O'DONOVAN, MICHAEL, 1903–1966

See O'Connor, Frank, pseud.

O'FLAHERTY, LIAM, 1897–

4359a **Doyle, Paul A.** A Liam O'Flaherty checklist. Twent Cent Lit 13:49–51 Ap '67.

Classified checklist of books and booklets; essays; short stories in periodicals; and ana.

OLDMIXON, JOHN, 1673–1742

4366d **Rogers, Pat.** The printing of Oldmixon's histories. Library ser5 24:150–4 Je '69.

Quasifacsim. TP transcrs., collations and bibliogr. notes on 2v. History, 1729.

OLIPHANT, MARGARET OLIPHANT (WILSON), 1828–1897

4366h **Colby, Vineta** and **R. A. Colby.** 'Chronology of mrs. Oliphant's principal works' *in* The equivocal virtue; mrs. Oliphant and the Victorian literary market place [Hamden, Conn.] 1966. p.245–9.

Chronol. checklist, 1849–56.

OMAN, SIR CHARLES WILLIAM CHADWICK, 1860–1946

4366m **Fowler, J. E. H.,** 1954: no.123b.

OPPENHEIM, EDWARD PHILLIPS, 1866–1946

4369d **Brown, Wray D.** Bibliography of E. Phillips Oppenheim. Bk Coll & Lib Mthly 11:324–30 Mr '69.
Title checklist with some bibliogr. notes.

OSBORNE, JOHN JAMES, 1929–

4376a **Carter, Alan.** 'Bibliography' *in* John Osborn. Edinburgh, 1969. p.187–91.
Classified checklist of works and ana.

O'SULLIVAN, SEUMAS, *pseud. of* JAMES SULLIVAN STARKEY, 1879–1958

4377a **Denson, Alan.** Seumas O'Sullivan (James Sullivan Starkey), 1879–1958, a check-list of his publications. Kendal, 1969. 27p. 22cm.
Rev. from Dublin Mag 7no2/4 '68. Checklist of books and pamphlets written by and contrib. to; some periodicals to which he contributed; musical settings of some of his poems; and ana.

OWEN, WILFRED, 1893–1918

4390 **White, William.** Wilfred Owen, 1893–1918: a bibliography. [Kent, Ohio] Kent state U.P. [1967] 41p. 19cm. (Serif series in bibliography, no.1)
Rev. from Serif 2no4:5–16 '65. Classified checklist of works and ana.

PAXTON, SIR JOSEPH, 1801–1865

4401d **Stevenson, C. L.,** 1961: no.210a.

PEACOCK, THOMAS LOVE, 1785–1866

4402d **Roper, I. A.,** 1956: no.192a.

4402g **Young, Arthur Button.** Thomas Love Peacock: contributions to periodicals. N&Q ser10 8:2–3 Jl '07; W. E. A. Axon *ib.* 8:157 Ag '07.

4402h **Read, Bill.** Thomas Love Peacock, an enumerative bibliography. Bull Bib 24:32–4 S/D '63; 24:70–2 Ja/Ap '64; 24:88–91 My/Ag '64.
Checklist of works and ana.

4402i **Dawson, Carl.** 'Bibliography' *in* Thomas Love Peacock. London; New York, 1968. p.111–16.

PECHAM, JOHN, fl.1279–1292

4402p **Kingsford, Charles Lethbridge** and **A. G. Little,** *comp.* 'Bibliography of John Pecham's writings' *in* Kingsford, Charles L., A. G. Little and F. Tocco, *ed.* Johannes Pecham. Tractatus tres de pauperate. Aberdeen, 1910. (Repr. London, Gregg pr., 1966) p.1–12.
Classified checklist of mss. and ptd. works.

PEELE, GEORGE, 1558?–1597?

4406a **Johnson, Robert Carl.** . . . George Peele. . . . London, Nether pr., 1968. *See* no.3521a.

4406b **Ashley, Leonard R. N.** 'Bibliography. The works by and attributed to George Peele' *in* Authorship and evidence, a study of attribution and the renaissance drama. . . . Genève, 1968. p.162–70.

PENNANT, THOMAS, 1726–1798

4408a **Rees, Eiluned** and **G. Walters.** Pennant and the pirates. Nat Lib Wales J 15no4:423–35 '68.
'Bibliographical checklist of Dublin editions of Pennant's works and the English editions on which they were based' (p.423–4)

PICKERING, WILLIAM, 1796–1854

See under Presses and Printing.

PIELOU, PIERCE LESLIE, 1870–1962

4424d **Denson, Alan.** 'Pierce Leslie Pielou, a check-list of his writings published and unpublished' *in* James H. Cousins . . . a bio-bibliographical survey. Kendal, 1967. p.261–8.
Checklist of books and pamphlets; periodical contribs.; and mss., with some bibliogr. notes.

PIOZZI, HESTER LYNCH (SALUSBURY), 1741–1821

4425a **Clifford, James Lowry.** 'Chief published works' *in* Hester Lynch Piozzi (mrs. Thrale). Oxford, 1941. (2d ed., 1952; repr. [1968]) p.[462]–3.

PLAT, SIR HUGH, 1552?–1611?

4425x **Mullett, Charles F.** 'Hugh Plat, Elizabethan virtuoso' *in* Prouty, Charles T., *ed.* Studies in honor of A. H. R. Fairchild. Columbia [Miss.] 1946. p.90–118.
'Bibliographical note; a list of Plat's published works' (p.117–18)

POLIDORI, JOHN WILLIAM, 1795–1821

4432d **Viets, Henry R.** The printings in America of Polidori's The vampyre in 1819. Pa Bib Soc Am 62:434–5 '68.
Quasifacsim. TP transcrs., collations, and bibliogr. notes and locations of copies for 5 ed. of Polidor's short story, attrib. to Byron.

4432e —— The London editions of Polidori's The vampyre. Pa Bib Soc Am 63:83–103 '69.
'Bibliography' (p.101–3): quasifacsim. TP transcrs., collations, bibliogr. notes and locations of copies for 5 ed., 1819.

POPE, ALEXANDER, 1688–1744

4442a **Beckwith, F.** Audra: les traductions françaises de Pope, 1717–1825. Mod Lang R 29:70–2 Ja '34.

4443a **Sibley, Agnes Marie.** 'American editions of An essay on man, 1747–1850' *in* Alexander Pope's prestige in America, 1725–1835. New York, 1949. p.[137]–43.

'Some American editions of Pope's other works, to 1835'; 'Pope's poetry in English poetical miscellanies known in the colonies' (p.143–7); 'The sale of Pope's works by booksellers' (p.[148]–53)

4446 **Maslen, Keith Ian Desmond.** New editions of Pope's Essay on man, 1745–48. Pa Bib Soc Am 62:177–88 '68.

'London printed editions of the Essay on man with frontispiece, 1745–48' (p.184–8): quasifacsim. TP transcrs., collations, bibliogr. notes and refs. with locations of copies.

4447 **Guerinot, J. V.** Pamphlet attacks on Alexander Pope, 1711–1744, a descriptive bibliography. [London] Methuen [1969] lxxi,36op. facsims. 22cm.

Annotated chronol. checklist with some bibliogr. notes. 'A chronological list of Popiana' (p.[lxi]–lxxi)

Rev: TLS 12 F '70:155.

POTOCKI, GEOFFREY WLADISLAS VAILE, COUNT POTOCKI DE MONTALK, 1903–

4448 'Summary bibliography of count Potocki's published works' *in* A letter from Richard Aldington and a summary bibliography. . . . Draguigan, 1961. p.[4]

4448a **Graham, Rigby.** A tentative checklist of the work of Geoffrey count Potocki. Priv Lib 8no1:23–6 '67.

Annotated checklist, 1923–66.

POTTER, HELEN BEATRIX, 1866–1943

4450a **Linder, Leslie Charles.** Beatrix Potter, 1866–1943: centenary catalogue, 1966. London, National book league, 1966. 109p. illus., facsim. 22cm. (Not seen)

POVEY, KENNETH, 1898–1965

4450m **Cook, D. F.** and **A. N. Ricketts,** 1968: no.249.

POWELL, LAWRENCE FITZROY, 1881–

4450q **Simmons, John Simon Gabriel,** *comp.* 'A list of the published writings of Lawrence Fitzroy Powell' *in* Johnson, Boswell and their circle; essays presented to Lawrence Fitzroy Powell. . . . Oxford, 1965. p.[320]–8.

Chronol. checklist of 127 items, 1908–64.

POWER, SIR D'ARCY, 1855–1941

4450t 'A short-title bibliography of the writings of sir D'Arcy Power' *in* Sir D'Arcy Power: selected writings, 1877–1930. Oxford, 1931. p.330–55.

POWYS, JOHN COWPER, 1872–1963

4453 **Anderson, Arthur J.** John Cowper Powys, a bibliography. Bull Bib 25:73–8, 94 S/D '67.
Chronol. checklist of works and ana.

PRINGLE, THOMAS, 1789–1834

4464a **[Hutchison, B.]** Books by and about Thomas Pringle. Bk Coll & Lib Mthly 8:229–30 D '68.

QUARLES, FRANCIS, 1592–1644

4478 **Horden, John.** Francis Quarles, 1592–1644, a bibliography of his works to the year 1800. Oxford, 1953. x,83p. port. 25cm. (Oxford Bib Soc Pub new ser 2)
Quasifacsim. TP transcrs., collations, bibliogr. notes and locations of copies.
Rev: TLS 22 Ja '54:64; 5 F '54:89.

QUICK, JOHN, 1636–1706

4479 **Dredge, John Ingle,** 1889–99: no.886.

RACKHAM, ARTHUR, 1867–1939

4483a **Baughman, Roland.** The centenary of Arthur Rackham's birth, September 19, 1867. An appreciation of his genius and a catalogue of his original sketches, drawings and paintings in the Berol collection. New York, Columbia university libraries, 1967. 48p. illus. (part col.) 30cm.
'Text illustrations' (p.21–38)

4483b **[Hutchison, B.]** Arthur Rackham: prices at Sotheby's on 7 October. Bk Coll & Lib Mthly 8:244–5 D '68.

RALPH, JAMES, 1705?–1762

4485d **Shipley, John B.** James Ralph's pamphlets, 1741–1744. Library ser5 19:130–46 '64.
'I. Works by Ralph, 1741–1744.—II. Works probably not by Ralph, 1741–1744.—III. Works definitely not by Ralph, 1741–1748' (p.138–45): chronol. checklists, with bibliogr. notes.

RANDOLPH, THOMAS, 1605–1635

4487a **Day, Cyrus Lawrence.** Three notes on Randolph. Mod Lang N 46:507–10 D '31.
Checklist of songs and poems supplementing Parry, no.4487, p.509–10.

4488a **Guffey, George Robert.** . . . Randolph. . . . London, Nether pr., 1968.
See no.3650a.

RAY, JOHN, 1627–1705

4491a **Barr, C. B. L.** and **Mary Pollard.** The Historia plantarum of John Ray. Cambridge Bib Soc Trans 3pt4:335–8 '62.

Addendum to Keynes.

RICARDO, DAVID, 1772–1823

4513d **Franklin, Burt** and **G. Legman.** David Ricardo and Ricardian theory, a bibliographical checklist. New York, B. Franklin, 1950. vi,88p. 23cm. (Burt Franklin bibliogr. ser., no.1)

Chronol. checklist of works, 227 items, 1809–1940, and ana.

RICHARD DE BURY (RICHARD AUNGERVILLE), 1287–1342?

4513h **Hogan, Charles Beecher.** The Bement collection of the Philobiblon. Yale Univ Lib Gaz 6:25–30 Oc '31.

Detailed descrs. of first eight ed., except for fifth and sixth not in Yale, and checklist of later ed.

4513i **Zeitgeist,** *pseud.* The first English bibliophile. Am Bk Coll 4:233–6 N '33.

'Short bibliography of Bury's Philobiblon' (p.235–6): checklist with some bibliogr. notes.

4513k **Altamura, Antonio,** *ed.* 'Stampe' *in* Philobiblon, edizione critica. Napoli, 1954. p.40–6.

4513l **Maclagan, Michael,** *ed.* 'Bibliography of printed editions and manuscripts' *in* Philobiblon. Oxford, 1960. p.xxxvii–lxxiii.

Discursive checklist.

RICKETTS, CHARLES DE SOUSY, 1866–1931

4520d **Harvard university. Library. Houghton library.** An exhibition of books designed by Charles Ricketts, from the collection of A. E. Gallatin. [Cambridge, Mass., 1946] [5]p. 24cm.

Checklist of 40 works exhibited.

ROBIN HOOD

4527a **Fawcett, J. W.** Robin Hood. N&Q 166:266 Ap '34.

4527b **Gable, J. Harris.** Bibliography of Robin Hood. [Lincoln, Neb., 1939] 163p. facsims. 22cm.

Author checklist with location of copies, and indexes.

4527c **Simeone, William E.** More Robin Hood bibliography. N&Q 196:4–5 Ja '51; P. W. F. Brown 196:86 F '31; O. F. Babler 196:130,394 Mr,S '51.

ROBINSON, HENRY CRABB, 1775–1867

4527p **Baker, John Milton.** 'Items for a bibliography of Henry Crabb Robinson' *in* Henry Crabb Robinson of Bury, Jena, The Times and Russell square. London [1937] p.[245]–8.

ROBINSON, RICHARD, fl.1576–1600

4527t **Greg, sir Walter Wilson.** Richard Robinson and the Stationers' register. Mod Lang R 50:407–13 Oc '55.

4527u ——— [Same]: *in* Collected papers, ed. by J. C. Maxwell. Oxford, 1966. p.[413]–23.
Checklist of 19 items, 1576–[1598] with some bibliogr. notes and refs., and locations of copies.

ROCHESTER, JOHN WILMOT, 2D EARL OF, 1647–1680
See Wilmot, John, 2d earl of Rochester.

ROGET, PETER MARK, 1779–1869

4530d **Emblen, D. L.** Peter Mark Roget: a centenary bibliography. Pa Bib Soc Am 62:436–47 '68.
'The published works of Peter Mark Roget' (p.438–47): chronol. checklist of 96 items, 1798–1922, with locations of copies, and some notes.

ROHMER, SAX, *pseud. of* ARTHUR SARSFIELD WADE, 1883–1959

4530g **[Hutchison, B.]** Sax Rohmer, 1883–1959. Bk Coll & Lib Mthly 14:39–41 Je '69.
Title checklist.

ROLFE, FREDERICK WILLIAM SERAFINO AUSTIN LEWIS MARY ('BARON CORVO'), 1860–1913

4533a **Woolf, Cecil, co. ltd.,** LONDON. A Corvo library comprising first editions . . . assembled by rabbi Bertram W. Korn. London [1965] 23p. 22cm.

4533b **Woolf, Cecil.**

ROSE, JOHN HOLLAND, 1855–1942

4537g **Hully, P. M.,** 1955: no.144a.

ROSS, SIR RONALD, 1857–1932

4540a **Rees, Margaret J.,** 1966: no.189d.

RUSKIN, JOHN, 1819–1900

4557 **Dearden, James S.** The production and distribution of John Ruskin's Poems, 1850. Bk Coll 17no2:151–67 '68.
'Synopsis of copies of Poems 1850' (p.166–7): checklist of 40 items, recording original and present owners, sales, and bindings.

4558 **Halladay, Jean.** Some errors in the bibliography of the library edition of John Ruskin's Works. Pa Bib Soc Am 62:127–9 '68.
Additions and corrections to Cook and Wedderburn, no.4556.

RUSSELL, BERTRAND ARTHUR WILLIAM, 3D EARL RUSSELL, 1872–
1970

4559g **Jacob, Gertrude.** Bertrand Russell, an essay towards a bibliography.
Bull Bib 13:198–9 S/D '29; 14:28–30 My/Ag '30.
Classified checklist of works and ana.

4559h **Ruja, Harry.** Bertrand Russell, 1929–1967. Bull Bib 25:182–90,192 S/D
'68; 26:29–32 Ja/Mr '69.

RUST, BP. GEORGE, d.1670

4560 **Guffey, George Robert,** 1969: no.4976g.

RYMER, JAMES MALCOLM, fl.1842–1856

4567m **[Hutchison, B.]** Varney the vampire. Bk Coll & Lib Mthly 9:266 Ja
'69; rf. A. E. R. M. Stevens ib. 10:312 F '69.
Title checklist of works sometimes attrib. to Thomas Peckett.

RYMER, THOMAS, 1641–1713

4567q **Zimansky, Curt Arno,** ed. 'The canon of Rymer's works' in The critical
works of Thomas Rymer. New Haven; London, 1956. p.277–88.
Discursive checklist.

SACHEVERELL, HENRY, 1674?–1764

4567x **Simpson, W. Sparrow.** The Sacheverell controversy. N&Q ser8 5:3–4,
44–5,102–3,181–3,364–5 Ja–Ap '93.

SASSOON, SIEGFRIED LORRAINE, 1886–1967

4582a **Farmer, David.** Addenda to Keynes's Bibliography of Siegfried Sassoon.
Pa Bib Soc Am 63:310–17 '69.

SCOGAN, JOHN, fl.1565

4587m **Farnham, William Edward.** John (Henry) Scogan. Mod Lang R 16:120–8
Ap '21.
Discursive checklist of 7 items, c.1565–1796 (p.121–2)

SCOTT, SARAH, 1723–1795

4595k **Crittenden, Walter Marion.** 'Literary works by mrs. Sarah Scott' in The
life and writings of mrs. Sarah Scott, novelist, 1723–1795. Philadelphia,
1932. p.98–9.

SCOTT, SIR WALTER, 1771–1832

4595x **Corson, James Clarkson.** Verses on the death of Scott. N&Q 177:417–19 D
'39.
Checklist of 29 items.

4609a **Corson, James Clarkson.** Scott's novels, dramatized versions. N&Q
189:17–18 Jl '45.
Author checklist.

SHAW, GEORGE BERNARD, 1856–1950

4631a **Heydet, Xavier,** *ed.* 'Bibliographisches' *in* Shaw-Kompendium. . . .
Paris, 1936. p.[151]–224.

SHELLEY, PERCY BYSSHE, 1792–1822

4642a **Peck, Walter Edwin.** Publications of the Shelley society. TLS 22 N '23:
790.

4645a **White, William** [and] **L. Verkoren.** Shelley scholarship, 1939–1950. Eng
Stud 32:112–16, 222 '51.

4652a **Carlton, William Newnham Chattin.** Shelley's Adonais, 1821. Am Coll
5:25–31 Oc '27.

4653 **De Ricci, Seymour Montefiore Roberto Rosso.** A bibliography of Shelley's
letters, published and unpublished. [Bois-Colombes] Privately ptd., 1927.
(Repr. New York, B. Franklin, 1967) 296p. facsims. 26cm.

SHERIDAN, THOMAS, 1719–1788

4673 **Sheldon, Esther K.** 'Sheridan's works' *in* Thomas Sheridan of Smock-alley,
recording his life as actor and theater manager. . . . Princeton, N.J., 1967.
p.492–5.
Alphabetical checklist, with some locations of copies.

SHIEL, MATTHEW PHIPPS, 1865–1947

4676a **[Hutchison, B.]** M. P. Shiel, 1865–1947. Bk Coll & Lib Mthly 13:4–7 My
'69.
Title checklist.

SHIRLEY, JAMES, 1596–1666

4677b **Tannenbaum, Samuel Aaron** and **Dorothy R. Tannenbaum.** James Shirley,
a concise bibliography. New York, 1946. 42l. 28cm. (Elizabethan bibliographies, no.34) (Duplicated typescript)
Classified checklist of works, and ana.

4677c **Pennel, Charles A.** and **W. P. Williams.** . . . James Shirley. London,
Nether pr., 1968. *See* no.2413a.

SHORTHOUSE, JOSEPH HENRY, 1834–1903

4680h **Madden, John L.,** 1964: no.165a.

SIDNEY, SIR PHILIP, 1554–1586

4684a **Guffey, George Robert.** . . . Sir Philip Sidney. . . . London, Nether pr., 1967. *See* no.2948a.

SKELTON, JOHN, 1460?–1529

4696a **Pollet, Maurice.** 'Bibliographie' *in* John Skelton, c.1460–1529; contribution à l'histoire de la prérenaissance anglaise. Paris, 1962. p.[259]–77.
Classified checklist of mss., books, and ana.

4696b **Kinsman, Robert S.** and **T. Yonge.** John Skelton, canon and census. Darien, Conn., Monographic pr., 1967. 88p.   cm. (Renaissance society of America. Bibliographies and indexes, no.4) (Not seen)
Rev: Pa Bib Soc Am 62:636 '68.

SMITH, CHARLES MANBY, 1804–1880

4707p **Howe, Ellic,** *ed.* 'C. M. Smith's known publications, a chronological check-list [1822–68]' *in* Smith, Charles M. The working man's way in the world. London, 1967. p.xvi–xviii at end.

SMITH, DAVID NICHOL, 1875–1962

4707r **Wilson, Frank Percy,** *comp.* 'A list of the writings of David Nichol Smith, 1896–1945' *in* Sutherland, James R. and F. P. Wilson, *ed.* Essays on the eighteenth century presented to David Nichol Smith. Oxford, 1945. p.[274]–83.

4707s **Brissenden, R. F.,** *ed.* 'Bibliography of works by and about David Nichol Smith' *in* Studies in the eighteenth century; papers presented at the David Nichol Smith memorial seminar, Canberra, 1966. Canberra, 1968. p.307–13.
Checklist of works, 1898–1959, mss., and ana.

SMITH, JOHN, 1618–1652

4710m **Guffey, George Robert,** 1969: no.4976g.

SMITH, WILLIAM, 1769–1839

4714m **Sheppard, Thomas.** William Smith, his maps and memoirs. Yorkshire Geol Soc Proc 19:75–253 '17.

4714n **Cox, Leslie Reginald.** New light on William Smith and his work. Yorkshire Geol Soc Proc 25:1–99 '42.

4714o **Eyles, Joan M.** William Smith, 1769–1839: a bibliography of his published writings, maps and geological sections, printed and lithographed. J Soc Bib Nat Hist 5no2:87–109 '69.
Chronol. checklist of 51 items, 1801–64, with some bibliogr. notes and refs., and locations of copies.

SMITH, WILLIAM HENRY, 1808–1872

4714s **Davis, Kenneth W.** A bibliography of the writings of William Henry Smith. Library ser5 19:162–74 '64.

'I. Contributions to Blackwood's magazine' (p.163–72): chronol. checklist, 1839–71; 'II. Contributions to other periodicals'; 'III. Books by Smith' (p.173–4): chronol. checklist, 1834–79.

SMOLLETT, TOBIAS GEORGE, 1721–1771

4717b **Korte, Donald M.** An annotated bibliography of Smollett scholarship, 1946–68. [Toronto] University of Toronto pr. [1969] 54p. 19cm.

4721a **Jones, Claude Edward.** 'Attacks on the Critical, 1756–1771' *in* Smollett studies, Berkeley, 1942. p.107–10.

4721b —— Contributors to the Critical review, 1756–1785. Mod Lang N 61:433–41 N '46.
Annotated author list.

4723a **Spector, Robert Donald.** Further attacks on the Critical review. N&Q 200:535 D '55; 201:425 Oc '56; 202:121 Mr '57.
Additions to Jones's no.4721a.

4723b —— Attacks on the Critical review in the Court magazine. N&Q 203:308 Jl '58.

SNOW, CHARLES PERCY, BARON SNOW, 1905–

4732a **Rabinovitz, Rubin,** 1967: no.1724a.

SOANE, GEORGE, 1790–1860

4732p **Bowman, W. P.** Some plays by George Soane. Mod Lang N 54:278–9 Ap '39.
Checklist of 5 plays, recorded as of unknown authorship by Nicoll.

SOUTHCOTT, JOANNA, 1750–1814

4735n **Wright, Eugene Patrick.** A catalogue of the Joanna Southcott collection at the University of Texas. Austin, University of Texas [Humanities research center, 1968] 138p. illus., facsims. 26cm.
Classified catalogue of ptd. material; manuscript material; paintings; engravings; and photographs.

SOUTHEY, ROBERT, 1774–1843

4743 **Curry, Kenneth.** The published letters of Robert Southey, a checklist. N.Y. Pub Lib Bull 71:158–64 Mr '67.

SPENSER, EDMUND, 1552?–1599

4753a **Atkinson, Dorothy F.** Edmund Spenser, a bibliographical supplement. Baltimore, Johns Hopkins pr., 1937. (Repr. New York, Haskell house, 1967) xiv,242p. 23cm.
Supplements Carpenter, no.4752.

STARKEY, JAMES SULLIVAN, 1879–1958

See O'Sullivan, Seumas, pseud.

STERRY, PETER, d.1672

4794p **Guffey, George Robert,** 1969: no.4976g.

STEUART, SIR JAMES, afterwards DENHAM, 1712–1780

See Denham, sir James Steuart.

STEVENSON, ROBERT LOUIS, 1850–1894

4796 **Williamson, George Millar.** Catalogue of a collection of the books of Robert Louis Stevenson in the library of George M. Williamson. . . . Jamaica, N.Y., Marion pr., 1901. [96]p. port., facsims. 26cm.
Largely from the library of Charles B. Foote.

STOPES, CHARLOTTE (CARMICHAEL), 1841–1929

4816p **Murphy, Gwendolen.** A bibliographical list of the writings of Charlotte Carmichael Stopes. Essays by divers hands new ser 10:95–107 '31.
Classified checklist.

STRACHEY FAMILY

4818k **Sanders, Charles Richard.** 'Some contributions of the Stracheys to the Spectator, 1875–1925' *in* The Strachey family, 1588–1932; their writings and literary associations. [Durham, N.C.] 1953. p.298–321.
Chronol. checklist of articles by sir Edward, George, sir Arthur, St.Loe, sir Charles, Henry, mrs. St.Loe, Frances (mrs. W. H. C. Shaw), Giles Lytton, and James Strachey.

SUMMERS, ALPHONSE MONTAGUE JOSEPH-MARY AUGUSTUS, 1880–1948

4825a **[Smith, Timothy d'Arch]** 'Bibliographical check-list' *in* Jerome, Joseph. Montague Summers, a memoir. London, 1965. p.91–4.

SWIFT, JONATHAN, 1667–1745

4825y **Webster, C. M.** The satiric background of the attack on the puritans in Swift's A tale of a tub. Pub Mod Lang Assn 50:210–23 Mr '35.
Annotated chronol. checklist of non-dramatic satire, 1621–1700.

4826b **Mayhew, George P.** 'Recent Swift scholarship' *in* McHugh, Roger J. and P. Edwards. Jonathan Swift, 1667–1967, a Dublin tercentenary tribute. [Dublin, 1967] p.210–17.
Bibliogr. notes to survey article (p.187–97)

4826c **Stathis, James J.** A bibliography of Swift studies, 1945–1965. Nashville, Vanderbilt U.P., 1967. xi,110p. 24cm.

4838 **Craig, Maurice James,** *comp.* 'Short catalogue of the exhibition' *in* Dublin. St.Patrick's hospital. The legacy of Swift, a bi-centenary record of St. Patrick's hospital. . . . [Dublin] 1948. p.49–70.

4844 **Lenfest, David S.** A checklist of illustrated editions of Gulliver's travels, 1727–1914. Pa Bib Soc Am 62:85–123 '68.
Chronol. checklist of 48 items, with bibliogr. notes and refs.

SWINBURNE, ALGERNON CHARLES, 1837–1909

4845 **Faverty, Frederic Everett,** *ed.*, 1968: no.2017a.

TAYLOR, BP. JEREMY, 1613–1667

4877a **Hardy, Robert Gathorne-.** Jeremy Taylor [additions to his Bibliography] TIS 15 S '32:648.

TENNYSON, ALFRED, 1ST BARON TENNYSON, 1809–1892

4886 **Faverty, Frederic Everett,** 1968: no.2017a.

4888a **Wise, Thomas James.** Tennyson bibliography. Athenæum 417–18,479–80,543–4,681–2 Mr–My '97; 388–9,419–20 S '97.

4893a **Haney, John Louis.** Tennysoniana. Athenæum 4269:153–4 Ag '09.
Addenda to Wise's ana in no.4892.

4902 **Tennyson, sir Charles Bruce Locker** and **Christine Fall.** Alfred Tennyson, an annotated bibliography. Athens, University of Georgia pr. [1967] viii, 126p. 22cm.
Not indexed.
Rev: Pa Bib Soc Am 62:638 '68.

THACKERAY, WILLIAM MAKEPEACE, 1811–1863

4906a **Flamm, Dudley.** Thackeray's critics, an annotated bibliography of British and American criticism, 1836–1901. Chapel Hill, University of North Carolina pr. [1967] 184p. 22cm.

4921a **Ray, Gordon Norton,** *ed.* 'Articles newly identified as Thackeray's' *in* The letters and private papers of William Makepeace Thackeray. Cambridge, Mass.; London, 1945–6. V.2 (1945), p.844–7.

THEOBALD, LEWIS, 1688–1744

4928 **Jones, Richard Foster.** 'A chronological list of Theobald's works' *in* Lewis Theobald, his contribution to English scholarship. New York, 1919. p.[347]–55.

THOMAS, DYLAN MARLAIS, 1914–1953

4929 **Thomas, sr. Lois Theisen.** Dylan Thomas, a bibliography of secondary criticism. Bull Bib 26:9–28,32 Ja/Mr '69; 26:36,59–60 Ap/Je '69.

4937 **Maud, Ralph.** Dylan Thomas in Welsh periodicals. Nat Lib Wales J
15no3:265–89 '68.

THOMAS, PHILIP EDWARD, 1878–1917

4944 **Oxford. University. Bodleian library.** Edward Thomas, 1878–1917; an
exhibition held in the Divinity school, Oxford, 1968. Oxford, 1968. 38p.
21cm.
Rev: TLS 16 My '68:512.

THOMSON, JAMES, 1834–1882

4963 **Walker, Imogene B.** 'Bibliography. I. Works of James Thomson' *in* James
Thomson (B.V.), a critical study. Ithaca, N.Y., 1950. p.175–95.
Classified checklist of books and pamphlets; periodical contribs.; and mss.

THRALE, MRS. HESTER, 1741–1821
See Piozzi, Hester Lynch (Salusbury).

TICKELL, RICHARD, 1751–1793

4966 **Butterfield, Lyman Henry,** *ed.* Anticipation, by Richard Tickell. New York,
King's crown pr., 1942. xi,97p. facsim. 23cm. (Not seen)
'Bibliography of Tickell's writings'

TOMLINS, ELIZABETH SOPHIA, 1763–1828

4970j **Povey, Kenneth.** Elizabeth Sophia Tomlins, 1763–1828. N&Q 154:115–16
F '28.
Checklist of 4 items, 1785–98.

TOURNEUR, CYRIL, 1575?–1626

4971a **Tannenbaum, Samuel Aaron** and **Dorothy R. Tannenbaum.** Cyril Tourneur,
a concise bibliography. New York, 1946. 14l. 28cm. (Elizabethan bibliographies, no.33) (Duplicated typescript)
Classified checklist of works and ana.

4971b **Donovan, Dennis G.** . . . . Cyril Tourneur. . . . London, Nether pr. [1967]
See no.2996a.

TRAHERNE, THOMAS, 1637–1674

4976g **Guffey, George Robert.** Traherne and the seventeenth-century platonists,
1900–1966. London, Nether pr., 1969. 110p. 23cm. (Elizabethan biblio-
graphies supplements, XI)
Checklists for Ralph Cudworth, Nathaniel Culverwel, Henry More, John Norris,
George Rust, John Smith, Peter Sterry, Traherne, Benjamin Whichcote and John
Worthington.

TRYON, THOMAS, 1634–1703

4990p **Foster, John C.** Thomas Tryon, 1634-1703. Baptist Hist Soc Trans
2no3:182–9 My '11.
'Bibliography' (p.188–9)

VANDERBANK, JOHN, 1694–1739

4994i **Hammelmann, Hanns A.** Eighteenth-century illustrators: John Vanderbank, 1694–1739. Bk Coll 17no3:285–99 '68.

'Handlist of books illustrated by J. Vanderbank' (p.294–9): chronol. checklist, 1729–42, with some bibliogr. notes.

VAUGHAN WILLIAMS, RALPH, 1872–1958

See Williams, Ralph Vaughan.

WADE, ARTHUR SARSFIELD, 1883–1959

See Rohmer, Sax, pseud.

WALEY, ARTHUR DAVID, 1889–1966

5003a **Johns, Francis A.** A bibliography of Arthur Waley. New Brunswick, N.J., Rutgers U. P.; London, Allen & Unwin [1968] xi,187p. port., facsim. 20cm.

Classified checklist of books; first appearance of trans.; articles; original poetry and prose; book reviews; miscellaneous; some appearances in anthologies; and ana; with some bibliogr. notes.

Rev: TLS 2 My '68:464; Pa Bib Soc Am 62:481 '68; E. Lucie-Smith Priv Lib ser2 2:35–7 '69; R. J. Roberts Bk Coll 18:251–2 '69; Pa Bib Soc Am 63:354 '69; B. C. Bloomfield Library ser5 25:172–3 '70.

WALLACE, RICHARD HORATIO EDGAR, 1875–1932

5005r **Lofts, William Oliver Guillemont** and **D. Adley.** The British bibliography of Edgar Wallace. London, H. Baker [1969] [11]246p. 21cm.

Unindexed chronol. checklist of books by year of pub.; short stories; rare ed.; first ed.; works pub. in book form; autobiographies and biographies; collections of stories; stories in short story collections; True crime articles; miscellanea; works contained in magazines and newspapers; first London magazine stories.

WARBURTON, BP. WILLIAM, 1698–1779

5015e **Evans, Arthur William.** [Appendices II–V] *in* Warburton and the Warburtonians, a study in some eighteenth-century controversies. London, 1932. p.[284]–306.

Chronol. checklist of works; works ed.; works contrib. to; and books and pamphlets connected with the Warburtonian controversies.

WARD, MARY AUGUSTA (ARNOLD), MRS. HUMPHRY WARD, 1851–1920

5025a **Chesterton, Gilbert Keith.** Mrs. Humphry Ward. Eng Illus Mag new ser 31:293–5,299–300 Je '04.

'Bibliography' (p.294,299–300): checklist of works, translations, prefaces and introductions; plays; and ana.

5025b **Keogh, Andrew,** 1910: no.662.

WARLOCK, PETER, *pseud. of* PHILIP ARNOLD HESELTINE, 1894–1930

5025t **Rattenbury, S. K.,** 1959: no.189c.

WEBSTER, JOHN, 1580?–1625?

5051a **Easton, Judith M.,** 1937: no.115a.

5052a **Donovan, Dennis G.** . . . . John Webster, 1940–1965. London, Nether pr., 1967. *See* no.4216a.

WEDGWOOD, DAME CICELY VERONICA, 1910–

5052x **Flew, G. S. M.,** 1957: no.123a.

WELLESLEY, ARTHUR, 1ST DUKE OF WELLINGTON, 1769–1852

5053q **Paine, J.** A bibliography of the duke of Wellington. N&Q 152:222–4 Mr '27; J. Ardagh; A. J. H. *ib.* 152:226–7 Ap '27; J. F. B. 152:302 Ap '27.

WELLINGTON, ARTHUR WELLESLEY, 1ST DUKE OF, 1769–1852
See Wellesley, Arthur.

WELLS, HERBERT GEORGE, 1866–1946

5060 **H. G. Wells society,** LONDON. H. G. Wells, a comprehensive bibliography. [2d ed., rev.] London [1968] (First ed. 1966) vi,70p. 19cm.

Classified checklist of works; short stories; miscellaneous writings by and about; films, stage productions, etc., with some bibliogr. notes.

Rev: H. E. Gerber Eng Lit Transit 11:86 '68.

WESLEY, JOHN, 1703–1791

5068a **Judson, S.,** 1963: no.148b.

WESTERMAN, PERCY FRANCIS, 1876–1959

5072f **Butts, Dennis.** Percy F. Westerman. Bk Coll & Lib Mthly 6:186–8 Oc '68.

'The first editions of Percy F. Westerman, a provisional list' (p.187–8)

WHICHCOTE, BENJAMIN, 1609–1683

5075n **Guffey, George Robert,** 1969: no.4976g.

WHITE, GILBERT, 1720–1793

5082 **Prance, Claude Annett.** Some uncollected authors XLIII: Gilbert White, 1720–1793. Bk Coll 17no3:300–21 '68.

'List of the principal editions of The natural history of Selborne' (p.310–11); 'Checklist of the principal editions of The natural history of Selborne' (p.311–20); 'Other writings . . .' (p.320–1)

5083 **Scott, W. S.** Gilbert White's The natural history of Selborne. (Note 304). Bk Coll 18no1:89–90 '69.

Some foreign additions to Prance.

WILKES, JOHN, 1727–1797

5107 **Rhodon,** *pseud.* Anonymous works relating to John Wilkes. N&Q 164:208 Mr '33.

Chronol. checklist of 26 items, 1763–70.

5108 **A select** list of works in Guildhall library by, and relating to, John Wilkes. Guildh Misc 3:75–84 Oc '69.

WILKES, WETENHALL, fl.1730–1747

5109 **Williams, sir Harold.** The rev. Wetenhall Wilkes. N&Q 184:315–16 My '43.

Chronol. checklist, 1730–47.

WILLARD, EDWARD SMITH, d.1915

5111d **Harting, Hugh.** Edward Smith Willard; bibliography. N&Q 163:402–4 D '32.

Chronol. checklist of works about, 1882–1930.

WILLIAMS, CHARLES, *pseud. of* CHARLES WALTER STANSBY, 1886–1945

5111p **Dawson, Lawrence R.** A checklist of reviews by Charles Williams. Pa Bib Soc Am 55:100–17 '61.

Chronol. checklist of 280 items, 1918–45, with indexes.

WILLIAMS, EDWARD, 1750–1813

5112g **Owen, William Thomas.** 'Bibliography of Edward Williams's publications' *in* Edward Williams, D.D., 1750–1813, his life, thought and influence. Cardiff, 1963. p.[162]–6.

Chronol. checklist with some locations of copies.

WILLIAMS, RALPH VAUGHAN, 1872–1958

5114x **De la Mare, Judith,** 1949: no.108a.

WILMOT, JOHN, 2D EARL OF ROCHESTER, 1657–1680

5120x **Vieth, David Muench,** *ed.* 'Rochester studies, 1925–1967' *in* The complete poems of John Wilmot, earl of Rochester. New Haven, 1968. p.lii–lxix.

5126 **Vieth, David Muench.** 'Lists of early texts and ascriptions' *in* Attribution in restoration poetry, a study of Rochester's Poems of 1680. New Haven, 1963. p.[363]–477.

WILSON, ANGUS FRANK JOHNSTONE, 1913–

5127 **Rabinovitz, Rubin,** 1967: no.1724a.

WILSON, FRANK PERCY, 1889–1963

5128 [Bennett, Henry Stanley] *comp.* 'A select list of the writings of F. P. Wilson' *in* Davis, Herbert J. and dame Helen Gardner, *ed.* Elizabethan and Jacobean studies presented to Frank Percy Wilson. Oxford, 1959. (Repr. 1969) p.[339]–48.
Chronol. checklist, 1914–59.

WILSON, JOHN DOVER, 1881–1969

5129 [Butt, John Everett and J. C. Maxwell] 13 July, 1961, a list of his published writings presented to John Dover Wilson on his 80th birthday. Cambridge, C.U.P., 1961. 32p. 18cm.

5130 —— [Same]: . . . With later additions by the author *in* Wilson, John D. Milestones on the Dover road. London [1969] p.[287]–309.
Classified checklist of 237 items.

WISE, THOMAS JAMES, 1859–1937

5147 **Dearden, James S.** Wise and Ruskin, III. Bk Coll 18no3:318–39 '69.
'Handlist of T. J. Wise's Ruskin publications, etc.' (p.338–9): table of forgeries, binary editions, letters and miscellaneous, with dates, number and locations of copies, and bibliogr. refs.

5148 **Todd, William Burton.** Some Wiseian advertisements. Bk Coll 18no2:219–20 '69.
Checklist of 8 prospectuses, 1894–1908.

5149 **Carter, John Waynflete.** Thomas J. Wise's Verses, 1882/1883. Library ser5 24:247–9 S '69.
Expands Todd's census of copies (no.5141), with bibliogr. notes and discussion.

WODEHOUSE, PELHAM GRENVILLE, 1881–

5153a **Voorhees, Richard Joseph.** 'Selected bibliography' *in* P. G. Wodehouse. New York [1966] p.191–7.
Checklist of books, selections and ana.

WOLFE, JAMES, 1727–1759

5154p **Paine, J.** A bibliography of Wolfe. N&Q 157:259–60 Oc '29; G. H. W. *ib.* 157:304 Oc '29; J. Ardagh 157:320 N '29.
Chronol. checklist of works about Wolfe.

WOOLF, ADELINE VIRGINIA (STEPHEN), 1882–1941

5159 **Kirkpatrick, Brownlee Jean.** A bibliography of Virginia Woolf. Rev. ed. London, R. Hart-Davis, 1967. xi,212p. port., facsims. 23cm. ([Soho bibliographies, IX])
Adds section G on the location of mss. and autograph letters, to no.5158.

WORDSWORTH, WILLIAM, 1770–1850

5159x **Ward, William Smith.** Wordsworth, the Lake poets, and their contemporary magazine critics, 1798–1820. Stud Philol 42:87–113 Ja '45.

Chronol. list of reviews in British magazines, 1798–1820, of Wordsworth's works (p.109–13)

5175a **Coe, Charles Norton.** Wordsworth and the literature of travel, a bibliography. N&Q 197:429–33,457 S,Oc '52.

63 titles of poems and the travel books from which they were drawn.

WORTHINGTON, JOHN, 1618–1671

5183 **Guffey, George Robert,** 1969: no.4976g.

WRANGHAM, FRANCIS, 1769–1842

5187a **May, Frederick.** Archdeacon Francis Wrangham: addenda to Sadleir. Library ser5 19:238–42 '64.

WRIGHT, JOHN BUCKLAND, 1897–1954

5188m **Reid, Anthony.** A check-list of the book illustrations of John Buckland Wright, together with a personal memoir. Pinner, Private libraries association, 1968. 94p.+plates. illus. 26cm.

Checklist of published and unpublished work and dust-wrapper designs, with some bibliogr. notes.

Rev: S. Carter Library ser5 25:175–6 '70.

WRIGHT, JOSEPH, 1734–1797

5188t **Hope, Alison.** Joseph Wright of Derby, a bibliography. Derby, Public library, 1967. 13p. 25cm. Covertitle. (Duplicated typescript)

Classified author checklist of works relating to Wright.

YEATS, WILLIAM BUTLER, 1865–1939

5197u **Saul, George Brandon.** Thread to a labyrinth; a selective bibliography in Yeats. N.Y. Pub Lib Bull 58:344–7 Jl '54.

5197v **Jochum, Klaus Peter S.** W. B. Yeats's plays, an annotated checklist of criticism. Saarbrücken, Anglistisches Institut, Universität des Saarlandes, 1966. 180p. 20cm. (Duplicated typescript)

5207a **Alspach, Russell K.** Additions to Allan Wade's bibliography of W. B. Yeats. Irish Bk 2no3/4:91–114 '63.

5207b **Ó Haodha, Micheál.** Unrecorded Yeats contributions to periodicals. Irish Bk 2no3/4:129 '63.

5209b **Wade, Allan.** A bibliography of the writings of W. B. Yeats. 3d ed., rev. and ed. by Russell K. Alspach. [London] R. Hart-Davis [1968] (First pub. 1951) 514p. port., facsims. 22cm. ([Soho bibliographies, I])

See no.5207. 'The Cuala press, first called the Dun Emer press' (p.451–7).

YONGE, CHARLOTTE MARY, 1823–1901

5209y **Madden, J. L.,** 1964: no.165a.

CORRECTIONS AND ADDITIONS TO THE BIBLIOGRAPHY OF BRITISH LITERARY BIBLIOGRAPHIES

Items which have been greatly corrected or added to have been reprinted in full in the Supplement; such items are noted here so users of the first volume may amend their copies. Consequential alterations to the Index have been incorporated in the present Index and also recorded in the list of corrections to the Index of the previous volume, which follows this.

This list also includes reviews of items in the first volume; these are not so important usually to warrant reprinting the whole entry and are best treated as corrections, as they are here. The following list gives the item or page number together with the correction, in text order.

p.[xxiii] Comparée
1   See Supplement for revision.
3   See Supplement.
34   Annually, 1952–67. From 1968, issued separately.
45   dictionary (replacing 'alphabetical author-subject')
56   See Supplement.
57   See Supplement.
58   D–Mr
74   Angliæ notitia,
103   (See no.4462)
107   Fallodon.
110   **Doughty, Dennis W.**
119   **Fanstone, Ruth I.**
189   (See no.1775)
199   **Skerl, Margaret.**
217   **Symons, L. Eleanor.**
247   LeFanu
270   36cm. (delete 'Not seen')
282   See Supplement.
294   See Supplement.
301   See Supplement.
312   See Supplement.
313   See Supplement.
325, before. *See also* period divisions under *Drama, Fiction, Newspapers and periodicals, Pamphlets,* and *Poetry.*
334   Add '*Rev*: Athenæum 4255:579–80 '09; *rf*. F. Karslake *ib*. 4256:617 '09.'
343   Add '*See* nos.325, 399.'
348   See Supplement.
350   Add '*See* no.376.'
399   Add '*See* no.343.'
426   **Minns, sir Ellis Hovell.**
442   Advocates' (twice); Pub (for Pa)
443   Add '*Rev*: TLS 6 N '24:708.'
445   Add '*Rev*: TLS 31 Ja '18:54.'
449   **sir W. D. Ross.**
455   Add '*See* no.487.'

472   Bühler
490   See Supplement.
518   Transfer line starting '*Rev*:' to follow no.517, and add 'TLS 11 S '24:560'.
523   After '27cm.' add '(Duplicated typescript)'.
524   Transfer line starting '*Rev*:' to follow no.522 and see Supplement.
588   See Supplement.
590   See Supplement.
623   Add 'The Constance Meade collection is now in the Bodleian library, Oxford.'
624   Add '*Rev*: Pa Bib Soc Am 62:642 '68; J. Horden Library ser5 24:67–8 '69.'
627   See Supplement.
634   Add 'The collection is now in the library of Trinity college, Cambridge.'
654   See Supplement.
657b   viii,87p.
658   Add 'Rf. C. M. Falconer; J. S. C. Acad 45:250–1 '94; J. H. Slater *ib*. 45:270–1 '94.
     Rev: Athenæum 3474:673–4 '94.'
664   Change 'every' to 'each'.
667   See Supplement.
670   See Supplement.
714   Pub 1pt4:
745   **Rendel.**
748   Pub
753   Change 'the previous item'to 'no 752'..
762   (p.35–6).
777   After '1952.' insert '(2d ed., 1969)'.
811–13 See Supplement under Mandeville.
822   Chapel Hill
824   Add 'The Copinger collection of the Imitatio Christi is now in the library of Harvard university.'
855   Add 'The ms. of Anderson's bibliography was brought more or less up

to date and deposited in 1925 at Baillie's Institution, Glasgow.'
858   Add 'Rev: TLS 3 My '17:212.'
914   Add 'Rev: N&Q 163:466–7 '32.'
935a Add 'Rev: TLS 28 Mr '12:124.'
937   After 'by' add 'Fanny E. L. and'.
938   Somersetensis
948   **Barnsley. Public library.**
961   See Supplement.
1068 Remove space between 2d and 3d lines.
1167 bibliographies
1186 **Nicolas J.**
1197 See Supplement.
1201a '**Census**
1211 See Supplement.
1233 See Supplement.
1248 See Supplement.
1251 Add 'See also no.1256.'
1272 'Pub' for 'Proc'.
1313 Add 'Rev: TLS 12 Ap '17:178–9.'
1323 Pub 1pt4:1–15 [i.e. 41–55] Oc '94.
1329 See Supplement.
1341 12pt2:97
1356 Remove to Authors.
1359 See Supplement.
1368 Insert space before line starting 'Rev:'.
      Insert 'PRESSES — MORES, EDWARD ROWE, 1731–1778
      See under Authors.'
1377, after. Insert 'PRESSES — OXFORD UNIVERSITY PRESS
      See Authors — Fell, bp. John, 1625–1686.'
1382 See Supplement.
1384 **Rendel**
1394 'Bibliography' (p.53–88): chronol.
1401b cm.
1406a TEGG, THOMAS,
1408a Add 'Rev: W. R. McDonald Biblioth 5:77–8 '67; R. Donaldson Library ser5 23:173–4 '68.'
1416 Pub 1pt1
1420 After '1952.' insert '(2d ed., 1969)'.
1421 12pt1:
1425 Add 'Rev: TLS 3 Ja '18:4.'
1448 Add 'Rev: TLS 20 My '15:170.'
1460 Add 'Rev: Acad 38:318 '90.'
1471 See Supplement, no.1499.
1507 [Ballinger, sir John]
1522 Add 'The collection is now in the Henry E. Huntington library.'
1530 Insert space before 'A . . .'.
1585 Pub 1pt2:
1586 1pt5:
1592 Add 'Rev: C. J. Stratman Library ser5 19:297–300 '64.'
1600 After 'New York', add 'Burt Franklin'.
1614 Add 'Rev: J. Fuzier Langues Mod 59:205–6 '65; J. C. Maxwell N&Q 211:314–15 '66.'
1664 *in*
1699 Add 'Rev: C. J. Rawson N&Q 211:278–9 '66.'
1795 See Supplement.
1813 See Supplement.

1832 Add 'Rev: TLS 17 Je '04:190.'
1845, before. — 1601
1875a Take in no.1966 Collins as no.1875a.
1903 Simonds.
1925 Replace as no.1940a.
1960 Add 'Rev: Athenæum 3874:114 '02; rf. S. J. Reid ib. 3876:179–80 '02.'
1966 Replace as no.1875a.
2016 See Supplement, no.2017a.
2022 See Supplement.
2035b p.[355]–62.'
2045 Add 'Rev: Athenæum 4339:788–9 '10.'
2069, after. Add 'TRANSLATIONS
      See Foreign books published in English in Britain.'
2085, after. See also Botany; Gardening.'
2118 See Supplement.
2129 Add 'Rev: A. C. Townsend Library ser5 19:265–7 '64.'
2130 See Supplement.
2136 Add 'Rev: TLS 4 N '60:715.'
2144 See Supplement.
2158 'Pub' for 'Trans'.
2160 'Pub' for 'Trans'.
2168 index; ed.
2189, after. Move the reference GLENDOWER to here.
2190 Add 'Rev: TLS 29 Oc '38:700.'
2201 (Repr. New York, Hafner, 1961)
2203 8. Treatises; and see Supplement.
2210 Add 'Rev: TLS 17 F '27:107.'
2230 Add 'Rev: R. S. Wilkinson Bk Coll 15:506–9 '66; A. G. Debus Brit J Hist Sci 3:191–2 '66.'
2231, before. MILITARY BOOKS
2240, after. Insert 'NAVAL BOOKS
      See Military books.'
2245 See Supplement.
2250 **Moorehead.** Coatesville
2255 For 'New York, 1961)' subst. 'New York, B. Franklin, 1962)'.
2269 [**Davies, John H.**]
2289, after. TRAVEL BOOKS
      Insert 'VETERINARY SCIENCE
      See Medicine.'
2290 3pt2:37–124 D '97.
2300 See Supplement.
2360–2 See Supplement under 'Richard de Bury.'
2365 Goldwin.
2370 Add 'rf. ib. 2n05:348–50 My '03.'
2388 'Bibliography' (p.34–8): checklist
2397 Add 'Rev: TLS 15 N '28:864.'
2414, before. BECKETT, SAMUEL BARCLAY
2415 1930; New York, Bowker, 1931.
2432 **Gallatin, Albert Eugene** and **L. M. Oliver.** 27cm. (Soho bibliographies, III)
2481 See Supplement.
2485 Add 'Rev: D. V. Erdman J Eng Germ Philol 64:744–7 '65.'
2491 See Supplement.
2493 *ib.* 29 Oc '25.
2517 Add 'Note also [Cleverdon, Douglas] Unrecorded editions of Robert Boyle.

(Notes on sales). TIS 18 Ag '32:584; sir G. L. Keynes *ib*. 25 Ag '32:596.'
2549–50 Add '(Soho bibliographies, IV)'.
2556 See Supplement.
2563 Transpose numerals.
2563a Transpose numerals.
2612 Dublin
2613 Bunyan
2614 **Harrison,**
2625 **Mogg, William Rees-.**
2642 Add '*Rev*: W. S. Mitchell N&Q 211: 233–4 '66; G. R. Roy Mod Philol 64:357–61 '67; Pa Bib Soc Am 62:156 '68.'
2661–2 See Supplement.
2688 Add '*Rev*: TLS 21 S '33:636.'
2698 Argyle's . . . Pub
2770 Add '*Rev*: TLS 15 My '34:308.'
2810 p.[570]–7.
2816a Add '*Rev*: J. Horden Bk Coll 17:518, 521–2 '68; Pa Bib Soc Am 62:480 '68.'
2819 See Supplement.
2823 **Heal, sir Ambrose.**
2856, before. TEODOR JÓZEF
2891 no.181.
2896 Add '*Rev*: E. A. Bloom Mod Lang R 59:463–4 '64; C. Ryskamp Library ser5 19:316–18 '64.'
2900 **Ward, sir Adolphus.**
2913 Add '*Rev*: R. Girvan Mod Lang R 48:235 '53.'
2914 **Skerl, Margaret,**
2921 Add '*Rev*: TLS 14 N '29:921.'
2934 Add '*Rev*: TLS 6 N '24:716; *cf*. A. M. Cohn *ib*. 13 N '24:731.'
2945 Add '*Rev*: F. Greenaway Am Sci 22:141–2 '66; A. Thackray Brit J Hist Sci 3:194 '66; K. D. C. Vernon Lib R 20:397–8 '66.'
3025, before. DE VERE
3030 Add '*Rev*: R. McLean Connois 162:274 '66.'
3167 15pt2:35–54 Oc '34.
3178 See Supplement.
3276 See Supplement.
3283b See Supplement, no.3283c.
3301 Holmes.
3315 Add '*Rev*: M. L. Turner Library ser5 19:328–30 '64.'
3319–26 FitzGerald throughout.
3330 See Supplement.
3331 'Pub' for 'Proc'
3334, before. FLEURE . . . 1877–1969
3335 **Bell, sir Harold Idris.**
3337 D '91.
3348, before. FORSTER . . . 1879–1970.
3351 After '1965.' insert '(2d [rev.] impression, 1968)'.
3448 Critical
3494a no.4417a.
3502 Add '*Rev*: P. Toynbee Mod Lang R 13:343–5 '18.'
3622 **Barker, Nicolas J.**
3632 'Pub' for 'Proc'
3657 **Tannenbaum,**

3668 For line starting '*Rev*:', substitute '*Rev*: TLS 24 Ap '53:276; L. W. Hanson, H. Macdonald and J. M. Hargreaves *ib*. 8 My '53:307; sir F. C. Francis'.
3757 4pt2:
3816m See Supplement, no.3816m.
3838 Add '*Rev*: TLS 17 Je '15:206; P. Toynbee Mod Lang R 13:345–6 '18.'
3841 For 'Extensive . . .' substitute 'Extensive facsims.; the collection, once in the library of the University of Rochester, N.Y., is substantially contained in no.3850.'
3843 *See* no.3845.
3850 Catalogus
3899 Transpose numerals.
3903–10 See Supplement where the entries for Keats have been rearranged in this order:
3904 Forman (1900)
3905 English association (1912)
3905a Marsh (1934)
3906 Forman (1938)
3907 MacGillivray (1949)
3907a Raysor (1956)
3908 Rice (1965)
3909 Boston (1921)
3968, after. TEODOR JÓZEF
4017 new graph ser 1no4:
4122a 12:252–5 Oc '37.
4161 Simmons
4166 26cm. (Cambridge Bib Soc Monographs, no.1)
4218a See Supplement, no.4219a.
4244 Fletcher, nos.4231, 4232.
4265 **Gerber, Helmut E.**
4282 recusants
4316 Add '*Rev*: P. H. Priv Lib ser2 1:84 '68.'
4318 subsecivae. Add 'Also ptd. in Glasgow Bib Soc Rec 12:41–81 '36. p.60–81.'
4377, before. 1879–1958
4424 after. Insert 'PICKERING, WILLIAM, 1796–1854
See under Presses and Printing.'
4448 Lib
4455a Add '*Rev*: B. C. Bloomfield Library ser5 23:269–70 '68; F. G. F. Priv Lib ser2 1:184–5 '68.'
4462 Add '*Rev*: TLS 8 D '66:1160; D. H. Revill Lib Assn Rec 68:454–5 '66; K. D. C. Vernon 20:493–4 '66; Pa Bib Soc Am 61:159 '67; J. L. Marks Bk Coll 16:389–90,393 '67.'
4469 25cm.
4470 c.1727
4554 RUSKIN, JOHN
4554 1889–93. Insert space before next line.
4560, before. RUSSELL, 1872–1970
4595 Scot.
4621 copies of adaptation
4653 See Supplement, no.4652a.
4694 Add '*Rev*: T. Balston Library ser5 19:331–2 '64.'
4697 'Pub' for 'Proc'

4756 tions of
4768, after. 1879–1958 . . . *Seumas*
4796 See Supplement.
4825 After '1964', insert 'New Hyde Park, N.Y., University books [1964]'
4838 See Supplement.
4843 Mr
4845 **Faverty** . . . *ed.*,
4884 Add '*Rev*: D. Roper N&Q 211:240 '66.'
4886 **Faverty** . . . *ed.*,
4966 See Supplement.
5003a See Supplement.
5017 Add '*Rev*: N&Q 151:197–8 '26.'
5022–3 See Supplement, nos.5025a–b.
5058 Wells's
5074 **Robertson, sir Charles Grant**
5130, before. 1881–1969
5145 Sotheby's, 1967
5156 Elizabethan
5157, before. VIRGINIA (STEPHEN),
5158 See Supplement.
5190 **Doughty, Dennis William.**
5207 See Supplement.

INDEX CORRECTIONS

510 ALKEN, Henry Thomas, 1785–1851. 1738
    Altschul: move to follow Altick.
    ANGLESEY.
    ANGLIÆ NOTITIA.
512 Ballinger, sir John.
    BANFFSHIRE: move to follow Bandy.
    BANK OF ENGLAND: move to follow Bangs.
    Barker, N. J.: delete.
    Barker, Nicolas J. 1186 3622
513 BECKETT, Samuel Barclay.
    Bell, sir Harold Idris.
514 After *Bibliographica*, add *Bibliographica Celtica*. 1181
517 After BRANDE, add BRASH, James, 1758–1835. 2022
    BRITISH BOOKS PUBLISHED ABROAD *see also* PILGRIM PRESS; ST. OMER'S PRESS.
518 BROWNE, Samuel
    After Bury, J. B., add BURY, Richard de, 1287–1342? *see* AUNGERVILLE, Richard (Richard de Bury)
519 CARLYLE
520 Carr, sr.
    CARROLL . . . **2720–35**
    Casaide, Seumas.
522 CONJURING. **2139–41a** 2241
    CONRAD . . . Teodor Józef . . .
523 Under Damer, George . . ., indent Carlow.
524 D'ARBLAY, Frances . . .
    Darlington, James: delete.
    Darton, Frederick J. Harvey.
    After De Bhaldraithe, insert DE BURY, Richard, 1287–1342? *see* AUNGERVILLE, Richard (Richard de Bury)
    DE LA MARE, Walter John, 1873–1956. 684 **2998–3006**

De Vane,
    After De Vane, insert DE VERE, Aubrey Thomas, 1814–1902. **3025–6**
DE LA MARE: delete entry.
DEVERE: delete entry.
D'Ewes, sir Simonds.
526 Dudden . . . Holmes.
527 Under Edinburgh,—Society of writers. . . .
528 *English literary history see ELH*: move to after *English fiction*. . . .
    Escott, . . . Sweet-.
    EVELYN, sir John, 1682–1763.
    Fanstone, Ruth Isabel.
529 FLEURE . . . 1877–1969.
530 FORSTER . . . 1879–1970.
531 Replace Gathorne-Hardy, Robert by *see* Hardy, Robert Gathorne-.
    GIBSON, Edward: change to GIBBON, and insert before GIBBON, Lewis.
535 Harris, James Rendel.
    After HERALDRY, delete Herbert, Robert. . . .
536 After HERBERT, George, insert HERBERT, Robert. 1100 3673
537 After HOWELL, James, insert Howgego, James. 1795
539 Jones, S. K.: expand to Stephen, and place after Jones, Sheila.
540 Kern, Jerome David. 400
    Kern, John D. 1922 1937 2552
    Kitton
    KORZENIOWSKI, Teodor Józef. . . .
543 Under London, delete space in — Corporation.
546 Under MEDICINE, add 586
547 Minns, sir Ellis Hovell.
551 O'SULLIVAN, Seumas . . . 1879–1958.
552 PATERSON, Daniel. . . .
553 *POETRY ORIGINAL AND SELECTED*.
554 Price, Lawrence Marsden.
556 After REID, Thomas, add REID, William, 1764–1831. 2022
    Robertson, William: read Roberton.
557 Robertson, sir Charles Grant.
    Ross, sir W. D.
558 RUSSELL . . . 1872–1970.
559 Sands: place before SANDYS.
561 Skerl, Margaret.
    Smith, Goldwin.
    Smith, Lloyd Logan Pearsall: read 5185 for 5135.
    Smith, Wilbur Moorehead.
562 SOMERSET. **938–9**
    STARKEY, Seumas, 1879–1958.
564 After *Sweet* &, add Sweet-Escott, Thomas Hay *see* Escott, Thomas Hay Sweet-.
565 . . . TULLIS PRESS.
568 WEDGWOOD, dame Cicely. . . .
    WESLEY, John,
569 WILSON, John Dover, 1881–1969.
570 Worshipful company of stationers, London.

LIST OF REPRINTS

This list of bibliographies in the first volume which have been reprinted gives the item number, indication of the compiler and subject, and the details of the reprint. Where no publisher is given, it is to be understood that the reprint is by the publisher of the original volume.

45	Bigmore	Printing	Hildesheim, G. Olms, 1969
245	Mumby	Bookselling	Metuchen, N.J., Scarecrow, 1967
330	Grolier club	One hundred books	New York, Kraus reprint, 1968
331	„	Bibliographical notes	New York, Kraus reprint, 1968
338	Harvard university	Widener collection	New York, Arno pr. [1968]
340	De Ricci	Book collector's guide	New York, B. Franklin, 1967
345	Schwartz	1100 obscure points	Bristol, Chatford House pr., 1969
410	Peddie	Fifteenth century books	New York, B. Franklin, 1967
425	Abbott	„	New York, B. Franklin, 1968
445	Duff	„	London, 1964
496	Grolier Club	Books—1475–1640	New York, Cooper Square pub., 1963
521	Pollard & Redgrave	S.T.C.	Menston, Scolar pr., 1969
596	„	Books—1641–1700	New York, Cooper Square pub., 1963
628	Cordasco	18th century bibliogrs.	Detroit, Mich., Gale research, 1968
633	Williams	„ „ „	New York, B. Franklin, 1967
634	Rothschild	Books—1701–1800	London, Dawsons, 1969
652	Ehrsam	Books—1801–1900	New York, Octagon books, 1968
713	Dickson	Books—Scotland—1475–1640	Amsterdam, Philo pr., 1969; Hildesheim, G. Olms, 1969; New York, B. Franklin, 1970
715	Forbes-Leith	Pre-reformation scholars	New York, B. Franklin [1967]
716	Aldis	Scottish books	New York, B. Franklin, 1970
731	Bradshaw Irish collection, Cambridge	Irish books	New York, B. Franklin [1967]
827	Scott	Elizabethan translations	New York, B. Franklin, 1966; Hildesheim, G. Olms, 1969
855	Parker	Topography	Amsterdam, Theatrum orbis terrarum, 1966
1068	Dix	Dublin books	New York, B. Franklin, 1967
1072	„	„	New York, B. Franklin, 1967
1179	Lynam	Irish character	Shannon, Irish U.P., 1969
1185	Dobell	Privately published books	Detroit, Mich., Gale research, 1966
1245	Ashendene press	Ashendene press	New York, B. Franklin, 1967
1282	Aurner	Caxton	New York, Russell and Russell, 1965
1307	Courtney	Dodsley's Collection	New York, B. Franklin [1969]
1308	Straus	Dodsley	New York, B. Franklin, 1967
1414	Smith	Walsh	London, 1968
1449a	De Ricci	English collectors	New York, B. Franklin, 1967
1450–2	New York. Public library	Auction catalogues	Detroit, Mich., Gale research, 1967
1463	Rollins	Ballads	Hatboro, Pa., Tradition pr., 1967
1510	Stauffer	18th century biography	New York, Russell & Russell [1970]
1534	Edmond	Broadsides	New York, B. Franklin [1965]
1541	Harvard	Chapbooks	Detroit, Mich., Gale research, 1968
1552	Barry	Children's books	Detroit, Mich., Gale research, 1968; Detroit, Mich., Singing Tree pr., 1969

1561	Muir	Children's books	London, 1969
1575	Heal	Writing-masters	Hildesheim, G. Olms, 1962
1588	Clarence	Stage cyclopedia	New York, B. Franklin [1968]
1685	Esdaile	Tales and prose romances	London, 1969
1690	Cordasco	18th century novel	*See* no.628a.
1697	Block	Novel, 1740–1850	London, Dawsons; Dobb Ferry, N.Y., Oceana, 1967
1707	Parrish	Victorian lady novelists	New York, B. Franklin [1967]
1713	Summers	Gothic literature	London, Fortune pr. [1969]
1736	Lewine	Illustrated books	Amsterdam, Philo pr., 1969
1741-2	Levis	Engraving	Hildesheim, G. Olms, 1969
1762	Chubb	Maps of Great Britain	London, Dawsons, 1966
1783,90	Fordham	,,	London, Dawsons, 1969
1831	Kidson	British music publishers	New York, B. Blom, 1966
1850	Times	Tercentenary handlist	London, Dawsons, 1966
1885	Crane	British newspapers	Hildesheim, G. Olms, 1969
1888	Press club, London	Newspapers	New York, B. Franklin [1967]
1970	Lincoln's inn	Pamphlets	New York, B. Franklin [1967]
2035	O'Donoghue	Poets of Ireland	Detroit, Mich., Gale research, 1968
2038a	Hoskins	Primers	London, Gregg international, 1969
2039	Merritt	,,	Freeport, N.Y., Books for Libraries pr. [1967]; New York, B. Franklin, 1968
2045	Lindsay	Proclamations	New York, B. Franklin [1966]
2075	Corns	Unfinished books	Detroit, Mich., Gale research, 1968; New York, B. Franklin, 1968
2090	McDonald	Agriculture	New York, B. Franklin [1967]
2095	Rothamsted	,,	New York, B. Franklin, 1969
2160	Scott	Darien	New York, B. Franklin [1967]
2163	Wagner	Economics	New York, B. Franklin [1967]
2197	Schwerdt	Hunting, hawking . . .	Hildesheim, G. Olms, 1969
2284	Slater	Sport	Detroit, Mich., Gale research, 1969
2287	Whitman	Tennis	Detroit, Mich., Gale research, 1968
2336	Smart	Arnold	New York, B. Franklin, 1968
2350	Tannenbaum	Ascham	Port Washington, N.Y., Kennikat pr. [1967]
2366	Keynes	Austen	New York, B. Franklin [1967]
2368	Chapman	,, .	Oxford, 1969
2398	Cutler	Barrie	New York, B. Franklin 1967
2412-13	Tannenbaum	Beaumont and Fletcher	Port Washington, N.Y., Kennikat pr. [1967]
2472	Keynes	Blake	New York, Kraus reprint, 1968
2481	,,	,,	New York, Kraus reprint, 1968
2505	Wise	Borrow	London, Dawsons, 1966
2524	Tannenbaum	Breton	Port Washington, N.T., Kennikat pr. [1967]
2528	McKay	Bridges	New York, Ams pr., 1966
2538	Brontë society	Brontë family	New York, B. Franklin, 1967
2589	Broughton	Browning	New York, B. Franklin, 1967
2620	Cordasco	Burke	*See* no.628a
2647	Stisted	Burton	London, W. Lock, 1970
2648	Jones	,,	New York, B. Franklin [1967]
2649	Wright	,,	New York, B. Franklin [1967]
2650	Panzer	,,	New York, B. Franklin, 1967; London, Dawsons, 1967
2667	Hoppé	Butler	New York, B. Franklin, 1967
2670	Harkness	,,	New York, B. Franklin, 1967
2689	Newstead abbey	Byron	New York, B. Franklin [1967]
2708	Dyer	Carlyle	New York, B. Franklin, 1967
2724-5	Williams and Madan	Carroll	New York, B. Franklin [1967]
2758-9	Tannenbaum	Chapman	Port Washington, N.Y., Kennikat pr. [1967]
2778	Hammond	Chaucer	New York, P. Smith, 1933
2850	Parrish	Collins and Reade	New York, B. Franklin [1967]

2876	N.S.W. Public library	Cook	New York, B. Franklin, 1967
2878	Holmes	Cook	New York, B. Franklin, 1969
2918	Shaw	Creighton	New York, B. Franklin, n.d.
2929	Harvard university	Cruikshank	New York, Arno pro. [1968]
2948	Tannenbaum	Daniel	Port Washington, N.Y., Kennikat pr. [1967]
2996	,,	Dekker	Port Washington, N.Y., Kennikat pr. [1967]
3018	Green	De Quincey	New York, B. Franklin, 1967
3029	Cordasco	Dibdin	See no.628a
3032	Kitton	Dickens	Westmead, Farnborough, Gregg international, 1970
3053	,,	,,	Westmead, Farnborough, Gregg international, 1970
3057	Wilkins	,,	New York, B. Franklin [1967]
3067	Harvard University	,,	New York, Arno pr. [1968]
3069	Cowan	,,	New York, Johnson reprint corp., 1969
3151	Murray	Dobson	New York, B. Franklin [1967]
3153	Dobson	,,	New York, B. Franklin [1967]
3188	Tannenbaum	Drayton	Port Washington, N.Y., Kennikat pr. [1967]
3194a	Turnbull	Drury	London, Gregg pr., 1969
3201	Macdonald	Dryden	London, Dawsons, 1967
3276	Keynes	Evelyn	London, Dawsons, 1966
3298	Cordasco	Fielding	See no.628a
3323	Prideaux	FitzGerald	New York, B. Franklin, 1967
3345	Tannenbaum	Ford	Port Washington, N.Y., Kennikat pr., [1967]
3361	Besterman	Frazer	London, Dawsons, 1968
3383	Marrot	Galsworthy	New York, B. Franklin, 1967
3401	Tannenbaum	Gascoigne	Port Washington, N.Y., Kennikat pr. [1967]
3420	Cordasco	Gibbon	See no.628a
3423	Norton	,,	New York, B. Franklin, 1967
3431	Searle	Gilbert	New York, B. Franklin, 1967
3461	Cordasco	Godwin	See no.628a
3520–1	Tannenbaum	Greene	Port Washington, N.Y., Kennikat pr. [1967]
3575	Weber	Hardy	New York, Russell and Russell, 1965; New York, B. Franklin, 1967
3582	Webb	,,	New York, B. Franklin [1967]
3598	Purdy	,,	London, 1968
3614a	Turnbull	Hartlib	London, Gregg pr., 1969
3643	Tannenbaum	Herbert	Port Washington, N.Y., Kennikat pr. [1967]
3650	,,	Herrick	Port Washington, N.Y., Kennikat pr. [1967]
3657	,,	Heywood, J.	Port Washington, N.Y., Kennikat pr. [1967]
3659	,,	Heywood, T.	Port Washington, N.Y., Kennikat pr. [1967]
3747	Wilson	Hudson	Port Washington, N.Y., Kennikat pr., n.d.
3758	Jessop	Hume	New York, Russell and Russell, n.d.; New York, B. Franklin, 1967
3763	Brewer	Hunt	New York, B. Franklin [1967]
3803	Phillips	James	New York, B. Franklin, 1968
3829	Gosse	Johnson	New York, B. Franklin, 1967
3838	Courtney	,,	Oxford, 1968
3841	Adam	,,	New York, B. Franklin, 1969
3864	Tannenbaum	Jonson	Port Washington, N.Y., Kennikat pr. [1967]
3947–9	Livingston	Kipling	New York, B. Franklin, n.d.
3969	Tannenbaum	Kyd	Port Washington, N.Y., Kennikat pr. [1967]

4007	Collins	Laud	New York, B. Franklin, 1969
4069	Christophersen	Locke	New York, B. Franklin [1969]
4074	Tannenbaum	Lodge	Port Washington, N.Y., Kennikat pr. [1967].
4082	,,	Lyly	Port Washington, N.Y., Kennikat pr. [1967]
4118c	Mantz	Mansfield	New York, B. Franklin, 1967
4122–4	Tannenbaum	Marlowe	Port Washington, N.Y., Kennikat pr. [1967]
4137	,,	Marston	Port Washington, N.Y., Kennikat pr. [1967]
4151	,,	Mary Stuart	Port Washington, N.Y., Kennikat pr. [1967]
4159	Simmons	Masefield	New York, Ams pr., n.d.
4168	Shaw	Massie	New York, B. Franklin [1967]
4169	Tannenbaum	Massinger	Port Washington, N.Y., Kennikat pr. [1967]
4216	,,	Middleton	Port Washington, N.Y., Kennikat pr. [1967]
4224	[Sayle]	Milton	New York, B. Franklin, 1967
4231	Stevens	,,	New York, Russell and Russell, 1967
4298	Forman	Morris	New York, B. Franklin, 1967
4317	Tannenbaum	Munday	Port Washington, N.Y., Kennikat pr. [1967]
4325	,,	Nashe	Port Washington, N.Y., Kennikat pr. [1967]
4336	Gray	Newton	London, Dawsons, 1966
4406	Tannenbaum	Peele	Port Washington, N.Y., Kennikat pr. [1967]
4440	Griffith	Pope	New York, B. Franklin [1970]
4481	Latimore	Rackham	New York, B. Franklin, 1967
4484	Brushfield	Raleigh	New York, B. Franklin, 1967; Hildesheim, G. Olms, 1969
4488	Tannenbaum	Randolph	Port Washington, N.Y., Kennikat pr. [1967]
4517	Cordasco	Richardson	*See* no.628a
4519	Sale	,,	Hamden, Conn., Archon books, 1969
4596	Corson	Scott	New York, B. Franklin, 1967
4684	Tannenbaum	Sidney	Port Washington, N.Y., Kennikat pr. [1967]
4715–16	Cordasco	Smollett	*See* no.628a
4718	Anderson	,,	*See* no.628a
4757	Johnson	Spenser	London, Dawsons, 1966
4788	Cordasco	Sterne	*See* no.628a
4797	Prideaux	Stevenson	New York, B. Franklin, 1967
4799	Harvard University	,,	New York, Arno pr. [1968]
4828	Hubbard	Swift	New York, B. Franklin, 1967
4852	Wise	Swinburne	London, Dawsons, 1966
4859	Babington	Symonds	New York, B. Franklin, 1967
4892	Wise	Tennyson	London, Dawsons, 1967
4915	Van Duzer	Thackeray	New York, B. Franklin [1967]
4983	Irwin	Trollope	New York, B. Franklin, 1967
5037	Cordasco	Watt	Detroit, Mich., Gale research co., 1969; *see also* Supplement no.628a.
5052	Tannenbaum	Webster	Port Washington, N.Y., Kennikat pr. [1967]
5056	Wells	Wells	New York, B. Franklin, 1967
5214	Cordasco	Young	*See* no.628a

INDEX TO SUPPLEMENT

The Index to the Supplement to the *Bibliography of British Literary Bibliographies* incorporates the corrections and additions listed at the end of the Supplement.